# Junior Certificat
# Second and Third-Year English

Take the Plunge!

## Second Edition

DIVE IN!    TAKE THE PLUNGE!    WHY DON'T YOU...    THRASH IT OUT!    TEST THE WATERS!

## Edel O'Donovan
## Fiona Kirwan

**FOLENS**

| *Editor* | *Design* | *Layout and Cover* | *Picture Research* | *Illustrations* |
| --- | --- | --- | --- | --- |
| Julie O'Shea | Liz White | Karen Hoey | Aisling Hanrahan | Bronagh O'Hanlon, Helmut Kollars, Jenni Desmond |

© 2010 Edel O'Donovan, Fiona Kirwan

ISBN 978–1-84741-568-4

Produced in Ireland by Folens Publishers, Hibernian Industrial Estate, Greenhills Road, Tallaght, Dublin 24

# Introduction

In this Second Edition of *Take the Plunge!* you will find:

- An **extensive selection** from time-honoured pieces to recently published material.

- A comprehensively revised **Reading and Writing Unit** where the sections correspond to the essay styles featured on the exam paper: Personal, Descriptive, Storytelling/Narrative and Discursive writing.

- **Skill-building exercises,** such as pre-writing exercises and paragraph planning.

- Excerpts that highlight **key techniques** of particular styles of writing.

- **Exam questions integrated** with relevant material throughout the book in the **Test the Waters** questions.

- **Functional Writing** tasks **linked** directly to appropriate exam questions.

- Updated **Media Studies** chapter with the use of active methodologies.

- Key **Drama** concepts explored using exciting extracts in preparation for both Studied and Unseen Drama sections.

- A wide-ranging **Poetry** selection thematically arranged, encompassing modern and classic poems, from Irish and non-Irish poets.

- A diverse cross-section of **Short Stories** covering multiple aspects of the genre.

- **Revision Pages** – the **Exam Lifeboat** – a unique feature which pulls all of the key techniques covered in a section into a few pages for quick revision.

## Remember!

- Do not feel that you have to use *all* the material in this book.
- Every class should *select* material and exercises to suit its needs and preferences.
- Most extracts are followed by four sets of activities:

|  |  |  |  |  |
| --- | --- | --- | --- | --- |
| Short exploratory questions | Questions to make you think | Activities for *you* to do! | Things for the class to talk about | Exam-style questions relevant to the material covered |

## Don't Forget!

Use the **Exam Lifeboat** revision pages to revise for the exam!

# Contents

# 2. Functional Writing

# 3. Media Studies

# 4. Drama

# 5. Poetry

# 6. Fiction

# 7. Grammar

# Reading and Writing

In this chapter you will come across many types of *writing*, including:

- Personal writing
- Descriptive writing
- Storytelling/Narrative writing
- Discursive writing

You will *learn* how to:

- Brainstorm
- Plan paragraphs
- Improve your own writing

# Personal Writing

## Swimming with a Dolphin

Patricia O'Reilly

*A* few evenings ago a television holiday programme showed a picture of a glamorous blonde, make-up immaculate, swimming with a group of dolphins. She was a stressed career woman. And this was her way of unwinding.

But, long before dolphins became fashionable and even before I even knew the meaning of the word stress, much less experienced it, I had a swim with a dolphin.

It was the year I was fourteen. On holidays in Kerry. Smitten with Mikey, the local heart-throb and sick of being labelled a Dublin jackeen. Without hesitation, I took Mikey up on his dare to 'borrow' my uncle's kayak. In return he'd introduce me to the neighbourhood dolphin. My butterfly fears at what would happen if my uncle found out were well worth Mikey's instant attention.

As he rowed out into the bay, the pink-streaked sunset turned to gold. When he stopped, the kayak seemed to rest in a pool of cold flame. I put down my hand and stroked the sea's calm surface. I wasn't sure why. Perhaps for luck? Or maybe to call up the dolphin?

After a few moments of silence, a dorsal fin, curved like a gondola, broke the smooth water. In the early twilight, the dolphin arched upwards, its body burnished bronze. We watched in wonder as it romped near the boat. Bending, curving, emitting sounds of pleasure.

Mikey yanked off his shirt, kicked off his shoes, started undoing his fly. Omigod. I averted my eyes as he slithered out of his tight, black drainpipes. His togs were blue. Like my uncle's.

With a fierce rocking movement, he disappeared over the side of the kayak to be immediately joined by the dolphin.

'Come on,' he said.

I hesitated. But only for a moment. Kicking off my sandals, I jumped in as I was, my skirt umbrella-ing around me.

With a great whoosh, the dolphin was in front of me. Seeming to tread water. So close that I could have reached out and touched his snout. And his eyes were soft and gentle, his mouth curved in a smile.

He was full of playful cavortings, leaping balletically, trumpeting joy.

'This one sure likes the women,' said Mikey, looking at me with new respect.

The dolphin kneaded water in front of me, watching me through his button eyes, his mouth now wide open in a laugh. He'd little pearly teeth, just like a baby's, and I laughed back at him.

Switching mood, he gave off a series of squeaks and high pitched sounds.

'He's talking to you,' said Mikey, swimming beside me, his limbs long and pale in the water. 'Answer him.'

I talked back with incomprehensible sounds that came from I knew not where. But at the time they made sense.

Then the magic was over. The dolphin hooted, leapt once more in the air, dove into the sea and was gone. With his passing, I was bereft. The journey back was shiveringly miserable. But nothing compared to the reception I got from my uncle. Yet swimming with the dolphin was an experience I wouldn't have missed for the world.

1. What does the writer see on television that brings back her memory?

2. Why does the writer go out in the kayak, even though she knows she'll get into trouble?

3. What time of day is it?

4. How do the teenagers feel when the dolphin is there?

5. How does the writer feel when the dolphin has left?

● When you answer questions, it is important that you prove and explain your answer fully. For example, if you were asked, 'How does the writer show us that the dolphin has a personality?' you should answer using the following method:

● You begin your answer using words from the question to make your main

*The writer shows us that the dolphin has a personality when she describes the details of his face.*

● Then you must use evidence directly from the extract to prove your point. This is called a

*The writer says, 'his eyes were soft and gentle, his mouth curved in a smile.'*

Remember to use 'inverted commas' when you quote from the extract.

● Lastly, you must  how this quote proves your point.

*The dolphin's expression suggests that he has a kind and friendly personality.*

● So your completed answer should look like this:

*The writer shows us that the dolphin has a personality when she describes the details of his face. The writer says, 'his eyes were soft and gentle, his mouth curved in a smile.' The dolphin's expression suggests that he has a kind and friendly personality.*

● From now on you will see this code next to many questions: **PQE**. This is to remind you to use the **PQE** method.

Point.

Quote.

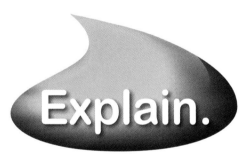

Explain.

# The Secret World of the Irish Male

Joe O'Connor

*Joe O'Connor is on a plane travelling to America to see Ireland play in the 1994 World Cup Finals. The plane is full of Irish football fans.*

I go down the back of the plane and find myself sitting beside a nine-year-old child, my worst nightmare on a long flight. He is very self-confident too, which makes it worse. 'I'm going to America,' he says. I contemplate telling him that he's on the wrong plane, and that he's actually going to Siberia, but his parents are sitting just across the aisle. 'Ireland are cool,' he says, 'aren't they?' I agree that Ireland are cool. 'I have a girlfriend,' he says, 'and I'm going to marry her when I grow up.' I offer heartiest congratulations. 'I kiss her,' he says, 'I kiss her and everything.' I say I think he's a bit young to be kissing girls. 'I am not,' he says, 'you put your tongue in their mouths but you don't swop spits.' I suddenly realise what I've been doing wrong all these years. Down the back the fans are chanting 'Irela-hand, Irela-hand, Irela-hand.' 'Do you kiss girls?' the kid says. I ignore him. 'DO YOU KISS GIRLS?' he shrieks. 'Not as often as you do,' I say. 'I bet you do,' he sniggers, his little voice gurgling with malevolent pleasure, 'can I try on your glasses, fatso?' It is going to be a very long flight.

1. What is the child obsessed with?
2. Why does Joe think that this is going to be a long flight?
3. Would you like to be sitting next to this child?

Re-write this extract from the child's point of view. Remember to imagine that you are only nine years old and that you see adults differently.

**OR**

Write down three of the best football chants that you know, or make one up for your favourite team. No bad language!

**OR**

Write a description of a really annoying child that you know. (HINT: There are some ideas below.)

# Brainstorm

Before you write a paragraph, it helps if you BRAINSTORM. This means scribbling down all your ideas roughly before you write. It can be done in one or two minutes. You will see this logo to remind you when to brainstorm.

Brainstorm

Do a paragraph **Brainstorm** like this for your chosen person (real or imaginary). Decide:

- who they are,
- what they look like, and
- why they are annoying.

Notice that adjectives are in red and verbs are in blue.

## ACTIONS
tells tales
shrieks, screams
whines
constantly asking questions
sucks up to adults
tags along
'borrows' stuff
breaks things

- an annoying child
- KEVIN
- brother

## APPEARANCE
snotty nose
gaps in teeth
sticky out ears
flat nose
freckles
sellotaped glasses
scabby knees

## PERSONALITY
greedy
spoilt
serious
bold
stubborn

# Kathmandu

Michael Palin

*Michael Palin is a famous television presenter and writer who travels around the world and reports back from exotic places. In this extract he has just left India and arrived in the capital city of Nepal, Kathmandu. He is describing a very important Hindu religious ceremony to which he has been invited.*

We arrived here last night from Delhi on the penultimate night of Dasain, a big Nepali festival, and though badly in need of some rest and recuperation after our Indian adventure, the final day's celebrations cannot be missed.

To start the day we've been asked by Pratima Pande, a formidable, energetic, Gordonstoun-educated Nepali, to watch a *puja*, a ritual act of worship, at the home of one of her in-laws. This being the first time I've ever been to Nepal, I'm craning my head out of the car window as we drive there. I have a sense of streets that are less hectic and a city much easier on the eye than those we've seen these past few weeks.

*penultimate –* second last

*Gordonstoun –* famous school in England

*auspicious –* favourable

*hierarchical –* in order of importance

Buildings look like buildings rather than structures for supporting billboards.

The house is comfortable but not opulent. As we arrive a group of musicians are parading around the garden before taking up a position on the far side of a small swimming pool. It's a bit of a squeeze, as two of them are wielding large, curved horns.

I'm told that this is Bijaya Dasami, the 'victorious tenth day' of the Dasain festival, and Pratima and her husband, mother-in-law, brothers-in-law, nephews, nieces and cousins are here to celebrate King Rama's victory over the demon Ravana, helped by Shiva's escort, Durga.

I'm desperately trying to get all this down in my notebook when the music starts and the family priest, an unassuming, modestly dressed figure, who looks as if he might have come to fix the plumbing, steps forward. The exact timing of the *puja* is very auspicious and it cannot be delayed for foreign film crews. He sets the ball rolling by applying a dab of yellow to the forehead of the oldest member of the family, Pratima's 82-year-old mother-in-law. Today, Pratima tells me, everyone in Nepal, from the King downwards, will wear this mark, the *tika*.

After some light family argument over the exact order of things, the ceremony continues, in strictly hierarchical fashion, with the five brothers, and then the children, kissing the feet of their elders and giving each other the male *tika*, made from a preparation of curd, rice and vermillion powder. *Jamara*, shoots of barley, are placed on the head or in a garland around the neck as a symbol of fertility and longevity.

As an outsider I'm struck by how seriously all this is taken. Pratima's brothers-in-law are hard-nosed, professional people, one a doctor, one a banker, two others in the army. They're dressed in the *labada salwar*, a knee-length tunic, with tight leggings and black leather shoes, but over it they wear a Western-style sports jacket.

Many of them have been educated in Britain or America, their children speak fluent English and go to private schools. Yet here they are taking part in an ancient and rural ritual with a thoroughness that one can't imagine among their counterparts in the West.

The first thing to remember, says Pratima, is that not only is Hinduism the religion of 90 per cent of Nepal, the Nepalis take pride in being more scrupulous in their observance of festivals. The Indians, she says, have shortened their ceremonies.

'We take three days to get married. They do it in a day!'

She herself is off to a private audience at which she will be given *tika* and blessed by the King, who is some sort of relative (they're both from the Rana family). This afternoon, he will be doing the same for the public in the grounds of the palace. Would I like to come along?

*surreal –*
*strange and bizarre,*
*dreamlike*

The prospect of meeting the king of a country I've only been in for 12 hours appeals in a surreal sort of way, and I scurry back to the Yak and Yeti Hotel to find a tie and get my only jacket pressed.

1. Who has invited Palin to watch a *puja*?

2. What is the name of the victorious tenth day, and what does it celebrate?

3. How does the priest begin the ceremony?

4. What happens as the ceremony continues?

5. Why does Palin feel he needs to change clothes?

6. What did you think of the description of the ceremony in the house?

7. How does Palin show us the contrast between ancient and modern Nepal? **PQE**

8. Michael Palin is famous for his sense of humour. Can you see any evidence of this in the extract? **PQE**

Brainstorm

Write a journal entry describing your imagined experience in one of the following situations:

- Waiting in a very hot and crowded airport for a delayed flight

- Standing on a train from Dublin to Cork

- A bus journey next to an unpleasant fellow passenger

- A stormy ferry crossing

- A long and tense family car journey

**OR**

Write a letter of complaint to a travel company about an unsatisfactory journey you made recently. (See page 144 in Chapter 2 for help.)

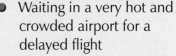

9

# Perfect Your Paragraphs!

*If you can write a good paragraph, then writing a good essay is easy!*

- A paragraph should get across one main idea or theme. This is usually found in a sentence called the **TOPIC SENTENCE.**

- A **TOPIC SENTENCE** can be at the beginning, the middle or the end of the paragraph.

So, how do you find it? Here is an example of a **TOPIC SENTENCE** at the beginning of a paragraph:

## My Family and Other Animals

Gerald Durrell

I have attempted to draw an accurate and unexaggerated picture of my family in the following pages; they appear as I saw them. To explain some of their more curious ways, however, I feel that I should state that at the time we were in Corfu the family were all quite young: Larry, the eldest, was twenty-three; Leslie was nineteen; Margo eighteen; while I was the youngest, being of the tender and impressionable age of ten. We have never been very certain of my mother's age, for the simple reason that she can never remember her date of birth; all I can say is that she was old enough to have four children. My mother also insists that I explain she is a widow for, as she so penetratingly observed, you never know what people might think.

*Notice how the topic idea is introduced in the first sentence, which is that the writer wants to draw an accurate picture of his family for us. The remainder of the paragraph explains who the members of his family are.*

This is probably the easiest type of **TOPIC SENTENCE** to identify.

- Another type of paragraph builds up the reader's anticipation by putting the **TOPIC SENTENCE** right at the end. Read the following opening paragraph from *Down with Pigeons*, p. 54.

# Down with Pigeons
Robert Benchley

St Francis of Assisi (unless I am getting him mixed up with St Simeon Stylites, which might be very easy to do as both their names begin with 'St') was very fond of birds, and often had his picture taken with them sitting on his shoulders and pecking at his wrists. That was all right, if St Francis liked it. We all have our likes and dislikes, and I have more of a feeling for dogs. However, I am not *against* birds as a class. I am just against pigeons.

*Here the writer seems to be rambling; however, he is gradually making his way to his main point at the end of the paragraph, which is that he hates pigeons, unlike St Francis of Assisi!*

Perhaps the most difficult **TOPIC SENTENCE** to identify is the one in the centre of a paragraph. Read the example below.

# Not on the Label
Felicity Lawrence

In an idle moment I decided to reconstruct the contents of a 99p bag of washed and ready-to-eat salad. Of course you are not meant to do this, the whole point of bagged salad being that we are too busy to wash our own lettuce leaves, let alone count them. But I wanted to know how many you get for your money. Erring well on the side of generosity, I reckoned that for roughly £1 I had bought two leaves of frisée, one leaf of red radicchio, and two leaves of a pale green crunchy variety of lettuce. This portion was livened up by eighteen tiny whole leaves and seven torn pieces of dark green leaves about the size of a 2p coin.

*Which sentence do you think is the topic sentence? In order to identify it you must ask, what's the main point the writer is making? Here, the writer wants to know how many leaves she gets for her money; therefore, the topic sentence is, 'But I wanted to know how many you get for your money.' Were you right?*

1. Write a paragraph about any of the following topics. Begin with a quick **Brainstorm**. Experiment with the order in which you introduce your ideas before you actually begin writing properly.

2. Then try to write three different paragraphs on the same topic, just varying the location of the TOPIC SENTENCE, not the ideas themselves.

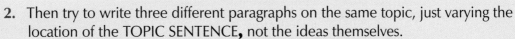

- The smoking ban works, but for whom?
- My pet hates
- Fashion is frivolous, but necessary.
- Drugs and sports don't mix.
- My family

# Reading in an Exam

In the Junior Cert English exam you will be asked to read a passage and answer questions in a very short amount of time.

Here are five steps to the perfect answer!

**STEP ONE**    SKIM READ the paragraphs, numbering them if they are not already numbered. Skim reading means reading as quickly as you can.

**STEP TWO**    CLOSE READ the passage, underlining what you think is the **topic sentence** or phrase in each paragraph. Close reading means reading carefully.

**STEP THREE**    READ THE QUESTIONS

**STEP FOUR**    SCAN READ the passage for the answers, noting quotes relevant to the different questions.

**STEP FIVE**    RE-READ question one. Jot down the key word in your rough work. Jot down a quick arrow plan of your main points. You are now ready to write your answer using **PQE**.

Look at the next page to see an example of how a student approached a question using this method.

## I wish I was in Dixie

**Aoife Ní Oistín**

1. The day crawls grey and blurry into my brain as I push the sleeping mask from my eyes. For a moment I'm not even aware of what has woken me. I check the clock. Half-past one. Then the insidiously merry sound breaches my earplugs and launches its attack. Awoken again by my Nemesis, another day's sleep disturbed. The natural enemy of the night-shift worker is the cheerful ice-cream man and his chirpy ice-cream van.

2. Sunny days like this he must feel himself King of the World, or at least of a small section of Bray. Everyone smiles to hear him coming. Little children rush toward him with bright faces, loose change jangling in their pockets. He is holidays and sand and raspberry sauce. He is shorts and sandals and chocolate flake. He is the sound of summer and the whole world loves him. Little does he suspect the resentment and loathing that oozes out between the slats of the Venetian blinds in No. 24. He has no idea that far from smiling, I curse and seethe with frustrated sleep when he and his noisemobile turn down my street. Never will he guess the hideous tortures I have devised for him. He doesn't know yet that an innocent ice-cream cone can be an instrument of pain.

3. Some days I dream of running, still pyjamaed, out into the street, the sleeping mask perched on my forehead, and, like a deranged Lone Ranger, shouting at the happy faces and the gorging children to please BE QUIET! A brief stunned silence as I march back to bed, followed by the shrill wail of the fattest child of all as his ice-cream drops in a soft splat by the side of the road.

4. It used to be the old *Match of the Day* theme tune he played, then 'The Yellow Rose of Texas'. Once I could have sworn I heard Brahm's 'Lullaby', but surely not even he could be so cruel? Day after day, broken sleep after broken sleep, his latest jangling nightmare winds itself into my beleaguered brain: 'I wish I was in Dixie'. I wish one of us was in Dixie and if I ever get my hands on him he'll wish it too. Pulling the sleeping mask down over my eyes, I turn over and plot as I wait for silence and sleep. I'm saving to buy myself an ice-cream van. We'll soon see how well everyone loves the sleep-splitting sound of the summer as I drive around the estates of Bray at half-past one in the morning, blaring the *Lone Ranger* theme music and looking for the ice-cream man's house.

**Question 1.** What is your impression of the writer of this passage? (15 marks)

Q. 1  My <u>impression</u> of writer? ...tired ...paragraph 1...'the natural enemy'...

...frustrated... para 3... 'I dream of'...

...sense of humour... para 5 ...plotting.

My impression of the writer is that she is extremely tired and frustrated but still has a sense of humour. I saw that she was very tired when she said, 'The natural enemy of the night-shift worker is the cheerful ice-cream man and his chirpy ice-cream van.' The ice-cream van is ruining her sleep and making her tired so she calls it her enemy. I got the impression that she was extremely frustrated when she imagined what she would like to do. '... I dream of running, still pyjamaed, out into the street ... like a deranged Lone Ranger, shouting at the happy faces and the gorging children to please BE QUIET!' The fact that she imagines herself shouting at happy, innocent children shows that she is angry and frustrated. But I also saw that the writer still has a sense of humour about the situation from the fact that she is plotting to buy herself a van, find the ice-cream man's house and blare music to wake him up. This gives me the impression that despite being tired and frustrated she also has a sense of humour about the situation.

Try out this method when you are answering the *Take the Plunge* questions after this extract.

# Shakespeare: The Lost Years 1585–1592

Bill Bryson

We don't know when Shakespeare first came to London. Ever a shadow even in his own biography, he disappears, all but utterly, from 1585 to 1592, the very years we would most like to know where he was and what he was up to, for it was in this period that he left Stratford (and, presumably, wife and family) and established himself as an actor and playwright. There is not a more tempting void in literary history, nor more eager hands to fill it.

> A biography is the story of a person's life, written by somebody else.
>
> An autobiography is the story of a person's life, told by the person themselves.

*effluvia* – unpleasant smell or vapour given off by waste or decaying matter

*perennial* – constant, continual

City life then had a density and cosiness that we can scarcely imagine now. Away from the few main thoroughfares, streets were much narrower than now, and houses, with their projecting upper floors, often all but touched. So neighbours were close indeed, and all the stench and effluvia that they produced tended to accumulate and linger. Refuse was a perennial problem (Houndsditch, according to John Stow, got its name from the number of dogs thrown in it; even if fanciful, the story is telling). Rich and poor lived far more side by side than now. The playwright Robert Greene died in wretched squalor in a tenement in Dowgate, near London Bridge, only a few doors from the home of Sir Francis Drake, one of the wealthiest men in the land.

Among the other differences we would notice between then and now was much to do with dining and diet. The main meal was taken at midday and, among the better-off, often featured foods that are uneaten now – crane, bustard, swan and stork, for instance. Those who ate well ate at least as well as today. A contemporary of Shakespeare's (and a friend of the family) named Elinor Fettiplace left to posterity a household management book from 1604 – one of the first of its type to survive – that contains recipes for any number of dishes of delicacy and invention: mutton with claret and Seville orange juice, spinach tart, cheesecakes, custards, creamy meringues. Other contemporary accounts – not least the plays of Shakespeare and his fellow writers – show an appreciation for dietary variety that many of us would be pressed to match today.

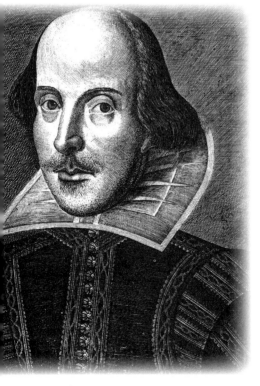

*bustard* – large, long-legged bird

For poorer people, not surprisingly, diet was much simpler and more monotonous, consisting mainly of dark bread and cheese, with a little occasional meat. Vegetables were eaten mostly by those who could afford nothing better. The potato was an exotic newcomer, still treated sceptically by many because of the similarity of its leaves to those of poisonous nightshade (to which it is in fact related). It wouldn't become a popular food until the eighteenth century. Tea and coffee were yet unknown.

People of all classes loved their foods sweet. Many dishes were coated with sticky sweet glazes, and even wine was sometimes given a generous charge of sugar, as were fish, eggs and meats of every type. Such was the popularity of sugar that people's teeth often turned black, and those who failed to attain the condition naturally sometimes blackened their teeth artificially to show that they had had their share of sugar, too. Rich women, including the queen, made themselves additionally beauteous by bleaching their skin with compound of borax, sulphur and lead – all at least mildly toxic, sometimes very much more so – for pale skin was a sign of supreme loveliness. (Which makes the 'dark lady' of Shakespeare's sonnets an exotic being in the extreme.)

Beer was drunk copiously, even at breakfast and even by the pleasure-wary Puritans (the ship that took the Puritan leader John Winthrop to New England carried him, ten thousand gallons of beer and not much else). A gallon a day was the traditional ration for monks, and we may assume that most others drank no less. For foreigners, English ale was an acquired taste even then. As one Continental visitor noted uneasily, it was 'cloudy like horse's urine'. The better-off drank wine, generally by the pint.

Tobacco, introduced to London the year after Shakespeare's birth, was a luxury at first but soon gained such widespread popularity that by the end of the century there were no fewer than seven thousand tobacconists in the city. It was employed not only for pleasure but as a treatment for a broad range of complaints, including … migraine and even bad breath, and was seen as such a reliable prophylactic against plague that even small children were encouraged to use it. For a time pupils at Eton faced a beating if caught neglecting their tobacco.

*prophylactic –*
protective device

1. Why are the years 1585–1592 known as Shakespeare's lost years?
2. How do we know London was very overcrowded in these years?
3. What types of food did rich people eat in Shakespeare's time?
4. What effect did sugar have on people?
5. How do you know tobacco was popular in London?

6. Were you surprised by the attitude to tobacco at the time? Why or why not? **P Q E**

7. A good biographer recreates the time and place their subject lived in. Do you think Bill Bryson does a good job of creating sixteenth century London in this extract? **P Q E**

8. Would you like to have lived in Shakespeare's world? **P Q E**

Choose your favourite pop/sports/soap opera star and write a short biographical piece about them.

**OR**

Consider the fact that we now know that smoking is very bad for you. Look at the rules in your own school.

- Imagine that you are a school child from Shakespeare's time.
- Write a reaction to the modern rules.
- Start with the line:

    *It seems strange that there is no mention of beatings …*

**OR**

Create a magazine ad for a make-up product that guarantees either beautiful black teeth, or perfect pale skin.

# Touching the Void

Joe Simpson

*This extract is from an **autobiography** written by Joe Simpson. He and his friend Simon Yates, two young but experienced climbers, set out to ascend a 21,000-foot mountain in the Peruvian Andes. They make it to the summit but on their descent they run into difficulties. Joe badly breaks his leg. Despite this, Simon comes up with a way of getting Joe down a 3,000-foot snow face by lowering him again and again on a 300-foot length of rope. But just when they are 200 feet from the bottom of this steep section disaster strikes. Without knowing it, Simon has lowered Joe over an overhanging section of ice cliff; beneath him is a crevasse, a huge hole in a glacier. Joe cannot get off the rope and Simon cannot continue to hold him. He holds him for as long as he can but he is gradually slipping down himself.*

**Simon:**

It had been nearly an hour since Joe had gone over the drop. I was shaking with cold. My grip on the rope kept easing despite my efforts. The rope slowly edged down and the knot pressed against my right fist. I can't hold it, can't stop it. The thought overwhelmed me. The snow slides and wind and cold were forgotten. I was being pulled off. The seat moved beneath me, and snow slipped away past my feet. I slipped a few inches. Stamping my feet deep into the slope halted the movement. God! I had to do something!

The knife! The thought came out of nowhere. Of course, the knife. Be quick, come on, get it.

The knife was in my sack. It took an age to let go a hand and slip the strap off my shoulder, and then repeat it with the other hand. I braced the rope across my thigh and held on to the plate with my right hand as hard as I could. Fumbling at the catches on the rucksack, I could feel the snow slowly giving way beneath me. Panic threatened to swamp me. I felt in the sack, searching desperately for the knife. My hand closed round something smooth and pulled it out. The red plastic handle slipped in my mitt

*Map by Tom Richardson, from* Touching the Void *by Joe Simpson, published by Jonathan Cape. Used by permission of The Random House Group Ltd.*

KEY.
1  1st snow hole
2  2nd snow hole
3  3rd snow hole
4  4th snow hole
A  Accident site
X  Rope cut
C  Cliff and crevasse
a  1st snow hole on crawl
b  2nd night alone
B  Bomb alley
---- Ascent & lowers

The crawl-out from the face

and I nearly dropped it. I put it in my lap before tugging my mitt off with my teeth. I had already made the decision. There was no other option left to me. The metal blade stuck to my lips when I opened it with my teeth.

It needed no pressure. The taut rope exploded at the touch of the blade, and I flew backwards into the seat as the pulling strain vanished. I was shaking.

Leaning back against the snow, I listened to a furious hammering in my temple as I tried to calm my breathing. Snow hissed over me in a torrent. I ignored it as it poured over my face and chest, spurting into the open zip at my neck, and on down below. It kept coming. Washing across me and down after the cut rope, and after Joe.

I was alive, and for the moment that was all I could think about. Where Joe was, or whether he was alive, didn't concern me in the long silence after the cutting. His weight had gone from me. There was only the wind and the avalanches left to me.

**Joe:**

I lolled on the rope, scarcely able to hold my head up. An awful weariness washed through me, and with it a fervent hope that this endless hanging would soon be over. There was no need for the torture. I wanted with all my heart for it to finish.

The rope jolted down a few inches. How long will you be, Simon? How long before you join me? It would be soon. I could feel the rope tremble again; wire-tight, it told me the truth as well as any phone call. So! It ends here. Pity! I hope somebody finds us, and knows we climbed the West Face. I don't want to disappear without trace. They'd never know we did it.

The wind swung me in a gentle circle. I looked at the crevasse beneath me, waiting for me. It was big. Twenty feet wide at least. I guessed that I was hanging fifty feet above it. It stretched along the base of the ice cliff. Below me it was covered with a roof of snow, but to the right it opened out and a dark space yawned there. Bottomless, I thought idly. No. They're never bottomless. I wonder how deep I will go? To the bottom … to the water at the bottom? God! I hope not!

Another jerk. Above me the rope sawed through the cliff edge, dislodging chunks of crusty ice. I stared at it stretching into the darkness above. Cold had long since won its battle. There was no feeling in my arms and legs. Everything slowed and softened. Thoughts became idle questions, never answered. I accepted that I was to die. There was no alternative. It caused me no dreadful fear. I was numb with cold and felt no pain; so senselessly cold that I craved sleep and cared nothing for the consequences. It would be a dreamless sleep. Reality had become a nightmare, and sleep beckoned insistently; a black hole calling me, pain-free, lost in time, like death.

My torch beam died. The cold had killed the batteries. I saw stars in a dark gap above me. Stars, or lights in my head. The storm was over. The stars were good to see. I was glad to see them again. Old friends came back. They seemed far away; further than I'd ever seen them before. And bright: you'd think them gemstones hanging there, floating in the air above. Some moved, little winking moves, on and off, on and off, floating the brightest sparks of light down to me.

Then, what I had waited for pounced on me. The stars went out, and I fell. Like something come alive, the rope lashed violently against my face and I fell silently, endlessly into the nothingness, as if dreaming of falling. I fell fast, faster than thought, and my stomach protested at the swooping speed of it. I swept down, and from far above I saw myself falling and felt nothing. No thoughts, and all fears gone away. So this is it!

A whoomphing impact on my back broke the dream, and the snow engulfed me. I felt cold wetness on my cheeks. I wasn't stopping, and for an instant blinding moment I was frightened. Now, the crevasse! Ahhh … NO!!!

The acceleration took me again, mercifully fast, too fast for the scream which died above me …

The whitest flashes burst in my eyes as a terrible impact whipped me into stillness. The flashes continued, bursting electric flashes in my eyes as I heard, but never felt, the air rush from my body. Snow followed down on to me, and I registered its soft blows from far away, hearing it scrape over me in a distant disembodied way. Something in my head seemed to pulse and fade, and the flashes came less frequently. The shock had stunned me so that for an immeasurable time I lay numb, hardly conscious of what had happened. As in dreams, time had slowed, and I seemed motionless in the air, unsupported, without mass. I lay still, with open mouth, open eyes staring into blackness, thinking they were closed, and noting every sensation, all the pulsing messages in my body, and did nothing.

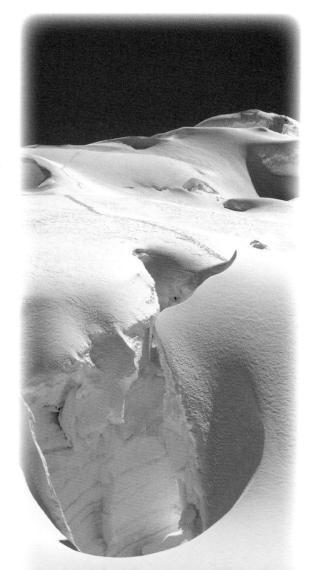

I couldn't breathe. I retched. Nothing. Pressure pain in my chest. Retching, and gagging, trying hard for the air. Nothing. I felt a familiar dull roaring sound of shingles on a beach, and relaxed. I shut my eyes, and gave in to grey fading shadows. My chest spasmed, then heaved out, and the roaring in my head suddenly cleared as cold air flowed in.

I was alive.

1. Why is Simon panicking?

2. How can you tell that it is very difficult for him to make even tiny movements?

3. What is his first thought when he cuts the rope?

4. Why is Joe disappointed that he will disappear without trace?

5. What are his thoughts about the crevasse?

6. How do we know that it's a shock for Joe when the rope is cut?

7. How is suspense created as Simon takes the knife out of the bag? 🅟🅠🅔

8. Look at all the questions that Joe is asking himself as he hangs off the rope. What do they tell you about him? 🅟🅠🅔

9. The description of the stars creates a lull in the tension. Why do you think the writer did this?

10. Re-read the account of Joe's fall. What verbs and adjectives make this dramatic?

11. Identify what Joe sees, hears and feels while falling and upon landing.

12. Would you like to know what happens next to Joe and Simon? Why?

Write a letter to Joe Simpson telling him what you thought of this extract. His address would not be very hard to find if you actually wanted to post the letter to him!

**OR**

Imagine you are hanging on to the end of the rope, over the crevasse, with a broken leg, freezing to death! What thoughts about your life are going through your head? What special moments are passing before your eyes? What are your regrets?

**OR**

Simon and Joe both survived (you have to read the rest of the book or watch the film made of it to find out how) and they are still friends. Write the conversation that they might have had when they met again.

# Why my brother never became a professional footballer

Kevin McDermott

My Dad was a man of strong conviction and like all true Dubs he confessed to certain articles of faith.

'Phoenix Park,' he'd say, 'is the biggest enclosed park in Europe.'

This was always followed by:

'And O'Connell Street is the widest street in Europe.'

And then he'd complete his trinity:

'And never forget, son, that your brother is playing in the world's greatest soccer academy, the Dublin and District Schoolboy's League.'

Now, I never considered it a matter of filial disloyalty that I gave no credence to the claims made for the Phoenix Park and O'Connell Street, but I inherited my Da's faith in the Dublin Schoolboy's League so, when I tell you that my brother was one of the finest players ever to grace that league, you'll know that I am talking 'quality' with a capital 'Q'.

He was a centre-half. He could turn on a sixpence, play off either foot, strike the ball with finesse. For a tall, gawky young fellow, he was beautifully balanced and had an unflappable temperament. He could outleap opposing forwards and he delivered the ball forward with the vision of a Franz Beckenbauer.

In short, the brother was a class act. I couldn't wait till he began to play at Under-Sixteen Level, for then the scouts would come knocking on our door, and he'd be off to England to play for Leeds United, alongside Johnny Giles and Billy Bremner. And how I'd bask in the reflected glory.

After each match, Eddie, the team manager would just say, 'Macer, me ole flower'. And we all knew what he meant.

But then my Ma took an unwitting hand in the proceedings, and all our might-have-beens crumbled to dust. Ma had her own guiding principle, and clung to it with a frightening tenacity. 'A mother's love expresses itself in the food you put on the table.'

And my Ma was in the *haute couture* league when it came to dressing up ordinary cuts of meat, and we ate like French Kings.

Well, summer faded into autumn and the new soccer season was upon us. Me, Da and my brother were mad with excitement. This was going to be *the* year.

'I'm off, Ma,' the brother called, on the first Sunday in September.

'Where are you going, love?'

'I've a match at two o'clock.'

'But your dinner?'

These were the fatal words. 'Your dinner.'

'You can't play on an empty stomach,' said Ma, 'and a beautiful dinner all ready for you.'

'I'll have it when I come back.'

'Don't be silly! I'll lift yours now. It'll only take a minute.'

'Ma!'

But the brother's protestations were in vain. Up came the dinner and he sat chewing like a condemned man, on his last meal. Every Sunday, the same. The brother chewing in grim silence. Da and me helpless. My Ma hovering, heaping his plate and fussin'.

I felt for him, watching from the sidelines.

'What's wrong with your brother, he's stuffed!'

'If only you knew, pal.'

Turn on a sixpence? The brother couldn't turn in the centre circle! Leap like a salmon? He couldn't get off the ground. The loss of form was as complete as it was baffling. Soon the scouts stopped coming. And after the game, when Eddie, the manager, said, 'Macer, me ole flower,' his words carried the ineffable sorrow of 'what-might-have-been'.

Really, it was a situation worthy of a Greek tragedy – a son's ambitions dragged to the ground by an excess of maternal love. (I wonder if Sophocles follows Bohemians? Now, that's a real case of tragedy.)

In this extract, dialogue, or direct speech, is used to good effect. 'Where are you going, love?'

What the person *actually said* goes inside the inverted commas. Notice that the question mark also goes inside the inverted commas. This is because it is telling you how the person spoke.

The other important thing to remember is that when a new person speaks you must begin a **new** line. Look at the above extract and you will see this.

**DIVE IN!**

1. What were the writer's Dad's 'articles of faith'?

2. Did the writer believe them?

3. What footballing skills did his brother have?

4. What effect did his mother's actions have on the brother's abilities?

**TAKE THE PLUNGE!**

5. How do you know that Kevin is really proud of his brother? **P Q E**

6. How can you tell from the dialogue between Kevin's brother and his mother that she will get her way? **P Q E**

7. Why does the writer compare the situation to a tragedy? **P Q E**

8. What aspects of this writer's style appealed most to you?

**WHY DON'T YOU...**

Write about your greatest sporting ambition. If you really hate sport, and your greatest ambition is to always avoid it, write about that!

**OR**

Think about a time someone tried to help you, but ended up making matters worse. Write an account of that time. Try to include some dialogue in your story.

**OR**

Pick someone who you would consider to be a great sporting hero and give reasons for your choice.

# God's Pockets

Rita Curran Darby

I had just turned six and wanted to know where babies came from. And my Aunt Kate, who raised me, said they came out of Holy God's pocket. That satisfied me. But on reaching the age of reason I began to wonder. After all, God would want huge pockets to hold all them babies. So I approached Aunt Kate again while she was hanging out the washing.

'Ah what ails ye at all,' she said, 'sure didn't I tell ye He had two pockets – one for the boys and one for the girls.'

I still wasn't convinced.

'Well then, why can't you get one?' I whinged. She let the washing pole drop.

'Will ye ge long ou' o' dat with ye,' she said. 'You're givin' me a splitting headache.'

Well, I thought, that's the end of that, and decided I'd ask my cousin, the one who gave me the low-down on Santy. It was while we were on our way to the Banyo that I asked her about it. She boasted about knowing everything about babies but she said she wasn't telling me because I was a tell-tale-tattler. My lip dropped while I tried to convince her I'd never tell again, but she wouldn't give in.

On our way home from the Banyo we swapped shoes and I told my cousin she could stay with me that night if she told me all about how you get babies. Then I remembered the last time she stayed with me, the time when she said the Sacred Heart was

winking at me from His picture on the wall, and when I screamed and Aunt Kate came running in, didn't she deny it and told Aunt Kate I was only dreaming. So this time I made her say 'honest to God' and cross her throat with a spit, that she wouldn't do it again. When we were washed for bed and Aunt Kate had given us bread with sugar on it along with fair warning about trick-acting, we got into bed. We made a few tumbles then tried to see who could stand on their head the longest, and when we both fell down with the laughing, didn't Aunt Kate shout in at us to go asleep. Eventually we settled down and when our whispered chat finally came around to babies didn't I learn the real truth once and for all, and it had nothing to do with Holy God's pocket.

'Ye see,' said my cousin, 'when your mammy wants a new baby she had to take a little white tablet and when she wants twins, well then she has to take two.'

I fell asleep plotting ways and means of getting Aunt Kate to take a right good handful of them little white tablets.

Even though English is spoken in many countries, the words people use, the way they pronounce them, and even their grammar, can vary. These variations are called **dialects**. Think of the differences between the way Irish people speak English and the way Americans speak it. For example, we say 'rubbish', they say 'garbage'. Can you think of any other examples?

**DIVE IN!**

1. Why doesn't the child believe her aunt's explanation about God's pockets?
2. Why does the aunt let the washing pole drop?
3. Who does the writer decide to ask next, and why?
4. How did her cousin scare her the last time she had stayed?
5. How does her cousin say babies are made?

**TAKE THE PLUNGE!**

6. What do we learn about Aunt Kate from what she says? PQE
7. In the extract the words are spelled as they would sound, for example, 'Will ye ge long ou' o' dat with ye'. Why does the writer do this?
8. Can you find another example of this?
9. What evidence can you find in this extract to prove that both children are very young and innocent? PQE
10. Did you find this story amusing in any way? Explain your answer.

Write a short story beginning with the line,
*I thought that the child would never stop asking questions ...*

### OR

Even in a country as small as Ireland there are many different dialects. Write a conversation between any combination of the people below, using whatever dialect is local to your area. You must use direct speech as in the extract.

| | | | |
|---|---|---|---|
| *Garda* | *Hippy* | *Coach* | *Soldier* |
| *Rock star* | *Priest* | *Dancer* | *Driver* |
| *Shopkeeper* | *Teacher* | *Mother* | *Nurse* |
| *Granny* | *Vet* | *Actor* | *Farmer* |
| | *Teenager* | *Ice-cream man* | |

Remember there are lots of words that you can use instead of 'said' when you are writing dialogue. Here are some examples that you could use to make your writing livelier:

*spluttered, shouted, announced, declared, claimed, answered, queried, whinged, moaned, asked, muttered, whispered, mumbled, giggled, screamed, replied, barked, commented, laughed, suggested.*

# Nits

Winifred Power

I hate it when Mum does my nits.

I brought a nit note home from school. I read it to Mum from the back of the car.

'*We are sorry to inform you that there has been an outb …*'

'*OUTBreak,*' said Mum.

'*… of head lice in the school,*' I read. '*This is a comm ….*'

'*COMMunity,*' said Mum.

'*…problem and we ask parents to follow these simple inst …*'

'*INSTructions,*' said Mum.

'*below.*'

That meant another fight. I kick and scream and Mum shouts and tells me if I don't stop moving she is going to cut my hair short. It *hurts* when she combs my hair. She uses a small metal comb and *drags* it through my hair. She puts conditioner through it to make it easier she says. She says I'm lucky I'm not in pain all the time, and this will prepare me for when I am an adult – it will make me stronger.

It's not fair. I get nits all the time. Mum says I go to school nit-free and come home *crawling with them*. She says they're having parties on my head and that they are learning their spellings with me. We think my nits can read.

She says I could be a spy and find out if my friends at school's parents do their nits.

'No,' I shouted, 'I won't.'

'But you could be a detective,' she says. 'Wouldn't you like that? You just watch out for who is scratching, and then ask them if their mum or dad do their nits.'

'I won't spy on my friends,' I say.

Mum's friend Anne is a nurse, and Mum got her to explain to me exactly how the nits work. Anne said nits can have baby nits every seven hours. So if I have five nits at four o'clock, I could have twenty-five by the time I go to bed and even more when I wake up in the morning. Nits just grow and grow.

Mum hates the nits. She shouts at them and gives out to them when she's combing my hair. She says it's hard on her because she's a *vegetarian* and it's not really in her to kill living things. (What about carrots? I don't ask.)

Mum gives out because she has to check *all* our heads, and she says it's hard because she's a *single parent*, so there's nobody to check her head. Then she's worried her friends

will get them too, so she tells them to check *their* hair. Then everybody goes *Ugh* and starts scratching, and Mum goes red.

When Conor and I went on holidays to Granny's, Mum spent ages telling Gran how to check my hair, and how she would pack my special nit comb, and could Granny please check me *every day*. When we come back from Granny's, Mum checks my hair. I am fine.

But Mum has forgotten to ask Granny to check Conor – he is crawling with them.

1. How do you know that a young child is speaking at the beginning of the extract?

2. What happens when the mother tries to check the child's hair?

3. How does Anne explain the way that nits spread?

4. Why does the mother hate killing nits?

5. How does Conor end up with nits?

6. Do you think it is fair that the mother asks her daughter to spy on her friends?

7. What impression did you get of the mother in this extract? **P Q E**

8. Did you enjoy this extract? Why or why not? **P Q E**

Write the script for a radio broadcast advising the public that there has been an outbreak of a serious infectious disease in their area.

- Describe the symptoms of the disease.
- Warn people to stay indoors.
- Explain how they should react if they think they're infected.
- Try to reassure them so they don't panic.

### OR

Imagine that you are the school principal and you have to write a letter to the parents informing them that there has been an outbreak of head lice. Don't forget to list the instructions to the parents.

Write a composition with the title:

*The best or worst holiday I've ever had*                    2005 H.L. Paper

### OR

You have spent the summer travelling around Ireland. Write a number of diary entries recording your impressions.                    2005 H.L. Paper

# Friday Night Treat

Clodagh O'Donoghue

When I was a little girl – we're talking six or seven here – my bedtime was at 7.30 p.m., the same as my younger brother. I was acutely aware of the injustice of this because, at two and a half years his senior, I should have commanded a later bedtime – eight o'clock, say. However, my little brother was what was commonly known back then as a 'holy terror' and the idea that he would go to bed quietly while I was still up and about was simply laughable. In contrast, as the rule-abiding and biddable eldest child, I could be prevailed upon to overlook my seniority and go up at 7.30 p.m. I may have been a goody-goody, and I may have done as requested without making a fuss, but it didn't mean I was happy about it; it didn't mean I didn't see the unfairness of it. My parents,

recognising this and appreciative of my obliging nature, devised a form of compensation. And it was this: on Friday nights, if my little brother could be got to sleep by ten o'clock, then I could sneak downstairs in my jimjams and watch *Come Dancing*.

And so it was that from Sunday to Thursday (Saturdays operated differently again), I submitted to an embarrassingly early bedtime with as much grace as I could muster. My brother and I shared a room at the time and I would retreat behind an Enid Blyton paperback and endeavour to ignore his antics as he fought to sleep manfully. These included jumping on the bed, badgering me to have a feet fight, and trying to tunnel out of the house through the wall with the aid of a dessert spoon. All of this I endured in stony silence with an air of long-suffering martyrdom. However, on Friday nights, I became a different person. I became a caring and solicitous big sister. I was all sweetness and light. I plumped his pillow; I listened to his prattle; I read to him until I was hoarse; I may even have sung to him – anything to get him to sleep before *Come Dancing* kicked off.

Of course, probably if I'd done nothing at all he would still have been asleep by ten o'clock, as being a holy terror is tiring work – but I was not prepared to leave it to chance.

And so, at the witching hour, my mammy and daddy would creep upstairs, help me into my dressing gown and slippers, and bring me down in time for the theme music.

In those days, the show was presented by the elegant Judith Chalmers, and regional teams from various parts of the UK would compete for the final. As a young man, my daddy had been a keen ballroom dancer and so he could pronounce authoritatively on the technique of the couples as they glided across the floor. I would nod sagely to indicate my agreement with his assessments but really, I was there for the dresses.

There were two distinct sections in the competition – oldtime and Latin – and the dresses worn for the Latin dances were frankly alarming.

The female contestants – all of whom had implausibly orange tans considering they hailed from such locations as Bristol and Leeds – seemed to have eschewed frocks in favour of spraying a few bits of glitter in strategic places and hoping for the best. At age seven, I was something of a prude – my most fervent wish back then was that crinolines would be back in fashion by the time I was a teenager and that discos would have been replaced by formal balls complete with dancing cards. So, you can imagine that the skimpy Latin creations, made up of a lot of flesh-coloured nylon and a few sequins, were not my cup of tea.

No, it was the old-time dresses that excited me. Yards and yards of floaty material made up of layers and layers of petticoats that stood out almost at right angles to the body. The men in their white tie and tails had to somehow negotiate these voluminous skirts and engage in a fight with the fabric to get close to their partners. Even more than the dresses' shapes, I loved their colours – the peacock blues, the deep pinks, the sherbet lemons – and all with high-heeled court shoes of the same shade for a perfectly co-ordinated look.

I notice that there has been a recent revival and rejuvenation of ballroom dancing as an early evening Saturday family television entertainment. Only now, of course, in keeping with the television practices of today, there must be celebrities involved – however minor or obscure – who are partnered with professionals and sent on a crash course to learn the foxtrot or the samba or whatever. And there has to be an elimination process in which the public have their say and get to vote for their favourite.

Although it is interesting to see how the ballroom dancing genre has been reinvented for today's TV audiences, for me, it has lost a lot of its magic. Maybe it is because it lacks that staying-up-late thrill or maybe it is because my sleeping holy terror of a brother is not upstairs, oblivious to his big sister's secret. But it does serve as a pleasant reminder of an almost-forgotten Friday night treat. And I still like the dresses.

1. Why was the writer's bedtime so early?

2. How did her parents make this up to her?

3. What was it that the writer really loved about *Come Dancing*?

4. How has the programme changed?

5. Does the writer still enjoy it as much?

6. From your reading of the first paragraph, what is your impression of the writer? PQE

7. Would you like to have shared a room with her little brother? Why or why not? PQE

8. Which type of dress most appeals to the writer? PQE

9. Nostalgia is a sentimental longing for a time in the past. Can you find evidence of a nostalgic tone in this passage? PQE

10. What's your favourite TV programme at the moment?

Write the script for an advertisement promoting your favourite television show. Remember, you will have to use persuasive language to convince people that your programme is worth watching.

*OR*

Imagine you are writing twenty years from now. Pick out the things – clothes, music, activities, objects, words and phrases – that you think you will look back on with embarrassment or nostalgia.

# That's Entertainment

Nancy Wilson

The summer before my senior year of college, I rented a place at the Jersey shore with some friends. One Tuesday night at about 9.30, I walked out of the house and went down to the beach. No one was around, so I pulled off all my clothes, left them in a pile, and dove into the surf. I swam around for twenty minutes and then rode a wave back to the shore.

When I came out of the water, my clothes were missing. As I stood there pondering what to do, I heard the sound of voices. It was a group of people walking along the beach – and all of them were walking in my direction. I decided to make a dash for it and run back to the house, which was fifty or sixty yards away. I could see that the door was open, or at least that light was coming out of the doorway. But as I ran closer, I realised at the very last second that there was a screen. I ran right through it.

Now I'm standing in the middle of a living room. There's a father and two little kids sitting on a couch watching TV, and I'm in the middle of the room without a stitch on. I turned around and ran through the busted-up screen door and tore back down the beach. I went right and kept on running and eventually found my pile of clothes. I didn't know that there was an undertow. It had carried me about four blocks from where I had gone into the water.

The next morning, I walked the beach looking for the house with the broken screen door. I find the house, and as I'm walking up to knock on what's left of the door, I see the father inside, walking toward me. I start stammering and finally manage to say, 'You know, I feel really bad about what happened, and I want to give you some money for the screen door.'

The father cuts me off and very dramatically throws up his hands and says – 'Honey, I can't take anything from you. That's more entertainment than we've had all week.'

1. Why does the girl panic when she comes out of the water after her swim?

2. Is the door into the house really open?

3. Who is in the house and what are they doing?

4. Why couldn't the swimmer find her clothes?

5. Why won't the father take any money for the damage the girl caused?

Write an account of the most embarrassing thing that has ever happened to you (that you are willing to share with your class!).

If you have had the good fortune to escape embarrassment all your life, invent something, but try to make it sound real and believable.

**OR**

Write out the conversation you think happened between the father and his children after the girl ran away.

**OR**

Write a County Council notice to be posted on a beach for swimmers, warning them of the dangers of the beach and informing them of safety precautions they should take.

In groups of four, prepare a freeze-frame of a moment from this story.

A **freeze-frame** is like a scene from a film that has been paused. You are going to pretend that you are frozen in a moment in the story. You decide what character each person in your group is playing. Remember to think about posture, gesture, expression and positions.

- Practise your moment.
- The teacher will call each group to the top of the classroom in turn.
- On the count of three, freeze your moment and hold it still for 30 seconds.
- When the teacher points to you, you must explain who you are and what you are thinking at this moment in time.

For homework, pretend you are the director of this scene. Write out in full sentences how you would position the actors, what gestures and expressions they should use, and what lighting, music or props they would need.

# From My Bedroom Window

Mick Ransford

'What I see from my bedroom window.'

So went the title of the composition our first year English teacher announced to the class moments before the bell rang out and released us into the blissful freedom of the weekend.

'Describe in detail,' he told us, 'everything you see when you look out your bedroom window. I'll read the best four and the winner will be given a prize.'

The compositions were to be written over the weekend and turned in to him on Monday. The weekend flew by, like they all did in those days, and Monday afternoon found us watching as the teacher stood up to read, his hands clasping either side of his high desk, the four copies he'd chosen stacked one atop the other in front of him. With a smile on his face he told us he intended to read them in ascending order, like they do on *Top of the Pops*, he said.

Everybody but the three runners-up and the winner had had their copies handed back earlier. Mine was safely tucked away in my school bag. The room was hot. The smell of chalk dust hung on the air. The class gave the teacher the benefit of its tired attention.

I was sitting next to Martin McCreash, and what caught my interest was that Martin actually seemed to be listening. It was then that I realised his copy had not been returned. We all knew that Martin was more than capable of writing, or of doing anything else he set his mind to, but he didn't seem to care about school at all. His was what would now be termed a 'dysfunctional' family and he came from one of the toughest estates in the town. But on that lazy September afternoon, he was all ears.

The teacher opened the first copy. He began each composition by reading out the title and the author's name. They were pretty much what you'd expect from thirteen-year-olds, full of green fields and songbirds and trees, but were mercifully not more than two or three pages long. Whenever he finished a composition its author would collect the work to a half-hearted round of applause.

One after the other the teacher went through them all and still Martin's copy hadn't been returned. I was all ears by this time myself.

As the teacher neared the bottom of the stack Martin seemed to become more and more uncomfortable. He'd gone a little red in the face and he shifted around on the seat of the bench we both shared.

When the teacher opened the last copy Martin stiffened visibly, and I could have sworn I heard him mutter, 'At least I wrote the truth.'

'What I see from my bedroom window, by Martin McCreash.'

The whole class fell still.

The teacher paused before reading on, 'I see houses, all just like mine.'

1. In what order does the teacher read the essays?

2. Why is Martin listening?

3. What did the first three essays describe?

4. What is Martin's reaction when the teacher gets close to reading his composition?

5. Were you surprised by the ending?

6. What is the atmosphere in the classroom? **P Q E**

7. What type of person do you think Martin is? Why do you think this? **P Q E**

8. Why do you think Martin's English teacher picks his essay as the best?

9. Would you like to be taught by this English teacher? Why or why not? **P Q E**

10. What is the best English essay title you were ever given?

The **atmosphere** of a story is linked to the setting of the story. It depends on where the action is taking place. You need to pay attention to the sights, sounds and smells that the writer describes.

Write the conversation that Martin has with his parents when he returns home with his prize.

*OR*

Describe what *you* can see from your bedroom window. Remember, it doesn't need to be a long description to be effective!

*OR*

Write about any time when your work or behaviour was praised or criticised. This could be from sports, a part-time job, at home or in school. How did this make you feel?

# Rock 'n' Roll

James Cotter

In February 1992, Guns N' Roses announced they'd play Slane Castle later that year. As soon as I heard it, I knew with the absolute certainty of a fifteen-year old that it would be the best day of my life.

The tickets went on sale one Saturday morning. Me and Ed, my best mate, decided we should queue before the shops opened. Sure Slane could only hold about 80,000 and

there'd be at least 2 million who wanted to see the best rock 'n' roll band ever. I mean, even the Pope got a million.

So when that Saturday arrived, we got up at 4.30 a.m. and Eamonn, my long-suffering dad, drove us into Grafton Street. Although not quite a million, there were several hundred people in the queue. It was an intriguing slice of society; long-haired students and leather clad ne'er do-wells mixed with Axl-Rose-loving schoolgirls and the occasional down-and-out, who, although not particularly interested in paying £50 to go to a field in Meath, seemed to enjoy the whole queuing process. Especially the yelling at passers-by bit …

Now, queuing today isn't what it used to be – these days if you are fifteen and stuck in a queue, you'd probably have your Sony mini-games console with you to play wireless *Hyperkill-Murder-Deathball 3000* with the other queuers and when your batteries wore out you could always hook yourself up to your MP3 player. If the worst came to the worst, you could amuse yourself by texting all your mates with wake-up messages.

But this was 1992 and all those gadgets were but distant gleams in the eyes of Japanese designers. We had nothing. We stared glumly at the queue ahead of us; then, after an hour or so, just to shake things up, we turned round and stared glumly at the queue behind us. There were a few nice-looking rocker girls there but, despite our long hair and moody stares, they didn't seem to want to talk to us. To be fair to them, if you saw what I looked like back then, you wouldn't want to talk to me either.

Ed, combining the worst of both his geek and rocker tendencies, had fitted two small speakers inside his jacket which he hooked up to his Walkman. Preparing to impress the crowd with this futuristic clothing, he pressed play. Unfortunately, he'd forgotten to change the batteries. The tortured noise that squeaked from his jacket may once have been Metallica, but forced out of a Walkman at quarter speed through two tinny South

Korean speakers, it sounded nothing so much as a funeral dirge being sung by Alvin and the Chipmunks after six pints and a valium.

Eventually, the shop opened and, to our great relief, when we reached the front of the queue, they still had tickets. It later turned out that if we'd wandered along on the morning of the concert, they still would have been able to spare oh, 9,000 or 10,000 for us – a point my dad didn't tire of making for months afterwards.

When the day of the concert came, me and Ed were on the first bus down to Slane and, when the gate opened, we raced down that long green field and got to the very front of the stage. As I looked up at the hundred-foot-tall stack of speakers that towered above me, I knew this really was going to be the best day of my life.

The sun beat down and the first supporting band came onto the stage with a yell of 'Bishop Eamon Casey, fair fecks to ya!' The crowd cheered, Ed and I looked at each other and nodded, yup, we were rebels against society, fearlessly rocking out and laughing at the establishment.

The day went by in a haze of screaming and sweat, scary toilets and noise. Noise so loud, every time a cymbal hit I felt a physical pain in my chest. I loved it.

As we made our way home afterwards, two red faces in a sea of sweaty black denim, we agreed it was probably the best gig ever performed by anyone, anywhere. We knew we were at the defining event of our generation, the Woodstock for rockers. In the back of the bus, we heard people talking about an upcoming Nirvana gig. We scoffed quietly, Nirvana were all very well, but they didn't speak for our generation, sure this whole grunge thing was just some Johnny-come-lately fad. But Poodle-haired rock, we knew, was eternal.

When I got home, hard-as-nails-rocker that I was, I told my mum all about the perfect day I'd had. The only problem, I frowned, was a bit of ringing in the ears – but it was a small price to pay and, sure, it was bound to go in a day or two.

Fifteen years later and I'm still waiting for the ringing to go. But if that's the worst thing I did to myself during my teenage years, I got off lightly. After all, one of my mates has a Def Leppard tattoo.

I got a call from Ed the other day; he lives in Spain now and is in the middle of starting his own company. I waited to hear him complaining about the cost of this, or the time it takes to do that. But all he said was – Guns N' Roses are playing in June; man, get tickets quick, they're bound to sell out!

1. Why do the writer and his friend decide to queue so early?
2. What kind of people are in the queue?
3. Why do you think no one wanted to talk to the writer and his friend?
4. What did the writer's dad like to remind him of?
5. Is the writer still a Guns N' Roses fan?

6. Would you agree with the writer's description of queuing today?

7. Did you think the description of the writer's friend Ed was good? Why or why not? PQE

8. Did the day live up to the writer's expectations? PQE

Write an essay using the line:

*I knew this **really** was going to be the best day of my life.*

**OR**

Write a paragraph about your favourite music at the moment. You can write about the music, the lyrics, the video or the personalities in your favourite group. Try to get across why they appeal to you.

**OR**

Try to write a description of a place and an occasion, like the writer above. It might help to look at the photographs below and use the following questions to start you off.

Someone has just left each of these places. You must decide the following:

● **Where** is it?

● **Who** was here?

● **What** has happened?

● **Why** have they left?

After you have decided these things, write a story based on your thoughts.

# One Day in the Life of Ivan Denisovich

Alexander Solzhenitsyn

*Ivan Denisovich, nicknamed Shukhov, is a prisoner in a Russian gulag. People were sent to these terrible prisons in Siberia if they disagreed with the government. Millions of people died in the gulags between 1930 and 1989. Here Shukhov eats a typical meal.*

Then he took off his cap from his clean-shaven head – however cold it might be, he couldn't bring himself to eat with his cap on – and, stirring the now cold gruel, took a quick look to see what was in the bowl. A medium haul. It had not been poured from the top of the cauldron, nor from the bottom either. Fetyukov wouldn't be above pinching a potato while he was guarding the bowl.

The only decent thing about the gruel was that it was usually hot, but Shukhov's had grown completely cold. However, he began to eat it as slowly and deliberately as always. No need to hurry – even if the roof caught fire. Not counting sleep, a prisoner lived for himself only for ten minutes in the morning at breakfast, five at lunch break and five at supper.

The gruel did not change from day to day – it depended on the type of vegetable stored for use in the winter. Last year it was salted carrots – which meant nothing but carrots in the gruel from September to June. And this year – black cabbage. The most satisfying time of the year for the prisoner was June, out of season for vegetables, when they substituted groats. The worst time was July: shredded nettles in the cauldron.

Bones were mostly all that remained of the fish, the meat having been boiled off the bones and reduced to nothing except for odd bits on the head and tail. Not leaving a single scale or the tiniest piece of meat on the brittle skeleton, Shukhov still crunched his teeth, sucked the bones dry – and then spat them out onto the table. He ate everything of a fish – the gills, the tail, the eyes, when they had not fallen out of their sockets but when they had been boiled out and floated separately in the bowl – great fish-eyes! – then he did not eat them. He was laughed at for that.

Today Shukhov economised: because he hadn't been back to the barracks, he had not received his bread ration, and now he ate without bread. The bread – he would be able to eat that later, it could even be more satisfying.

After the gruel there was magara porridge. That had frozen into a single, solid lump, and Shukhov had to break it into little pieces. It was not only that the porridge was cold – even when it was hot, it was tasteless, and quite unfilling: it was just grass, only yellow and looked like millet. They had had the idea of giving them it instead of groats. It was said to come from China. 300 grams of it boiled a day – that was the ration. It certainly wasn't porridge, but it passed for porridge.

Licking his spoon and returning it to the same place in his felt boot, Shukhov put on his cap and set off for the infirmary.

1. What is the first thing Shukhov does when he gets his gruel, and why?
2. How does he eat his meal?
3. What are the best and worst vegetables found in the gruel?
4. What part of the fish does Shukhov not eat? Why do you think this is? **PQE**
5. Where does Shukhov keep his spoon? What does this tell us about life in the camp?

6. Shukhov always eats with his cap off. What do you think this tells us about him as a person?
7. Solzhenitsyn uses very descriptive writing. Re-read the paragraph where Shukhov eats the fish. What senses does the writer use to convey the experience? Focus on textures and sounds. **PQE**
8. Does the magara porridge sound appetising? What words tell you that it is not a very nice food? **PQE**
9. Why are mealtimes the highlight of the prisoners' day? What does this tell you about their lives in the camp? **PQE**

Imagine you are the producer of a reality TV show. The contestants must eat a variety of disgusting food combinations in order to win points for their team. Devise a number of options to present to the director, for example, *rotten fish heads in a squid ink sauce garnished with hopping ants.*

**OR**

Describe an everyday meal in your life. Don't forget to include information about your surroundings. **Brainstorm** about the taste, smell, appearance and texture of the food and the sounds that you make while eating.

# Notes from a Small Island

Bill Bryson

*Bill Bryson is an American travelling around England. He visits a traditional
English hotel and begins to think about the way people write menus.*

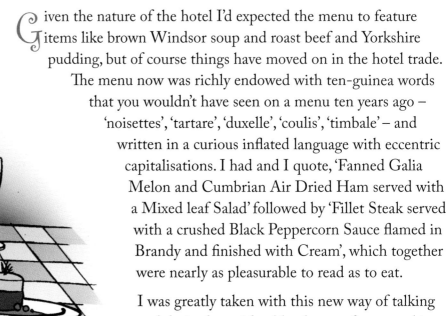

Given the nature of the hotel I'd expected the menu to feature items like brown Windsor soup and roast beef and Yorkshire pudding, but of course things have moved on in the hotel trade. The menu now was richly endowed with ten-guinea words that you wouldn't have seen on a menu ten years ago – 'noisettes', 'tartare', 'duxelle', 'coulis', 'timbale' – and written in a curious inflated language with eccentric capitalisations. I had and I quote, 'Fanned Galia Melon and Cumbrian Air Dried Ham served with a Mixed leaf Salad' followed by 'Fillet Steak served with a crushed Black Peppercorn Sauce flamed in Brandy and finished with Cream', which together were nearly as pleasurable to read as to eat.

I was greatly taken with this new way of talking and derived considerable pleasure from speaking it to the waiter. I asked him for a lustre of water freshly drawn from the house tap and presented *au nature* in a cylinder of glass, and when he came round with the bread rolls I entreated him to present me a tonged rondel of blanched wheat, oven baked and masked in a poppy-seed coating. I was just getting warmed up to this and about to ask for a fanned lap coverlet, freshly laundered and scented with a delicate hint of Omo, to replace the one that had slipped from my lap and now lay recumbent on the horizontal walking surface anterior to my feet when he handed me a card that said 'Sweets Menu' and I realised that we were back in the no-nonsense world of English.

It's a funny thing about English diners. They'll let you dazzle them with piddly duxelles of this and fussy little noisettes of that, but don't mess with their puddings, which is my thinking exactly. All the dessert entries were for gooey dishes with good English names. I had sticky toffee pudding and it was splendid. As I finished, the waiter invited me to withdraw to the lounge where a caisson of fresh-roasted coffee, complemented by the chef's own selection of mint wafers, awaited. I dressed the tabletop with a small circlet of copper specie crafted at the Royal Mint and, suppressing a small eruction of gastro-intestinal air, effected my egress.

1. What type of food does Bill Bryson expect the menu to offer?

2. What do you think he means by the phrase 'ten-guinea words'?

3. What do you think a 'Fanned Galia Melon and Cumbrian Air Dried Ham with a Mixed leaf Salad' might be?

4. What does the writer start to do to amuse himself in the second paragraph?

5. What two things does he ask for?

6. How do the descriptions of the desserts differ from the earlier descriptions?

7. Does Bill Bryson leave a tip? **PQE**

8. What does he do as he leaves the restaurant?

9. How would you react if you were waiting on a person who spoke to you like this?

10. Did you think this extract was funny? Why or why not? **PQE**

Write a description of three items from your favourite fast-food restaurant in the language Bryson uses in this extract, for example,
*regular chips: A modicum of delicately golden slivers of pomme de terre served in a crisp paper receptacle accompanied by a noisette of sun-blushed tomato puree.*

**OR**

Look again at the way Bill Bryson describes the napkin and the floor. Pick five everyday objects and, using a dictionary or a thesaurus (if you have one), describe these objects in the most complicated language you can. You could then play a guessing game with the rest of the class to see if they can figure out what objects are being described.

This extract is funny mainly because Bill Bryson mocks the way menus are written using words which are unnecessarily complicated. We use different **types of language** depending on our audience. For example, if you were explaining to a group of five year olds what to do if a fire broke out, you would use very **simple and clear language**. But if you were explaining the same procedures to a fire inspector you might use much more **technical language** because he would understand it and also because you want to impress him.

Write the instructions that you would give to a class of five year olds in case of a fire. Then re-write the same set of instructions which are to be presented to a fire inspector. Read out both sets of instructions to your class, and see if they can tell which set is for which group.

**OR**

Choose one of the scenarios below. Pretend that you are telling one of the people in the second column about the scenario you've chosen. Your class must try to guess, from your use of language, who is listening to you.

| Scenario | Person |
| --- | --- |
| You broke a window | Best friend |
| You were at a disco | Parent |
| Your first time surfing | School principal |
| You were fired from your job | Complete stranger |
| You were at a match | Non-English speaker |
| You failed a test | Small child |
| Death of family pet | TV interviewer |

Write an essay in which you describe a restaurant you love to visit. Try to give details that appeal not just to your readers' senses of sight and sound, but to all of their senses.

**OR**

You arrive home from a party at 3 a.m. having promised your parents you would be in by 11.30 p.m. You overhear your parents' conversation. Write out what you have heard in dialogue form. You may give the conversation a relevant setting and, if you wish, intersperse the dialogue with unspoken observations of your own on what is said.

# Don't use big words

Anon.

*pestiferous*

*cogitations*

*concatenated*

*prurient*

In promulgating your esoteric cogitations, or articulating your superficial sentimentalities and amicable, philosophical or psychological observations, beware of platitudinous ponderosity. Let your conversational communications possess a clarified conciseness, a compacted comprehensibleness, coalescent consistency, and a concatenated cogency. Shun double entendres, prurient jocosity, and pestiferous profanity, obscurant or apparent.

*platitudinous*

# Imeldas, and How to Spot Them

Marian Keyes

*Imelda Marcos was the wife of the ruler of the Phillipines in the 1980s. After her corrupt husband was overthrown, the rebels were astounded at the number of shoes they discovered in Imelda's palace. There were rooms and rooms full of shoes!*

I remember the first time I fell in love. I was fifteen years old and in a department store. Suddenly the breath was knocked from my body, as my eyes fixed on the object of my desire – a pair of four-inch, black-patent platform wedges with an ankle strap.

I wanted them desperately. I felt they'd change me into someone sophisticated and beautiful and make me completely irresistible to Eddie Jackson. But by the time I'd saved up my babysitting money, the shoes were long gone and Eddie Jackson was sporting several hickies that had Karen Baker's teeth marks on them.

Then, to my surprise, I became obsessed by a pair of navy clogs and I learnt a valuable lesson. Men will come and men will go, but there will always be shoes. I'm definitely a shoe woman. Or an Imelda, as we like to be called.

I used to think I was the only one. I lined the floor of my wardrobe with five-inch-heeled gold stilettos, eau-de-nil embroidered leather sandals and flowery Dr Martens and thought I was the only person who had ever slept with their new pair of green nubuck clogs.

Until a new girl started at work, wearing ox-blood pumps with back-to-front heels. 'I love shoes,' she admitted. 'All my friends call me Imelda. After Imelda Marcos.'

I was really upset. I had thought I was Imelda. But it transpired that there are lots of us out there and it's better to befriend each other. We're like collectors of rare artefacts. Only an Imelda would murmur, 'I've got a pair of rather special cone-heeled ankle boots that I think you might find interesting.' And only another Imelda wouldn't think she was a total nutter.

If they can't get shoes in the right size, Imeldas will still buy them, if they're sufficiently fabulous. Because there are remedies. Too big? Hey, that's why God invented insoles! Too small? What's a small piece of excruciating agony when your feet are well dressed?

Imeldas pamper their footwear as if they were loyal pets, buying them little tidbits, like colour-protect and rain-guard and all the rest of the crap they try to flog you every time you buy shoes. I've got *tons* of those plastic things you stick in shoes to help them keep their shape. And I've spent at least three years of my life holding suede boots over boiling kettles, in a labour of love.

Although recently I met an Imelda who keeps her shoes in their original boxes, and I don't know about you, but I think that's going too far.

Unlike other garments, shoes don't suddenly become too tight one week out of every four. Shoes will still fit you snugly even if you haven't gone to the gym for over three weeks and you've been having curries and pizzas every night. You see, shoes deserve your loyalty because they return it.

How to know if you're an Imelda:

- If you've bought shoes and never worn them because you *didn't want to damage them.*

- If you structure your day around the shoes you want to wear, staying in when you want to go out, just so you can wear your duck-egg-blue grosgrain slippers.

- If you've ever spent more on a pair of shoes than you would on a holiday.

- If you own around ten almost identical black pairs.

- If you've ever sustained injury falling off a high pair *and don't mind.*

- If you would rather lie and say you have athlete's foot than loan your shoes to your flatmate.

1. Why does Marian Keyes fall in love with shoes?

2. Why does she call herself 'Imelda'?

3. How do you know that Imeldas are mad about shoes?

4. In what way do Imeldas treat their footwear?

5. Look carefully at the tips on how to spot an Imelda. Do you know anyone who fits the description?

6. How does Marian Keyes describe the sensation of falling in love?

7. Look closely at the adjectives that the writer uses to describe her shoes. How do these help her to show us that she considers her shoes to be precious objects? **P Q E**

8. Why is Marian Keyes upset when she meets another Imelda?

9. How are shoes unlike other garments? **P Q E**

10. What part of this extract did you find funniest and why?

**WHY DON'T YOU...**

Think of your own biggest obsession. It might be a football team, make-up, Playstation, a particular band. Write your own list to help people recognise fellow obsessives. If *you* are also an Imelda, add five further points to Marian Keyes's list.

**OR**

Write a letter to Marian Keyes telling her what you think of her obsession.

**OR**

Describe your favourite footwear at the moment and think up an appropriate nickname for the style.

**THRASH IT OUT!**

- Divide into groups of four to six.

- The group must choose one of the photos above.

- The entire group should look silently at the photo. Each person must write one line of dialogue which they think the person who owns the shoes might say.

- When everyone has written their line, the group may share them.

- You must now come up with a story incorporating everyone's lines.

- When you have finished writing your story, report back to the class.

# You'll Never Watch Alone

John O'Donnell

Like many others of his age, my son had no choice. His news that day was a burden he had to share. 'Dad,' he said awkwardly, as if confessing to a fatal illness or life-changing desire, 'I'm Liverpool.' His fate had been decided not by a virus or rogue gene but by a cocky classmate. When my son's turn came to choose which football team to support, this knowing nine-year-old loftily declared, 'We've enough United. Tell you what: you can be Liverpool.'

What was I supposed to do? Should I persuade him of the virtues of a local team rather than some foreign legion? Should I cajole him to switch allegiance to the dodgy East End London team I'd supported through thick and – mostly – thin for over thirty years? I did what anyone would do. Heading for the nearest sports shop, I forked out a succession of notes in exchange for the official shirt, shorts and socks. On the shop floor, my son twirled, demanding to wear his new kit on the way home.

I could have said that in choosing Liverpool he was following a long tradition of Irish supporters and Irish players: Heighway, Lawrenson, Aldrige, Houghton. So what if some of these were, as it were, 'adopted' Irishmen? Liverpool had long supported us. In the thirteenth century, King John had used the port as a base for his Irish campaigns, but by 1885, the city had elected an Irish nationalist MP to Westminister and, in 1918, a Sinn Féin candidate won a seat. Sometimes, Liverpudlians seemed more Irish than the Irish: spirited, contrary, resourceful and brimming with ironic, self-lacerating humour. Like us, Scousers have been accused of wallowing in 'victim' status; they've certainly had their share of it in recent years: Toxteth, Hysel, Hillsborough. When the city mourned the execution of Ken Bigley in Iraq, Conservative MP Boris Johnson drew howls of protest as he told them they were hooked on grief.

If it was grief my son was looking for, he'd come to the right place. Being a football fan is far more about the agony than the ecstasy, no matter who you support. How could I explain to him that in signing up for this, he was signing up for a lifetime of affliction; days and nights of groans and tears, and only the occasional trophy? But as it happened, that season 2004–2005, Liverpool was in the hunt for one trophy; the Champions League, the greatest football prize in Europe. After we watched Liverpool's first match, my son insisted we make a pact; we would watch every European game the team played in, on TV, together.

How could I say no? Aside from naked self-interest, wasn't this a perfect opportunity for father and son to bond together? Two dents began appearing in the couch. I told myself this was education in action, a practical way of learning the geography of Europe; like watching Eurovision. We toured Europe from our living room, gazing at games in Austria and Monaco, Greece and Spain and Germany. In the quarter-finals, they knocked out favourites Juventus of Turin; in the semi-finals, they disposed of Chelsea, thanks to a single flukey (perhaps illegal) goal. Somehow, against many predictions, Liverpool made it to the final, against AC Milan in May in Istanbul.

Perhaps this was as good a time as any for my son to learn a lesson: that in life there are very few happy endings. I tried to explain. Milan were the aristocrats, flashy, suave sophisticates; Liverpool were grunt and honest effort. Of course, I hoped they'd win, but really it was piano-players against piano-shifters. We took up our positions and waited.

A goal in the first minute for Milan seemed ominous; two further goals were the last nails in the coffin. An optimist by nature, my son enquired, 'Dad, do you think

they could still win?' I shook my head, preparing to comfort the afflicted. At half-time, 3-nil up, Milan's squad were already celebrating. Should I send him to bed now, or allow him to endure and thereby learn from what was certain to be a long night of the soul? Resigned, we watched on.

A goal by Liverpool ten minutes into the second half. 'What do you think now, Dad?' More head-shaking; a consolation prize. Then, a minute later, another. 'Well, Dad?' I sighed, knowing coming close would only make the pain of losing worse. Five minutes further on, a Liverpool penalty was parried by the keeper, but a red shirt stuck the rebound into the roof of the net. Three all. Liverpool fans who'd left the stadium at half-time begged taxis to turn back. In our house, a small red-shirted figure danced around the furniture, 'Well Dad … what do you think *now*?' Elder lemon to the last, I soberly assured him. 'Even if they make it to the end, they've got no chance on penalties.'

One of the milestones in a child's life is the moment when he learns his parents are not infallible; perhaps a milestone in the parent's life as well. Astonishingly, they survived a barrage on their goal in extra time. Thanks to their rubbery-legged Polish goalkeeper and three coolly taken spot-kicks later, Liverpool won the Champions League – on penalties – in a match which has been described even by non-Liverpool fans as the greatest-ever game.

We sat joyously together as the screen filled with pictures from the far-off Turkish night of delirious fans singing their team's anthem, 'You'll Never Walk Alone'. Incandescent with delight, my son crowed and whooped; not only had his team won, but his dad had been proved wrong. It's hard to know which mattered to him more. In the future, there would be days when things did not go right; days when we would both be wrong. But, for now, we cheered for happy endings; for how in the most unlikely places the lost innocence of childhood is sometimes rediscovered.

1. Why did the writer's son choose to support Liverpool?

2. What does the father do when his son tells him about his choice?

3. What pact do the father and son make?

4. What does the father expect to happen during the match?

5. Who wins the match and how?

6. What connections does the writer make between Liverpool and Ireland? PQE

7. Why does the father agree to watch all the matches with his son? PQE

8. The father uses imagery to explain the different footballing styles of Milan and Liverpool. Can you explain this imagery? PQE

9. How does the relationship between the father and son change during this extract? PQE

10. Would you give this extract to somebody else to read? Who and why?

Re-read this line from the extract:

*Being a football fan is far more about the agony than the ecstasy, no matter who you support.*

Write about the best or worst moment you've experienced as a supporter of a team.

**OR**

Write a story starting with the line:

*How could I say no?*

**OR**

In groups, rehearse and perform the 'happy dance' that you perform when your team scores a goal or wins a match. (If you don't have a 'happy dance' make one up!)

# Marathon Man

Paul Cullen

I have a woman waiting for me in Kimmage tomorrow morning. She'll be there from early morning, with a bottle of holy water in one hand and a hard-boiled sweet in the other, I don't know her personally, but that won't stop her shouting at me in public. That's all right, though, because she'll be shouting at all the runners in tomorrow's Dublin City marathon.

I normally go for the sweet. The glucose gives a small sugar high, sustenance for another stretch of road as the last miles approach. The benefit is more psychological than real, I'm sure, but any distraction from the hardship of running twenty-six miles has to be welcome.

The start will be fun, 10,000 of us setting off in giddy spirits, cheering at the cameras and our loved ones. Those early miles will glide along, plenty to see as we travel the city's empty thoroughfares. Familiar faces from previous years are sure to pop up – the tartan-clad Scotsman with the orange wig or members of that small and dwindling band of men (and one woman) who have run all twenty-six previous Dublin marathons.

Then, there's the middle stretch, when the race meanders through outer suburbs and the going gets tougher. A strange silence will descend, broken only by the footfall of expensive trainers. This being Dublin at the end of October, a sudden squall will blow up to buffet us and prick our earlier confidence, and there'll be few spectators.

This is payback time for all those hours of training. The endless circuits of the park, the sweat-racked runs on now-distant summer days, the nightly trudges through mounds of fallen leaves as autumn and the day of the race draw near. Reservoirs of stamina built up for sudden dissipation on this bank holiday marathon.

Now, as the strength drains from my legs, my body starts listing and I slow to a crawl, I'll be asking the same question I asked last time I ran a marathon, and the time before that, and before that again – why? This can't be good for us – after all, didn't the first marathon-runner, Pheidippides in ancient Greece, drop dead at the end of his exertions? Why inflict such pain on myself? Why subject my body to such shocks? And what was it I said last time? – 'Never again.'

Pounding the streets of suburban Dublin while the rest of the city rests, I'll have plenty of time to come up with an answer of sorts.

Because? Because I can. Because I'm here and I'm healthy. Because this discomfort, being self-inflicted, has an end. Because I have a short memory. Because the guy in the white T-shirt who I passed a few miles back has just caught up with me. And, finally, now that I've twenty miles of running behind me, because stopping is arguably more painful – physically and psychologically – than continuing.

And so I'll go on, on to the finish, now looming, with the cheering of the crowds a fuzzy din, as though I'm hearing it from under water. I'll be struggling, now, listing like a sunken trawler, my face contorted in pain and my brain telling me to pack it in. Tightening muscles will force a shortening of my stride, the lightness in my head, the only counterpoint to the dead weight of tired limbs. I might hear a friend call my name from the crowd, but I'll be too weary to look.

Most of the city centre shops will be closed, but their appearance will be comforting nonetheless, for it means the end is nigh.

Suddenly, I'm rounding the corner onto Merrion Square, striding with new-found energy to the succour of the finishing line. Hands aloft, I'll pass under the bright clock and crumple once I'm on the other side. It's over now, once again. I've done it. That's that.

But as the pain subsides, optimism will grow. Within minutes, I'll start thinking about next year. Just one more go. For my woman cheering in Kimmage. Only this time I might ask her for the holy water.

1. Why is the woman in Kimmage waiting for the writer?

2. Why does the writer 'normally go for the sweet'?

3. According to the writer, what are the three main stages of the marathon?

4. How does the writer feel at the end of the extract?

5. Why does the writer say he runs marathons?

6. What details does the writer use to capture the atmosphere during the first half of the race? **P Q E**

7. How does the atmosphere change in the second half? **P Q E**

8. Do you think the writer will run another marathon? **P Q E**

In groups, make a list of the sports played by people in your group. Discuss whether or not you feel sport is important in people's lives. For homework, write a paragraph outlining your feelings on the importance or otherwise of sport.

What do you think is the greatest Irish sporting moment of them all?

- Was it local, national or international?

- Why do you think it is such a special moment?

- How did it make you feel?

### OR

Imagine that you are about to run the Dublin Marathon for a charity of your choice. Write the letter that you would send to companies looking for corporate sponsorship.

- Before you begin, look at the guidelines for writing formal letters, starting on p. 141.

- Remember to introduce yourself.

- Explain the work of your charity.

- Describe the hard work you have already done.

- Point out the positive publicity the company will get if it sponsors you.

### OR

Write a story, fictional or real, inspired by this saying:

*Quitters never win, and winners never quit.*

# Down with Pigeons

Robert Benchley

St Francis of Assisi (unless I am getting him mixed up with St Simeon Stylites, which might be very easy to do as both their names begin with 'St') was very fond of birds, and often had his picture taken with them sitting on his shoulders and pecking at his wrists. That was all right, if St Francis liked it. We all have our likes and dislikes, and I have more of a feeling for dogs. However, I am not *against* birds as a class. I am just against pigeons.

I do not consider pigeons birds, in the first place. They are more in the nature of people; people who mooch.

Probably my feeling about pigeons arises from the fact that all my life I have lived in rooms where pigeons came rumbling in and out of my window. I myself must have a certain morbid fascination for pigeons, because they follow me about so much – and with evident ill will. I am firmly convinced that they are trying to haunt me.

Although I live in the middle of a very large city (well, to show you how large it is – it is the largest in the world) I am awakened every morning by a low gargling sound which turns out to be the result of one, or two, or three pigeons walking in at my window and sneering at me. Granted that I am a fit subject for sneering as I lie there, possibly with one shoe on or an unattractive expression on my face, but there is something more than just a passing criticism in these birds making remarks about me. They have some ugly scheme on foot against me, and I know it. Sooner or later it will come out, and then I can sue.

This thing has been going on ever since I was in college. In our college everybody was very proud of the pigeons. Anyone walking across the Yard (Campus to you, please) was beset by large birds who insisted on climbing up his waistcoat and looking about in his wallet for nuts or raisins or whatever it is you feed pigeons (bichloride would be my suggestion, but let it pass).

God knows that I was decent enough to them in my undergraduate days. I let them walk up and down my back and I tried to be as nice as I could without actually letting them see that I was not so crazy about it. I even gave them chestnuts, chestnuts which I wanted myself. I now regret my generosity, for good chestnuts are hard to get these days.

But somehow the word got around in pigeon circles that Benchley was anti-pigeon. They began pestering me. I would go to bed at night, tired from overstudy, and at six-thirty in the morning the Big Parade would begin. The line of march was as follows: Light on Benchley's window sill, march once in through the open window, going 'Grumble-grumble-grumble' in a sinister tone. Then out and stand on the sill, urging other pigeons to come in and take a crack at it.

There is very little fun in waking up with a headache and hearing an ominous murmuring noise, with just the suggestion of a passing shadow moving across your window sill. No man should be asked to submit to this *all* his life.

I once went to Venice (Italy), and there, with the rest of the tourists, stood in awe in the centre of St Mark's Piazza, gazing at the stately portals of the church and at the lovely green drinks served at Florian's for those who don't want to look at the church all of the time.

It is an age-old custom for tourists to feed corn to the pigeons and then for the pigeons to crawl all over the tourists. This has been going on without interruption ever since Americans discovered Venice. So far as the records show, no pigeon has ever failed a tourist – and no tourist has ever failed a pigeon. It is a very pretty relationship.

In my case, however, it was different. In the first place, the St Mark's pigeons, having received word from the American chapter of their lodge, began flying at me in such numbers and with such force as actually to endanger my life. They came in great droves, all flying low and hard, just barely skimming my hat and whirring in an ugly fashion with some idea of intimidating me. But by that time I was not to be intimidated, and, although I ducked very low and lost my hat several times, I did not give in. I even bought some corn from one of the vendors and held it out in my hand, albeit with bad grace. But, for the first time in centuries, no pigeon fell for the corn gag. I stood alone in the middle of St Mark's Square, holding out my hand dripping with kernels of golden corn, and was openly and deliberately snubbed. One or two of the creatures walked up to within about ten feet of me and gave me a nasty look, but not one gave my corn a tumble. So I decided the dickens with them and ate the corn myself.

Now this sort of thing must be the result of a very definite boycott, or, in its more aggressive state, an anti-Benchley campaign. Left to myself, I would have only the very friendliest feelings for pigeons (it is too late now, but I might once have been won over).

But having been put on my mettle, there is nothing that I can do now but fight back. Whatever I may be, I am not yellow.

Here is my plan. I know that I am alone in this fight, for most people like pigeons, or, at any rate, are not antagonised by them. But single-handed I will take up the cudgels, and I hope that, when they grow up, my boys will carry on the battle on every cornice and every campus in the land.

Whenever I meet a pigeon, whether it be on my own window sill or walking across a public park, I will stop still and place my hands on my hips and wait. If the pigeon wants to make the first move and attack me, I will definitely strike back, even to the extent of hitting it with my open palm and knocking it senseless (not a very difficult feat I should think, as they seem to have very little sense).

If they prefer to fight it out by innuendo and sneering, I will fight it out by innuendo and sneering. I have worked up a noise which I can make in my throat which is just as unpleasant sounding as theirs. I will even take advantage of my God-given power of speech and will say, 'Well, what do you want to make of it, you waddling, cooing so-and-sos?' I will glare at them just as they glare at me, and if they come within reach of my foot, so help me, St Francis, I will kick at them. *And* the next pigeon that strolls in across my window ledge when I am just awakening, I will catch with an especially prepared trap and will drag into my room, there to punch the living daylights out of him.

I know that this sounds very cruel and very much as if I were an animal hater. As a matter of fact, I am such a friend of animals in general that I am practically penniless. I have been known to take in dogs who were obviously impostors and put them through college. I am a sucker for kittens, even though I know that one day they will grow into cats who will betray and traduce me. I have even been known to pat a tiger cub, which accounts for my writing this article with my left hand.

But as far as pigeons go, I am through. It is a war to the death, and I have a horrible feeling that the pigeons are going to win.

1. What do you think is the most important sentence in the first paragraph?

2. To what type of person does the writer compare the pigeons?

3. How do the pigeons annoy him in the morning?

4. When did his bad relationship with the pigeons start?

5. In your own words, describe the relationship between pigeons and tourists in Venice.

6. What happens to the writer when he arrives in St Mark's Square?

7. How does he decide to fight back?

8. How does Benchley prove that he is not an animal hater?

9. Do you think pigeons really dislike Benchley, or is he being paranoid? **PQE**

10. Which part of the passage did you find most humorous and why? **PQE**

11. Is the ending of the extract effective?

12. If you were listening to Benchley reading this essay aloud, what tone of voice do you think he would be using at different stages? Try to identify three moments that would require three different tones. **PQE**

13. Find three words that you did not understand in this passage and look them up in the dictionary.

14. Examine the verbs that Benchley uses to describe the pigeons throughout the passage. List them and say why they are effective. **PQE**

Write an essay with the title 'Down with …' Think of something that really annoys you, and try modelling your essay structure on Benchley's. Read the points below for help.

- Plan a good opening, only revealing your pet hate at the very end of the paragraph.
- Classify your dislike.
- Give a specific example of an encounter with your pet hate.
- Outline the history of your dislike, stating its origins.
- Explain how your hatred worsened over time, using exaggeration.
- Be paranoid!
- State your plan and seek support.
- Look at how this student modelled his essay on Benchley's.

### Fir trees aren't all they're cracked up to be
### by Ryan Leahy

You often hear stories of people who go to an area full of trees (a forest, if you will) that is scheduled to be cut down (deforested, if you will), and they chain themselves to the trees to prevent them from being cut down. This is fine; if you want to risk your life for a few trees then more power to you; one less idiot in the world to bother me. That said, I am not 'anti-tree'; I quite like them; I am just 'anti-fir tree'.

Now, you may think (as many before you have) that this is absurd. How can someone hate a type of tree? Well, before I explain, I would like to clear something up: I don't consider fir trees to even be trees. They are more like children. Do you remember primary school? Do you remember the one child you hated with a burning passion? The child everyone else adored because he was always happy and nice. The child your parents invited over to your house and constantly asked, 'why can't you be more like him?' The child who knocked your books on the floor when nobody was watching, and who picked his nose and flicked it at you when everyone's attention was elsewhere. This is exactly what fir trees are like.

I remember the first time I experienced the evil of the fir tree. I was no older than seven at the time. My friend and I had gone up to a nearby pine plantation to play. Being the tireless young boys we were, 'playing' usually meant climbing the trees and jumping off. I had climbed quite a large fir tree (large by a seven-year-old's standards) and prepared myself to jump. I scanned the landing zone, making various calculations to do with wind velocity, grass to stone ratio and other such factors that need to be considered before making such a jump.

I made sure that there was no possible way that I could injure myself from the leap. I instructed my friend to clear a patch for my landing and I took a deep breath. Then I leapt. For one moment everything was clear and I felt ecstatic. Suddenly my trouser leg caught on a branch, a branch that sure as hell wasn't there when I made my oh-so-careful analysis. This one simple snag sent me hurtling towards the ground. Luckily the fall was low enough to escape serious injury (the tree's plan had been foiled). I examined the tree carefully, even climbing it again to investigate anything that could have caught me like that. After minutes of tireless study I came to the conclusion that the tree must have moved, and with malicious intent. It was attempted murder (dendrocide?).

Of course there's nothing out of the ordinary about a young boy hurting himself while playing in the woods, and that's what the fir tree had intended. I looked like a lunatic trying to explain it. I could tell you about other such incidents (including every single Christmas in memory; I know the fir tree convinced Santa not to give me that bike!) but I want to explain other reasons for hating fir trees. First of all, they smell – the vile, sickly sweet odour that permeates the entire building in which the tree is situated. I don't know anyone else who finds this noxious odour unpleasant so it's obvious that the pine tree has created it just to bother me. I've spent many a Christmas with my nose buried in an old sock; pungent in its own right, yet infinitely more enjoyable than the gruesome scent exuded by the firs. We now have an artificial tree. Sadly, having an artificial tree doesn't save me from sitting into cars with pine-scented air fresheners, or walking onto buildings with the scent having leached into every fabric after years of it being consistently sprayed throughout.

Have you ever had to move a fir tree? If you have then you'll know exactly how unpleasant it is. There is, of course, the obvious handicap of thousands upon thousands of needles covering every available surface. Any attempt at getting a decent grip is foiled, and your hand has now got a lot more holes in it than before. If, by some extraordinary feat of good luck, you manage to grab a surface that isn't too densely packed with needles, and haul the hulking conifer to where it needs to go, more often than not your hands will be coated in a layer of sap. This viscous, amber liquid is like glue without any of the useful applications. It will not wipe off, and it will transfer to anything you touch like some sort of sticky virus. You have to make your way to the nearest bathroom (and wash your hands with hot water and soap) without touching anything at all. Being the devious creatures the fir trees are, they also take this opportunity to somehow make your nose itchy. It is torture, plain and simple.

These so called 'fir-trees' don't even have fur. Their name makes no sense, it defies logic. It's like the time my sister named her (gold) goldfish 'Purple'. Fir trees are covered in spindly needles, the very opposite of fur. It is a form of propaganda. When people think of fur they think of cute little cats and dogs and rabbits that are cuddly and playful. So fir trees are subconsciously linked with cute little animals. A cunning ruse, I must say. But now, anyone like me who dares to speak up against these pernicious trees is instantly deemed insane. People ask 'how can you hate fir trees?' It's like hating roses they say. (Don't even get me started on roses!) But the truth is fir trees plan to take over the world.

Now you're probably saying to yourself 'this guy really is insane' but let me explain. Fir trees have already made their way into the houses of anyone who celebrates Christmas (which, as an aside, is the time of year when suicide rates are highest; tell me that's not linked to fir trees). They have also gotten their smell into almost every car and house ever made. It's only a matter of time. Have you ever wondered why they don't lose their so called 'leaves' in winter? It's a defence mechanism. If they lost their leaves, not only would they lose a powerful weapon, but they would be bare and we could all see whatever evil it is that they are concealing all year round.

There is only one viable course of action; we must eradicate all fir trees (and rose bushes, if we have time). These are not the ravings of a madman; these are the ravings of a man who wants to save the world. I ask of you, my brethren, to throw out your Christmas trees, burn your pine-scented air fresheners and grab your nearest chainsaw. March with me to the nearest woodland and we will wreak havoc upon fir trees. Anyone who stands in our way is an ally of the firs and should be treated with severe prejudice. Faced with this, the fir trees will be forced to come out of hiding. A war will follow, but we will emerge victorious!

Write a composition entitled:

*The time I was … sick OR lucky OR embarrassed OR sad.*        2002 O.L. Paper

**OR**

Write a composition entitled:

*Things that make me angry.*        2009 H.L. Paper

**OR**

Write a composition about a hobby or activity that you love.

**OR**

Write a composition with the following title:

*A day in my life that I would like to relive.*        2006 H.L. Paper

# Descriptive Writing

## Being There

Tim Clancy

I am standing in my summer pajamas, the lightest of cotton. The top buttons up to a flat lapel collar that lies open at my neck, like a sport shirt my grandfather might have worn. The bottoms are held up by an elastic waistband that I tug and release, snapping it gently against my clean body, fresh from a bath on a Saturday evening in June. A faint breeze curls through the baggy openings of the pajamas and swirls over me like a soft electric charge. I feel weightless.

My father has just finished cutting the grass. I hear the crunch of gravel and the rattly echo of the mower's hard wheels as he pushes them over the driveway and into the grey cinder-block garage. He is wearing what he always wears in my childhood memories of him in the summer: a white V-neck T-shirt and baggy grey work pants. His hair is black and cut flat on top. He is a lean six-footer with neck and arms browned and freckled by the sun, his left arm more so because of the way he angles it out of the window of the car whenever he is driving. Parking the mower marks the end of his labour for the week. In my memory he is smiling that jaunty off-to-the-side smile, one I could never confuse with anyone else's.

Sounds drowned by the roar of the mower begin to return: the cooing of an evening dove, muted by hazy stillness drifts on the air. I look in the direction of the cooing, but see only a field of knee-deep grass surrounded by a boggy woods. From their already darkening depths comes the steady croaking drone of frogs, invisible but as present as the cool grass beneath my feet.

My mother is sitting in an old metal lawn chair holding a white-haired baby, my brother Pat. She wears a breezy summer housedress, one that she made herself, and she is singing softly, a song about sitting on top of the world and the street where you live and a yellow bird.

I smell lilac blossoms, the freshly cut grass, cow manure, Ivory soap.

I hear the rhythmic squeak of the rope swing as my sister Marianne glides back and forth under the massive cedar tree in the front yard, her red-blond hair and nightgown flowing together like flags in the wind.

My sister Sharon, in her pajamas, sits on the edge of the porch, petting a black-and-white kitten.

> Good writers don't just describe what they SEE! They use all the SENSES. Think about this as you read the next couple of extracts.

The tractor is parked in front of the garage. My brother Mike has climbed up into the seat and is holding on to the steering wheel. He thinks he's a big man driving down the road. Mike's hair is like mine. Mom has given us our summer haircuts with the electric clippers so that what we have left is more like suede than hair. My brother Kevin is standing a few feet away, feeding handfuls of grass to Jerry, our spotted pony. Kevin has the suede look, too. He and Mike are both wearing their pajamas.

I have other memories of the farm, memories that seem to be there for the obvious reason: they might be dramatic or humorous or frightening. But my pajama night memory is different. In it, I am simply standing barefoot on the lawn. I remember the dove, the rope swing, my mother and father, sisters and brothers, the barn, the lilacs, the woods – all bathed in the diffuse radiance of fading summer light.

1. What time of day is it at the opening of this extract?

2. What are the child's father and mother doing?

3. What are his brothers and sisters doing?

4. Is this a happy memory?

5. What can the child feel at the start of the extract?

6. What can he hear? **PQE**

7. What does he smell?

8. Why do you think this memory is special for the writer? **PQE**

Divide your copy page into four columns. Put one of the headings SOUND, SIGHT, TOUCH and SMELL on each column. In the first column make a list of every sound described in the extract. Do the same for the senses in the other columns.

### OR

Choose a memory from your own childhood. **Brainstorm** under the headings above, but also include the sense of TASTE. Try to capture the atmosphere of the moment in your piece of writing. It need not be as long as this extract.

### OR

Draw or paint a picture of a scene inspired by the Tim Clancy extract.

# Follow Me Down

Julie Hearn

It was the stench seeping in through the car windows that bothered Tom the most. Rank and beefy, it reminded him of the way dogs smell after a walk in the rain. Smelly dogs made him think of Goldie, left behind in Dorset, and for a moment the page of the London A to Z he was supposed to be reading blurred and swam in front of his eyes.

Quickly, he knuckled the wet from his face. Had his mother noticed? If she had, he would say it was sweat. And that he felt sick. It was late morning, the middle of August, and hot enough for even a skinny twelve year old to be melting like a lolly. Add the stink of Smithfield meat market, leaching through the traffic fumes, and anyone with nostrils and a stomach in working order was bound to feel bad.

His mother, in profile, looked surprisingly fit considering she was driving in circles, unable to remember where her own mother lived, and had more reason than most people to feel like throwing up, with or without a pong in the air.

'You all right, Mum?' His voice was gruff. A 'yes' or 'no' answer would do him.

'Tired. Just tired. I'll be glad to stop.'

They came to a roundabout. It was somewhere Tom recognised. 'We've done this one,' he said. 'Twice.' His mother circled it three times more, looking for signs.

Go round again, thought Tom, and I really will chuck. The smell was getting worse. He tried breathing through his mouth. Tasted offal on his tongue. Liver without the onions. His mother, he knew, had a brilliant sense of smell; could recognise anything from gas to a bunch of flowers through several closed doors. How come she wasn't complaining?

'Can't stand much more of this stink,' he muttered.

**DIVE IN!**

1. What is bothering Tom?
2. What does the smell remind him of?
3. Why does he get upset?
4. Where is the smell coming from?
5. Why are Tom and his mother driving in this area?

**TAKE THE PLUNGE!**

6. Pick what you think is the most disgusting smell described in the extract.
7. Identify all the words in the passage used to convey the sense of smell.
8. The smells have a terrible effect on Tom. How does the writer get this across?

**P Q E**

**WHY DON'T YOU...**

Describe entering one of the following places, focusing particularly on including a specific smell or aroma:

A crowded lift                A bakery

An empty house          A hospital

A changing room         The local butcher's

A spring meadow         An amusement arcade

An expensive department store         An outdoor market

**OR**

Think about a smell that always brings to mind a certain memory (for example, a perfume or aftershave might remind you of a particular person). Describe the smell and the effect it has.

# Q&A

Vikram Swarup

By three a.m. the firing stopped completely and there was a deathly silence. A sudden gust of wind rustled the trees nearby. I inched towards the Pakistani bunker, no more than two hundred feet away. Suddenly, in front of me, I heard the sound of muffled footsteps. I strained to hear over the pounding of my heart as I raised my rifle. I cocked it, ready to fire, but hoping that I wouldn't have to use it. Firing in the darkness produces a bright muzzle flash that would betray my position to the enemy. I tried to suppress even the sound of my own breathing. Something thin and slippery crawled over my back. It felt like a snake. I had a desperate urge to shake it off, but fear of alerting the enemy made me close my eyes and hope that it would not bite me. After what seemed like an eternity, it slithered down my leg and I heaved a sigh of relief. My back was drenched in sweat and my arms were aching. My rifle felt as if it was made of lead. The footsteps started coming again, coming closer and closer. I peered into the darkness, trying to decipher the outline of the enemy, but could see nothing. I knew that death was lurking close by. I would either kill or be killed. A twig crunched and I could even detect faint breathing. It was an agonizing wait. I debated whether I should wait for the enemy to make the first move. Suddenly, I saw the flare of a match and the back of a head floated into view, like a disembodied ghost, not more than ten feet away. I immediately leapt out of the grass and rushed forward with open bayonet.

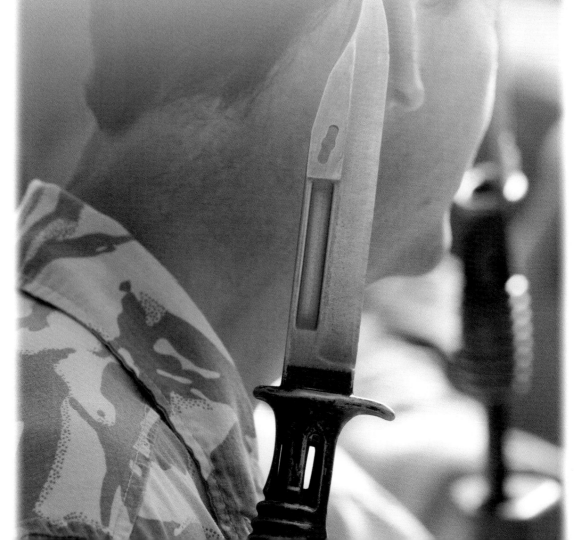

1. What is the first sound that the soldier hears?

2. How do you know that he is nervous?

3. How do you know that the enemy soldier is very close?

4. Why is the sense of sound so important in this extract? **P Q E**

5. What other senses are used as part of the description in the extract? **P Q E**

6. Would you like to read more of this book?

Imagine that you are taking a ride on a very scary ghost train. Describe the experience, paying special attention to the sounds that you hear, and those that you make!

**OR**

Bring some instrumental music (music without words) into class. This can be any type of music, from classical to pop, jazz to hip hop. Play the music three times.

- The first time you hear the music, write down any **words** that come into your head. They can be anything at all.

- The second time you listen, look at the words you have written and try to think of a **place**.

- After the third time you have heard the music, write a paragraph describing a **place**, a **moment** or a **situation**. Remember to use all your senses!

**OR**

Think of a sound that really, really annoys you. Describe it in as much detail as possible

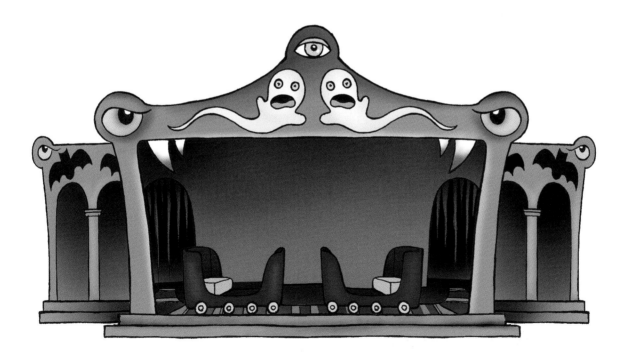

# I Know Why the Caged Bird Sings

Maya Angelou

On Sunday mornings Momma served a breakfast that was geared to hold us quiet from 9.30 a.m. to 3 p.m. She fried thick pink slabs of home-cured ham and poured the grease over sliced red tomatoes. Eggs over easy, fried potatoes and onions, yellow hominy and crisp perch fried so hard we would pop them in our mouths and chew bones, fins and all. Her cathead biscuits were at least three inches in diameter and two inches thick. The trick to eating catheads was to get the butter on them before they got cold – then they were delicious. When, unluckily, they were allowed to get cold, they tended to a gooeyness, not unlike a wad of tired gum.

We were able to reaffirm our findings on the catheads each Sunday that Reverend Thomas spent with us. Naturally enough, he was asked to bless the table. We would all stand; my uncle, leaning his walking stick against the wall, would lean his weight on the table.

Then Reverend Thomas would begin. 'Blessed Father, we thank you this morning …' and on and on and on. I'd stop listening after a while until Bailey kicked me and then I cracked my lids to see what had promised to be a meal that would make any Sunday proud. But as the Reverend droned on and on and on to a God who I thought must be bored to hear the same things over and over again, I saw that the ham grease had turned white on the tomatoes. The eggs had withdrawn from the edge of the platter to bunch in the centre like children left out in the cold. And the catheads had sat down on themselves with the conclusiveness of a fat woman sitting in an easy chair. And still he talked on. When he finally stopped, our appetites were gone, but he feasted on the cold food with a non-talking but still noisy relish.

**DIVE IN!**

1. How many main ingredients are there in the breakfast?

2. What happened to the cathead biscuits when they went cold?

3. What effect does Reverend Thomas's blessing have on the food?

**TAKE THE PLUNGE!**

4. Pick out the adjectives that describe
   - the ham
   - the tomatoes
   - the perch

5. What words make the cold food sound unappetising?
   **PQE**

6. The writer gives the food human characteristics. See if you can pick out these examples of personification.

**WHY DON'T YOU...**

Write a description of your favourite breakfast, concentrating on the textures and flavours of the food.

**OR**

Describe the most disgusting thing you have ever eaten.

**OR**

Write out a menu that you might find in an Irish hotel or guesthouse.

> When something that isn't human is given human characteristics it is called personification.

# The Poisonwood Bible

Barbara Kingsolver

*This passage is set in the jungle in the African Congo.*

This awful night is the worst we've ever known: the *nsongonya*. They came on us like a nightmare. Nelson bang-bang-banging on the back door got all tangled up with my sleep, so that, even after I was awake, the next hours had the unsteady presence of a dream. Before I even knew where I was, I found myself pulled along by somebody's hand in the dark and a horrible fiery sting sloshing up my calves. We were wading through very hot water, I thought, but it couldn't be water, so I tried to ask the name of the burning liquid that had flooded our house – no, for we were already outside – that had flooded the whole world?

'*Nsongonya*,' they kept shouting, '*Les fourmis! Un corps d'armée!*'

*Ants.* We were walking on, surrounded, enclosed, enveloped, being eaten by *ants*. Every surface was covered and boiling, and the path like black flowing lava in the moonlight. Dark, bulbous tree trunks seethed and bulged. The grass had become a field of dark daggers standing upright, churning and crumpling in on themselves. We walked on ants and ran on them, releasing their vinegary smell to the weird, quiet night. Hardly anyone spoke. We just ran as fast as we could alongside our neighbours. Adults carried babies and goats; children carried pots of food and dogs and younger brothers and sisters, the whole village of Kilanga. I thought of Mama Mwanza: would her sluggish sons carry her? Crowded together we moved down the road like a rushing stream, ran till we reached the river, and there we stopped. All of us shifting from foot to foot, slapping, some people moaning in pain but only the babies shrieking and wailing out loud. Strong men sloshed in slow motion through waist-deep water, dragging their boats, while the rest of us waited our turn to get in someone's canoe.

**DIVE IN!**

1. What wakes the writer?

2. What are the people being attacked by?

3. Where are they all running to?

**TAKE THE PLUNGE!**

When writing descriptions, people often forget about the sense of **touch**. The word used to describe things connected to our sense of touch is **tactile**. Good descriptive writing is very tactile.

4. What do you think is the most tactile moment in the first paragraph? **P Q E**

5. The first two sentences of the second paragraph are very dramatic. Why?

6. What does the writer compare the grass to and why?

**WHY DON'T YOU...**

Choose an object and describe it using only the sense of touch. You have five minutes in which to do this. Then take it in turns to read your description out to your class. People must guess what the object is.

**OR**

Re-read the description of the colony of ants attacking the village, and try to imagine yourself there. If you hate any type of insect this is probably your worst nightmare, or is it? What is the worst tactile experience you can think of? Write a brief description of it.

**OR**

Re-write this passage from the point of view of the ants!

# Descriptive Essay Writing

In the last few extracts you read some great descriptive writing. You will have noticed that the writers concentrated on using all of the senses – smell, sound, taste, touch and sight. In the Junior Certificate you are often asked to write your own descriptions. The best essays will always use more than one sense. It is best if you plan these using a brainstorm, but think about the specific areas that you see in the sample brainstorm on the next page. Here are some sample exam essays.

Write a composition on 'A Day in the Country' OR 'A Day in the City'.

2002 O.L. Paper

*OR*

Write an essay in which you describe a place you love to visit. Try to give details that appeal not just to your readers' senses of sight and sound, but to all senses.

2002 H.L. Paper

*OR*

Write a composition with the title:

'The most interesting place OR places I've ever been'.

2008 H.L. Paper

1. Begin by placing your essay title in the centre of the page. In the brainstorm on the opposite page the person has decided the place they love to visit is an art gallery.

2. Note how the brainstorm is divided into sights, sounds, smells, tastes and touch.

3. First, brainstorm things that you can see, hear, smell, taste and touch in the place that you have chosen. (Note, these are written in **black**.)

4. Then, brainstorm words that will describe the things you have chosen. Normally these words will be adjectives or verbs. (Note, these are written in **red**.)

5. You don't have to colour code your brainstorm, but it can be very helpful in reminding you to use descriptive words! Did you spot that the writer of this brainstorm deliberately went into the café so that they could include some tastes in their brainstorm? Not something you'd expect in an art gallery!

6. When you have finished your brainstorm, try writing a sample paragraph. Remember, you can take ideas from any part of the brainstorm at any time. Cross out ideas as you use them.

7. Always make out a paragraph plan for your essay, no matter how rough it is.

# Brainstorm

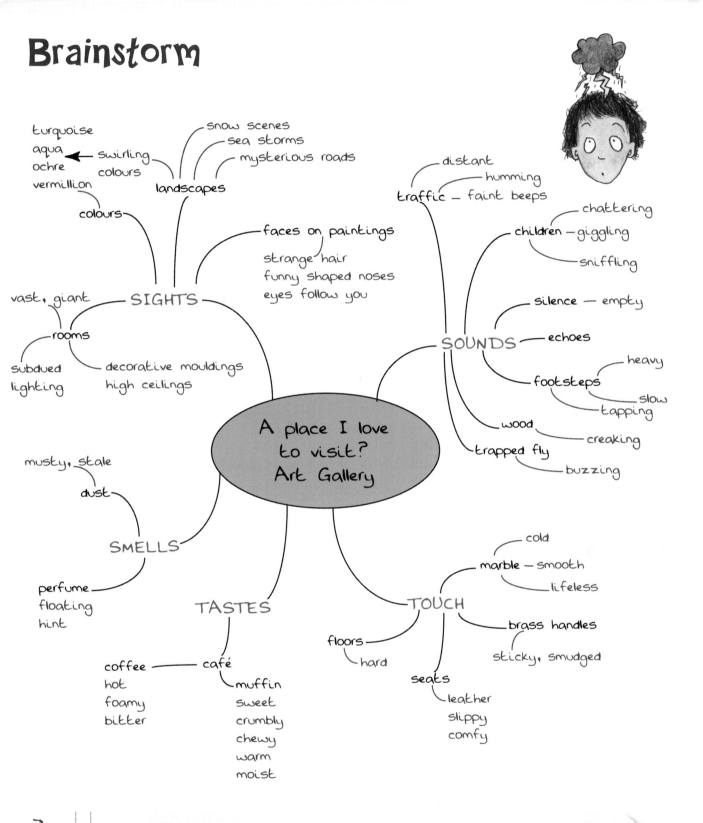

**Colours:** turquoise, aqua, ochre, vermillion ← swirling colours

**landscapes:** snow scenes, sea storms, mysterious roads

**SIGHTS**
- faces on paintings — strange hair, funny shaped noses, eyes follow you
- vast, giant rooms
- subdued lighting
- decorative mouldings, high ceilings

**SOUNDS**
- traffic — distant, humming, faint beeps
- children — chattering, giggling, sniffling
- silence — empty
- echoes
- footsteps — heavy, slow, tapping
- wood — creaking
- trapped fly — buzzing

**A place I love to visit? Art Gallery**

**SMELLS**
- dust — musty, stale
- perfume — floating hint

**TASTES**
- café — coffee (hot, foamy, bitter), muffin (sweet, crumbly, chewy, warm, moist)

**TOUCH**
- marble — cold, smooth, lifeless
- brass handles — sticky, smudged
- floors — hard
- seats — leather, slippy, comfy

Wandering through the echoing halls of the art gallery, I listened contentedly to the distant hum of the busy traffic. Here in the silent, subdued lighting I stared in wonder at mysterious roads and violent sea storms. The musty, stale smell of forgotten dust mixed with the fragrant aroma of coffee drifting from the café.

# Storytelling/Narrative Writing

The following are the features of good storytelling:

## ▪ Narration

- Narrative writing tells a story.
- The **narrator** is the person telling the story.
- **First-person narration** is when a person in the story tells the story: 'As I walked out the door I slammed it loudly behind me.'
- Third-person narration is when someone who is not in the story tells the story: 'As he walked out the door he slammed it loudly behind him.'

## ▪ Plot

- The opening of a story must **catch the reader's attention**. It may do this by introducing the main characters, raising questions in the reader's mind or creating an unusual setting (time and place).
- Every good story has a **complication**. Normally this is caused by conflict, either between characters or within a character. The complication is what moves the story along as the reader wonders how it will be resolved.
- The **climax** is the moment that all the tension has been building up to. It is an important, vital moment in the story.
- The **resolution** is how the story ends; all the main issues are resolved.

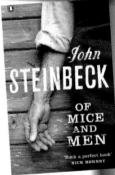

## ▪ Character

- The **personalities** of characters are revealed through what they say, what they do and what others say about them.
- The main person in a story is called the **protagonist**. If we admire this character and want them to succeed in overcoming obstacles we call them the **hero** or **heroine**. If they are evil and obstruct the hero, we call them the **villain**.

# Slam

Nick Hornby

So things were ticking along quite nicely. In fact, I'd say that good stuff had been happening pretty solidly for about six months.

– For example: Mum got rid of Steve, her rubbish boyfriend.

– For example: Mrs Gillett, my art and design teacher, took me to one side after a lesson and asked whether I'd thought of doing art at college.

– For example: I'd learned two new skating tricks, suddenly, after weeks of making an idiot of myself in public. (I'm guessing that not all of you are skaters, so I should say something straight away, just so there are no terrible misunderstandings. Skating = skateboarding. We never say skateboarding, usually, so this is the only time I'll use the word in this whole story. And if you keep thinking of me messing around on ice, then it's your own stupid fault.)

All that, and I'd met Alicia too.

I was going to say that maybe you should know something about me before I go off on one about my mum and Alicia and all that. If you knew something about me, you might actually care about some of those things. But then, looking at what I just wrote, you know quite a lot already, or at least you could have guessed a lot of it. You could have guessed that my mum and dad don't live together, for a start, unless you thought that my dad was the sort of person who wouldn't mind his wife having boyfriends. Well, he's not. You could have guessed that I skate, and you could have guessed that my best subject at school was art and design, unless you thought I might be the kind of person who's always being taken to one side and told to apply for college by all the teachers in every subject. You know, and the teachers actually fight over me. 'No, Sam! Forget art! Do physics!' 'Forget physics! It would be a tragedy for the human race if you gave up French!' And then they all start punching each other.

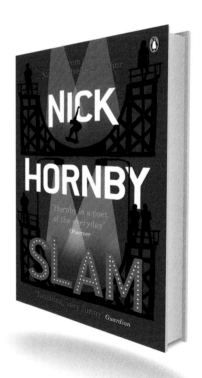

Yeah, well. That sort of thing really, really doesn't happen to me. I can promise you, I have never caused a fight between teachers.

And you don't need to be Sherlock Holmes or whatever to work out that Alicia was a girl who meant something to me. I'm glad there are things you don't know and can't guess, weird things, things that have only ever happened to me in the whole history of the world, as far as I know. If you were to guess it all from that first little paragraph, I'd start to worry that I wasn't an incredibly complicated and interesing person, ha, ha.

**DIVE IN!**

1. What did Sam's Mum do?
2. Why did Mrs Gillett take Sam to one side?
3. How do you know that the narrator takes skating seriously?

**TAKE THE PLUNGE!**

4. What is your impression of Sam?
5. How does the first-person narration used here help you to understand more about Sam's character? **P Q E**
6. Would you like to read more of this book? Why or why not?

**WHY DON'T YOU...**

Re-write this extract with Sam's mum as the narrator.

**OR**

Write a story beginning with the words:

*So things were ticking along quite nicely.*

**OR**

Imagine you are a skater. Local residents have objected to your group skating in the nearby park. Write the letter you would send to your local government representative defending your right to skate.

# Memoirs of a Geisha

Arthur Golden

Hatsumomo turned back to face the mirror and sang quietly to herself as she opened a jar of pale yellow cream. You may not believe me when I tell you that this cream was made from nightingale droppings, but it's true. Many geisha used it as a face cream in those days, because it was believed to be very good for the skin; but it was so expensive that Hatsumomo put only a few dots around her eyes and mouth. Then she tore a small piece of wax from one of the bars and, after softening it in her fingertips, rubbed it into the skin of her face, and afterward of her neck and chest. She took some time to wipe her hands clean on a rag, and then moistened one of her flat makeup brushes in a dish of water and rubbed it in the makeup until she had a chalky white paste. She used this to paint her face and neck, but left her eyes bare, as well as the area around her lips and nose. If you've ever seen a child cut holes in paper to make a mask, this was how Hatsumomo looked, until she dampened some smaller brushes and used them to fill in the cutouts. After this she looked as if she'd fallen face-first into a bin of rice flour, for her whole face was ghastly white. She looked like the demon she was, but even so, I was sick with jealousy and shame. Because I knew that in an hour or so, men would be gazing with astonishment at that face; and I would still be there in the okiya, looking sweaty and plain.

Now she moistened her pigment sticks and used them to rub a reddish blush onto her cheeks. Already during my first month in the okiya, I'd seen Hatsumomo in her finished makeup many times; I stole looks at her whenever I could without seeming rude. I'd noticed she used a variety of tints for her cheeks, depending on the colours of her kimono. There was nothing unusual in this; but what I didn't know until later was that Hatsumomo always chose a shade much redder than others might have used. I can't say why she did it, unless it was to make people think of blood. But Hatsumomo was no fool; she knew how to bring out the beauty in her features.

# Take the Plunge!

1. Why does Hatsumomo only use a few dots of the face cream around her eyes and mouth?

2. What colour of make-up does she use on her face?

3. What is unusual about the colour of blush that she uses?

4. What comparisons does the writer make in order to help us visualise what Hatsumomo looked like with the white paste on? **P Q E**

5. How does the narrator feel about Hatsumomo? **P Q E**

6. How does the writer help us see so many details in this passage? **P Q E**

Invent a name for a new make-up product. Design a poster to sell it and include a caption, a slogan and copy to accompany it. (Have a look at Chapter 3 on Media Studies for ideas.)

### OR

Imagine that you are adapting this passage as a scene for a film. Write out the director's notes in point format, telling the actors exactly what to do in what sequence.

### OR

Write a description of a clown putting on his make-up.

In pairs, prepare a mime of this scene – if you have never worn make-up, pay attention to the detailed instructions!

# Across the Barricades

Joan Lingard

Kevin was not allowed to go back to work for another two weeks. His job involved too much heavy lifting, the doctor said. The days were long for Kevin. The house was too small; the street, in daytime hours, was the prerogative of the women and young children. The women gossiped in their doorways, arms folded, their eyes sharp for any speck of interest. When he came by they called out to him, willing him to stop, but he seldom did. He talked less to anyone now than he ever had.

'There's a real change come over your Kevin,' said Mrs Kelly to Mrs McCoy when she called to see her. 'He used to be a right cheery boy, always ready for the craic.'

Mrs McCoy lifted another shirt from the wash basket and carried on ironing. She was hot, even though the back door stood wide open to let in the air, or what air there was in the small spaces between the houses. She thought of the green fields of County Tyrone and thought she should try to take the baby there for a week or two after he was born so that his lungs could fill with fresh country air.

'Kevin got a right beating up, you know.'

'There's some that say he was asking for it.'

Mrs McCoy lifted her head and looked Mrs Kelly straight in the eye.

'And what are you meaning by that?'

Another type of narration is **third-person narration**. This is when someone who is not in the story tells the story using 'he', 'she' and 'they'. This allows us to see the story from many **points of view**.

**DIVE IN!**

1. Why were the days long for Kevin?

2. How does Mrs Kelly think Kevin has changed?

3. What makes Mrs McCoy think of Co. Tyrone?

**TAKE THE PLUNGE!**

4. A third-person narrator can see inside any character's mind. How can we tell this from this extract? **P Q E**

5. How many points of view are we shown in this passage?

6. A third-person narrator can tell us about the characters' thoughts, feelings and knowledge. What does the narrator choose to tell us about Kevin and Mrs McCoy in this extract? **P Q E**

**WHY DON'T YOU...**

Briefly re-write this story using first-person narration. You can use any of the characters mentioned as your narrator.

**OR**

Write a short story beginning with the following line: *The women gossiped in their doorways, arms folded, their eyes sharp for any speck of interest …*

> A **synonym** is a word or phrase that means the same thing as another word, for example, hungry, ravenous and peckish are all synonyms.

**OR**

Look at the list of verbs below.

| | | |
|---|---|---|
| ran | wrote | fought |
| said | sat | asked |
| ate | drank | carried |
| looked | walked | searched |
| thought | danced | got |

Try to think of three synonyms for each verb. Write a short paragraph using some of these synonyms.

UDU MEMBER — U.F.F MEMBER — UDA MEMBER

ULSTER DEFENCE UNION FORMED 1893. — ULSTER DEFENCE ASSOCIATION FORMED 1972.

# Nineteen Eighty-Four

George Orwell

It was a bright cold day in April, and the clocks were striking thirteen. Winston Smith, his chin nuzzled into his breast in an effort to escape the vile wind, slipped quickly through the glass doors of Victory Mansions, though not quickly enough to prevent a swirl of gritty dust from entering along with him.

The hallway smelt of boiled cabbage and old rag mats. At one end of it a coloured poster, too large for indoor display, had been tacked to the wall. It depicted simply an enormous face, more than a metre wide: the face of a man of about forty-five, with a heavy black moustache and ruggedly handsome features. Winston made for the stairs. It was no use trying the lift. Even at the best of times it was seldom working and at present the electric current was cut off during daylight hours. It was part of the economy drive in preparation for Hate Week. The flat was seven flights up, and Winston, who was thirty-nine and had a varicose ulcer above his right ankle, went slowly, resting several times on the way. On each landing, opposite the lift shaft, the poster with the enormous face gazed from the wall. It was one of those pictures which are so contrived that the eyes follow you about when you move. BIG BROTHER IS WATCHING YOU, the caption beneath it ran.

Inside the flat a fruity voice was reading out a list of figures which had something to do with the production of pig-iron. The voice came from an oblong metal plaque like a dulled mirror which formed part of the surface of the right-hand wall. Winston turned a switch and the voice sank somewhat, though the words were still distinguishable. The instrument (the telescreen, it was called) could be dimmed, but there was no way of shutting it off completely. He moved over to the window: a smallish, frail figure, the meagreness of his body merely emphasised by the blue overalls which were the uniform of the Party. His hair was very fair, the face naturally sanguine, his skin roughened by coarse soap and blunt razor blades and the cold of the winter that had just ended.

Outside, even through the shut window-pane, the world looked cold. Down in the street little eddies of wind were whirling dust and torn paper into spirals, and though the sun was shining and the sky a harsh blue, there seemed to be no colour in anything, except the posters that were plastered everywhere. The black-moustachio'd face gazed down from every commanding corner. There was one on the house-front immediately opposite. BIG BROTHER IS WATCHING YOU, the caption said, while the dark eyes looked deep into Winston's own. Down at street level another poster, torn at one corner, flapped fitfully in the wind, alternately covering and uncovering the single word INGSOC. In the far distance a helicopter skimmed down between the roofs, hovered for an instant like a bluebottle, and darted away again with a curving flight. It was the police patrol, snooping into people's windows. The patrols did not matter, however. Only the Thought Police mattered.

Behind Winston's back the voice from the telescreen was still babbling away about pig-iron and the overfulfillment of the Ninth Three-Year Plan. The telescreen received and transmitted simultaneously. Any sound that Winston made, above the level of a very low whisper, would be picked up by it; moreover, so long as he remained within the field of vision which the metal plaque commanded, he could be seen as well as heard. There was of course no way of knowing whether you were being watched at any given moment. How often, or on what system, the Thought Police plugged in on any individual wire was guesswork. It was even conceivable that they watched everybody all the time. But at any rate they could plug in your wire whenever they wanted to. You had to live – did live, from habit that became instinct – in the assumption that every sound you made was overheard, and, except in darkness, every movement scrutinised.

Winston kept his back turned to the telescreen. It was safer; though, as he well knew, even a back can be revealing. A kilometre away the Ministry of Truth, his place of work, towered vast and white above the grimy landscape. This, he thought with a sort of vague distaste – this was London, chief city of Airstrip One, itself the most populous of the provinces of Oceania. He tried to squeeze out some childhood memory that should tell him whether London had always been quite like this. Were there always these vistas of rotting nineteenth-century houses, their sides shored up with baulks of timber, their windows patched with cardboard and their roofs with corrugated iron, their crazy garden walls sagging in all directions? And the bombed site where the plaster dust swirled in the air and the willowherb straggled over heaps of rubble; and the places where the bombs had cleared a larger patch and there had sprung up sordid colonies of wooden dwellings like chicken houses? But it was no use, he could not remember: nothing remained of his childhood except a series of brightly-lit tableaux, occurring against no background and mostly unintelligible.

The Ministry of Truth – Minitrue, in Newspeak – was startlingly different from any other object in sight. It was an enormous pyramidal structure of glittering white concrete, soaring up, terrace after terrace, three hundred metres into the air. From where Winston stood it was just possible to read, picked out on its white face in elegant lettering, the three slogans of the Party:

# WAR IS PEACE

# FREEDOM IS SLAVERY

# IGNORANCE IS STRENGTH

1. When do you first realise that this novel is not set in the present time?

2. How do you know that Victory Mansions is not a nice place to live?

3. What device is in Winston's flat and what is its purpose?

4. What do you think the Thought Police do?

5. Winston lives in London. How is the London in this story different from present-day London? What is the writer suggesting has happened?

6. Are the three slogans on the Ministry of Truth's walls 'true'?

7. What physical details do we learn about Winston in the first three paragraphs? **P Q E**

8. What did you think are the most unfamiliar and strange aspects of Winston's world? **P Q E**

9. Why do you think George Orwell decided to tell this story using the third-person narration?

10. Is there anything about this world that reminds you of our world today?

Write a blog entry, or twitter, telling people about your first impressions of Winston and his world.

### OR

Look at the slogan 'Big Brother is Watching You'. This is now a very well known catch-phrase, but it was invented by George Orwell. We see slogans every day – they are part of 'media-speak'. Think of three of the best slogans you know and explain why you think they are catchy.

In groups, discuss the following points:

- First-person narration allows the reader to get to know the main character well.

- We get more involved in the story with first-person narration because we feel as if the story is happening to us.

- There is more suspense with first-person narration, because we only know what the main character knows.

- In third-person narration the reader can know the thoughts and feelings of many characters. Is this more interesting?

- We can see events from different viewpoints with third-person narration. Does this make the story more exciting?

- With third-person narration we sometimes know more than the characters inside the story. This can also create suspense.

For homework, decide which style of narration you prefer and say why. Use examples from the extracts you have studied in class to reinforce your points.

# Of Mice and Men

John Steinbeck

When creating a setting, the writer must think about the following:

- The **overall setting** where the story will take place.
- Will there be a **variety** of settings?
- The **atmosphere** of the setting, for example, a church can be a happy setting for a wedding or a sad setting for a funeral.
- The **time**: Will the story be set in the past, present or future?
- **Descriptive words** that will help to create a believable location in the reader's mind.

A few miles south of Soledad, the Salinas River drops in close to the hillside bank and runs deep and green. The water is warm too, for it has slipped twinkling over the yellow sands in the sunlight before reaching the narrow pool. On one side of the river the golden foothill slopes curve up to the strong and rocky Galiban mountains, but on the valley side the water is lined with trees – willows fresh and green with every spring, carrying in their lower leaf junctures the debris of the winter's flooding; and sycamores with mottled, white, recumbent limbs and branches that arch over the pool. On the sandy bank under the trees the leaves lie deep and so crisp that a lizard makes a great skittering if he runs among them. Rabbits come out of the brush to sit on the sand in the evening, and the damp flats are covered with the night tracks of 'coons, and with the spread pads of dogs from the ranches, and with the split-wedge tracks of deer that come to drink in the dark.

There is a path through the willows and among the sycamores, a path beaten hard by boys coming down from the ranches to swim in the deep pool, and beaten hard by tramps who come wearily down from the highway in the evening to jungle-up near water. In front of the low horizontal limb of a giant sycamore there is an ash pile made by many fires; the limb is worn smooth by men who have sat on it.

Evening of a hot day started the little wind to moving among the leaves. The shade climbed up the hills toward the top. On the sand banks the rabbits sat as quietly as little grey, sculptured stones. And then from the direction of the state highway came the sound of footsteps on crisp sycamore leaves. The rabbits hurried noiselessly for cover. A stilted heron labored up into the air and pounded down river. For a moment the place was lifeless, and then two men emerged from the path and came into the opening by the green pool.

1. What colours can you see in the first paragraph?

2. What animals does the writer mention?

3. Who has made the path? **P Q E**

4. What are the rabbits compared to? **P Q E**

5. What kind of story do you think will take place in this setting?

Brainstorm

Write a description of a river setting with which you are familiar. Use a **Brainstorm** to help. Refer back to the descriptive brainstorm on p. 71 of this chapter.

***OR***

Imagine that you are a presenter on a wildlife show. Write the commentary that you would use if you were showing a film of this setting.

# The Great Stink

Clare Clarke

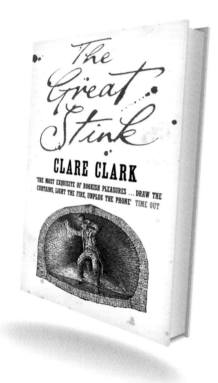

Where the channel snaked to the right it was no longer possible to stand upright, despite the abrupt drop in the gradient. The crown of William's hat grazed the slimed roof as he stooped, holding his lantern before him, and the stink of excrement pressed into his nostrils. His hand was unsteady and the light shuddered and jumped in the darkness. Rising and rushing through the narrower gully, the stream pressed the greased leather of his high boots hard against the flesh of his calves, the surge of the water muffling the clatter of hooves and iron-edged wheels above him. Of course he was deeper now. Between him and the granite-block road was at least twenty-feet of heavy London clay. The weight of it deepened the darkness. Beneath his feet the rotten bricks were treacherous, soft as crumbled cheese, and with each step the thick layer of black sludge sucked at the soles of his boots. Although his skin bristled with urgency, William forced himself to walk slowly and deliberately the way the flushers had shown him, pressing his heel down hard into the uncertain ground before unrolling his weight forward on to the ball of his foot, scanning the surface of the water for rising bubbles. The sludge hid pockets of gas, slop gas the flushers called it, the faintest whiff of which they claimed could cause a man to drop unconscious, sudden as if he'd been shot. From the little he knew of the toxic effects of sulpheretted hydrogen, William had every reason to believe them.

The pale light of his lantern sheered off the black crust of the water and threw a villain's shadow up the curved wall. Otherwise there was no relief from the absolute darkness, not even in the first part of the tunnel where open gratings led directly up into the street. All day the fog had crouched low over London, a chocolate-coloured murk that reeked of sulphur and defied the certainty of dawn. In vain the gas-lamps pressed their circles of light into its upholstered interior. Carriages loomed out of the darkness, the stifled skitters and whinnies of horses blurring with the warning shouts of coachmen. Pedestrians, their faces obscured by hats and collars, slipped into proximity and as quickly out again. On the river the hulking outlines of the penny steamers resembled a charcoal scrawl over which a child had carelessly drawn a sleeve. Now, at nearly six o'clock in the evening, the muddy brown of afternoon had been smothered into night.

1. How do you know that William is in a cramped tunnel?

2. What tells you that this is a dangerous place?

3. What kind of weather is there above ground?

4. Choose a word from the list below that you think best describes the atmosphere of this setting:

   *depressing, gloomy, claustrophobic, dangerous, calm*

5. Pick three details that tell you this story is set in the past. Explain your choices.
   ⓟⓠⓔ

6. How did this writer use descriptive words to create a believable location?
   ⓟⓠⓔ

Choose your favourite setting from a novel, film or story that was unusual or memorable. Could you say what struck you most about that setting?

**OR**

Think of a moment in your life when you felt one of the following:

*claustrophobic, excited, frightened, peaceful, exhilarated*

Write a description of that moment, trying to recapture the atmosphere and setting.

# Martyn Pig

Kevin Brooks

*Martyn Pig is telling us about his life.*

This – what I'm going to tell you about – it all happened just over a year ago. It was the week before Christmas. Or Xmas as Dad called it. Exmas. It was the week before Exmas. A Wednesday.

I was in the kitchen filling a plastic bin-liner with empty beer bottles and Dad was leaning in the doorway, smoking a cigarette, watching me through bloodshot eyes.

'Don't you go takin' 'em to the bottle bank,' he said.

'No, Dad.'

'Bloody emviroment this, emviroment that … if anyone wants to use my empty bottles again they'll have to pay for 'em. I don't get 'em for nothing, you know.'

'No.'

'Why should I give 'em away? What's the emviroment ever done for me?'

'Mmm.'

'Bloody bottle banks …'

He paused to puff on his cigarette. I thought of telling him there's no such thing as the *emviroment*, but I couldn't be bothered. I filled the bin-liner, tied it, and started on another. Dad was gazing at his reflection in the glass door, rubbing at the bags under his eyes. He could have been quite a handsome man if it wasn't for the drink. Handsome in a short, thuggish kind of way. Five foot seven, tough-guy mouth, squarish jaw, oily black hair. He could have looked like one of those bad guys in films – the ones the ladies can't help falling in love with, even though they know they're bad – but he didn't. He looked like what he was: a drunk. Fat little belly, florid skin, yellowed eyes, sagging cheeks and a big fat neck. Old and worn out at forty.

He leaned over the sink, coughed, spat and flicked ash down the plughole. 'That bloody woman's coming on Friday.'

'That bloody woman' was my Aunty Jean. Dad's older sister. A terrible woman. Think of the worst person you know, then double it, and you'll be halfway to Aunty Jean. I can hardly bear to describe her, to tell you the truth. Furious is the first word that comes to mind. Mad, ugly and furious. An angular woman, cold and hard, with crispy blue hair and a face that makes you shudder. I don't know what colour her eyes are, but they look as if they never close. They have about as much warmth as two depthless pools. Her mouth is thin and pillar-box red, like something drawn by a disturbed child. And she walks faster than most people run. She moves like a huntress, quick and quiet, homing in on her prey. I used to have nightmares about her. I still do.

She always came over the week before Christmas. I don't know what for. All she ever did was sit around moaning about everything for about three hours. And when she wasn't moaning she was swishing around the house running her fingers through the dust, checking in the cupboards, frowning at the state of the windows, tutting at everything.

'My *God*, William, how can you *live* like this.'

Everyone else called my dad Billy, but Aunty Jean always called him by his full name, pronouncing it with a *wover-wemphasis* on the first syllable – *Will*-yam – that made him flinch whenever she said it. He detested her. Hated her. He was scared stiff of the woman. What he'd do, he'd hide all his bottles before she came round. Up in the loft, mostly. It took him ages. Up and down the ladder, arms full of clinking bottles, his face getting redder and redder by the minute, muttering under his breath all the time, 'Bloody woman, bloody woman, bloody woman, bloody woman …'

Normally he didn't care what anyone thought about his drinking, but with Aunty Jean it was different. You see, when Mum left us – this was years ago – Aunty Jean tried to get custody of me. She wanted me to live with her, not with Dad. God knows why, she never liked me. But then she liked Dad even less, blamed him for the divorce and everything, said that he'd driven Mum to the 'brink of despair' and that she wasn't going to 'stand by and let him ruin an innocent young boy's life too'. Which was all a load of rubbish. She didn't give a hoot for my innocent life, she just wanted to kick Dad while he was down, kick him where it hurts, leave him with nothing. She despised him as much as he despised her. I don't know why. Some kind of brother/sister thing, I suppose. Anyway, her plan was to expose Dad as a drunkard. She reckoned that the authorities would decide in her favour once they knew of Dad's wicked, drunken ways. They'd never allow me to live with a boozer. But she reckoned without Dad. His need for me was greater than hers. Without me, he was just a drunk. But with me, he was a drunk with responsibilities, a drunk with child benefit, a drunk with someone to clear up the sick.

After he was given notice that Aunty Jean had applied for custody he didn't so much as look at a bottle for two months or more. Not a drop. Not a sniff. It was remarkable. He shaved, washed, wore a suit, he even smiled now and then. I almost grew to like him.

Aunty Jean's custody case was dead in the water. She didn't stand a chance. As far as the rest of the world was concerned, Mr William Pig was the *ideal father*.

The day I was officially assigned to Dad's loving care, he went out drinking and didn't come back for three days. When he did come back – unshaven, white-eyed, stinking – he slouched into the kitchen where I was making some tea, leaned down at me, grinning like a madman, and slurred right into my face: 'Remember me?'

Then he stumbled over to the sink and threw up.

So that's why he hid the bottles. He didn't want to give Aunty Jean any excuse for re-opening the custody debate. It wasn't so much the thought of losing me that worried him, it was the thought of staying off the drink for another two months.

1. What is your first impression of Martyn's dad?

2. Aunty Jean is a 'terrible woman'. What makes her so terrible?

3. How does Martyn's dad prepare for his sister's visit?

4. What did Aunty Jean do when Martyn's mother left?

5. Why does Martyn think his father bothers keeping him?

Write a description of Martyn and his dad from Aunty Jean's point of view.

*OR*

Imagine that you were the judge at Martyn's custody case. Prepare your final statement, comparing the characters of Aunty Jean and William Pig, and explain why you are granting custody to William.

6. How does what the father says at the beginning of the passage tell us something about his character?

7. What does Martyn tell us directly about his dad? **P Q E**

8. Do you think the description of Aunty Jean is effective? Explain your answer. **P Q E**

9. The father says and does certain things to keep custody of his son. Do these words and actions really reflect his character? **P Q E**

10. What kind of person do you think Martyn is? **P Q E**

# Across the Nightingale Floor

Lian Hearn

*This story is set in the past, in a country very like Japan.*

Lord Shirakawa's eldest daughter, Kaede, went to Noguchi castle as a hostage when she had just changed her sash of childhood for a girl's, and she had now lived there for half her life – long enough to think of a thousand things she detested about it. At night, when she was too tired to sleep and did not dare even toss and turn in case one of the older girls reached over and slapped her, she made lists of them inside her head. She had learned early to keep her thoughts to herself. At least no one could reach inside and slap her mind, although she knew more than one of them longed to. Which was why they slapped her so often on her body or face.

She clung with a child's single-mindedness to the faint memories she had of the home she had left when she was seven. She had not seen her mother or her younger sisters since the day her father had escorted her to the castle.

Her father had returned three times since then, only to find she was housed with the servants, not with the Noguchi children, as would have been suitable for the daughter of a warrior family. His humiliation was complete: he was unable even to protest, although she, unnaturally observant even at that age, had seen the shock and fury in his eyes. The first two times they had been allowed to speak in private for a few moments. Her clearest memory was of him holding her by the shoulders and saying in an intense voice, 'If only you had been born a boy!' The third time he was permitted only to look at her. After that he had not come again, and she had had no word from home.

She understood his reasons perfectly. By the time she was twelve, through a mixture of keeping her eyes open and engaging the few people sympathetic to her in seemingly innocent conversation, she knew her own position: she was a hostage, a pawn in the struggle between the clans. Her life was worth nothing to the lords who virtually owned her, except in what she added to their bargaining power. Her father was the lord of the strategically important domain of Shirakawa; her mother was closely related to the Maruyama. Since her father had no sons, he would adopt as his heir whoever Kaede was married to. The Noguchi, by possessing her, also possessed his loyalty, his alliance, and his inheritance.

> The main person in a story is called the **protagonist**. If we admire the **protagonist** and want them to succeed and to overcome obstacles, we call them the **hero** or **heroine**. If they are evil and obstruct the hero, we call them the **villain**.

She no longer even considered the great things – fear, homesickness, loneliness – but the sense that the Noguchi did not even value her as a hostage headed her list of things she hated, as she hated the way the girls teased her for being left-handed and clumsy, the stench of the guard's room by the gate, the steep stairs that were so hard to climb when you were carrying things … And she was always carrying things: bowls of cold water, kettles of hot water, food for the always ravenous men to cram into their mouths, things they had forgotten or were too lazy to fetch for themselves. She hated the castle itself, the massive stones of the foundations, the dark oppressiveness of the upper rooms, where the twisted roof beams seemed to echo her feelings, wanted to break free of the distortion they were trapped in, and fly back to the forest they came from.

**DIVE IN!**

1. Why did Kaede have to go to Noguchi castle?

2. How do the other girls treat her?

3. Why is her father humiliated when he visits?

4. What do the Noguchi gain by possessing Kaede?

5. What does she hate most about the castle?

**TAKE THE PLUNGE!**

6. In your opinion is Kaede a likeable protagoinist? **PQE**

7. This is an extract from an early stage in the novel, can you find any evidence to suggest that Kaede will be the heroine of the story? **PQE**

8. How does the writer create the world in which Kaede lives? Is the description of the setting effective?

**WHY DON'T YOU ...**

Write about your favourite fictional hero or heroine. You can choose from a film, a novel or a short story.

**OR**

● Put an empty chair at the top of the class. This is now the hot seat!

● When a person sits in the hot seat they become a character from the story.

● The teacher will select people to sit in the hot seat.

● Divide a page of your copybook into two columns. In one column write the questions you would like to ask Kaede. In the other the questions you would like to ask the Noguchi family.

● Re-read the extract to get ideas for these questions.

● Take it in turns to ask the person in the hot seat questions.

● Afterwards, write a brief description of either character based on their answers.

# The Bodhrán Makers

John B. Keane

At seventy-eight Canon Peter Pius Tett sat, blue-eyed and clear-skinned, at the head of the table, belying his age by a dozen years or more, awaiting the arrival of his housekeeper and senior curate. The latter was the first to enter: meekly he took his place at the bottom of the table.

'Good morning, Father.' Canon Tett was the first to speak. It was one of a number of unspoken rules of the presbytery that the first word of the day belonged to the Canon. New curates were so informed immediately after their arrival and those who forgot the edict were greeted with a stony silence until they exited and entered again and awaited their turn in the order of conversation. They never forgot thereafter.

'Good morning, Canon,' Father Butt returned and then, 'it's a hard day outside, Canon.'

'The thing then,' Canon Tett threw out without a smile, 'is to be hard enough for it.'

Father Butt was a pasty-faced, rather self-effacing man in his early fifties. Physically he contrasted with his superior. The Canon stood six foot three in his stockinged feet, was spare as a whippet, his peach-red face glowing with rude health, his whole being still exuding nervous energy, irreversible in his outlook, impervious to contradiction however justified and quite capable of traversing several miles of rough countryside before his breakfast.

Father Butt was a mere five foot four, flabby although not obese with dark hollows beneath his eyes which gave him an almost saintly look but for a lower lip, puck and full and drooping which detracted in the final analysis from his appearance of sanctity.

In his early years he had flirted briefly with golf and badminton but abandoned both after failing abysmally to make the least leeway in either. The people of Trallock would tell you that he was not a man of the world. It was their way of justifying his timidity. They liked and respected him. They might have liked him even more had they known that he lived in constant fear of Canon Tett, a fact not unknown to the Canon who relished keeping his curates on their toes.

1. Who enters the room first?

2. What is one of the unspoken rules of the presbytery?

3. What happens to people who break the rule?

4. How does Father Butt feel about Canon Tett?

5. What does Canon Tett's appearance tell us about him as a person? P Q E

6. How does his treatment of Father Butt tell us more about him? P Q E

7. Which priest do the people of Trallock prefer? P Q E

8. How does Father Butt's appearance contrast with that of the Canon?

9. What does Father Butt's 'flirtation' with golf and badminton tell you about him? P Q E

10. How would you deal with someone like Canon Tett if you had to work with him?

Describe the breakfast from the point of view of either Canon Tett or Father Butt.

**OR**

Write about a meeting between two characters, one of whom is more powerful than the other, imitating the style of this extract. You can use one from the following list if you like:

● *A criminal and a judge*

● *A bully and a victim*

● *A journalist and a politician*

● *A mother and a child*

● *A terrorist and a hostage*

**OR**

Choose a person. It could be an actor, sportsperson, character in a book, film or television programme. Tomorrow, bring in an object that you think could represent that person. Write a sentence in your copybook explaining why you chose that object, for example:

*The person I chose was Marilyn Monroe. The object I chose to represent her was a cracked mirror. I think the mirror represents her because she was considered to be very beautiful, but she had a lot of problems. The crack represents the fact that she wasn't perfect.*

*The person I chose was Roy Keane. The object I chose to represent him was a boiled egg! I think the egg represents him because he has a very tough shell but it is easily cracked. He looks hard on the outside, but underneath he is very kind and soft. He does a lot of charity work.*

# Plot Creation
# Shane

Jack Schaefer

The plot is the basic storyline. Read the next four extracts to see some of the ingredients needed for a good plot.

He rode into our valley in the summer of '89. I was a kid then, barely topping the backboard of father's old chuck-wagon. I was on the upper rail of our small corral, soaking in the late afternoon sun, when I saw him far down the road where it swung into the valley from the open plain beyond.

In that clear Wyoming air I could see him plainly, though he was still several miles away. There seemed nothing remarkable about him, just another stray horseman riding up the road toward the cluster of frame buildings that was our town. Then I saw a pair of cowhands, loping past him, stop and stare after him with a curious intentness.

He came steadily on, straight through the town without slackening pace, until he reached the fork a half-mile below our place. One branch turned left across the river ford and on to Luke Fletcher's big spread. The other bore ahead along the right bank where we homesteaders had pegged our claims in a row up the valley. He hesitated briefly, studying the choice, and moved again steadily on our side.

As he came near, what impressed me first was his clothes. He wore dark trousers of some serge material tucked into tall boots and held at the waist by a wide belt, both of a soft black leather tooled in an intricate design. A coat of the same dark material as the trousers was neatly folded and strapped to his saddle-roll. His shirt was finespun linen, rich brown in colour. The handkerchief knotted loosely around his throat was black silk.

His hat was not the familiar Stetson, not the familiar grey or muddy tan. It was a plain black, soft in texture, unlike any hat I had ever seen, with a creased crown and a wide curling brim swept down in front to shield his face.

All trace of newness was long since gone from these things. The dust of distance was beaten into them. They were worn and stained and several neat patches showed on the shirt. Yet a kind of magnificence remained and with it a hint of men and manners alien to my limited boy's experience.

Then I forgot the clothes in the impact of the man himself. He was not much above medium height, almost slight in build. He would have looked frail alongside father's square, solid bulk. But even I could read the endurance in the lines of that dark figure and the quiet power in its effortless, unthinking adjustment to every movement of the tired horse.

He was clean-shaven and his face was lean and hard and burned from high forehead to firm, tapering chin. His eyes seemed hooded in the shadow of the hat's brim. He came closer, and I could see that this was because the brows were drawn in a frown of fixed and habitual alertness. Beneath them the eyes were endlessly searching from side to side and forward, checking off every item in view, missing nothing. As I noticed this, a sudden chill, I could not have told why, struck through me there in the warm and open sun.

He rode easily, relaxed in the saddle, leaning his weight lazily into the stirrups. Yet even in this easiness was a suggestion of tension. It was the easiness of a coiled spring, of a trap set.

1. Where is this story set?
2. Who is speaking to us?
3. How do the cowhands react to the stranger?
4. What does the narrator first notice about the man?
5. How do you know that the man has been travelling for a long time?
6. What does the narrator notice about the stranger's face?

7. Do you want to know more about the stranger who is introduced in this opening? Explain your answer.
8. The writer not only describes the stranger's appearance, he also suggests things about his personality. What kind of person is this stranger? **PQE**
9. What details did you notice about the place where this story is set? Do these details suggest what type of book this is going to be? **PQE**
10. Write down three questions about this story that you would like answered.

The **opening** of a novel is very important. If it doesn't catch our attention we won't read on. How many books have you started and then put down? Maybe they didn't have good openings. A good opening should have some of the following:

- A **character** that the reader wants to know more about.
- A **description** of a place that is different or mysterious.
- **Questions** that the reader wants answered.
- An **exciting** or **unusual** event.
- A **conversation** that pulls the reader into the story.
- **Vivid descriptions** that make the reader see something ordinary from a new viewpoint.

Pick what you think was a really good opening to either a film, novel or short story, and write a paragraph about it, using some of the points given to explain why you thought it was so good.

**OR**

Re-write the opening of this novel from the point of view of the horseman. Remember, you see many of the same details as the original narrator but from a different angle. Try to convey your impression of:

- the approach to the town
- the young boy
- your feelings.

# August '44

Carlo Gébler

*Saul and his family are in hiding from the Nazis during World War II. They are safe while they stay in their cave in the forest, but they must avoid the road running through the forest in case a passing truck spots them. Saul's sister Nelly and their cousin Leon have disobeyed the rules and secretly crossed the road. Saul is about to follow them when a German truck drives by.*

A rumble sounded like the noise an engine made. He started and looked up. He saw a lorry hurtling towards him. He saw the driver behind the windscreen, his hands gripping the steering wheel. He wore a blue-grey uniform. The driver was a German soldier.

Saul dropped to his belly. The verge was dry and hard and the grass that grew out of it was hard and coarse. It scratched his bare knees, his chin and his face. The taste in his mouth was part pine, part earth.

Had the driver seen him? The noise made by the lorry's engine, as it rolled towards him, was constant. It wasn't braking. It wasn't stopping. It was also loud. Loud meant Leon and Nelly would hear it in the storehouse. They would stay in there, wouldn't they?

He slid back. He decided to retreat into the forest and run as fast as he could. And in case the driver decided to stop and have a look, he would not stop until he got to the cave.

Slithering off the sun baked verge and into the forest he felt the temperature change from warm to cold, and the ground from dry and dusty to damp and musty. He went on going backwards until at last he judged it was safe to stand. Then he sprang to his feet, turned and sprinted off, twisting his body around tree trunks and ducking under low branches as he fled.

As he ran he listened. Were the Germans in pursuit?

There was a hollow in front of him. He jumped over the lip and landed on the soft bed of pine rubbish that had collected inside over the years. He folded his knees and sank to his haunches.

He froze. Was there any sound behind? His breathing was so loud he couldn't hear anything. He swallowed a great mouthful of breath and closed his lips. He felt his heart pushing against his ribs. He heard no sound behind.

He turned and lifted his head over the lip. He squinted along the forest floor. Nothing stirred between the trees rising like bars all around him. He had not been seen. He had not been followed.

He felt his breath slowing. He must go to the cave now. He must get back before Nelly and Leon. But he must not arrive looking hot or out of breath. The grown-ups would only ask what had happened and why was he running? He could not tell anyone a German driver saw him.

Saul set off for the cave. He was filled with a vague sense of dread. He was a bad dissembler and his father always seemed to know when he wasn't being truthful. What if his father interrogated him? It was this dreadful thought, Saul assumed, that explained why he felt as he did.

However, when he got to the rock they had named the Cube which was close to their cave, he realised what was wrong. He'd gone and left his beloved spear by the road, hadn't he?

His throat went sore – it always did before he cried. Though he could hear the sound of the grown-ups talking inside the cave he couldn't see them. Nor could they see him. He spun round on the spot, rushed back into the forest and went straight to the small dusty hole where he always ran when he was morose or troubled. It lay in the middle of the trees that had tumbled one on top of the other.

He got into the hole, sunk right down so he could not be seen and began to cry. His tears were hot and salty. He wanted to hit himself he was so angry. What an idiot he had been. He had left his treasure behind and now he dare not go back for it. To do so was unsafe, it was against the rules and he might meet his sister and his cousin. How could he have been such a fool?

Later, he stopped crying. He remained curled up in his hole, nursing his grief. At some point he fell asleep.

Every good story has a **complication**. Normally this is caused by **conflict** either between characters, or within a character. The **complication** is what moves the story along as the reader wonders how it will be resolved.

Choose a film or novel in which you thought the complication was excellent. Explain how the conflict was built up and explain how it made you feel.

**OR**

Write your own description of a moment of conflict in your school life. The obvious example might be when you got caught breaking a school rule, or maybe even when you experienced inner conflict at the thought of breaking a rule?

1. How does Saul react when the truck passes by?

2. Why does he decide to retreat into the forest?

3. Why must he not arrive back to the cave looking hot or out of breath?

4. When he gets near the cave what is upsetting him?

5. How do the events in this passage complicate life for Saul and his family?

6. In this extract the writer emphasises the complication by letting us hear Saul's thoughts. Saul doesn't know if he has been spotted by the German driver, and neither do we. Make a list of all the questions Saul asks that show us the inner conflict he feels.

7. Why do you think Saul doesn't just confess to the adults what has happened?
PQE

8. What do you think will happen next?

In groups, prepare a short scene to dramatise one of the following conflicts:

- The conversation between a teenager whose parents have forbidden them to go to the best party of the year
- Two best friends, one of whom has stolen the other's boyfriend/girlfriend
- Someone whose luggage is overweight trying to avoid paying the extra money
- Someone who has accidentally walked out of a shop with something they didn't pay for in their bag, explaining the situation to the manager and store detective
- A class prefect trying to keep a rowdy group under control.

For homework, write a description of the event you have dramatised. Remember to:

- create the setting
- introduce your key characters
- build up the atmosphere and tension.

# The Defender

Alan Gibbons

*Kenny Kincaid and his son, Ian, are on the run from paramilitaries who want Kenny to return money that he took with him when he disappeared. In this extract, the house Kenny and Ian are in has been surrounded by paramilitaries. Unknown to any of them, an Armed Response Unit is ready and watching.*

When the attack comes, it comes fast, with the thunder of running feet on uncarpeted floors, the appearance of two dark shapes at the bottom of the stairs, finally with the explosion of a gun in the narrow stairwell and a cascade of plaster and painted woodwork. Ian has heard gunshots before – hundreds, thousands of them in countless movies and TV dramas. But nothing has prepared him for this – the deafening report that fills the air and cannons round your skull. In almost the same split-second that the gun goes off – whose, Ian can't tell – Dad is yelling at him.

'Get down! Stay down!'

A figure is halfway up the stairs, roughly silhouetted against the half-light of streetlamps cast through the downstairs windows.

'Stop right there, Billy! So help me, I'll fire!'

McClean doesn't stop but there is something odd about his approach. Then Ian understands. He is a right-handed man holding a gun in his left. Ian sees Dad take aim and fire. A shriek of pain detonates through the crazed blackness. Ian can make out the wolfman clutching his thigh. It's obvious to Ian that Dad fired low deliberately. He knows what killing a man feels like. He doesn't want to do it again. But the attack isn't over. Another figure clambers over his groaning comrade. Another explosion rips open the fabric of the night. It's Dad's turn to cry out.

'Dad!'

Ian reaches for his father but his hand is shrugged away. Dad gets off a shot with shaking hand. Barr ducks down but he hasn't been hit. He watches with satisfaction as Dad's trembling fingers lose their grip on the gun.

Barr steps forward to finish the job.

\*\*\*\*\*\*\*\*\*\*\*\*\*\*\*\*

At the sound of shots Lomas and Hagan exchange glances.

'Sounds like it's going down,' says Lomas.

There's a quiver in his voice. This isn't the kind of incident that he's used to in his quiet little town. Hagan doesn't reply. He is already on the radio, talking to the Armed Response Unit's officer-in-charge.

'Deploy your men immediately,' he said. 'If my information is correct, we've got four men, four firearms being used. Almost certainly we've got a fourteen-year-old boy in the house.'

But as the vehicles screech to a halt there is the sound of shattering glass. An upstairs window has blown out, followed by a body.

*******************

Barr is standing over Dad. He is panting.

'So where's the money, Kenny boy?'

Dad is holding his side. Ian can see the blood seeping between his fingers – thick, dark streams, separating, spreading. For all the pain etched on his face, Dad still manages a show of defiance.

'Find it yourself, Chubby.'

Dad's gun is on the second stair. Barr kicks it out of reach.

'Oh, I will, believe me.'

Straightening up, Chubby points the gun barrel at Kenny's head.

'I'll count to three.'

Ian doesn't count that far. Grabbing the baseball bat, he swings it. He hears the crack as it crunches into Barr's shoulder joint. Tears running down his face, Ian swings again. He hears the oddest sound.

Clunk!

It's almost funny, but he knows what it is. Bone. The bat has caught Barr on the skull.

He goes down.

Even then the nightmare isn't over. Barr is slumped against the wall, semi-conscious, but McClean is hobbling up the stairs. Behind him McCullough had entered the house and is already climbing.

'Dad!' Ian cries. 'Are you all right? Can you move?'

Dad nods.

'But there's nowhere to go, son.'

Ian knows different. Grabbing the frame of the camp bed, he hurls it through the window. Snatching a glance at McClean's lumbering form, he starts shoving the mattress through the window.

'Give me a hand,' he yells.

Normal time crumples. Events occur like camera shots, the sequence too fast to order. Dad is at his side, shoving desperately at the mattress. McClean is at the top of the landing, gun in hand. McCullough is coming up behind.

'Go!' Ian screams, seeing the injured McClean struggling to aim his revolver. 'I'll follow you out.'

In the same split second three things happen: the mattress has hit the ground outside, Dad tumbles through the window, blood spitting out between his fingers; Ian follows him out.

In the next split second there is an exchange of shouts, then another gunshot and a cry. A life had ended.

1. What sounds does Ian hear when the attack comes?

2. Who gets hit first?

3. Who is Lomas and why is he nervous?

4. How does Ian save his father?

5. How do Kenny and Ian get out of the house?

6. The opening of this passage is very dramatic. What makes it so dramatic? **P Q E**

7. Lots of things happen very quickly in this extract. In your own words say what happens up to the end of the first section.

8. Why do you think the writer takes the reader to a different location in the second section? What is the effect of this?

9. How do you know that this is an important, vital moment in this story? **P Q E**

10. The writer says, 'Events occur like camera shots.' How has he captured this in his description?

Think about how this story will end. There are only eight pages left to the end of the novel from these events. Do you think Kenny and Ian will survive? Write a brief summary of what you would like to happen next.

A **climax** is the moment that all the tension has been building up to. It is an important, vital moment in the story.

*OR*

Re-read this extract and state whether or not you thought it was a good climax to a novel. Was it exciting enough? Would it make you want to read more? Give reasons for your answer.

*OR*

Imagine that you are the director of a film adaptation of this extract. Prepare the storyboard that will help you with your filming. (A storyboard is like a cartoon showing all the different shots that a director will include in a scene.)

# Genesis and Catastrophe

Roald Dahl

'Everything is normal,' the doctor was saying. 'Just lie back and relax.' His voice was miles away in the distance and he seemed to be shouting at her. 'You have a son.'

'What?'

'You have a fine son. You understand that, don't you? A fine son. Did you hear him crying?'

'Is he all right, Doctor?'

'Of course he is all right.'

'You are certain he is all right?'

'I am quite certain.'

'Is he still crying?'

'Try to rest. There is nothing to worry about.'

'Why has he stopped crying, Doctor? What happened?'

'Don't excite yourself, please. Everything is normal.'

'I want to see him. Please let me see him.'

You need to read a whole story in order to appreciate its **ending**. Try this one.

'Dear lady,' the doctor said, patting her hand. 'You have a fine strong healthy child. Don't you believe me when I tell you that?'

'What is the woman over there doing to him?'

'Your baby is being made to look pretty for you,' the doctor said. 'We are giving him a little wash, that is all. You must spare us a moment or two for that.'

'You swear he is all right?'

'I swear it. Now lie back and relax. Close your eyes. Go on, close your eyes. That's right. That's better. Good girl …'

'I have prayed and prayed that he will live, Doctor.'

'Of course he will live. What are you talking about?'

'The others didn't.'

'What?'

'None of my other ones lived, Doctor.'

The doctor stood beside the bed looking down at the pale exhausted face of the young woman. He had never seen her before today. She and her husband were new people in the town. The innkeeper's wife, who had come up to assist in the delivery, had told him that the husband worked at the local customs-house on the border and the two of them had arrived quite suddenly at the inn with one trunk and one suitcase about three months ago. The husband was a drunkard, the innkeeper's wife had said, an arrogant, overbearing, bullying little drunkard, but the young woman was gentle and religious. And she was very sad. She never smiled. In the few weeks that she had been here, the innkeeper's wife had never once seen her smile. Also there was a rumour that this was the husband's third marriage, that one wife had died and that the other had divorced him for unsavoury reasons. But that was only a rumour.

The doctor bent down and pulled the sheet a little higher over the patient's head. 'You have nothing to worry about,' he said gently. 'This is a perfectly normal baby.'

'That's exactly what they told me about the others. But I lost them all, Doctor. In the last eighteen months I have lost all three of my children, so you mustn't blame me for being anxious.'

'Three?'

'This is my fourth … in four years.'

The doctor shifted his feet uneasily on the bare floor.

'I don't think you know what it means, Doctor, to lose them all, all three of them, slowly, separately, one by one. I keep seeing them. I can see Gustav's face now as clearly as if he were lying here beside me in the bed. Gustav was a lovely boy, Doctor. But he was always ill. It is terrible when they are always ill and there is nothing you can do to help them.'

'I know.'

The woman opened her eyes, stared up at the doctor for a few seconds, then closed them again.

'My little girl was called Ida. She died a few days before Christmas. That is only four months ago. I just wish you could have seen Ida, Doctor.'

'You have a new one now.'

'But Ida was so beautiful.'

'Yes,' the doctor said. 'I know.'

'How can you know?' she cried.

'I am sure she was a lovely child. But this new one is also like that.' The doctor turned away from the bed and walked over to the window and stood there looking out. It was a wet grey April afternoon, and across the street he could see the red roofs of the houses and the huge raindrops splashing on the tiles.

'Ida was two years old, Doctor … and she was so beautiful I was never able to take my eyes off her from the first time I dressed her in the morning until she was safe in bed again at night. I used to live in holy terror of something happening to that child. Gustav had gone and my little Otto had also gone and she was all I had left. Sometimes I used to get up in the night and creep over to the cradle and put my ear close to her mouth just to make sure that she was breathing.'

'Try to rest,' the doctor said, going back to the bed. 'Please try to rest.' The woman's face was white and bloodless, and there was a slight blueish-grey tinge around the nostrils and the mouth. A few strands of damp hair hung down over her forehead, sticking to the skin.

'When she died … I was already pregnant again when that happened, Doctor. This new one was a good four months on its way when Ida died. "I don't want it!" I shouted after the funeral. "I won't have it! I have buried enough children!" And my husband … he was strolling among the guests with a big glass of beer in his hand … he turned around quickly and said, "I have news for you, Klara, I have good news." Can you imagine that, Doctor? We have just buried our third child and he stands there with a glass of beer in his hand and tells me that he had good news. "Today I have been posted to Braunau," he

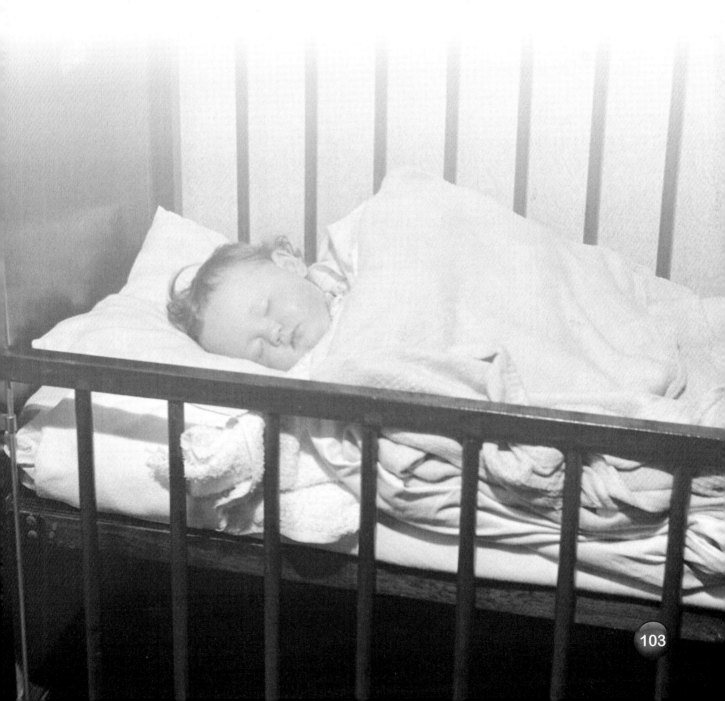

says, "so you can start packing at once. This will be a new start for you, Klara," he says. "It will be a new place and you can have a new doctor …"'

'Please don't talk anymore.'

'You *are* the new doctor, aren't you, Doctor?'

'That's right.'

'And here we are in Braunau.'

'Yes.'

'I am frightened, Doctor.'

'Try not to be frightened.'

'What chance can the fourth one have now?'

'You must stop thinking like that.'

'I can't help it. I am certain there is something inherited that causes my children to die in this way. There must be.'

'That is nonsense.'

'Do you know what my husband said to me when Otto was born, Doctor? He came into the room and he looked into the cradle where Otto was lying and he said, "Why do all my children have to be so small and weak?"'

'I am sure he didn't say that.'

'He put his head right into Otto's cradle as though he were examining a tiny insect and he said, "All I am saying is why can't they be better *specimens*? That's all I am saying." And three days after that, Otto was dead. We baptised him quickly on the third day and he died the same evening. And then Gustav died. And then Ida died. All of them died, Doctor … and suddenly the whole house was empty …'

## Do NOT read any further

- Do you feel sorry for the woman? Why or why not?
- How do you think this story will end? How do you want it to end?

**When you have answered these questions, continue reading …**

'Don't think about it now.'

'Is this one so very small?'

'He is a normal child.'

'But small?'

'He is a little small, perhaps. But the small ones are often a lot tougher than the big ones. Just imagine, Frau Hitler, this time next year he will be almost learning to walk. Isn't that a lovely thought?'

She didn't answer to this.

'And two years from now he will probably be talking his head off and driving you crazy with his chatter. Have you settled on a name for him yet?'

'A name?'

'Yes.'

'I don't know. I'm not sure. I think my husband said that if it was a boy we were going to call him Adolfus.'

'That means that he will be called Adolf.'

'Yes. My husband likes Adolf because it has a certain similarity to Alois. My husband is called Alois.'

'Excellent.'

'Oh no!' she cried, starting up suddenly from her pillow. 'That's the same question that they asked me when Otto was born! It means he is going to die! You are going to baptise him at once!'

'Now, now,' the doctor said, taking her gently by the shoulders. 'You are quite wrong. I promise you you are wrong. I was simply being an inquisitive old man, that is all. I love talking about names. I think Adolphus is a particularly fine name. It is one of my favourites. And look – here he comes now.'

The innkeeper's wife, carrying the baby high up on her enormous bosom, came sailing across the room towards the bed. 'Here is the little beauty!' she cried, beaming. 'Would you like to hold him, my dear? Shall I put him beside you?'

'Is he well wrapped?' the doctor asked. 'It is extremely cold in here.'

'Certainly he is well wrapped.'

The baby was tightly swaddled in a white woollen shawl, and only the tiny pink head protruded. The innkeeper's wife placed him gently on the bed beside the mother. 'There you are,' she said. 'Now you can lie there and look at him to your heart's content.'

'I think you will like him,' the doctor said, smiling. 'He is a fine little baby.'

'He has the most lovely hands!' the innkeeper's wife exclaimed. 'Such long delicate fingers!'

The mother didn't move. She didn't even turn her head to look.

'Go on!' cried the innkeeper's wife. 'He won't bite you!'

'I am frightened to look. I don't dare to believe that I have another baby and that he is all right.'

'Don't be so stupid.'

Slowly, the mother turned her head and looked at the small, incredibly serene face that lay on the pillow beside her.

'Is this my baby?'

'Of course.'

'Oh … oh … but he is beautiful.'

The doctor turned away and went over to the table and began putting his things into his bag. The mother lay on the bed gazing at the child and smiling and touching him and making little noises of pleasure. 'Hello, Adolfus,' she whispered. 'Hello, my little Adolf …'

'Ssshh!' said the innkeeper's wife. 'Listen! I think your husband is coming.'

The doctor walked over to the door and opened it and looked out into the corridor.

'Herr Hitler!'

'Yes.'

'Come in, please.'

A small man in a dark-green uniform stepped softly into the room and looked around him.

'Congratulations,' the doctor said. 'You have a son.'

The man had a pair of enormous whiskers meticulously groomed after the manner of Emperor Franz Josef, and he smelled strongly of beer. 'A son?'

'Yes.'

'How is he?'

'He is fine. So is your wife.'

'Good.' The father turned and walked with a curious little prancing stride over to the bed where his wife was lying. 'Well, Klara,' he said, smiling through his whiskers. 'How did it go?' He bent down to take a look at the baby. Then he bent lower. In a series of quick jerky movements, he bent lower and lower until his face was only about twelve inches from the baby's head. The wife lay sideways on the pillow, staring up at him with a kind of supplicating look.

'He has the most marvellous pair of lungs,' the innkeeper's wife announced. 'You should have heard him screaming just after he came into this world.'

'But my God, Klara …'

'What is it, dear?'

'This one is even smaller than Otto was!'

The doctor took a couple of quick paces forward. 'There is nothing wrong with that child,' he said.

Slowly, the husband straightened up and turned away from the bed and looked at the doctor. He seemed bewildered and stricken. 'It's no good lying, Doctor,' he said. 'I know what it means. It's going to be the same all over again.'

'Now you listen to me,' the doctor said.

'But you do *know* what happened to the others, Doctor?'

'You must forget about the others, Herr Hitler. Give this one a chance.'

'But so small and weak!'

'My dear sir, he has only just been born.'

'Even so …'

'What are you trying to do?' cried the innkeeper's wife. 'Talk him into the grave?'

'That's enough!' the doctor said sharply.

The mother was weeping now. Great sobs were shaking her body.

The doctor walked over to the husband and put a hand on his shoulder. 'Be good to her,' he whispered. 'Please. It is very important.' Then he squeezed the husband's shoulder hard and began pushing him surreptitiously to the edge of the bed. The husband hesitated. The doctor squeezed harder, signalling him urgently through fingers and thumb. At last, reluctantly, the husband bent down and kissed his wife lightly on the cheek.

'All right, Klara,' he said. 'Now stop crying.'

'I have prayed so hard that he will live, Alois.'

'Yes.'

'Every day for months I have gone to the church and begged on my knees that this one will be allowed to live.'

'Yes, Klara, I know.'

'Three dead children is all that I can stand, don't you realise that?'

'Of course.

'He *must* live, Alois. He *must*, he *must* … Oh God, be merciful unto him now …'

1. What event has taken place at the beginning of this story?

2. What is the mother afraid will happen?

3. How did the innkeeper's wife describe the woman's husband?

4. At what point did you realise who the baby was?

5. Did this change your attitude towards how you wanted the story to end?

6. The writer uses dialogue to open this story. Do you think this is a good way to begin?

7. The writer shares information very slowly in this story. List the main pieces of information about the woman and baby that you are given in the first three pages.

8. What major revelation produces a complication on the fifth page?

9. This story plays with the reader's emotions. Describe how your feelings at the end of the story differed from your feelings in the middle.

10. Ask your teacher to explain the meaning of the title of this story. Do you think it is a good title? Why or why not?

Try reducing the plots of some books or films that you have studied to just six words. If you can do this before you start writing a story it probably means you have a good plot figured out! Look at the examples below to get you started:

| | |
|---|---|
| *Genesis and Catastrophe* | 'Mother loves weak baby. Becomes Hitler.' |
| *Hansel and Gretel* | 'Lost children. Gingerbread house. Dead witch.' |
| *Wizard of Oz* | 'Follow the yellow brick road. Home.' |
| *Twilight* | 'Girl loves vampire. Requited without bloodsucking!' |
| *Hamlet* | 'Maybe he will. Maybe he won't.' |

**OR**

Look at these examples of six-word autobiographies, and see if you can come up with one for your life!

*Asked for love. Received confusion. Waiting.*
*Bank robber, prison-humbled, confesses all.*
*I love food. Calories love me.*
*Learned. Forgot. Better off relearning anyway.*
*Got a pony, broke my arm.*
*Open road. No map. Great scenery.*
*Lived life. Played metal. Went deaf.*
*Must remember: people, gadgets. That order.*

Now write a story inspired by one of the six-word autobiographies (including your own).

**OR**

Choose one of the following scenarios and write your thoughts on what would have happened if …

- *Hitler and the Nazis had won World War II*
- *The Ice Age had never ended*
- *Television was made illegal*
- *Ireland won the World Cup*
- *Mankind had never invented the wheel*

## Even Hitler had a Mother

Herbert Farjeon

Even Hitler had a mother,
Even Mussolini had a ma,
When they were babies they said
 Goo, goo, gooo
And sucked their thumbs, and got wet
 through.
Don't be hard upon the Blackshirts,
They may be rather Swastika
But
Even Hitler had a mother
And
Even Mussolini had a ma.

# Writing a Story

In the Junior Cert Exam you will have a chance to write a story. If you decide to do this, you will be given a number of 'triggers' on the paper. These might include:

- A *sentence*, describing a situation or a moment
  *The day started the same as any other, nobody could have known that by evening …*
- A *photograph* of a person and/or a place

Look at the steps that the student below has taken to write a story based on the trigger from the 2009 paper:

Write a composition including the line:
*That really was the last straw …*

First of all, decide who you are, where you are, and how you ended up in the position you are in.

**Read the brainstorm on the page opposite while following the numbered sequence below.**

1. This student decides that they are a teenage runaway – this is creating a character.

2. The writer then decides that they are on a bus, in a city, in Ireland – this is creating a setting.

3. Next the student decides that they are running away from home because of a fight with their parents – this is creating a conflict.

4. Most importantly, the writer thinks about the beginning, middle and end of the story. This is creating a plot. You should never begin writing a story until you have decided on your plot.

5. The writer also thinks about the other characters he or she will meet in the story, and how their relationships will develop. Notice that the brainstorm also contains ideas about how to describe these characters.

6. Always do a paragraph plan after your brainstorm to help you organise your story. Remember you don't have to include everything from the brainstorm; notice how this writer has scribbled out some of the options.

# Brainstorm

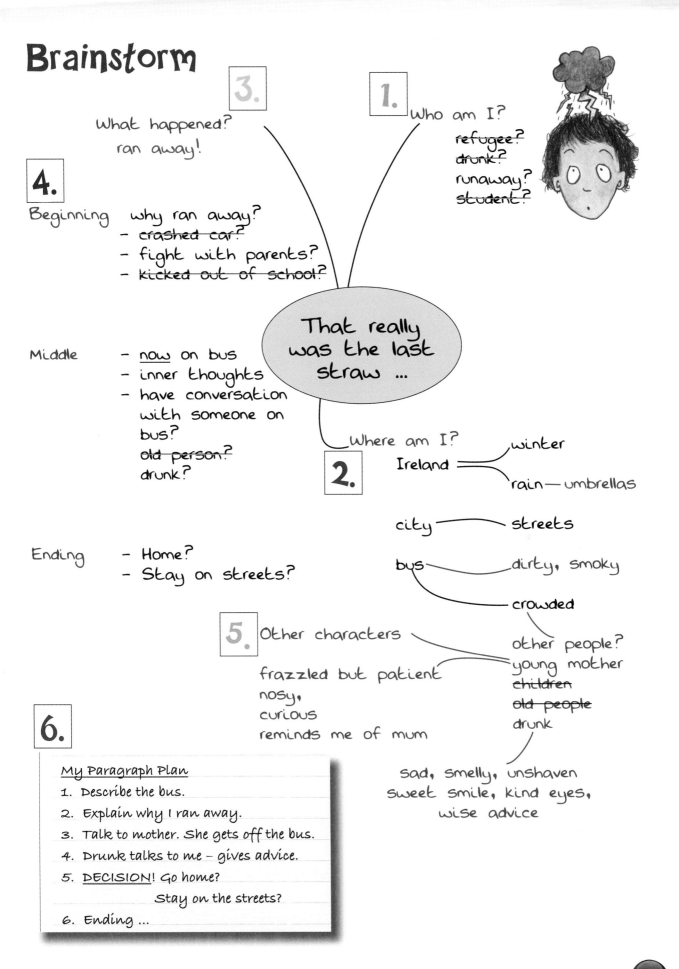

**3.** What happened?
ran away!

**1.** Who am I?
~~refugee?~~
~~drunk?~~
runaway?
~~student?~~

**4.**
Beginning    why ran away?
– ~~crashed car?~~
– fight with parents?
– ~~kicked out of school?~~

*That really was the last straw ...*

Middle
– <u>now</u> on bus
– inner thoughts
– have conversation with someone on bus?
~~old person?~~
drunk?

**2.** Where am I?
Ireland ═══ winter
       ═══ rain — umbrellas

city ──── streets
bus ──── dirty, smoky
     ──── crowded

Ending
– Home?
– Stay on streets?

**5.** Other characters
frazzled but patient
nosy,
curious
reminds me of mum

other people?
young mother
~~children~~
~~old people~~
drunk

sad, smelly, unshaven
sweet smile, kind eyes,
wise advice

**6.**

<u>My Paragraph Plan</u>
1. Describe the bus.
2. Explain why I ran away.
3. Talk to mother. She gets off the bus.
4. Drunk talks to me – gives advice.
5. <u>DECISION!</u> Go home?
           Stay on the streets?
6. Ending ...

**TEST THE WATERS!**

Write a story inspired by one of these photos:

'My mouth was dry and my heart beat so hard I thought it would beat from my chest …'

Continue this story.

2005 H.L. Paper

'The day started the same as any other, nobody could have known that by evening …'

Continue this story.

2007 H.L. Paper

'I could hardly sleep with excitement. Only three more days to go …'

Continue this composition.

2008 H.L. Paper

'Why can't I go? Everybody else is …'

Write a composition that includes the above sentences.

2008 O.L. Paper

Write a story which at some point includes the sentence: 'You should have seen the look on his/her face …'

2009 O.L. Paper

# Discursive Writing
## Thrashing It Out!

Nearly everyone has to make a **speech** at some time in their life, whether they want to or not, so it is as well to be prepared! Before writing a speech you should think about the following points:

- **Why** are you writing the speech? What occasion is it for?

- **Who** is going to be listening to you? Who is your audience?

- **How long** does it need to be?

- **What sort of language** must you use? Can it be funny, or should it be serious?

# Lou Gehrig's Farewell Speech to Baseball

*Lou Gehrig was one of the greatest baseball players of the early twentieth century. However, the discovery that he had an incurable disease forced him to retire early. Today the disease is actually called after him.*

Fans, for the past two weeks you have been reading about the bad break I got. Yet today I consider myself the luckiest man on the face of the earth.

I have been in ballparks for seventeen years and have never received anything but kindness and encouragement from you fans. Look at these grand men. Which of you wouldn't consider it the highlight of his career just to associate with them for even one day?

Sure I'm lucky.

Who wouldn't consider it an honor to have known Jacob Ruppert? Also, the builder of baseball's greatest empire, Ed Barrow? To have spent six years with that wonderful little fellow, Miller Huggins? Then to have spent the next nine years with that outstanding leader, that smart student of psychology, the best manager in baseball today, Joe McCarthy?

Sure I'm lucky.

When the New York Giants, a team you would give your right arm to beat, and vice versa, sends you a gift – that's something. When everybody down to the groundskeepers and those boys in white coats remember you with trophies – that's something.

113

## Take the Plunge!

When you have a wonderful mother-in-law who takes sides with you in squabbles with her own daughter – that's something.

When you have a father and a mother who work all their lives so you can have an education and build your body – it's a blessing.

When you have a wife who has been a tower of strength and shown more courage than you dreamed existed – that's the finest I know.

So, I close in saying that I might have been given a bad break, but I've got an awful lot to live for.

 **DIVE IN!**

1. Who is Lou Gehrig addressing in this speech?

2. What is the first reason he gives for being 'the luckiest man on the face of the earth'?

3. What other reasons does he give for feeling lucky?

4. Why do you think he mentions his family at the end of the speech?

5. How do you think the fans felt listening to this speech?

 **TAKE THE PLUNGE!**

6. What is surprising about the opening paragraph, when you remember that Lou Gehrig is being forced to retire from the game he loves? **PQE**

7. What phrase does Lou Gehrig repeat throughout this speech?

8. How many questions does he ask during the speech?

9. Why do you think he asks so many questions. **PQE**

10. Do you think this is a good speech?

A **rhetorical question** is a question where the answer is so obvious that there is no need to actually respond. Writers and speakers use this device to catch our attention and to emphasise their point. Lou Gehrig uses many rhetorical questions in his speech.

**Repetition** is also very useful because it allows a speaker to emphasise the most important points for the audience. Lou Gehrig used it by repeating the word 'lucky' throughout his speech.

 **WHY DON'T YOU...**

Think about your favourite sports star. Imagine that they have been forced to retire early due to illness or injury. Write their farewell speech. Copy the style of Lou Gehrig's speech; just change the names and details. Try to include one **rhetorical question** and some **repetition**.

 **THRASH IT OUT!**

Read your speech out to the class.

# Braveheart
## William Wallace's speech before the Battle of Stirling

*William Wallace was a Scottish Chieftain who led the Scots in a failed rebellion against the English in 1297. Here he is trying to convince his troops to go into battle against huge odds. Notice that sometimes a speech can be interrupted by hecklers!*

WALLACE: Sons of Scotland, I am William Wallace.

YOUNG SOLDIER: William Wallace is seven feet tall.

WALLACE: Yes, I've heard. Kills men by the hundreds, and if he were here he'd consume the English with fireballs from his eyes and bolts of lightning from his arse. I am William Wallace. And I see a whole army of my countrymen here in defiance of tyranny. You have come to fight as free men, and free men you are. What would you do without freedom? Will you fight?

VETERAN SOLDIER: Fight? Against that? No, we will run; and we will live.

WALLACE: Aye, fight and you may die. Run and you'll live – at least a while. And dying in your beds many years from now, would you be willing to trade all the days from this day to that for one chance, just one chance to come back here and tell our enemies that they may take our lives, but they'll never take our freedom!!!

WALLACE AND SOLDIERS: Alba gu bra! (Scotland forever!)

1. Why doesn't the young soldier believe that the speaker is William Wallace?

2. Why are the soldiers there, according to Wallace?

3. How does he convince them that it is better to fight and die, than to run away and live?

4. A good speaker appeals to the audience's feelings. How does Wallace make his audience feel? **P Q E**

5. Wallace shows the army that they have two options. How does this contrast make them want to fight? **P Q E**

6. Where does Wallace use humour to get his listeners' attention? **P Q E**

Imagine that you are losing a very important match by very little. You are the captain of the team. It is up to you to urge your team on to victory. Write the speech you will make in the dressing room at half-time. Remember, like William Wallace, you have to appeal to your team's feelings; you have to contrast the two options available to them.

Read your inspiring speech out to the class. See if you get the reaction you are looking for!

# The Coach's Last Word

Christopher Prendiville

Today is a very special day for you all. You will treasure it forever. But today is also a day that has already seen you succeed. You have all reached a point in your sporting lives that many only wish they could reach. You are representing your school, your friends, your teachers and your family in an All-Ireland final. You are the first in over thirty years to wear the proud colours of St Mary's in a national basketball final. Many great teams have gone before you. You have now joined them by being part of this wonderful occasion today. Regardless of how today goes, remember that your year has been a tremendous success and your lives have been enriched by the games, journeys and emotions felt so far.

It is hugely important that you enjoy the day and feed off the positive energy that comes from it. Enjoy the buzz of the National Arena and, believe me, the noise is deafening when it gets going. Enjoy the bus journey, the thumping music, the supporters singing, the dressing room and especially standing with your friends for the National Anthem.

These are the things that make this day one of the best of your lives. It's a whirlwind of happiness and excitement. You'll ride one serious emotional roller coaster from now until the final whistle is blown but it will stay with you forever. You want to win of course but whatever the result, you will all have a memory and experience that few others are lucky enough to encounter. It will pass you by so quickly but do your best to stop, take deep breaths and take it all in. Enjoy it!

As regards the game itself, the most important thing is to keep your cool. I've experienced two All-Ireland finals with other schools and the difference between the final we won and the final we lost was that the girls kept their nerve. You are as prepared as you can be, you know your moves and you know the opposition's strengths and weaknesses. But beware of the Tallaght factor! The occasion can overwhelm you and the atmosphere will cut you off from the umbilical cord that is your coach. In both other finals I couldn't get instructions to the players because of the noise. Some of the players didn't even know their own names when it was called. Try and stay focused and keep your job as a player in mind. I will talk to you before the game and during time-outs. I can't emphasise enough how important it is to listen carefully in those precious calm moments because when you go back out on court you are stepping back into a cauldron. Despite all the moves practised very few will get used. The game will become a case of just doing the simple things with the ball and keeping your head when all around you are losing theirs.

The two games you played to get to Tallaght prove that you are a team of character. Coming through from behind to win in extra time says so much about your ability. Let those games remind you of how you never need to panic and that you should never give up hope. You've proven you know how to win tight games. That experience will stand to you once more.

My final point is that what will win you the final is a cool, calm approach where you do the simple things you always did. As my old rugby coach used to say, 'Keep it Simple, Stupid!' Enjoy it all, bring home the memories, love the buzz and do your best. Best of luck and remember that all of Donegal is rooting for you.

1. Why is this All-Ireland final so important?

2. In the second paragraph what does the coach tell the team to enjoy?

3. What does he warn them about in the third paragraph?

4. In what tone of voice do you think this speech would be delivered? **P Q E**

5. How does the writer use details to create a sense of the importance of the occasion? **P Q E**

6. Identify three images used in this speech. Say which is your favourite and why. **P Q E**

7. How does the coach appeal to the team's emotions? **P Q E**

8. Do you think this speech would inspire you to perform well in a basketball All-Ireland final?

Write a speech to be delivered to a Junior Certificate class the week before the exams. Use the coach's speech as a model:

- Explain why the Junior Cert is so important.
- Praise the students for all their hard work.
- Remind them to enjoy the adrenalin and camaraderie.
- Point out possible pit-falls.
- Wish them luck!

# I Have a Dream

Martin Luther King

*Martin Luther King was a famous black civil rights leader in America in the 1960s. This is an excerpt from one of his most famous speeches.*

I say to you today, my friends, that in spite of the difficulties and frustrations of the moment I still have a dream. It is a dream deeply rooted in the American dream.

I have a dream that one day this nation will rise up and live out the true meaning of its creed: 'We hold these truths to be self-evident: that all men are created equal.'

I have a dream that one day on the red hills of Georgia the sons of former slaves and the sons of former slaveowners will be able to sit down together at the table of brotherhood. I have a dream that one day even the state of Mississippi, a desert state sweltering with the heat of injustice and oppression, will be transformed into an oasis of freedom and justice.

I have a dream that my four little children will one day live in a nation where they will not be judged by the colour of their skin but by the content of their character.

I have a dream today. I have a dream that one day the state of Alabama, whose governor's lips are presently dripping with the words of interposition and nullification, will be transformed into a situation where little black boys and little black girls will be able to join hands with little white boys and little white girls and walk away together as sisters and brothers.

I have a dream today. I have a dream that one day every valley shall be exalted, every hill and mountain shall be made low, the rough places will be made plains, and the crooked places will be made straight, and the glory of the Lord shall be revealed, and all flesh shall see it together.

This is our hope. This is the faith with which I return to the South. With this faith we will be able to transform the jangling discords of our nation into a beautiful symphony of brotherhood. With this faith we will be able to work together, to pray together, to struggle together, to go to jail together, to stand up for freedom together, knowing that we will be free one day.

This will be the day when all of God's children will be able to sing with new meaning, 'My country 'tis of thee, sweet land of liberty, of thee I sing. Land where my fathers died, land of the pilgrim's pride, from every mountainside, let freedom ring.'

And if America is to be a great nation this must become true. So let freedom ring from the prodigious hill-tops of New Hampshire. Let freedom ring from the mighty mountains of New York. Let freedom ring from the heightening Alleghenies of Pennsylvania!

Let freedom ring from the snowcapped Rockies of Colorado!

Let freedom ring from the curvaceous peaks of California!

But not only that; let freedom ring from Stone Mountain of Georgia!

Let freedom ring from every hill and molehill of Mississippi. From every moutainside let freedom ring.

When we let freedom ring, when we let it ring from every village and every hamlet, from every state and every city, we will be able to speed up that day when all of God's children, black men and white men, Jews and Gentiles, Protestants and Catholics, will be able to join hands and sing in the words of that old Negro spiritual, 'Free at last! Free at last! Thank God Almighty, we are free at last!'

1. In your own words, what does Martin Luther King say is his nation's creed?

2. What does he hope will happen between the sons of former slaves and slave owners?

3. How does he hope his children will be judged?

4. What does he want to happen in Alabama?

5. Can you find evidence of religious language in this speech? **P Q E**

6. Find the song quote that Luther King uses during his speech. What song is it from?

7. While listing the numerous states, Luther King uses striking imagery and adjectives. Choose two and say why you chose them.

8. What do you think it felt like to have been in the crowd listening to this speech?

9. This speech is full of powerful contrasts, for example: 'The state of Mississippi, a desert state sweltering with the heat of injustice and oppression, will be transformed into an oasis of freedom and justice.' Here a desert is contrasted with an oasis, while simultaneously injustice is contrasted with justice.

   Can you find another example of contrast and explain why it is effective?

10. There is a phrase repeated constantly at the start of this speech. What is it? Why do you think he uses it? What effect does this repetition have?

11. Imagery that is almost poetic is used here to help the audience visualise the dream of unity. Pick an image which you found moving and comment on it.

Pretend that you've been asked to make a speech at a political rally. You have a dream of what Ireland could be like. Imitate the structure of Martin Luther King's speech, but identify problems which you would like to see resolved. You will need to **Brainstorm** these issues before you write.

Read your speech to your class. Take notes as you listen to the speeches of others. Have a class discussion based on the different points raised.

# Speak Up

So far, you have read examples of good speech writing. So, remember, when writing speeches yourself you should try to include some of the following:

- **Attention-grabbing opening:** you need to get your audience's attention immediately. You can do this by surprising or shocking them with a statement or by using a good quote, if you have one.

- **Rhetorical questions:** these are very useful if you are trying to convince your audience of something. Lou Gehrig knew that people were feeling sorry for him, but he used rhetorical questions to show them that he still had things to be thankful for.

- **Repetition:** this is used to emphasise a point or create drama, as in Martin Luther King's 'I Have a Dream' speech.

- **Imagery:** this helps the audience to visualise what you are describing. For example, Wallace got his men to see that in years to come they would regret not fighting for their country's freedom.

- **Appeal to the emotions:** think about how you want your audience to feel. William Wallace wanted his men to feel determined so he makes them angry by almost insulting them.

- **Contrast:** if you describe both a pleasant and an unpleasant scene, it can convince people that you are right.

- **Humour:** if it is appropriate to the situation, humour always wins an audience over.

- **Epigrams** are short clever sayings, like *'Ask not what your country can do for you, but what you can do for your country.'* The American president John F. Kennedy once used this in a speech. It has since been borrowed and adapted by the GAA and others as it is so effective. Epigrams help to keep your main point in your audience's mind.

Imagine that one of the following people is moving away from your local community:

- A Sports Club President
- Someone who has raised money for a local charity over the course of twenty years
- The Leader of the Youth Club

Write the speech you would deliver to the club or community group on the occasion of their departure.

**OR**

A well-known writer or sports star is visiting your school. You have been nominated to prepare a welcome speech for the occasion. Write out the speech you would make to a gathering of staff and pupils welcoming the VIP.

**OR**

You have been asked to nominate a pupil in your class for the 'Student of the Year' award. Write in a persuasive style the nomination speech you would make in favour of this individual.

1999 H.L. Paper

# What's Your Opinion?

Often in newspapers and magazines, writers give their opinions on various issues. This is called DISCURSIVE writing, as the writers are discussing ideas. You can be asked to write like this in the Junior Cert Exam and often the passages you get to read are discursive in style. Watch out for the techniques that the following writers use.

*The Irish Independent*, Thursday, 9 July 2009

## Cuts mean writing is on the wall for literacy rates

### Martina Devlin

I'LL NEVER FORGET the first book I read on my own, at the age of five. *Have You Seen My Puppy?* was about a little boy who lost his dog, hunting high and low until he found him.

I remember the anxiety I felt about whether he would be reunited with his curly-tailed puppy. I remember ducking under my father's newspaper to ask him what a word meant. I remember the feeling of achievement at making it through to the end of the book, and also the prickle of loss.

It left me eager to read another book, then another. It introduced me to a world outside the family and classroom. It taught me empathy. It gave me confidence with schoolwork: I could look at the pages pointed out by the teacher and grasp what she wanted us to do.

That first book was one I borrowed from the school library, and I loved it so much I asked for a copy for my birthday. Later I graduated to *Anne of Green Gables* and *Just William* and *Little House on the Prairie*, all available in the school library.

I used the town library as well, and there were books in the house – Maurice Walsh was a fixture – but the school facility meant books which a child might be interested in reading were right there, under your nose, every day. We talked to each other in the playground about books, we recommended favourites to each other.

The school library helped form my reading habit. If you're a reader, you probably count this pastime as one of life's most enriching pleasures. You may resent how life interferes with your good intentions to catch up on reading. Maybe you're looking forward to packing some new releases in your luggage for the summer holidays.

But spare a thought for people with limited literacy, those for whom reading is a challenge and a source of anxiety, rather than a recreation.

If you don't learn to love books at a young age, chances are you may never develop that passion.

In an ideal world, every parent would foster a reading habit in their child; unfortunately, the world is far from ideal.

Schools have been picking up the slack. An initiative to stock school libraries has been running in Ireland since the late 1960s, guaranteeing books in the life of every child in the country, regardless of social background or family circumstances.

It didn't cost a lot, at around €2m a year, but it made a difference. It meant books – not textbooks but attractively packaged, recently-published novels and non-fiction books – were introduced into the classroom.

After almost 40 years, the scheme has now been discontinued. There is no School Library Grant for 2009 – the budget is gone. Not reduced but removed. Teachers and librarians expected some decrease, in view of economic circumstances, but to their dismay it has simply vanished.

The Department of Education explains it has reallocated the funds by increasing the capitation grant for schools. But teachers look at you pityingly when you suggest this will provide books. That money will go towards heating bills and day-to-day running costs, they say – it is not ring-fenced for books.

Meanwhile the books currently stocked in school libraries will grow increasingly tatty, and the excitement of new titles will be a distant memory.

There are public libraries, of course. But some families do not use them. There are parents who don't even make their children attend school, let alone rise to anything extracurricular like a library visit. There are households where children are left to get themselves up, dressed and breakfasted in the morning.

No doubt schools in towns and cities will organise classroom library visits, in an attempt to plug the gap, but schools in rural areas do not have easy access. Besides, there can be discipline problems associated with decanting a class of 30 or 35 primary school pupils into a public library.

Yet books are vital for a child's development. Dublin city librarian Rosemary Hetherington says: 'It's important that children are surrounded by a print environment – if there are books around them, they are more likely to pick them up and realise books are fun, and mean pleasure rather than pain. Once children gain reading confidence it improves every part of the school curriculum for them.'

But one in three children in disadvantaged areas leaves school with severe literacy and numeracy problems, according to children's charity Barnardos. This statistic shames us all.

A recent Barnardos report, 'Written Out, Written Off', eloquently notes how education 'can make all the difference to a child: the difference between believing in their own future and despairing of it; the difference between living in poverty and forging their own path out of it'.

We are submerged in recession and everyone agrees cutbacks are inevitable, although nobody wants to feel the pain. But victimising children in underprivileged circumstances is no way to proceed – educational cutbacks are a false economy.

Removing this funding is a retrograde step. Yet the figures involved in maintaining the scheme are tiny compared with the cost of our democratic trappings, such as ministerial cars and drivers. It has such a positive impact on children who may never see a book at home. Isn't democracy meant to be about ensuring equality of opportunity?

Imagine if there are children growing up in Ireland today who never have the opportunity to say: 'I'll never forget the first book I read …'

1. How did Martina Devlin's first book make her feel?

2. In what way does she feel that the school library encouraged her and her friends to read?

3. According to the writer, why do some people never learn to love reading?

4. What has happened to the school library grant scheme?

5. Why does Rosemary Hetherington say that books are vital to a child's development?

6. What does the Barnardos report note?

7. Why does the writer say the funding should be restored?

An **anecdote** is a short account of an interesting incident in a person's life. In discursive writing **anecdotes** are often used to gain the reader's interest before introducing more difficult information.

8. The writer uses an **anecdote** about her childhood to open this piece of writing. Is this effective? Why?

9. Can you find an example in this article of the writer addressing the reader directly? What effect does this have? **P** **Q** **E**

10. Would you describe the language in this piece as 'descriptive' or 'technical'? **P** **Q** **E**

11. Martina Devlin, the writer, includes many quotes in this article. Why does she do so? Do you think these quotes make the article reliable?

12. In this article the writer moves from a specific anecdote to a general point, to make her overall argument. Can you write a paragraph tracing her points in your own words?

Write a letter to the editor in response to this article. You will find more information on letters to the editor in Chapter 2.

*OR*

Read the following quote from Martina Devlin's article:

*Educational cutbacks are a false economy.*

Write an opinion piece about this statement. Structure your article like Martina Devlin:

– Brainstorm and research the areas you are interested in, for example, sport, science, drama or music.

– Begin with a personal anecdote.

– Move on to a general point.

– Use quotes and statistics to back up your argument.

– Appeal directly to your reader's emotions.

– Try to relate your closing paragraph to your opening anecdote.

*The Irish Independent*, Saturday, 4 July 2009

# Wimbledon fever proves tennis is a game of two halves

## David Robbins

ACROSS FROM WHERE I LIVE, there is a lovely old square which contains three lovely old tennis courts. For most of the year, they lie empty, their net cords sagging, their filaments billowing in the wind.

Occasionally, my wife and myself rouse ourselves and play a set or two. On Sundays, there is the pock-pock sound of a foursome arranged by one of our neighbours.

But mostly, the courts just stand there, idle and reproachful.

Until, that is, the second fortnight in June, Wimbledon fortnight, when people dig out their old racquets, buy a new tube of balls and sally forth, inspired by the game which Martin Amis recently called 'the most perfect combination of athleticism, artistry, power, style and wit'.

And he's right. Tennis has a grace about it that sets it apart from other sports.

Power isn't enough in tennis. You have to think as well.

And it has that quality, very important in sport, of allowing the once-a-year duffer to feel like a champion. For once in every match, even a very bad player will hit the perfect shot.

It might be a return of serve down the line, or a cross-court winner, or a one-in-a-million chance drop-shot or, heaven be praised, an ace, and the very bad player will think: 'OK, if I practised a little, I think I could be quite good, you know.'

As with most other sports I have taken up (and often given up), I am mediocre at tennis.

Not bad, mind you. I can be a pain in the ass to beat. But by no means good.

I have a home-schooled, self-taught style which a coach once described as 'effective'.

I like to think I play with the inventiveness of Ilie Nastase, but from the other side of the net, I probably look more like Virginia Wade.

The tennis bug, which had lain dormant for many years, suddenly sprang to life again last summer, while I was on holidays with a group of friends.

We were four families in all, and most days, in that time of the evening when people are pottering, we four dads used to sneak off for a quick set or two.

We soon worked out which combination of teams was the fairest, and then went at it hammer and tongs.

Every means to victory was deployed: sneaky short serves, attempts at decapitation, sledging, relentless seeking out of the weaker players' weakest shots.

I remember a vicious forehand drive straight at my partner's head. He ducked (the only time I have seen this tactic on a tennis court) and the ball passed neatly through the crease in his straw hat.

In the frequent breaks, we discussed the perennial topic of elite sports men: what is it with women and sport?

All present had played tennis against or alongside women, and we all had noticed certain common characteristics.

Firstly, they did not want to win. They did not want to expose any one of their number as being useless at tennis.

They wanted to be inclusive and nice, but found to their dismay that tennis, like all sports, is designed to throw up winners and losers.

'But you're good,' one might say to her partner. The implication was that being good at the game was somehow cheating. 'No I'm not,' the other might reply, 'just hit some lucky shots, that's all.'

They called balls in that were out. They said 'oh, take it again' if someone hit a ball into the net. They took deprecation to new levels. Praise was always deflected, never accepted.

Apologies flew back and forth. Sorry, they said, if a serve went out. Sorry, if it went in.

Sorry when they hit a rasping winner, and sorry if they put the ball out.

Some women, we concluded, just do not like to compete.

They do not want to be seen to be trying, perhaps because then, if they lose, they can pretend it doesn't matter.

They do not want to stand out, to push themselves forward, to break ranks with the others.

'Of course,' said one of us, 'then you play singles against them and they beat the pants off you.' Yup.

1. Does the writer play tennis often?
2. What makes tennis different from other sports in the writer's opinion?
3. What tactics do the 'four dads' use to try to win at tennis?
4. In what ways does the writer think women play tennis differently to men?
5. Do you agree that a person would not need to like tennis to enjoy this article?

6. The writer uses personification at the beginning of this extract. Identify and explain it.
7. Did this piece of writing make you smile? Why or why not? **PQE**
8. This writer contrasts the way men and women play tennis with each other in order to make a specific point. What is this point?
9. Can you find any examples of conversational language in this extract? What effect does this have? **PQE**
10. If you were the editor of this piece what alternative title would you give it? Explain why.

*Detested sport that owes its pleasure to another's pain.*

Write a serious or humorous article for the school magazine agreeing or disagreeing with this opinion.

## Don't forget to watch out for the following:

- **Openings:** Writers often use techniques like anecdotes, quotes or specific examples to catch our attention.
- **Structure:** Does the writer move from a specific example to a general point, or vice versa?
- **Language:** Is the language descriptive or technical? Is there imagery used to emphasise a particular point? Does the writer try to appeal to the reader's emotions?
- **Humour/Sarcasm:** Has the writer tried to make the reader laugh?
- **Compare/Contrast:** Are there comparisons or contrasts made in order to reinforce or simplify particular points?
- **Questions:** Does the writer use questions, rhetorical or otherwise, to draw us into the argument?

# Debate Writing

Here are some debating topics or motions:

**Co-education is the best education.**

*THE INFORMATION SUPER-HIGHWAY NEEDS TRAFFIC POLICE.*

A debate is a formal discussion or dispute on an agreed topic. Because it is formal there are rules which must be followed.

**The voting age should be reduced to 16.**

*We should say 'Yes' to nuclear power.*

We should rage against the machine!

**It Could Be You!**
**The National Lottery creates more problems than it solves.**

*School uniforms are a great idea.*

The Junior Cert should be abolished.

**Participation in PE should be voluntary.**

The death penalty for murder should be brought back.

Public figures have a right to private lives.

Science is a danger to civilisation.

The environment should come before economics.

**Sports stars are no longer heroes, merely fame and money hungry mortals.**

# Like all good battles a strategy is necessary:

## First ...

- Divide into teams. If you are 'For' the motion you are the proposition; if you are 'Against' the motion you are the opposition.

- Define the team's general argument. For example, if the topic is 'It is better to go abroad for your summer holidays than to stay in Ireland' the proposition's general argument might be:

  - *'Ireland has unreliable weather, expensive food, and no amenities, three reasons why it is better to go abroad on holidays.'*

- Discuss the topic that has been chosen.

  - What do you think the title or the motion means?

  - What points could prove or disprove your argument?

  - What areas do you need to research to find evidence to back up your points?

  - What points are the opposition likely to come up with?

    | For | Against |
    |-----|---------|
    | Weather | Skin cancer |
    | More amenities | Crime |
    | Exchange rates | Diseases, infections, insects |
    | Better value for money | Expense |
    | Practise language | Communication problem |
    | Experience new culture and histories | Support home industry |

# Second ...

- Assign each member of the team a specific area to research:
    - *Speaker A    Weather and amenities*
    - *Speaker B    Exchange rates and value for money*
    - *Speaker C    Language, culture and history*
- You can research almost any topic by:
    - going to the school or local library
    - going online; newspaper archives on the web are very useful
    - reading books, magazines or newspapers
    - listening to the radio or watching television
    - talking to people about your debate topic.

# Third ...

- You must write your speech! To win an argument you must have evidence or proof that your point of view is the correct one. You should begin each paragraph with a statement and then back it up with evidence. There are three types of evidence you should use.

    - Personal evidence, for example, *a description of your own experience of going abroad on holidays and how wonderful it was while everyone else sat at home in the rain.*

    - Anecdotal evidence, for example, *stories or accounts of other people's experiences taken from conversations, newspapers, travel programmes, etc.*

    - Factual evidence, for example, *a statistic, a scientific fact, a quote from a famous person, etc. You must tell the audience where you got your information from if you want to be convincing.*

- With this evidence you must persuade the audience that your argument is right, so you need to use entertaining language that they will enjoy.

    - It is good to use questions which will make the audience think, like, for example, *'Can anyone here in this room remember a summer in Ireland when it did not rain? (pause) I thought not!'* A question like this is called a rhetorical question. No one is expected to respond because the answer is obvious.

        - Try to use some jokes and quotes, if appropriate, to get the audience on your side.

        - You can disagree with speakers from the other team who have already spoken. This is called rebuttal. You should mention the speaker by name and use your information to knock theirs.

● In the opening of your speech, remind the audience of the topics discussed by previous teammates. This makes your team and argument stronger. In your conclusion, summarise your main points into two or three sentences, for example, '*To conclude, I described my sun-soaked adventure in Barbados, I recounted details of wonderful holidays seen on the travel programme* No Frontiers, *and I astounded you with the unbelievable statistic that it rains in Ireland 347 days out of 365! I leave it to your intelligence to decide whether it is better to holiday abroad or not.*'

Write out your argument for **OR** against the motion that:

Footballers OR Top Models OR Pop Stars are paid too much.

You should be either totally **for** or totally **against** this motion.

State clearly and convincingly the reasons for your opinion.

2003 O.L. Paper

### OR

Write a speech for or against the motion that: 'Teenagers should be called "screenagers" because they are addicted to screens – TV, phones, electronic games …'

You need to:

● decide whether you are for OR against the motion

● think about the points you want to make

● plan the order in which you will make them

Now write the speech in full.

2009 O.L. Paper

FOR or AGAINST

You have been chosen as a member of your class debating team. The motion for the debate is:

'Teenagers today are too easily influenced by celebrities.'

Write out your SPEECH in full.

2008 O.L. Paper

# The Great Debate

The **Chairperson** runs the debate.

- They introduce the topic and speakers.
- They keep the audience quiet.
- They open the discussion to the audience at the end.
- They take the vote.

Teams sit on two sides.

The **person who speaks** stands at the podium.

The **timekeeper** rings a bell or taps the table when a speaker's time is up.

After the speak finish, the top should be oper to the floor. This means th **audience** gets contribute. Th audience als votes to decide winners.

- If you are nervous, choose a point on the wall above the audience to look at. Make eye contact if you can.

- Use gestures to emphasise important points, but try not to fidget.

- You must try to look relaxed. Put your two feet shoulder width apart and firmly on the ground.

- Stand up straight.

- Use your notes for reference in case you go blank, but try not to read the entire speech.

- Try to project your voice to the back of the room. A good tip to help you slow down is to take a breath at every comma and to pause for the count of three at every full stop.

# D.I.Y. Debate

Here is a ready-made debate that you might like to do in class.

## WE DON'T CARE FOR OUR ENVIRONMENT.

## First ...

- The class divides into teams of three students.

- In groups, discuss the topic that has been chosen in the following way:

  - What do you think the title or the motion means? Think about the word 'We'. It could refer to the class, the Irish nation or the human race.

  - Try to structure your arguments on local, national and international topics.

  - Brainstorm a list of issues relating to the environment. Some of the following points might be worth thinking about:

| Proposition | Opposition |
|---|---|
| Management of waste | Improvements in recycling |
| Illegal dumping | New laws enforced |
| Pollution of inland waters | Restocking of fisheries |
| Business waste | Business conduct changing |
| Urban sprawl | Urban renewal |
| Overuse of fossil fuels | Alternative energy sources |
| Depletion of natural resources | |
| Greenhouse gases | CFC ban |
| Ozone layer | Ozone hole shrinking |
| Kyoto Protocol and US refusal to ratify | Kyoto Protocol |

## Second ...

- Assign each member of the team a specific area to research, for example:

  - *Speaker A*   *Illegal dumping and farming practices*

  - *Speaker B*   *Business practices and water schemes*

  - *Speaker C*   *Greenhouse gases and the Kyoto Protocol*

Remember to think about your topics in terms of local, national and international practice.

Some useful websites for material on greenhouse gases, Kyoto, etc., are:

www.epa.ie

www.earthwatch.org

www.foe.org

www.greenpeace.org

www.childrenoftheearth.org

An archive search of any national newspaper using the words 'environmental issues' gives instant access to the most recent environmental controversies.

# Third ...

Research your area outside of class. Remember to think about personal, anecdotal and factual evidence. There are examples of possible approaches below.

## Proposition:

### Speaker A  Topics:  Bad waste management, illegal dumping, farming

- Personal evidence: 'Last week I witnessed someone burning their household rubbish. Later, while out walking, I was appalled at the amount of casual litter that I saw. Someone had even left their baby's dirty nappies behind on the beach. How can you say that such people care for the environment?'

- Anecdotal evidence: 'Only yesterday evening on the news I saw a story about a huge fish kill in Co. Mayo. An investigation is underway, but experts are already saying that it was caused by farmers illegally dumping effluent, which is really pooey stuff, from their animals, into rivers! You may laugh now, but think about it the next time you eat a nice juicy fishfinger!'

- Factual evidence:  'According to a report by An Taisce there may be 300 illegal dumps in Ireland and approximately 100 of those are in Wicklow. And they call Wicklow the garden of Ireland? Not in my garden, thanks!'

Over the following pages there are some other useful facts on this topic that you might incorporate into your speech if you want to look very well informed! You may need to look up some of the technical words and the roles of certain agencies as part of your research.

## Proposition:

**Only 60% of group water schemes are at acceptable safety levels.**
**(*An Taisce*)**

●

**10% of the state's archaeological monuments have been destroyed in the last 10 years. (*Heritage Ireland*)**

●

Ireland scored 8 out of a potential 30 among EU member states in protecting its wildlife. *(World Wildlife Fund)*

●

Ireland is the 17th worst country out of 176 in its $CO_2$ emissions per capita. (OECD)

●

**31% of group water schemes contain e-coli.**
**(*Environmental Protection Agency, EPA*)**

●

Every year 98,000 tonnes of hazardous waste is dumped illegally in Ireland without being reported. *(An Taisce)*

●

**The budget to protect our architectural heritage has dropped 44% in the last year. (*Heritage Ireland*)**

●

Chlorine monitors and alarms are a vital part of the infrastructure of a drinking water plant. In August 2008 40% of public water supply had no such equipment in place. (EPA)

●

Ireland is producing twice as much municipal waste as it was 10 years ago. (EPA)

## Opposition:

**Compliance with a code of Good Farming Practice is now a condition for receiving CAP payments.**

●

Use of chemical phosphorus fertilizer has dropped dramatically since the introduction of local authority bye-laws in 1998.

●

**In 1997, the Government produced a policy document called *Sustainable Development: A Strategy for Ireland*.**

●

**A National Bio-Diversity Plan has been put in place to protect wildlife habitats.**

●

**The 2000 Planning Act puts the principle of sustainable development into law.**

●

**The 1996 Waste Management Act and the 2000 Wildlife Act make sure the environment is protected under the law.**

●

**In Ireland the packaging waste recovery rate was 60% in 2005 which exceeds the EU target of 50%.**

●

**70% of Irish rivers and 85% of lakes have a satisfactory water quality status and the level of serious pollution is 0.6%.**

●

From 2008 to 2018 the Government has committed itself to investing €30 billion in clean energy.

Examples of big businesses changing their waste practices are:

Coates Lorilleux. A manufacturer of printing inks, this company took on a project sponsored by the EPA. They replaced 200-litre ink containers with 1,000-litre drums and replaced metal pails with plastic liners so that solvents could be recovered and re-used, thus reducing its packaging waste by 74 tonnes.

Mallinckrodt Medical Imaging invested $3 million to recover and recycle what would otherwise have ended up as waste.

Write a speech for OR against the motion, 'Mobile phones should be banned in schools.'

> 2009 H.L. Paper

**OR**

Write a speech for OR against the motion, 'Young people are not taken seriously in Ireland.'

> 2008 H.L. Paper

**OR**

Write a speech for OR against the motion, 'Second level education in Ireland is a good preparation for life.'

> 2007 H.L. Paper

**OR**

Write a speech for OR against the motion, 'Having a job during the school year is bad for second-level students.'

> 2006 H.L. Paper

**OR**

Write a speech for OR against the motion, 'Transition Year should be made compulsory.'

> 2005 H.L. Paper

# Exam Lifeboat

You have by now practised many different types of writing. The exam questions in this section can be divided into four broad categories:

 Personal writing

 Descriptive writing

 Storytelling (narrative writing)

 Discursive writing

1. Choose your **essay title** based on the type of writing that you are best at. Some people are excellent at writing arguments and others are brilliant at writing stories.

2. Always, always, always begin with a **Brainstorm**. Even if you only spend 60 seconds at this it can make all the difference.

3. Decide the order in which you are going to present your ideas and number your brainstorm into **paragraphs**.

4. Spend a few moments thinking of an exciting **opening**. Remember you need to catch the examiner's attention!

5. Use all your **senses** when writing anything descriptive.

6. Try and make sure that your essay has a good, solid **closing**.

If you are writing:

### A Personal Essay

*Remember –*

- draw on your own experiences
- say what you really think and feel, and try to make your descriptions vivid
- recreate the event, place and people for your reader

### A Descriptive Essay

*Remember –*

- use all your senses – sight, sound, taste, touch and smell
- think about what verbs, adjectives and adverbs to use; try to use imagery (similes, metaphors, symbols)

### Storytelling (Narrative)

*Remember –*

- make sure that you have a beginning, middle and end before you start writing
- decide on a narrator, setting and characters while brainstorming

### Discursive Writing

*Remember –*

- don't just make general points
- use personal, anecdotal and factual evidence

# Functional Writing

In this chapter you will come across many types of *writing*, including:

- Letters
- Reports
- Reviews

17 St Michael's Terrace,
Barrack Street,
Ballyshannon,
Co. Donegal,
Ireland.
11 February 2011

Dear Pablo,

I have just received your address from my teacher Mrs Dunlevy. My name is Jack and I am fifteen years old. I live right at the top of Ireland in a small town called Ballyshannon. It rains a lot here; I suppose that is very different from Uruguay!

I have been learning Spanish for three years now, but I am afraid that I am not very good yet. I hope it is all right with you that I am writing in English. I would love to hear more about your country and your lifestyle. What subjects do you study in school?

I am the eldest of three children. I have a brother David, who is 10, and a sister Niamh, who is 7. They really get on my nerves sometimes, but I suppose they are O.K. Do you have any brothers or sisters?

My favourite sport is surfing. There are lots of brilliant beaches near my town. Some day I would love to go to Australia to Surfers' Paradise and catch a few waves. I know that soccer is very popular in South America; do you support a team?

That's all I can think of at the moment.
I am looking forward to getting a letter from you.

Best wishes,

Jack Hayes

You will *learn* how to:

- Compile a CV
- Give a factual description of a photo

# Personal or Informal Letter

A personal or informal letter is a letter we write to a close friend, but it should still obey certain rules. However, in the main body of the letter you can still be yourself.

Your teacher has provided you with the name and address of a new pen-pal in Uruguay. You might write an informal letter to introduce yourself.

17 St Michael's Terrace,
Barrack Street,
Ballyshannon,
Co. Donegal,
Ireland.
11 February 2011

Dear Pablo,

I have just received your address from my teacher Mrs Dunlevy. My name is Jack and I am fifteen years old. I live right at the top of Ireland in a small town called Ballyshannon. It rains a lot here; I suppose that is very different from Uruguay!

I have been learning Spanish for three years now, but I am afraid that I am not very good yet. I hope it is all right with you that I am writing in English. I would love to hear more about your country and your lifestyle. What subjects do you study in school?

I am the eldest of three children. I have a brother David, who is 10, and a sister Niamh, who is 7. They really get on my nerves sometimes, but I suppose they are O.K. Do you have any brothers or sisters?

My favourite sport is surfing. There are lots of brilliant beaches near my town. Some day I would love to go to Australia to Surfers' Paradise and catch a few waves. I know that soccer is very popular in South America; do you support a team?

That's all I can think of at the moment.
I am looking forward to getting a letter from you.

Best wishes,

Jack Hayes

Write a letter to one of the following:

- A new pen-pal, introducing yourself
- A friend who is sick in hospital and is not allowed a phone or visitors
- Your best friend who is away in Irish college
- Your brother or sister who is away in Australia for a year
- An exchange student who is coming to visit you soon
- A new friend who you met at a concert whose address you took

# Letter of Application

If you do Transition Year you will be expected to apply for work experience. Don't forget, you only get one chance to make a first impression!

Before writing, plan the information you need to include like this …

A formal letter is a business letter or a letter to someone you don't know. It must therefore be very polite and written according to very specific rules.

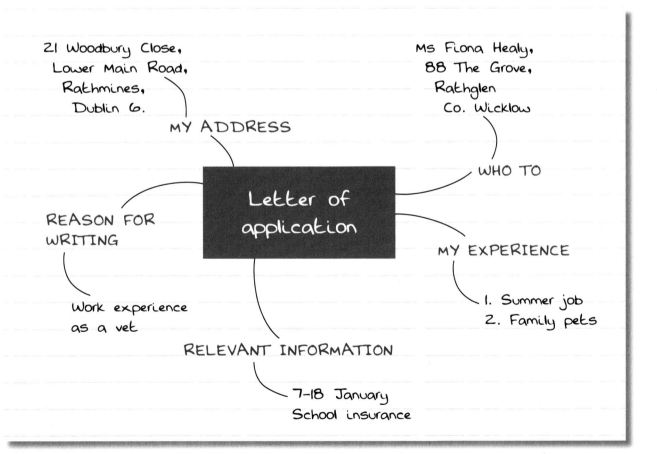

21 Woodbury Close,
Lower Main Road,
Rathmines,
Dublin 6.

MY ADDRESS

Ms Fiona Healy,
88 The Grove,
Rathglen
Co. Wicklow

WHO TO

REASON FOR WRITING

Work experience as a vet

Letter of application

MY EXPERIENCE

1. Summer job
2. Family pets

RELEVANT INFORMATION

7-18 January
School insurance

# Remember ...

- In your opening, if you do not know the person's name, write 'Dear Sir/Madam,'.
- When signing off, use 'Yours sincerely,' if you know the person's name, and 'Yours faithfully,' if you don't. Don't forget to use a capital 'Y' for 'Yours'!
- Watch out for errors in punctuation when writing addresses.
- This is a serious letter, so avoid slang, misspellings or inappropriate humour.
- If you are replying to an advertisement, state where and when you saw the ad.

21 Woodbury Close,
Lower Main Rd,
Rathmines,
Dublin 6.
10 October 2011

*Your address and the date (note punctuation)*

Ms Fiona Healy,
88 The Grove,
Rathglen,
Co. Wicklow.

*Name, position and address of the person you are writing to*

Dear Ms Healy,

*Greeting*

I am writing to enquire about the possibility of gaining work experience in your veterinary clinic. I am sixteen years of age and am presently in Transition Year in St Ignatius's Secondary School, Kilmacud.

Our work experience programme begins on Monday, 9 January and ends on Friday, 20 January. We are expected to spend two weeks working in an area of interest to our future careers. The school keeps a careful eye on our progress and we are insured under a school policy.

*Information you want the recipient to know*

I have some experience of working with animals since I had a summer job in nearby stables last year. I also have responsibility for the care of our family pets: a dog, two cats and a rabbit. I am a diligent and enthusiastic worker and would be very grateful for the opportunity to find out if I am suited to the veterinary profession.

I enclose my CV with further information and references. My work experience has to be confirmed by Monday, 14 November, so I would appreciate a response prior to that date. Thank you for your consideration in this matter.

*Concluding signature*

Yours sincerely,

Ciara Mulally

Write a letter applying for your choice of work experience for Transition Year.

**OR**

Write a letter in response to any one of the following advertisements.

---

**Daly's Diner requires**

An experienced
## DELI ASSISTANT
Supervisory experience an advantage

Applications to:
**Donal Daly**
**Woodview Park**
**Limerick**

*Irish Independent, 1 June*

---

# Cora's Café

*needs you!*

Are you a young, enthusiastic, hard-working person?
Join our team, and work in a busy, fun environment!

☞

Application forms available from:
Cora's Café, 22 High Street, Tipperary Town
*Limerick Leader, 23 May*

---

# SHOP ASSISTANT REQUIRED

For Cork City Centre Jewellery Store
Retail experience required
Tel: Maria between 10 a.m. and 5 p.m.
555-2349503
or please forward letter of application to:
Maria Moloney
Glitz Jewellers
63 Thomas Street, Cork
*Irish Examiner, 27 May*

---

# SALES PERSON REQUIRED

for busy Wexford music store

Experience essential

Reply in writing with CV to:
James MacMahon
**Funky Vibes**
Milltown Road, Wexford
*Munster Express, 22 July*

---

See pages 150–152 for advice on preparing your CV and filling in application forms.

# Letter of Complaint

Now look at this formal letter of complaint.

37 Summerfield Avenue,
Birr,
Co. Offaly.
12 March 2010

O'Leary's Hostel,
Clifden,
Co. Galway.

Dear Sir/Madam,

I am writing to inform you of my disappointment with a recent stay in your hostel. I am a student in Birr Community School, and as part of our Transition Year Programme we take part in an outdoor pursuits weekend. Normally this is one of the highlights of the year.

In this instance, I am sorry to say, it was one of the low points. There were a number of reasons for our dissatisfaction. Firstly, on our arrival, the hostel was locked and there was nobody around to let us in. When we finally gained entry, the rooms were dirty and the beds had not been made up. There was a most unpleasant smell of damp throughout the hostel.

Secondly, the food, for which we had paid an extra supplement, was utterly disgusting. On two occasions we had to travel to the local fast-food restaurant rather than eat the mess that was served up to us in the hostel. To add insult to injury, the food was invariably cold.

In my opinion your hostel is overpriced, and your food is a health hazard. For these reasons I will be reporting you to the Food Safety Authority and I will not be recommending your establishment to anyone else.

Yours faithfully,

Amy Farrell

Write a letter of complaint to one of the following:

- The Department of Education about the poor quality of the audiotape used in one of your aural Irish exams

- An electrical shop that sold you a faulty MP3 player

- The promoters of a rock concert where crowd control was non-existent

### OR

Look at the picture on the right. You are a resident in this locality and you are very upset by the dumping of all this rubbish.

Write a letter to your local county council or corporation.

In it, you should:

– describe the problem

– state your annoyance

– make suggestions for dealing with the situation.

**Don't forget to Brainstorm before you start writing!**

Brainstorm

# Letter of Enquiry

Here is a formal letter of enquiry.

9 Strand Hill,
Dunmore East,
Co. Waterford.
17 August 2011

The Dungarvan Dreadnoughts,
Dungarvan,
Co. Waterford.

Dear Sir/Madam,

I am writing to enquire about a pair of football boots that I lost during a recent away match at your club. I play with the Dunmore East Rangers, and we played a match at your club on the 15th of August.

On my return to Dunmore East I discovered that my favourite boots were missing. I am hoping that I left them in your clubhouse, and that they have been handed in to lost property. They are size nine, yellow with black trim.

I would be delighted to hear that you have recovered these boots as they are my lucky pair! My phone number is 555-234789. I can arrange for someone to come and collect the boots, if they have been found.

I hope you will be able to assist me in this matter. Thank you for your help.

Yours faithfully,

Colm O'Sullivan

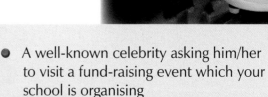

Write a letter of enquiry to one of the following:

- A person in a profession you would like to follow, asking for advice on getting started

- A pet shop, asking for advice on looking after the boa constrictor you got for your birthday!

- A well-known celebrity asking him/her to visit a fund-raising event which your school is organising

- An outdoor pursuits centre looking for details of their courses, prices and availability

*Don't forget to* Brainstorm *before you start writing!*

# Letter to the Editor

If you look in any of the broadsheet newspapers, near the centre, you will find a section called 'Letters to the Editor'. This is where people write to the editor of the newspaper expressing their opinions on various issues.

WHY DON'T YOU...

Gather a selection of broadsheet newspapers. In groups, go through the letters to the editor picking out any letters that you think are particularly interesting or well written. Share these with the class.

**OR**

Read this letter. Notice that the layout is slightly different from that of other letters.

Choose a topic or experience about which you feel very positive, or negative. Write a letter to the editor of a national newspaper outlining your opinion. Remember that your letter will be in the public eye so you must remain polite!

**OR**

Choose one of the letters from the selection that you read in class. Write a letter in response. Maybe you could even send it in to the editor?

Sir,– I recently travelled on a well-known low-cost air carrier. Now, I have often heard this company condemned in the past for its lack of customer care, so I was not expecting five-star treatment. However, my recent experience was such that I shall always go out of my way to avoid this company in future.

I have never encountered such rude and surly staff. The cabin crew were completely unprofessional, and treated the passengers with contempt. They all but threw items at passengers, items which I might add, the passengers were paying exorbitant prices to acquire.

The plane itself was filthy. I would go so far as to say that the toilets were a danger to health and safety. It was evident that ground crew never got on board to clean.

To add insult to injury, although we were seated on the plane at the correct time for take-off, we were left sitting on the runway for two hours, and we were given no explanation by the captain or his crew. This was terribly distressing for all passengers, but particularly for the elderly and children.

One is left asking the question: do low costs inevitably lead to low standards?

Yours etc.,

Aoife Stevens,
22 Greenfields Est.,
Oranmore,
Co. Galway.

# Take the Plunge!

**WHY DON'T YOU...**

Write your own letter to the editor on one of the following topics. Don't forget that it has to be a clear and concise expression of your own opinion.

- The problem of dog droppings on footpaths

- The lack of funding for sports and the arts

- The disappearance of your favourite childhood sweets from the shops

- The cancellation of an event that you were looking forward to

- A death row execution in Texas, USA

**OR**

Write a response to one of the letters to the editor below.

---

Sir, – I am writing to complain about the way builders and developers abandon new housing estates. Lazy builders fail to remove rubbish created while building.

Roads are left unfinished, green areas are not grassed and landscaping is not completed. The developers fail to consider basic amenities like shops, playgrounds or sports fields. Laws need to be passed to prevent these abuses, and they then must be enforced. I am sick of these urban jungles!

Yours etc.,

Seamus O'Sullivan,
Main Street,
Kilkenny.

---

Madam, – Recently I have been appalled at the skimpy apparel which is presently being worn by teenage girls. What are their parents thinking of, letting them out in such indecent clothing? Never mind the issue of modesty, the climate in this country does not facilitate the wearing of navel-revealing, off-the-shoulder garments. They'll all die of pneumonia! If they cannot be trusted to dress themselves appropriately perhaps a National Dress Code should be introduced?

Yours etc.,

Mary Minahane,
Bantry,
Co. Cork.

---

**TEST THE WATERS!**

A national newspaper has organised a 'Person of the Year' award. Write a letter to the editor nominating the person you think is most deserving of this award. You should explain why you think this person deserves the award.

# Letter to an Author

Sometime you might want to write to the author of a book you have really enjoyed or hated (NOTE: this question has come up in the Junior Certificate exam!). You could write the same style of letter to any celebrity you admired.

Read this sample letter.

Ballymore,
Ardtully,
Co. Laois.
12/09/2010

Dear Ms Rowling,

I have just finished reading *Harry Potter and the Prisoner of Azkaban* and I had to pick up a pen and write to you. I think that this book and all the other books in this series are brilliant. I wish that I could meet Harry Potter and his friends.

I wish that it were physically possible to visit Hogwarts. I have had dreams that I am playing a game of Quidditch, but of course I am not as good as Harry.

This book was far scarier than the first two. I was especially worried by the appearance of Sirius Black and I was concerned that Voldemort might finally defeat Harry, but I should have known better! As always, the ending was completely unexpected. I don't know where you get the ideas from.

While I am enjoying the film versions, I still prefer to read the books and have my own pictures in my head. I can't wait for the next instalment. Thank you for writing such fantastic books.

Yours sincerely,

Emily Byrne

Write a letter to the author of any text you have studied, telling him or her whether or not you enjoyed it, and explaining why.

2002 H.L. Paper

# Curriculum Vitae

A curriculum vitae, or CV, is a summary of the information
a future employer might need to know about you. It should be:

- very clearly laid out
- brief and to the point
- typed
- signed and dated.

Typically a CV should include the following information:

**Personal Details:**
    Name
    Address
    Telephone number
    Date of birth

**Education:**
    Primary school
    Secondary school
    Exam results to date

**Work Experience:**
    Start with the most recent position held
    Include jobs like babysitting, if relevant
    Mention duties and responsibilities

**Hobbies/Interests:**
    List activities you take part in
    Mention any clubs you are member of

**Achievements:**
    List any certificates or awards you have

**References:**
    Name, address and phone numbers of referees (two required)

**Personal Details:**

Name                 Regina O'Flynn
Address             Gleann Rua, Carlow
Telephone number   (077) 56438950
Date of birth        05/12/1995

**Education:**

Primary school
St Jude's National School, Gleann Rua, Carlow
Secondary school
Presentation College, Convent Road, Carlow
Exam results to date
Junior Certificate

| | | | | | | |
|---|---|---|---|---|---|---|
| English (H) | A | French (H) | B | Science (H) | B |
| Irish (O) | B | History (H) | A | Art (H) | C |
| Maths (O) | A | Geography (H) | C | Music (H) | B |

Currently taking part in Transition Year Programme

**Work Experience:**

**Waitress**:                 Murphy's Coffee Shop,
                      Hill Street,
                      Carlow.
June 2010–August 2010
Duties and responsibilities
Opening café, counting till receipts

**Babysitting**:    O'Boyle family,
                      11 Park View,
                      Carlow.
2008–present
Duties and responsibilities
Management of two children under 5

**Hobbies/Interests:**

Enjoy reading and going to the cinema
Member of Carlow Swimming Club
Member of Presentation Drama Society

**Achievements:**

Hold bronze medal in lifesaving
Took part in school production of *Annie*

**References:**

Sr Imelda McCarthy,
Principal,
Presentation College,
Convent Road,
Carlow.
Tel: (077) 58679023

Mr Declan Murphy (Owner),
Murphy's Coffee Shop
Hill Street,
Carlow.
Tel: (077) 39867670

**Signature:**    *Regina O'Flynn*      **Date:** 11/09/2010

# Application Form

You are often asked to fill in an application form rather than send in a CV.

● Fill it in using a pencil first in case you make mistakes.

● Use BLOCK capital letters unless the form says otherwise.

● If possible, keep a copy for yourself.

Try filling in this form. Count how many mistakes you make when you do it in pencil.

# Job Application Form

*(Please complete in block capitals in black or blue biro.)*

| First Name(s): | Surname:<br><br>Mr/Mrs/Ms | Date of Birth: | Place of Birth: |
|---|---|---|---|
| | | | Nationality: |
| Home Address: | | Correspondence Address (if different): | |
| Telephone No. (day time): | | Telephone No. (evening): | |
| E-mail: | | Application for position of: | |
| Details of qualifications: | | | |
| Details of previous experience or employment: | | | |
| Any other relevant information: | | | |

# Describing a Picture or Photograph

There will probably be a range of pictures or photos on your Junior Certificate paper. If you are asked to give a description of a picture or photo in the functional writing or media studies section you are probably being asked for a **factual description**.

- Take a few minutes to look carefully at the photo below.

- Jot down everything you can see, for example:

|  |  |  |
|---|---|---|
| Dolphin | Five people in a small boat | Calm sea |
| Clouds | Distant coastline | Dolphin watching |

- Begin by describing the picture in one sentence:

*This is a picture of a dolphin jumping out of the sea, being watched by people on a boat.*

● Next you must focus on the details in the picture if you are to give a full and factual description. To do this you need to look at different areas of the picture.

- *In the **foreground** on the **right-hand** side of the photo we can see a **dolphin** jumping out of the water. He appears almost black in colour and casts a black shadow on the water. We can see the outline of his nose and fin quite clearly.*

- *On the **left-hand** side of the photo we can see a small blue and white motorboat with five people on board. Some of them are watching the dolphin, while one man seems to be focusing his camera at the far shore.*

- *In the **background** on the right-hand side we can see a distant strip of grey coastline. Above it and dominating the top half of the picture is the sky, with long strips and tufts of soft white cloud.*

- *The **colour** of the boat matches the colour of the sea and sky. The sea is calm and there is a clam peaceful feel to the photo.*

● You can see that there are certain technical words which help you to describe the picture:

| | |
|---|---|
| foreground | centre |
| background | top |
| middle ground | bottom |
| left-hand side | right-hand side |

● You must also describe colours, even if the photo is in black and white, as there will still be areas of light and shade. You can also use details of people's facial expressions, postures, gestures and any activity you can see.

● A person should be able to draw a rough outline of your picture without actually seeing it.

● If you are asked to describe a picture in an advertisement you might need to say why you think that particular photo was chosen.

Get a photo from a newspaper or magazine at home. Bring it into class but don't show it to anyone. Split into pairs. Describe your photo to your partner without letting them see it! They have to try to draw a rough outline of your photo. Then change around.

**OR**

Describe any of the photos on the next page as accurately as possible. Remember, you are not asked how you feel about the photo, but solely to describe it objectively and clearly.

# Report

Most reports have four sections.

- **Introduction:**     Briefly outline the situation or problem and state the purpose of the report.

- **Information:**     Step by step, give the facts in detail, perhaps using statistics or examples.

- **Conclusion:**     Summarise the main points and explain why certain elements were successful or unsuccessful.

- **Recommendations:**   Suggest solutions for future problems; these must be realistic and practical.

Before writing, plan your report using the four headings above.

> Always bear in mind who will be reading the report!

Look at the following task:

Write a report for the School Principal on the litter problem in your school.

**1. Introduction**
- project CSPE
- survey

**Litter Report**

**3. Conclusion**
- bad places
- bad times
- bad classes

**2. Information**
- no. of students
- no. of bins
- locations
- recycling policy
- break times

**4. Recommendations:**
- more teachers
- more punishment
- more campaigns

# Report on the Litter Problem in Our School

## Introduction

The purpose of this report is to outline the causes of litter in our school, and to recommend some solutions. Interest in this project began in our CSPE class, and we became aware that there was a litter problem in our school. We decided to carry out a survey to measure the extent of the problem.

## Information

First, we found out the number of students in the school. We then counted the number of bins in the school and established their location. We discovered that there was one large bin for every twenty students. There is a bin in every classroom, and at least one bin on every corridor.

We then enquired about the school's recycling policy. Bins for cans only are available, but there are only three of them in the school.

Finally, we went around the school at both lunchtime and at four o'clock to see how much rubbish had been created during a typical day. In this way we identified the worst areas for litter.

## Conclusion

From our observations it is clear that there are certain 'hot spots'. The area around the sweet shop is particularly bad at lunchtime. The worst classroom was 3A, who left their room in a disgusting state at four o'clock. There were a sufficient number of bins around the school, but many of them had not been filled. The area around the Principal's office was the most litter free!

## Recommendations

As a result of these findings it is recommended that the following steps be taken:

1. A teacher should patrol the area around the sweet shop at lunchtime in order to discourage littering.

2. 3A should receive a punishment, such as removing the chewing gum from beneath their desks, in order to teach them the consequences of their actions.

3. A poster campaign should be organised to raise awareness of the litter problem, and to encourage students to use the bins provided.

4. Incentives and prizes should be offered to the class with the most improved attitude to litter.

# Review

**A** INTRODUCE ...

- What you are going to talk about
- The **title** of the book, film or CD
- The **type** of book, film or CD it is, e.g. *book or film:* horror, romance, drama, comedy, etc. *CD:* rock, pop, r 'n' b, etc.

**B** DESCRIBE ...   *Book/Film*

- **Where** and **when** the story takes place
- Who the main **character** or characters are
- The general outline of the **plot,** without spoiling the ending!
- The main point or **message** in one sentence, if possible

*CD*

- The types of songs, e.g ballads, instrumentals, and how many there are
- The lyrical value – what are the **messages** in the songs?

**C** JUDGE ...   *Book/Film*

- The main **strengths** and **weaknesses**, in your opinion
- How much you liked or disliked the characters
- How realistic the **dialogue** was
- Whether or not the descriptions of the **relationships** were believable
- Whether or not it kept your interest; was there good **suspense**?
- Whether or not the **ending** was satisfactory, without giving it away!
- The **language** or **camera shots and special effects** in the film

*CD*

- The overall **atmosphere** of the album
- Whether or not the **sequence** of the tracks works
- Which were the strongest and weakest **songs**
- Which tracks could be released as singles
- How it made you feel

**D** DECIDE ...

- To whom you would recommend the book/film/CD and why?
- Whether or not it is **suitable** for teenagers or younger children
- The **type of person** who would enjoy this particular book/film/CD
- The type of person who would not enjoy this book/film/CD

Read this example of a review.

*Shrek 2* is the highly anticipated sequel to the brilliant *Shrek*, and takes up where that film left off. We follow the story of Shrek, his bride Fiona and the irrepressible Donkey as they go to meet Shrek's new in-laws for the first time. Along the way, our heroes meet new friends and get into all manner of awkward situations.

The comedy begins when Shrek and Fiona return from their honeymoon to find themselves summoned to the Kingdom of Far Far Away, to meet Fiona's parents. In the first *Shrek* the filmmakers created a clever pastiche of the famous fairytales that we all know and love. This time they go a step further, and mock the superficiality and silliness of Hollywood and its celebrity culture. The Kingdom of Far Far Away is a thinly disguised portrait of the capital of American film in all its absurdity.

Unsurprisingly, Shrek, in all his green glory, is an unacceptable son-in-law so Fiona's father schemes to get rid of him.

This film is full of hilarious one-liners and ridiculous situations. New characters are introduced, like Puss-in-Boots, who almost steals the show from Donkey! The attention to detail in the animation, and state-of-the-art computer graphics only add to the viewers' enjoyment. In fact, there are so many good jokes that the film bears repeated viewing to try to catch them all!

I would highly recommend this film to all viewers between the ages of 6 and 106! Children will enjoy the fairytale aspect, while adults will get the subtle references to other movies. Somehow, I get the feeling that this won't be the last we'll be seeing of Shrek.

Most books and DVDs have a short blurb on the outside of the back cover. Typically this is a brief text which describes and praises the plot, characterisation, acting, etc. Write such a blurb for any book or DVD of your choice.

H.L. Paper 2006

**OR**

Write a review for a young people's magazine of any book, film, computer game or concert you have recently experienced. Your answer should include an introduction, description, evaluation and recommendation.

H.L. Paper 2004

# Writing Instructions or Rules

When you are writing instructions or rules you have to imagine that the person reading hasn't a clue what they are doing. Pretend that they are from another planet!

You need to begin with a **Brainstorm**, as giving instructions can be complicated.

● Make a list of everything that you will need.

● Go through all the actions step by step and number them.

● Use very simple and clear language.

● Use headings and sub-headings if necessary.

Look at the following task:

Brainstorm

> You plan to hold a PHOTOGRAPHY COMPETITION in your school. Write the rules of the competition.
>
> In the rules you could mention:
>
> ● the different groupings of pictures
> ● the different age groups involved
> ● the regulations about entries
> ● the prizes to be won.     2001 O.L. Paper
>
> ***Don't forget to* Brainstorm *before you start writing!***

## Rules for Photography Competition

**Equipment Needed:**

● Any camera          ● Black and white or colour film

**Photo Groupings:**

Photos will be accepted for the following groupings:

● Nature          ● People          ● Humour          ● Sport

**Age Groups:**

There are three age groups as follows:

● Juniors – 1st, 2nd and 3rd years     ● Transition Year     ● Seniors – 5th and 6th years

**Regulations:**

- The closing date is 28 February.

- The photo size should not be smaller that 12cm x 20cm or larger than 20cm x 30cm.

- The name and category of the entrant must be clearly written on the back of each photo.

- Each photo must be placed on a white paper background.

- Only two entries are permitted per person.

- The entry fee is €1.

- The decision of the judges (Mrs Joyce and Ms Friel – Art Department) is final.

**Prizes:**

- First prize in each category is €100.

- Second prize in each category is €75.

- Third prize in each category is €50.

Every entrant will receive a certificate of participation.

Write out a set of school rules to help first years settle into your school. (Remember, in functional writing, you must not be sarcastic or humorous, otherwise you lose marks in the exam!)

*OR*

Write a set of instructions for preparing your favourite food.

*OR*

Write a guide to explain your favourite sport to someone who has never seen or played it.

*OR*

Write a set of rules for a school field-trip.

Write a list of safety guidelines to be displayed on a poster EITHER in your school's Science Lab OR in the Woodwork, Metalwork or Home Economics room.

H.L. Paper 2007

# Brochures

Look at these photographs:

Imagine you have been asked to write the text that will accompany these photos in a tourist brochure.

##  VISIT CHARMING CLONDEL!

Now is your chance to make the most of our special weekend offer to visit the wonderful Clondel Palace. This hotel, surrounded by beautiful countryside, has fantastic  amenities and will offer a five-star welcome to you and your family.
Relax in our leisure centre before indulging in a delicious afternoon tea. Allow our staff to entertain your children in our fun kids' club, while you enjoy the sumptuous creations of our exclusive gourmet chef.
The hotel is a mere five minutes walk from the scenic coastline of Clondel. 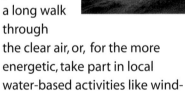 Here you can refresh yourself with a long walk through the clear air, or, for the more energetic, take part in local water-based activities like wind-surfing and scuba-diving.

Clondel is at the centre of some of the most famous mythical sites in Ireland.  Soak up the ancient culture on organised day trips, and experience the Ireland of the Fianna and Oisín.

The more energetic among you will be able to avail of a wide  range of sporting activities in the vicinity. From tennis to horse-riding, and golf to fishing, there's something to please everyone!

In the evenings, you can relax with a bit of 'ceol and craic',  as you make new friends and dance and sing the night away. The warmth of an Irish welcome awaits you in Clondel!

Gather a set of photos of your own locality, or an exotic location you would like to visit. Stick the photos onto an A4 page, leaving spaces for you to write your promotional text. **Brainstorm** the text in your copy and write it into your brochure. Present your brochure to the class and vote on the location your class would most like to visit.

# Interviews

If you read magazines you will often see interviews with famous people.

The writer normally introduces the piece by explaining:

- who the person is

- where and when they met

- what the writer was interviewing them about.

The interviewer will normally use a question and answer format.

Notice that although there are similarities, this is different to writing dialogue (look at the information on dialogue on page 23 of Chapter 1).

Look at the following task:

> Your school has won a National Final in some sporting event. You have interviewed the captain of the team for your school magazine. Write out the text of the interview as you would submit it for publication.

It is vital that you begin with a **Brainstorm**, otherwise you won't know what questions to ask, or what answers the person might have given.

Now read the interview on the next page (take note of the format).

*In an exclusive interview immediately after their historic victory in the Senior A Basketball Finals, I spoke to Emma Prendeville about her role as the team's captain, and her vital contribution to the game.*

**Interviewer: Emma, how do you feel now that it's all over? Are you relieved?**

Emma: Well, it was a bit nerve-wracking in the second half, but I knew that I could depend on the team to keep their heads up. I can't believe we've made it. It's brilliant!

**Interviewer: It was very close at the end, when you were a point down with only six seconds to go. Did you deliberately go for the foul?**

Emma: I was only conscious of getting to the basket, I didn't even hear the whistle blow.

**Interviewer: The pressure must have been awful when you had to take the two free shots. The entire game depended on you ...**

Emma: I tried not to think about it. The crowd was very quiet, I'm not sure if anyone was breathing! It felt like the ball would never fall into the basket on that final shot, it seemed to roll around the ring forever.

**Interviewer: How has the team reacted to the victory? You've all shown great team spirit throughout the championship.**

Emma: Well, as you know, this is my last year playing for the team. I really wanted this season to be special. All of the sixth years playing felt the same, and I think that the younger players really contributed to the team spirit. We've been together for a long time now, and we know each other really well. I'd depend on those girls for anything. I'll be so sorry to say goodbye to them.

**Interviewer: Coach Daly says his heart can't take the stress any more, and he's going to retire. Do you believe him?**

Emma (laughs): No way! That man loves the stress! He's the best coach in the world, he'll never stop coaching basketball!

**Interviewer: What are your plans for next year? Will you keep playing basketball when you leave school?**

Emma: Hopefully I'll be good enough to make the team in whatever college I get into, but there's a lot of competition out there.

**Interviewer: Thanks for taking the time out to talk to us Emma.**

Write an interview for your school magazine with any of the following:

- A poet or author whose work you really admire
- Your favourite musician
- Your local TD

- A prominent local businessperson who is paying for a new school gym
- A local or national sporting hero
- A famous actor

You have interviewed for your school magazine a poet or writer with whose work you are familiar. Write out the text of the interview as you would submit it for publication.

H.L. Paper 2000

# 3 Media Studies

In this chapter you will come across many types of **media**, including:

- Television
- Newspapers
- Magazines
- Advertising

You will **learn** how to:

- Identify the various media
- Analyse media techniques

# Mass Media

The modern media can be divided into two groups: print and electronic.

## Print Media

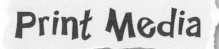

**Tabloid Newspapers**

**Billboards**

**Magazines**

**Posters**

**Broadsheet Newspapers**

## Electronic Media

**Internet (World Wide Web and e-mail)**

**Television**

**Cinema**

**USB key**

**Radio**

The purpose of the media is to **inform** and **entertain** large numbers of people, which is why they are called the **mass media**.

# Survey: The Mass Media and Me!

Answer the following questions **in your copybook**. Do them by yourself. If any of the questions don't apply to you just move on to the next one. When the class has completed the survey you will be working with everyone's results.

**On a typical day:**

1.  Approximately how many hours do you spend on the following?
    a)  Watching television ☐
    b)  Reading newspapers or magazines ☐
    c)  On the computer ☐
    d)  Listening to radio programmes ☐

2.  When watching television, which of the following do you mainly choose?
    a)  Entertainment programmes ☐
    b)  Documentaries ☐
    c)  News programmes ☐
    d)  Sports ☐
    e)  Other (please specify) ☐

3.  What is your favourite television programme? _____

4.  Name the main newspapers and/or magazines that are in your house.
    _____

5.  When you use the Internet do you mainly surf the web or use e-mail?
    surf the web ☐          use e-mail ☐

6.  When on the web, on which of the following do you spend most of your time?
    a)  Entertainment websites ☐
    b)  Research websites ☐
    c)  Other (please specify) ☐

7.  What radio station do you mainly listen to? _____

8.  How often, approximately, do you go to the cinema per month? _____

9.  Roughly how many billboard ads do you see on your journey to and from school? (Remember these can be on the sides of buses and trains and inside the carriage.)
    _____

10. What is your favourite ad (tv, radio, printed) at the moment? _____

When everyone in the class has answered these questions, make a giant poster or write on the board collating the class results like this:

| Question 1 | Television Newspapers Computers Radio | Average time | Least time | Most time | |
|---|---|---|---|---|---|
| Question 2 No. of students | Entertainment | Documentaries | News programmes | Sports | Other |
| Question 3 List five most popular programmes | | | | | |
| Question 4 List five most popular newspapers/ magazines | | | | | |
| Question 5 No. of students | Web | E-mail | | | |
| Question 6 No. of students | Entertainment | Research | Other | | |
| Question 7 List five most popular stations | | | | | |
| Question 8 Frequency of cinema visits | Average | Least | Most | | |
| Question 9 Billboards | Average | Least | Most | | |
| Question 10 List five most popular ads | | | | | |

R

**WHY DON'T YOU...**

Discuss the results of this class survey. Focus on the following key points:

- Identify the most popular medium in your class. What does this tell you about the media that appeals most to your age group?

- What programmes emerged as the most popular within your group? Why do you think they are so popular? Do you think that advertisers are aware that these programmes are popular with your age group? Have you any evidence to support your opinion?

- Why are certain types of programmes screened at certain times? Do you notice a big difference in the type of programme shown after the **watershed** of 9 p.m.?

- Compare the average time spent by your age group reading newspapers/magazines to the time you spend using other media.

- What do your age group use the Internet for? Do you notice any advertising on the most commonly visited websites?

- Talk about the issue of supervision. Does anyone check what you watch on TV, what you read or where you surf on the Internet? Do you have unlimited access to all media? Are there dangers associated with any of these media?

- What are the most popular radio stations listened to by your class? Are they local or national? Why do you think people prefer these stations?

- Do you think that where you live influences how much advertising you are exposed to?

- As a group, discuss whether you think the mass media is a positive or negative force in society.

*OR*

Ask an adult to give you his or her answers to the survey. Bring in the results to the class and compile the answers. Does this adult survey give you very different results to the class survey? Discuss why the results might be different. Think about age profiles and preferences for different media.

## Television

# War and the Simpsons

Hilary McKay

The really good thing about war is that they generally put
  it on at 6 o' clock
Same time as *The Simpsons.*

And nowadays, of course, war is quite safe.
It stays in the TV and makes no mess.
Even if it gets too noisy you can just turn down the sound.

(If you can find the remote.)

Also it is very clean,
No dust, nor smoke, nor blood leaks through the screen.
And when it gets boring you can switch over and watch
  *The Simpsons.*

(If you can find the remote.)

The only trouble is, it still goes on.
(The war, not *The Simpsons. The Simpsons* lasts for
  twenty minutes – unless it is a special.)
The war still goes on. The noise and the smoke and
  the leaking blood. The dirt and the boredom and the fear.
You cannot switch it off with the remote.

(Even if you can find the remote.)

You have to switch it off another way
You have to say, No
No
No war
You have to say No To War.

Then you can watch *The Simpsons*
In peace.

1. Is the war really only 'on' at six o'clock?
2. Who puts the war 'on' at that time?
3. What kind of person is speaking in the poem?

4. Do you change the TV channel (if you can find the remote!) when you see the news coming on? Why or why not?

5. What do you think the poet is saying about the way war is treated on television?

6. What effect does the frequent reporting of war have on the way we react to these news reports?

7. What does the poet mean when she says that you have to switch the war 'off another way'?

8. Did this poem make you think about your TV viewing habits?

### 'Young people watch too much television.'

Make three points in favour of or against this argument.

Based on your experience of media studies, what advantages do you think television has over radio and print media?

Based on your experience of media studies, how do you think television could be used for educational purposes?

2002 H.L. Paper

#### OR

Use what you have learned from your media studies to make a comparison between local and national radio.

Which do you prefer to listen to, local or national radio? Give reasons for your answer, referring to one or more radio stations.

If you were the programme controller for a radio station, what sort of programmes would you provide for teenage listeners?

2001 H.L. Paper

#### OR

(a) Explain fully the term watershed.

(b) Explain what kind of programmes can be shown before the watershed.

(c) Give reasons why you do or do not think that the watershed is a good idea.

#### OR

There is a perception that many young people only want to listen to music-based radio. Based on your experience of Media Studies, what do you think would make talk-radio more attractive to young people?

2009 H.L. Paper

#### OR

(a) An Irish athlete has won a gold medal at the Beijing Olympic Games. Write a script for a radio commentary on the event. Try to capture the excitement of the athlete's winning performance in your script.

(b) Would you have preferred to experience the gold medal winning by watching it on television or listening to it on the radio? Outline the advantages, as you would see them, of your preferred medium in this case.

2008 H.L. Paper

# Newspapers

Before you begin this section, bring some newspapers from home into class, or ask your local shop for some of yesterday's unsold newspapers. Swap and trade with others in the class so that you have more than one type of newspaper.

Have you noticed that there is more than one kind of newspaper?

# BROADSHEETS and TABLOIDS

A **broadsheet** is a 'quality' newspaper with serious and in-depth reporting on a wide range of important issues. It is usually A2 size. It uses **formal language** and tries to give the facts without exaggerating.

A **tabloid** newspaper reports mostly on scandals, gossip, celebrities and sport, all in a **sensational style**. It is A3 size, which is half the size of a broadsheet. It uses simple, exaggerated language and slang.

Look at this selection of words from a tabloid. Re-write them as words you might find in a broadsheet.

HUNK

Scum

Chat

BABE

Doc

Ace

Smash

PUNTER

LOONY

Hellraiser

Look at this selection of words from a broadsheet. Re-write them as words you might find in a tabloid.

Refuse

Consumer

Expulsion

VIRUS

EXPLOSION

Negotiations

Amateur

MURDERER

# Front Pages

A front page has to be eye-catching to get readers' attention, otherwise they won't buy the paper!

It has to use specific methods. You can tell the difference between a broadsheet and a tabloid just by looking at the front page.

## BROADSHEET

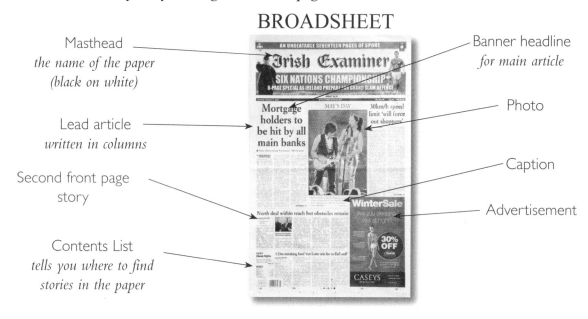

Masthead
*the name of the paper*
*(black on white)*

Lead article
*written in columns*

Second front page
story

Contents List
*tells you where to find*
*stories in the paper*

Banner headline
*for main article*

Photo

Caption

Advertisement

## TABLOID

Masthead
*the name of the paper*
*(red and white)*

Big headline
*dramatic and*
*sensational*

More of the page is
used for headlines
*in the tabloid*

Photo
*to illustrate the*
*lead article*

Lead article
*very short*

In two columns list the similarities and differences that you can see between the two examples above.

**OR**

Take an example of a broadsheet and a tabloid from people in the class and compare and contrast them, making notes in your copybook.

**OR**

Design your own front page for either a tabloid or broadsheet making sure that you have incorporated all of the main features.  Ⓡ

# Headlines

A headline should tell you what a story is about. If you look at the headlines on the previous page you will see that broadsheets and tabloids do this in different ways. For example, the broadsheet has a serious, informative headline: *Mortgage holders to be hit by all main banks.* In contrast, the tabloid uses simple and sensational language: *Roses are red, JT's a Blue, He's missing the Cup to say sorry to you.*

**BROADSHEETS** usually use **longer, more informative headlines**.

**TABLOIDS** use **specific techniques** to make their headlines eye-catching:

- **Puns**
- **Slang**
- **Alliteration**
- **Rhyme**
- **Clichés**

## Puns

When people play with words that sound similar or that mean the same thing in order to be funny, it is called a pun.

### SHEL SHOCK!
*(Shelbourne Football team win a surprise victory)*

### DEBS BALL TO BREAK DANCE
*(Debs ball broken up because of fighting)*

### Supermart Chiefs are sorry for 'mis-steak'
*(Supermarket apologises for mislabelling beef)*

## Alliteration

Headlines often repeat the same letter to make them sound dramatic.

### BOOKIES TAKE A BASHING

### LUCKY LOTTO NUMBERS

### JOCKEY ROCKS RIVALS

## ● Clichés

A cliché is an overused phrase that everyone knows. Often a tabloid will change it slightly to suit the story.

### MONEY CAN'T BUY ME DOVE
*(Pigeon-owning millionaire loses favourite bird)*

### ZOO LETS THE CAT OUT OF THE BAG
*(Zoo admits that panther is missing)*

### COP BETWEEN A ROCK AND HARD PLACE
*(Gardaí catch robbers on rocky cliffs)*

## ● Slang

Words that you would use informally in a chatty conversation are often called slang.

### <u>PUNTERS</u> PULL OFF €2M <u>STING</u>
*(Gamblers manage to win €2 million in bets)*

### BONO <u>HITS</u> STATES TO <u>NAG</u> BUSH AND KERRY
*(Bono goes to America to lobby the presidential candidates Bush and Kerry)*

## ● Rhyme

When words in a headline rhyme they also catch the reader's attention.

### HELL'S BELLS
*(Mr and Mrs Bell describe their horrific holiday)*

### SIMON'S AGE RAGE
*(Young man disqualified from claiming lotto because he was underage)*

Write a broadsheet and a tabloid headline to accompany five of the following stories:

- A gang uses a JCB to steal an ATM machine
- Four die in road deaths over a weekend
- Record temperatures in May
- Surprise victory for Irish soccer team
- Major financial institution announces bankruptcy
- Ireland wins Gold at the Olympics
- Fraudsters steal millions from pensioners
- New coach for county GAA team
- Famous movie star couple announces divorce
- Huge scientific discovery for the treatment of deadly disease

# Gutter Press

Paul Dehn

**News Editor:**   Peer Confesses,
Bishop Undresses,
Torso Wrapped in a Rug,
Girl Guide Throttled,
Baronet Bottled,
J.P. Goes to Jug

But yesterday's story's
Old and hoary.
Never mind who got hurt.
No use grieving
Let's get weaving.
What's the latest dirt?

Diplomat Spotted,
Scout Garrotted,
Thigh Discovered in Bog,
Wrecks Off Barmouth,
Sex in Yarmouth,
Woman in Love with Dog,
Eminent Hostess shoots her Guests,
Harrogate Lovebird Builds Two Nests.

**Cameraman:**   *Builds two nests?*
*Shall I get a picture of the lovebird singing?*
*Shall I get a picture of her pretty little eggs?*
*Shall I get a picture of her babies?*

**News Editor:**   No!
Go and get a picture of her legs.
Beast Slays Beauty
Priest Flays Cutie,
Cupboard Shows Tell-tale Stain,
Mate Drugs Purser,
Dean Hugs Bursar,
Mayor Binds Wife with Chain,
Elderly Monkey Marries for Money,
Jilted Junky Says 'I want my Honey'.

| Cameraman: | 'Want my honey?'<br>Shall I get a picture of the pollen flying?<br>Shall I get a picture of the golden dust?<br>Shall I get a picture of a queen bee? |
|---|---|
| News Editor: | No!<br>Go and get a picture of her bust.<br>Judge Gets Frisky,<br>Nun Drinks Whisky,<br>Baby Found Burnt in Cot,<br>Show Girl Beaten,<br>Duke Leaves Eaton – |
| Cameraman: | *Newspaper Man Gets Shot!*<br>*May all things clean*<br>*And fresh and green*<br>*Have mercy upon your soul,*<br>*Consider yourself paid*<br>*by the hole my bullet made –* |
| News Editor<br>*(dying)*: | Come and get a picture of the hole. |

The use and exaggeration of stories dealing mainly with violence, sex and scandal to shock and excite the public in order to sell news is called **sensationalism**. The motto 'If it bleeds, it leads' is often used in media circles. This means that a **sensational** story will always be reported first because it is attention-grabbing.

1. Who are the speakers in this poem?

2. Who is the boss?

3. What does the news editor think of 'yesterday's story'?

4. What kind of newspaper do you think he edits?

5. Why do you think the cameraman shoots the news editor?

6. Are all of the stories the news editor mentions sensational or are they being sensationalised?

7. The cameraman suggests the visual shots that he thinks should accompany the stories. What kind of visuals are these? What kind of visuals does the news editor want?

8. Do you think this news editor is interested in telling the truth? Give reasons for your answer.

Try to have a look at today's newspapers or the news. What do you think is the most sensationalised story at the moment?

**OR**

Write the sensationalist report that you think might accompany one of the news editor's headlines.

**OR**

Read the definition of bias below. Imagine that you have had a fight with your closest friend.

● Write two diary entries describing the fight. One from your point of view, one from your friend's.

● Now imagine that you are a teacher who has to write an objective account of the fight for the principal. Try to write an unbiased report.

We all see things from our own personal point of view; this is called being subjective. Good reporters try to be objective, which means that they try to report without involving their own personal feelings. Bias occurs when a story is deliberately distorted in order to convince the viewers or readers of a particular point of view. News reporters sometimes do this in a very subtle way so you have to watch out!

## Reports

The following two reports are about the same incident. Read them both carefully, and think about the different approaches of the broadsheet and tabloid journalists.

### Article from the Irish Daily Star

## PUNTERS PULL OFF €2M STING

BOOKIES THROUGHOUT IRELAND and the UK have been stung for almost €2 million in a huge gambling coup executed by a group of Irish gamblers.

A Co. Kerry-based gang carried out the feat with military precision – ensuring that they would not be rumbled.

It's estimated the group risked over €300,000 if the horse failed to win. But the horse romped home and Cork-based firm Cashmans paid out over €130,000 to punters, while Paddy Power was stung for €100,000.

The betting coup hurt Irish and UK bookmakers and online firm Betfair.

### ONLINE
Punters placed bets in shops throughout Ireland and online on a horse called Bocaccio – which duly won at Leopardstown 13 days ago.

It is understood that the brains behind the coup were canny north Kerry gamblers who instructed a handful of people to place bets of €500 on the horse on the day of the race.

Each member of the gambling hit squad put on bets of €500 on behalf of the group when the first show of betting appeared on betting shop screens.

The odds on the horse opened at 7/1 and – after each bet was placed – members of the group were then allowed to have a bet with their own money.

"There was only one bet per office at a variety of different locations, so as not to arouse suspicions," an insider told The Irish Daily Star.

The horse romped home an easy winner at odds of 6/4, although those behind the coup got higher prices.

### UNAWARE
The horse's trainer – Michael Grassick from Newbridge, Co. Kildare – told The Irish Daily Star last night he was totally unaware of the heavy betting on the horse.

"I only train the horse – I don't gamble," he said. "But I did hear some people made money on the horse at Leopardstown."

A spokesman for Paddy Power said: "It was the biggest gamble of the year and fair play to them. They caught us with our pants down and gave us a good spanking. And we deserved it."

WINNER ALRIGHT: Bocaccio romps home

### Big windfall for Irish gamblers

BOOKIES throughout Ireland and the UK have been stung for almost €2 million in a huge gambling coup executed by a group of Irish gamblers.

A Co Kerry-based gang carried out the feat with military precision — ensuring that they would not be rumbled.

It's estimated the group risked over €300,000 if the horse failed to win.

But the horse romped home and Cork-based firm Cashmans paid out over €130,000 to punters, while Paddy Power was stung for €100,000.

The betting coup hurt Irish and UK bookmakers and online firm Betfair.

#### Online
Punters placed bets in shops throughout Ireland and online on a horse called Bocaccio — which duly won at Leopardstown 13 days ago.

It is understood that the brains behind the coup were canny north Kerry gamblers who instructed a handful of people to place bets of €500 on the horse on the day of the race.

Each member of the gambling hit squad put on bets of €500 on behalf of the group when the first show of betting appeared on betting shop screens.

The odds on the horse opened at 7/1 and — after each bet was placed — members of the group were then allowed to have a bet with their own money.

"There was only one bet per office at a variety of different locations, so as not to arouse suspicions," an insider told The Star.

The horse romped home an easy winner at odds of 6/4, although those behind the coup got higher prices.

#### Unaware
The horse's trainer — Michael Grassick from Newbridge, Co Kildare — told The Star last night he was totally unaware of the heavy betting on the horse.

"I only train the horse — I don't gamble," he said. "But I did hear some people made money on the horse at Leopardstown."

A spokesman for Paddy Power said: "It was the biggest gamble of the year and fair play to them. "They caught us with our pants down and gave us a good spanking. And we deserved it."

TRAINER: Grassick

## Article from The Irish Times

# KERRY GAMBLERS CELEBRATE €2M COUP

Gamblers in north Kerry are believed to be celebrating a betting coup that netted them up to €2 million in winnings.

It has been estimated that the sting operation, which took place earlier this month, cost bookmakers in Ireland and the UK up to €2 million. However, other pundits say that this figure is pure speculation and estimated that it was lower.

The operation was based on a race in Leopardstown, Co Dublin, 12 days ago. In a well-planned affair, people placed bets in bookmakers around the country on a horse called Bocaccio, which went on to win.

It is understood that much of the gambling took place at bookmakers in the Munster area and that the coup was organised by a group from north Kerry.

It is believed that Cashman's bookmakers in Cork paid out some €130,000 to punters, while the Paddy Power chain paid out an estimated €100,000.

The betting coup also stung bookmakers in the UK and at the online betting site Betfair, as well as other independent bookmakers in Ireland and at the track. One Irish on-course better is believed to have netted €600,000.

It is understood that only a handful of people knew which horse was to be backed. Those who put money on the winner only got the name of the horse just minutes before the race. They were instructed to place bets of €500 on behalf of the group when the first show of betting appeared on TV screens in betting shops.

"There was only one bet per office at a variety of different locations so as not to arouse suspicions," said one racing insider.

The odds on the horse opened at 7/1. After each bet was placed members of the group were then allowed to have a bet with their own money.

The horse won at odds of 9/4. Between what was taken out of the betting shops and what was laid on the horse at the track, "bookmakers were easily stung for at least €2 million", the racing source stated.

1. **WHAT** happened?
2. **WHO** was involved?
3. **WHERE** did it happen?
4. **WHEN** did it happen?
5. **WHY** did it happen?
6. **HOW** did it happen?

The questions that you have just answered form what is known as the **inverted pyramid**.

## The Inverted Pyramid

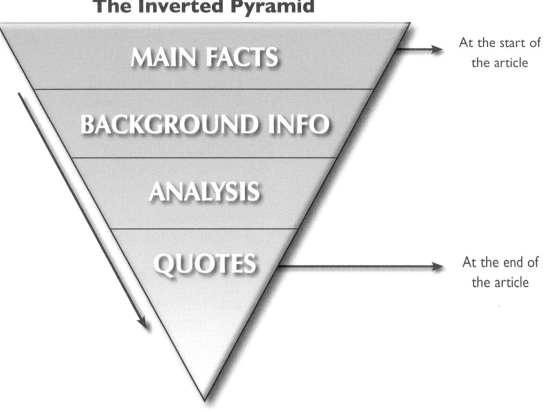

MAIN FACTS — At the start of the article

BACKGROUND INFO

ANALYSIS

QUOTES — At the end of the article

# Spot the Differences

| Article from **The Irish Times** (broadsheet) | Article from **The Irish Daily Star** (tabloid) |
|---|---|
| **KERRY GAMBLERS CELEBRATE €2M COUP**<br><br>This headline is more informative. It uses formal language, e.g. 'gamblers' and 'celebrate'. | **PUNTERS PULL OFF €2M STING**<br><br>The headline uses alliteration and slang. The headline is more dramatic. |
| The print used for the heading is black writing on a white background.<br><br>The font used is small bold type, with capital letters. | The print used for the heading is white writing on a black background.<br><br>The font is bold, with capital letters.<br><br>The headline takes up more space and is therefore more eye-catching. |
| This article attempts to be more accurate by using words such as 'estimated' and 'understood'. | This article presents the €2m coup as a definite fact, which it is not.<br><br>It is more sensational – it uses phrases like 'military precision' and 'gambling hit squad'.<br><br>It uses more controversial quotes from horse trainers and bookies. |
| There is no photo accompanying the article. | There are two photographs accompanying the article, which attract readers' attention. |
| It is reported that the horse won at odds of 9/4. | In this article, the winning odds are given as 6/4. |

Compare the style of writing and the layout in these reports using the grid on the previous page as a guide.

**The Hole In The Wall Gang struck again yesterday and almost demolished a bank after ripping out an ATM machine.**

The cocky criminals used a stolen digger to tear the cash till from the Bank of Ireland building in Borris, Co. Carlow, and then drove off with it.

But the thieves' luck ran out when Gardaí gave chase and the machine toppled off a trailer during the dramatic high-speed pursuit.

The officers escaped injury as gang members in a second car then rammed them at a junction close to Mount Leinster.

The drama began at around 3 a.m. when a number of men stole a JCB from a building site on the outskirts of Borris.

The racket they made was enough to wake a local man who followed the robbers in his car. When he saw them at the bank he contacted the Gardaí in Thomastown, Co. Kilkenny.

A squad car on patrol in the Graignamanagh area was alerted and arrived at the scene within five minutes.

By then the gang had managed to destroy the front wall of the bank and load the ATM on a trailer and drive it away.

The Gardaí gave chase and caught up with one of the getaway cars, a white Subaru, on a back road but lost the vehicle which was travelling at speeds well in excess of 100mph.

They came across the same car a short time later at another junction and were rammed by it. A front tyre on the squad car burst in the impact and the officers could only watch as the criminals, all wearing balaclavas, sped off.

At the same junction the Gardaí discovered the ATM machine which had fallen off the trailer as the car pulling it negotiated a narrow bend.

It was taken to Thomastown Garda station where it is being examined by forensic experts.

Chief investigating officer, Supt Aidan Roche, said his men were following a number of lines of enquiry.

The robbery is just the latest in a series of similar incidents in the South East in the past few weeks. A Garda spokesman said the thefts were being investigated separately although there were "obvious comparisons". He added: "There is no concrete evidence to link the incidents although there are similarities. We are keeping an open mind."

Early last Saturday a gang using a mechanical digger ripped a bank machine from a wall in Taghmon, Co. Wexford.

Gardaí initially thought they had made off with the till but it was later found buried under rubble with the cash still inside. And earlier this month raiders who tried to steal another ATM from a bank were foiled by Gardaí.

A stolen tractor was used by three men to prise the cash dispenser from the wall of the Bank of Ireland in Callan, 10 miles from Kilkenny city, on July 8. That robbery came 10 days after a similar incident in Rosslare, Co. Wexford, in which thieves used a digger to rip an ATM from a bank wall before making their getaway with €140,000.

CASH machine chaos is set to continue after Brinks Allied staff decided yesterday to carry on with their strike action.

SIPTU members at the security firm voted two to one to reject a settlement after talks at the Labour Relations Commission.

Union representative Kevin McMahon said there are still concerns with new safety arrangements put forward by the company.

# 'Hole-in-the-wall gang' strikes again but flees empty-handed

Sarah Murphy

THE 'Hole-in-the-wall gang' struck again in Co Carlow yesterday morning when they ripped out another automatic bank machine.

The latest raid – the fourth in just five weeks – occurred at around 3am at a Bank of Ireland branch in Borris, Co Carlow.

All of the banks targeted by the raiders since the first robbery on June 29 have been Bank of Ireland branches.

A stolen JCB, which was taken from a construction site in Rathanna, just two miles away, several hours before the incident, was used in the raid – following the gang's usual pattern.

Gardaí in the south-east and the National Bureau of Criminal Investigation (NBCI) are to join forces in a bid to apprehend the gang.

The Bank of Ireland branch, on the main street of Borris, is located directly opposite a number of homes.

It is understood one of the residents alerted gardaí after hearing the commotion outside.

A garda patrol car from Graighnamanagh, Co Kilkenny, just five miles from Borris, was on the scene within six minutes and disturbed the five raiders, who had used the JCB to load the ATM they had ripped from a wall on to a trailer which was being towed by a black car and accompanied by a white high performance car.

The two gardaí called for back-up from members in Thomastown and Kilkenny city while they chased the raiders for over a mile along a back road to Enniscorthy and on to the Dublin road.

However, the gang was forced to abandon the trailer and the ATM after the car towing it hit a ditch and lost a tyre.

The raiders then used the second car to ram the garda patrol car, disabling the vehicle, and fled empty-handed.

The gardaí in the patrol car were uninjured.

It is understood that up to €250,000 might have been in the stolen machine, although the ongoing dispute at Brinks Allied which has disrupted cash deliveries to bank machines nationwide is likely to have significantly reduced this amount.

Gardaí have now stepped up the number of late night patrols around the region, primarily around rural areas where ATMs are located.

They believe that a highly organised crime gang is working closely with other criminals in the region to carry out the daring raids.

The raiders are understood to target particular areas of the country for several weeks before pinpointing other parts of the country to hit.

The first of these raids took place in Rosslare Harbour on June 29 when €140,000 was successfully taken by the raiders. The money has not been recovered.

The second and third, unsuccessful raids occurred on July 8 in Callan, Co Kilkenny, and last Saturday in Taghmon, Co Wexford.

In the latter raid , a tractor and JCB broke down during their elaborate operations.

Security experts say that, while the ATMs offer rich pickings, significant expertise is required to open the machines.

The scene in Borris, Co C[...]

## 'Hole-in-the-wall gang' strikes again but flees empty-handed

Sarah Murphy

THE 'Hole-in-the-wall gang' struck again in Co. Carlow yesterday morning when they ripped out another automatic bank machine.

The latest raid – the fourth in just five weeks – occurred at around 3 a.m. at a Bank of Ireland branch in Borris, Co. Carlow.

All of the banks targeted by the raiders since the first robbery on June 29 have been Bank of Ireland branches.

A stolen JCB, which was taken from a construction site in Rathanna, just two miles away, several hours before the incident, was used in the raid – following the gang's usual pattern.

Gardaí in the south-east and the National Bureau of Criminal Investigation (NBCI) are to join forces in a bid to apprehend the gang.

The Bank of Ireland branch, on the main street of Borris, is located directly opposite a number of homes.

It is understood one of the residents alerted Gardaí after hearing the commotion outside.

A Garda patrol car from Graighnamanagh, Co. Kilkenny, just five miles from Borris, was on the scene within six minutes and disturbed the five raiders, who had used the JCB to load the ATM they had ripped from a wall on to a trailer which was being towed by a black car and accompanied by a white high performance car.

The two Gardaí called for back-up from members in Thomastown and Kilkenny city while they chased the raiders for over a mile along a back road to Enniscorthy and on to the Dublin road.

However, the gang was forced to abandon the trailer and the ATM after the car towing it hit a ditch and lost a tyre.

The raiders then used the second car to ram the Garda patrol car, disabling the vehicle, and fled empty-handed.

The Gardaí in the patrol car were uninjured.

It is understood that up to €250,000 might have been in the stolen machine, although the ongoing dispute at Brinks Allied which has disrupted cash deliveries to bank machines nationwide is likely to have significantly reduced this amount.

Gardaí have now stepped up the number of late night patrols around the region, primarily around rural areas where ATMs are located.

They believe that a highly dangerous Dublin-based organised crime gang is working closely with other criminals in the region to carry out the daring raids.

The raiders are understood to target particular areas of the country for several weeks before pinpointing other parts of the country to hit.

The first of these raids took place in Rosslare Harbour on June 29 when €140,000 was successfully taken by the raiders. The money has not been recovered.

The second and third, unsuccessful raids occurred on July 8 in Callan, Co. Kilkenny, and last Saturday in Taghmon, Co. Wexford.

In the latter raid, a tractor and JCB broke down during their elaborate operations.

Security experts say that, while the ATMs offer rich pickings, significant expertise is required to open the machines.

# Shaping the News

Divide into groups. Make sure that you have a mixture of tabloid and broadsheet newspapers.

1. Examine your newspapers for the following types of article:

- News stories and current affairs – national, international, political, financial, etc.

- Feature articles – these treat specific issues in more depth, for example, an investigation into teenage drug use, articles on fashion, music and the arts.

- Entertainment – arts, cartoons, horoscopes, ads, TV listings, weather.

- Sports.

- Letters to the editor.

- Editorial – the editor writes a piece giving his or her own opinion.

- Special supplements – e.g. health, education, property.

- Advertisements.

- Notices – births, deaths and marriages.

2. Carry out the following activities:

- List the differences you found between the tabloid and broadsheet newspaper in terms of content.

- Identify the sections which were given more space or emphasis in each paper.

- Make a note of items which appear in the broadsheet and not in the tabloid, and vice versa.

Divide into groups of approximately eight people. You are going to produce your own newspaper.

Decide who will do each of the following jobs:

The **EDITOR** has overall responsibility for the paper. They decide which articles are included and which are left out. They consult with sub-editors and the designers.

**SUB-EDITORS** edit a particular section of the newspaper, for example, the sports section. Often sub-editors are also journalists on the newspaper.

**JOURNALISTS** write the news reports for the paper, and submit them to the editor for publication. Sometimes they will have to re-write a report if the editor suggests changes. If they find a story that no-one else has, it is called **an exclusive**.

**PHOTOGRAPHERS** take photographs to illustrate the news articles.

**DESIGNERS** use computers to graphically lay out the page. They prepare the overall 'look' of the paper, decide where on the page the photos and articles will appear, and also what fonts will be used.

*These are only some of the important jobs carried out in the preparation of a newspaper.*

- Decide whether you are preparing a tabloid or a broadsheet newspaper.
- You cannot reproduce an entire newspaper, but try to cover the main areas.
- Don't worry too much about presentation, you're not trained graphic designers! But do think a little bit about the layout, and where different stories should be placed.
- Some suggestions:
  - Cut up the newspapers you have.
  - Use some of their photographs and ads.
  - Try to imitate their writing style.
  - Write about issues in your school or local area.
  - Use a blank white sheet of A3 paper as your background and stick your articles on it.

®

● **Remember, the following important features should appear in your paper:**

# Features of Broadsheets

## Layout and Content

- important global and national stories
- cover stories on politics, finance and current affairs

# Features of Tabloids

## Layout and Content

- sensational news
- cover stories about scandals, gossip, celebrities and sport

## Headlines

- informative
- factual
- serious language
- black print on white

KERRY GAMBLERS CELEBRATE €2M COUP

## Headlines

- dramatic
- exaggerated
- use of slang
- bold and colour print

**MONEY CAN'T BUY ME DOVE**

## Reports and Articles

- highly researched
- factual details
- neutral and unbiased
- few quotations
- few photographs
- small print

**Hundreds of complaints over abuse of disabled people**

Residential care staff accused of assault and mistreatment

## Reports and Articles

- some research
- less factual details, more speculation
- bias obvious
- many quotations
- large, eye-catching photographs
- large print

PUNTERS PULL OFF €2M STING

Big windfall for Irish gamblers

# Magazines

**WHY DON'T YOU...**

Do the following 'mini-survey' in class:

|  | Y | N |
|---|---|---|
| 1. Do you read magazines? | ☐ | ☐ |
| 2. Do you buy magazines? | ☐ | ☐ |

3. Name the magazines that you prefer.

_____

4. Do you prefer to read newspapers, magazines or books? Why?

_____

_____

5. Adults are sometimes critical of 'teenage' magazines.
   a) Why do you think this is?

   _____

   b) Do you agree with such criticisms?

   _____

**DIVE IN!**

1. Who do you think the magazines on this page are aimed at? Give reasons for your answer.

2. What information do you get from these covers?

3. What 'extras' do the magazines offer to try to persuade you to buy them?

4. Can you spot any 'buzz words'?

5. There are lots of different types of fonts. Why do you think this is?

**TAKE THE PLUNGE!**

6. Do you like the way these covers are presented? Give reasons for your answer.

7. Would you be interested in reading these magazines? Why or why not?

8. Do you think the issues raised in these magazines are relevant to Irish teenagers?

**WHY DON'T YOU...**

Choose a topic that you are interested in and write an article for submission to your school magazine.

**OR**

Design your own cover page for a magazine that you would like to read.

# Advertising

## Adman

Nigel Gray

I'm the new man
in the ivory tower
the new man
the man with the power
the old village chief
used to lay down the law
but the medicine man
had his foot in the door
he taught me the secret
of how you tick
to use psychology
like a conjuring trick
so I've found the doorway
into your brain
when you get a bargain
you lose – I gain
I can get in your bath
I can get in your bed
I can get in your pants
I can get in your head
you're like a man on the cross
you're like a priest at the stake
you're like a fish on the hook
make no mistake
I can tie you up

I can take you down
I can sit and watch
you wriggle around
'cos I'm the medicine man
with the media touch
the man with the power that's
too much

# Target Audience Identified

**Conduct a survey at home tonight.**

**1** **DIVIDE ...** the class into groups.

**2** **ASSIGN ...** each group one of the following times to watch the ads that appear on television. Or choose other times and channels depending on your access to satellite TV.

- 5.15 p.m. RTÉ 2
- 6.15 p.m. RTÉ 2
- 6.30 p.m. RTÉ 1
- 7.30 p.m. TV3
- 8 p.m. TG4
- 8.30 p.m. RTÉ 2
- 9 p.m. RTÉ 1

**3** **LIST ...** the ads that appeared in your time slot.

**4** **IDENTIFY ...** who you believe is the **target audience** for this time, and state why you believe this to be so.

**5** **COMPARE ...** results tomorrow in class.

For homework, choose one of the ads that you watched last night and write a paragraph profiling its target audience. ®

We are all **consumers**. In other words, we have to buy things. What makes us buy one brand of a product instead of another? Very often it is the **advertising**.

The purpose of an advertisement is to **persuade** us, the consumers, that we need a product or service. The advertisement will **target** different consumers for different products. They won't make an ad to sell health insurance policies to fifteen year olds, but they certainly will try to sell a fifteen year old trendy clothes.

Most ads have three elements which work together to make them persuasive:
1. Slogans and captions
2. Photos, pictures, cartoons or graphics (visuals)
3. Copy/Text

**Before beginning this section bring in some examples of advertisements from newspapers or magazines that you find at home.**

# 1. Slogans and Captions

- A **slogan** is a repeated catchphrase associated with a product.

- A **caption** is the main heading of an ad.

In pairs, look at the following products and slogans and see if you can match them up. Your teacher can time you to see who does it fastest!

| | |
|---|---|
| Beanz Meanz … | Rice Krispies |
| Let your fingers do the walking | Maybelline |
| Just do it! | McDonalds |
| Snap, crackle and pop! | Ronseal |
| Because I'm worth it. | Toyota |
| Does exactly what it says on the tin | Yellow Pages |
| I'm lovin' it. | Heinz Beans |
| Have a break, have a … | Nike |
| The best built cars in the world. | L'Oreal |
| Maybe she's born with it, maybe it's … | Kitkat |

®

**OR**

Look at the ads on the following pages (or elsewhere) and see if you can find examples of captions or slogans that do the following:

- Use **buzz words**, for example, *free, guaranteed, fresh, new, improved.*

- Make us laugh.

- Talk directly to the consumer, or ask the consumer a question, for example, *have you thought about …?*

- Make a statement as if it can't be contradicted, for example, *'the best built cars in the world'.* Who says they are the best built?

- Suggest that you will be worse off without the product, for example, *should have gone to …*

**OR**

Look at the products below.

Write a caption or a slogan to advertise one of the products. See if you can use any of the following techniques:

- **Strange spellings**, for example, *Kozy Kittens*

- **Alliteration**, for example, *best buys*

- **Repetition,** for example, *Less Drag. Less Pull. Less Irritation.*

- **Imagery**, for example, similes, *water as pure as mountain air*, or metaphors, *diamond nails*

- **Abbreviations**, for example, *Shake 'n' vac*

- **Rhyme**, for example, *spin 'n' win*

# 2. Visuals

Advertisers use photographs, pictures, cartoons, colours and graphics to:

- **show us** the product.

- make us associate the product with a **logo** – this is a symbol which is used to represent the product, e.g. *the Golden Arches of McDonalds* or the *Nike swoosh*.

- make the product seem **glamorous**.

- **shock us** into noticing the product.

- **warn us** that bad things will happen to us if we don't use the product.

- associate the product with someone famous. This is called **endorsement**.

- appeal to our **emotions**, e.g. *The Andrex puppy, cute babies in nappy ads*.

Mmm...Classic.

For homework, see if you can find five examples of well-known logos in magazines or online. Separate them from their product and bring them in tomorrow. See who can link the greatest number of logos and products.

### OR

Decide what your favourite ad is. If possible, bring it into the class, or describe it from a visual point of view. Explain why you think it is an effective, interesting ad.

# 3. Copy

Any writing in an ad is called **copy.** This includes captions and slogans, but can also refer to more detailed text. Normally the copy will try to:

- associate positive language with the product using **buzz words.**

- make **claims** and **promises** about the product, for example, *it will improve your looks …, it's scientifically tested …, it's a bargain …*, etc.

- associate **negative language** with not having the product, for example, *lonely, frizzy, spotty,* etc.

- appeal to our **emotions,** for example,
  *If you care about your children's future …*
      This copy is trying to make parents feel guilty.
  *Reassuringly expensive …*
      This copy appeals to people's need to show off.
  *Not for the average Joe …*
      This appeals to people's need to feel different.
  *Apple tart like your mother used to make …*
      This makes people feel nostalgic.

Can you think of any other emotions that advertisers appeal to? Can you back these up with examples?

- Also notice the design of the writing, the **typography** and the colour of it, as these give us other subtle messages about the product.

Choose an ad which you think uses copy effectively. Explain why you think it is so effective.

**OR**

Write the copy that you think might accompany one of the following pictures. Invent a product that you think the picture might be selling.

- You have been invited to present a product on the Dragons' Den.
- Divide the class into groups.
- Each group is going to brand one of the following products and devise an advertising campaign for it.
- The teacher will assign a product to each group.

**Firstly,** decide on a *product name*.

**Secondly,** establish your *target audience*.

**Thirdly,** design your advertisements for the following media:

- Print media, e.g. newspapers, magazines, billboards
- Television
- Radio
- Internet

**Finally,** use this checklist to make sure that you have used a sufficient number of *persuasive techniques*!

| Slogan and Caption | Visuals | Copy |
|---|---|---|
| Buzz words | Display the product | Buzz words |
| Rhyme | Logo | Promises |
| Unusual spelling | Glamour | Scientific jargon |
| Alliteration | Shock tactics | Striking typography |
| Repetition | Warnings | Emotional appeal |
| Imagery | Endorsement | Link to visual imagery |
| Abbreviations | Appeal to emotions | Associate negative language with lack of product |

Make your product presentation to the Dragons' Den and see who wins the contract for the ad campaign!

®

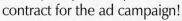

(a) Write the text for a radio advertisement for a new chocolate bar called 'Yummy'. Remember, the message is going to be heard not seen.

(b) Suggest the type of voice most appropriate for the voice-over for your advertisement. Indicate any music or sound effects you think might make it more effective. Explain your choices.

2007 H.L. Paper

1. Identify the caption in this advertisement. What is your opinion of it?

2. What is the slogan? How does it re-enforce the caption?

3. What is the purpose of the visual?

1. How does this ad talk directly to the consumer?

2. Does the ad suggest the consumer will be worse off without the product? In what way?

3. Say what you think of the use of cartoons in the visual. Do they make this ad different?

1. What is the effect of repetition in the main caption?

2. Why do you think the product is called Mach3? How does the visual reinforce the product's name?

3. How does the copy try to sell this product to the consumer?

1. What does this ad promise the consumer?

2. How is verbal and visual imagery combined in this ad?

3. Can you find any examples of alliteration in the copy? Why do you think it is used?

1. Why do you think this ad is in black and white?

2. Part of the ad isn't in black and white. Why do you think this is?

3. Who do you think is the target audience for this ad? Give reasons for your answer.

4. Do you think that Homer Simpson is a good celebrity to endorse this product? Give reasons for your answer.

1. What is the link between the caption and the visual in this ad?

2. Can you find any buzz words in this ad?

3. Who do you think this ad is aimed at? What kind of lifestyle does it promise?

DIVE IN!

1. How does this ad appeal to our emotions?

2. What does the visual suggest about Ariel non-bio?

3. What do you think of the use of colour in this ad?

Based on your knowledge of media studies, write an analysis of this advertisement.                    2002 H.L. Paper

*(Look back at the techniques listed earlier in this section to help you to structure your answer.)*

**OR**

Write a critical analysis of this advertisement. Your answer should deal with all the advertising techniques which you find in the text and the visual of the advertisement.

1996 H.L. Paper

*(Look back at the techniques listed earlier in this section to help you to structure your answer.)*

**OR**

Based on your reading of the advertisement, identify the target audience it is aimed at and explain how you arrived at this conclusion. You must refer to the advertisement in your answer.

2009 H.L. Paper

Design an ad for one of the following products. You could cut visuals out from other ads, but try to write your own copy using as many persuasive techniques as possible.

| | | |
|---|---|---|
| Lipstick | Health insurance | Dishwasher |
| Hair gel | Motorbike | Coffee |
| Chocolate bar | Adventure holidays | Grass seed |
| Dandruff shampoo | Anti-smoking chewing gum | Soft Drink |

# Stereotypes

# Stupid White Men

Michael Moore

I don't know what it is, but every time I see a white guy walking toward me, I tense up. My heart starts racing, and I immediately begin to look for an escape route and a means to defend myself. I kick myself for even being in this part of town after dark. Didn't I notice the suspicious gangs of white people lurking on every street corner, drinking Starbucks and wearing their gang colours of Gap Turquoise or J. Crew Mauve? What an idiot! Now the white person is coming closer, closer – and then – *whew*! He walks by without harming me, and I breathe a sigh of relief.

White people scare the crap out of me. This may be hard for you to understand – considering that I *am* white – but then again, my colour gives me a certain insight. For instance, I find *myself* pretty scary a lot of the time, so I know what I'm talking about. You can take my word for it: if you find yourself suddenly surrounded by white people, you better watch out. *Anything* can happen.

As white people, we've been lulled into thinking it's safe to be around other white people. We've been taught since birth that it's the people of the *other colour* we need to fear. *They're* the ones who'll slit your throat.

Yet as I look back on my life, a strange but unmistakable pattern seems to emerge. *Every* person who has ever harmed me in my lifetime – the boss who fired me, the teacher who flunked me, the principal who punished me, the kid who hit me in the eye with a rock, the other kid who shot me with a BB gun, the executive who didn't renew *TV Nation*, the guy who was stalking me for three years, the accountant who double-paid my taxes, the drunk who smashed into me, the burglar who stole my stereo, the contractor

who overcharged me, the girlfriend who left me, the next girlfriend who left even sooner, the pilot of the plane I was on who hit a truck on the runway (he probably hadn't eaten in days), the other pilot who decided to fly through a tornado, the person in the office who stole *checks from my *checkbook and wrote them out to himself for a total of $16,000 – every one of these individuals has been a white person! Coincidence? I think not!

I have never been attacked by a black person, never been evicted by a black person, never had my security deposit ripped off by a black landlord, never *had* a black landlord,

*American spelling of cheque*

never had a meeting at a Hollywood studio with a black executive in charge, never seen a black agent at the film/TV agency that used to represent me, never had a black person deny my child the college of her choice, never been puked on by a black teenager at a Mötley Crue concert, never been pulled over by a black cop, never been sold a lemon by a black car salesman, never *seen* a black

car salesman, never had a black person deny me a bank loan, never had a black person try to bury my movie, and I've never heard a black person say, 'We're going to eliminate ten thousand jobs here – have a nice day!'

I don't think I'm the only white guy who can make these claims. Every mean word, every cruel act, every bit of pain and suffering in my life has had a Caucasian face attached to it.

So, um, why is it *exactly* that I should be afraid of black people?

I look around at the world I live in – and, folks, I hate to tell tales out of school, but it's not the African-Americans who have made this planet such a pitiful, scary place to inhabit. Recently a headline on the front page of the science section of the *New York Times* asked the question 'Who Built the H-Bomb?' The article went on to discuss a dispute that had arisen between the men who claim credit for making the first bomb. Frankly, I could have cared less – because I already know the only pertinent answer: 'IT WAS A WHITE GUY!' No black guy ever built or used a bomb designed to wipe out hordes of innocent people, whether in Oklahoma City, Columbine, or Hiroshima.

No, my friends, it's *always* the white guy. Let's go to the tote board:

- Who gave us the black plague? A white guy.
- Who invented PBC, PVC, PBB, and a host of chemicals that are killing us? White guys.
- Who has started every war America has been in? White men.
- Who is responsible for the programming on Fox? White men.
- Who invented the punch card ballot? A white man.
- Whose idea was it to pollute the world with the internal combustion engine? Whitey, that's who.
- The Holocaust? That guy really gave white people a bad name (that's why we prefer to call him a Nazi and his little helpers Germans).

- The genocide of the Native Americans? White man.
- Slavery? Whitey!
- So far in 2001, American companies have laid off over 700,000 people. Who ordered the layoffs? White CEOs.
- Who keeps bumping me off the Internet? Some white guy, and if I find him, he's a dead white guy.

You name the problem, the disease, the human suffering, or the abject misery visited upon millions, and I'll bet you ten bucks I can put a white face on it faster than you can name the members of 'NSync.

And yet when I turn on the news each night, what do I see again and again? Black men alleged to be killing, raping, mugging, stabbing, looting, rioting, selling drugs … having too many babies, dropping babies from tenement windows, fatherless, motherless, Godless, penniless. 'The suspect is described as a black male … the suspect is described as a black male … THE SUSPECT IS DESCRIBED AS A BLACK MALE …' No matter what city I'm in, the news is always the same, the suspect always the same unidentified black male. I'm in Atlanta tonight, and I swear the police sketch of the black male suspect on TV looks just like the black male suspect I saw on the news last night in Denver and the night before in L.A. In every sketch he's frowning, he's menacing – and he's wearing the same knit cap! Is it possible that it's the same black guy committing every crime in America?

1. What reaction has Michael Moore when he sees a white man walking towards him?

2. Why does he think this reaction might be hard to understand?

3. Pick an example of a bad thing that a white person has done to him.

4. Name three things that Moore claims that only white people have done which make the world a more unpleasant place.

5. What point is Moore making about the portrayal of black people on the news?

6. In this piece Moore is arguing that black people are stereotyped. How are they stereotyped?

7. Does Moore agree with this stereotype? Why not?

8. *While Moore is making a serious point, he does it in a humorous way.* Do you agree with this statement?

Think about the way some of the following can be stereotyped:

- Age groups
- Races/nationalities
- Occupations
- Religions

Find examples of these stereotypes in any of the following areas:

- Advertising
- Newspapers
- TV programmes

### OR

Think about the fact that stereotyping is a way of labelling people. Advertisers often use labels to make their products more desirable, for example, certain brands of trainers are 'cooler' than others. Can you think of any examples of labels that are considered to be more desirable than others in any of the following areas:

- Clothing
- Footwear
- Food
- Cars

Many of the big label brands have been accused of exploiting labourers in the developing world. Have a class debate on the topic:

The moral cost of designer labels is too much!

You might have discussed this topic in CSPE class. There is lots of material on the Internet on this topic.

THE TEENAGE REBEL

THE BLONDE ?!*?*!

THE POLITICIAN

Do you have a favourite cartoon? Bring in some examples to show the class. Can you explain why you like the humour in the cartoon?

1. What kind of cat is Garfield?

2. Look at the way Garfield is drawn. How does this help to tell us about his character? What features are exaggerated?

3. Why is the final frame of the cartoon so funny?

4. The cartoon is about exercise. Why might it appeal to most people?

1. What aspect of classroom life is the cartoonist mocking?

Cartoons are generally intended to entertain us and make us laugh …

**off the mark** by Mark Parisi
w w w . o f f t h e m a r k . c o m

DIVE IN!

1. The humour in this cartoon comes from an unexpected reversal. What is it?

2. What underlying message is the cartoonist sending us?

... but sometimes they can have a serious message as well.

This next cartoon was published at a time when many Irish banks had been discovered to be overcharging their customers on a regular basis.

DIVE IN!

1. Is this cartoon a satire? Explain your answer.

Very often newspaper cartoonists will use **satire** to expose the ridiculous side of certain political or economic issues.

1. Do you recognise any of the people in the posters?

2. What is the cartoonist saying about politicians and elections?

Cartoonists also use **caricature** to make their images more humorous. This is a grotesque, exaggerated image of a person.

Martyn Turner's cartoon shows aliens viewing planet Earth in the future. Examine the cartoon and

1. State briefly what you think the cartoonist's message is. (20)

2. Imagine that one of the aliens in the cartoon is a journalist. Write a brief article that he/she/it might write for the front page of *The Martian Times* on his/her/its return home. (20)

*Note: The Stern Report mentioned in the cartoon refers to a report by economist Sir Nicholas Stern on the effect of human activity, such as global warming, on the world's climate.*

2007 H.L. Paper

# Drama

In this chapter you will read extracts from many different **plays**, encountering:
- Dramatic openings
- Unusual settings
- Interesting characters

You will **think** about:
- Staging scenes
- Tension and suspense
- Themes in drama

Over the next few pages you will read extracts from various plays, but this is not 'real' drama. If you read the script from your favourite TV programme it would not be the same as watching it. When you go to a play you *see* and *hear* things, you do not read. So remember, while you are reading the page you should be trying to see a stage.

The opening scene of a play, a TV programme or a film has to catch our attention or else we won't keep watching. In the following scene the writer introduces us to important characters and makes us wonder what is going to happen next.

# Big Maggie

John B. Keane

*(Action takes place in a graveyard. A near middle-aged woman dressed in black is seated on a headstone buttress smoking a cigarette, with her handbag clutched between her knees.*
*In the background can be heard the sound of earth falling on a coffin. A man and woman, both old, stop to pay their respects. In turn they shake hands with MAGGIE POLPIN.)*

| | |
|---|---|
| Old Man: | Sorry for your trouble, Maggie, he was a good man, God be good to him. |
| Maggie: | He was so. |
| Old Woman: | He was a good man, if he had a failing, Maggie, 'twas a failing many had. |
| Old Man: | He had a speedy release, God be good to him and that's a lot. |
| Old Woman: | Worse if he was after spending six or seven months in a sick bed. |
| Maggie: | He went quick and that was the way he wanted it. |
| Old Woman: | That was a blessing. |
| Old Man: | *(Emphatically)* That was a lot all right. Make no mistake! We can't all go the way we'd like. |
| Maggie: | We can't. |
| Old Man: | You may say we can't! There's no one can. |
| Old Woman: | He was a cheerful sort of a man. |
| Maggie: | Cheerful is the word. |
| Old Man: | What age was he? |
| Maggie: | He was just turned sixty. |
| Old Man: | He didn't get a bad share of it. |
| Old Woman: | There's a lot never saw sixty. |
| Old Man: | And a lot never will! We must be thankful for all things and accept the Holy Will of God. |

Maggie: We must indeed! Well, I won't be holding you up, if you're in a hurry.

Old Man: I understand, Maggie. You want your own about you at a time like this. I was wondering if you'd have any notion where Madge Gibbons is buried? There's no stone over her.

Maggie: I've no idea! Sure isn't one grave as good as another. 'Tis the thought that counts you know! *(Old man and old woman exit and GERT enters.)*

Gert: Won't you go over to lay on the wreaths?

Maggie: I won't.

Gert: But, Mother …

Maggie: Don't but me now, like a good girl. I'm in no humour for it.

Gert: I just thought it would be the correct thing to do.

Maggie: You're not old enough yet to know what is correct and what is not correct. God forgive me if there's two things I can't endure 'tis the likes of them two caterwaulin' about the dead and the other is the thump of clods on a timber coffin. I couldn't bear to watch that gang around the trench and they trying to look sorry.

Gert: Can I go over to help with the laying of the wreaths?

Maggie: No! Your brothers and sisters can do that. 'Tisn't that the wreaths will do him any good.

Gert: Oh, Mother, how can you say a thing like that!

Maggie: It's the truth! God forgive me 'tis a hard thing to say about my own husband, but that's what they'll be saying in the pubs after the funeral. 'Tis what everybody knows. I'm not a trained mourner, Gert. I can't olagón or moan or look for the arm of another hypocrite to support me.

Gert: He was no saint but he was my father. *(Rebelliously)* I'm going over to the grave.

Maggie: You will stay where you are. I have enough to contend with without my youngest wanting to desert me in my hour of need. Call Byrne there! He's on the verge of the crowd somewhere.

**DIVE IN!**

1. Was Maggie's husband sick for a long time?

2. What age was he when he died?

3. What does Maggie really think of the two old people?

4. Why does she refuse to put wreaths on the grave?

5. Why won't Maggie let Gert go to help?

**TAKE THE PLUNGE!**

6. What kind of person do you think Maggie is? P Q E

7. Do you think that she got on well with her husband? P Q E

8. How would you know that this play is set in Ireland?

9. Why does Gert speak angrily to her mother?

10. What questions does this opening scene make you want to ask?

**WHY DON'T YOU...**

Re-read the stage directions. How does John B. Keane tell us things about Maggie even before she speaks? Think about the position he describes her sitting in and the sort of expression that might be on her face. What advice would you give to the actor playing Maggie?

**OR**

Draw the stage set based loosely on the stage directions. How will you create the impression of a large graveyard on stage?

**OR**

Write the conversation you imagine that the old man and woman have after they leave Maggie.

# Much Ado About Nothing

## Act One, Scene One

William Shakespeare (abridged)

*This play is set in Italy. It begins with the arrival of a messenger to the house of Signor Leonato and he bears good news.*

*Before Leonato's House.*
*Enter Leonato, Hero and Beatrice, with a Messenger.*

| | |
|---|---|
| Leonato: | I learn in this letter that Don Pedro of Arragon comes this night to Messina. |
| Messenger: | He is very near by this: he was not three leagues off when I left him. |
| Leonato: | How many gentlemen have you lost in this action? |
| Messenger: | But few of any sort, and none of name. |
| Leonato: | A victory is twice itself when the achiever brings home full numbers. I find here Don Pedro hath bestowed much honour on a young Florentine called Claudio. |
| Messenger: | Much deserved on his part and equally remembered by Don Pedro. He hath borne himself with all the promise of his age, doing, in the figure of a lamb, the feats of a lion. He hath indeed better bettered expectation than you must expect of me to tell you how. |
| Beatrice: | I pray you, is Signior Mountanto returned from the wars or no? |
| Messenger: | I know none of that name, lady. There was none such in the army of any sort. |
| Leonato: | What is he you ask for, niece? |
| Hero: | My cousin means Signior Benedick of Padua. |

Messenger:   O, he is returned, and as pleasant as ever he was.

Beatrice:   I pray you, how many hath he killed and eaten in these wars? But how many hath he killed? For indeed I promised to eat all of his killing.

Leonato:   Faith, niece, you tax Signior Benedick too much – but he'll be meet with you, I doubt it not … You must not, sir, mistake my niece. There is a kind of merry war betwixt Signior Benedick and her. They never meet but there is a skirmish of wit between them.

Beatrice:   Alas, he gets nothing by that. Who is his sworn companion now? He hath every month a new sworn brother.

Messenger:   Is't possible?

Beatrice:   Very easily possible. He wears his faith but as the fashion of his hat, it ever changes with the next block.

Messenger:   I see, lady, the gentleman is not in your books.

Beatrice:   No, and he were, I would burn my study. But I pray you who is his companion? Is there no young squarer now that will make a voyage with him to the devil?

Messenger:   He is most in the company of the right noble Claudio.

Beatrice:   O Lord, he will hang upon him like a disease – he is sooner caught than the pestilence, and the taker runs presently mad. God help the noble Claudio. If he have caught the Benedick, it will cost him a thousand pound ere a' be cured.

Messenger:   I will hold friends with you, lady.

Beatrice:   Do, good friend.

Leonato:   You will never run mad, niece.

Beatrice:   No, not till a hot January.

Messenger:   Don Pedro is approached.

1. What do you think Don Pedro and his men were doing? Why is the news about them so good?

2. Why does Beatrice ask about Signior Benedick?

3. What does Leonato explain to the messenger about Beatrice and Benedick?

4. What does the messenger think of Beatrice?

5. What do you think will happen when Beatrice and Benedick meet?

6. Name three characters who were introduced in this scene. Choose one and say what you learnt about them. **PQE**

7. What do you think is going to happen next?

8. What other questions come into your head about the people in this play?

9. What sort of play do you think this is going to be (sad, happy, scary, funny, adventurous …)? Give reasons for your answer. **PQE**

10. Did you think this was a good opening scene? **PQE**

Write out three pieces of advice that you would give to the actor playing Beatrice if you were directing this scene.

**OR**

Design the costumes you would use to show that Leonato, Hero and Beatrice are wealthy people. A group of soldiers are about to enter the scene – how will you costume them? Remember, the costumes do not have to come from Shakespearean times!

**OR**

Imagine that, like the characters in this scene, you are receiving important news. Nowadays that news would often come by telephone. Take a couple of minutes to think about the conversation you will have. Your teacher will then call on volunteers to act out 30 seconds of listening to this news without giving away the actual details. The class must be able to tell from your expressions, gestures and tone what type of news you are receiving.

People's reputations can sometimes precede them. Do we sometimes judge people based on what we have heard about them? Is this a good thing? Should we always believe what we hear? Discuss this in groups and report back to the class.

**The Drama Continues …** Write the scene which you imagine took place immediately after either of these extracts from *Big Maggie* and *Much Ado About Nothing*.

# Staging and Setting

You go to 'see' and 'hear' a play, not to read it, which is why the following elements are so important:

- **Set** and **scenery** create a place on the stage.
- **Props** are any objects on stage that are moveable and that the actors use.
- **Costumes** and **make-up** worn by characters reveal when the play is taking place and what the characters may be like.
- **Lighting** creates atmosphere and mood as well as highlighting important moments in the play.
- **Sound effects** and **music** also add to the atmosphere and can make the play more realistic.

Is this a realistic set? Why do you think the designer used a set like this?

Where and when do you think this play might be taking place? Base your answers on what you can see on the set. Pay particular attention to costumes, background and any props you can find.

What do you think of the costumes in this production? Are they effective?

What do the costumes in this scene tell you about the world in which the characters live?

What do you think of the lighting effects in this scene?

How is mood and atmosphere created in this scene?

Judging from the expressions and gestures in this scene, what do you think might be happening?

Suggest what the relationship between these three men might be, based on the way they are positioned on stage.

Comment on the effectiveness of this scene under the following headings:
- Set
- Costumes
- Lighting
- Gestures
- Positioning

# Vampire Dawn

Dennis Horvitz

Simone: You killed Martine.

Etienne: Yes.

Simone: Etienne, she … she …

Etienne: She made you a vampire.

Simone: How did you know?

Etienne: Your footfall. Vampires move differently than mortals do. Your body isn't completely dead yet, and you already move like a vampire. I could hear your footsteps long before you came into the room.

Simone: This feeling! I've never experienced the night this way before! I can hear conversations on the street just by concentrating. The colours, the smells. Is this death?

Etienne: This is living death.

Simone: Etienne, why did Martine choose me?

Etienne: For two reasons. The first and most important, because she's a killer. Just like me. And now, just like you.

Simone: And the second.

Etienne: To get at me. She knew that I cared about you as a mortal. She knew that I would do anything to protect you. In her jealousy, she has chosen the one act that would hurt me. She knew that I could not bear the idea of you roaming the night, an unclean thing, needing to kill.

Simone: But Etienne! This sensation! This power! I think I'm beginning to understand.

Etienne: You haven't killed yet. If you haven't killed, you don't understand.

Simone: But why must I kill people? Couldn't I live off animals?

Etienne: You could, but for how long? What will you do when you've finally cleared the area of every rat and stray dog or cat? What will you do when the need becomes so intense that even the simplest motion is agony? I have seen vampires die of hunger, Simone. Your wildest imagination cannot conceive the sight – or the screams.

Simone:   But I don't feel like killing.

Etienne:   That is because Martine fed you as she made you. By this time tomorrow, you will do what you will be driven to do until the end of time.

Simone:   Is there no hope?

Etienne:   *(He takes her hand)* Hmmm … a very human gesture, really. A symbol of communication, of comfort, of strength. Yes, there is hope, because after all this time, I finally have the courage.

Simone:   Courage for what, Etienne?

Etienne:   To do what must be done.

Simone:   What do you mean? What must be done?

Etienne:   The first step is, we wait.

Simone:   Wait for what?

Etienne:   We wait for the sunrise.

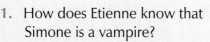

1.  How does Etienne know that Simone is a vampire?

2.  How does Simone feel?

3.  Why did Martine make Simone a vampire?

4.  Etienne says that Simone doesn't understand yet. What does he mean?

5.  What do you think Etienne has found the courage to do? What is supposed to happen to vampires at sunrise?

*Remember that the decisions you make when staging a scene must remain consistent. The choices you make when answering Question 6 below will affect the rest of the questions. For example, if you choose a modern set then your actors will have to wear modern costumes and you could use modern music.*

6.  There are no stage directions with this extract. Where do you think this scene might take place? What kind of set would you design? Try to keep it simple.

7.  Depending on **where** and **when** you set your scene, decide what costumes the characters should wear. Describe them and draw them.

8.  This scene obviously takes place at night, but the audience have to be able to *see* the actors, therefore, think about what kind of lighting you might need to use.

9.  What kind of sound effects do you think might go well with this scene? Bring in a piece of music that you think might help create the atmosphere.

# The Vampire Game

 Clear all chairs, tables and bags to the sides of the room.

 Everyone must stand in a circle and close their eyes. Anyone who opens their eyes is disqualified.

 The teacher will walk around the back of the circle. He or she will tap one student on the shoulder. That student becomes the 'vampire'. While the 'vampire' walks around, all students must keep their arms folded and their eyes closed.

 Now everyone walks around the room (still with their eyes closed, so walk slowly!). If the 'vampire' taps a student's shoulder he or she also becomes a 'vampire'. The 'vampire' must try to do this without being discovered.

 Students who are tapped on the shoulder must yell and stretch their arms out in front of them to show that they have been 'vampirised'. This will give everyone else a clue as to their whereabouts so they can avoid that area. The new 'vampire' should now try to 'vampirise' other students.

 If a 'vampire' accidentally tries to 'vampirise' another vampire this actually 'rehumanises' that person. The victim screams again and then folds his or her arms.

 The aim of the vampire is to have the entire room 'vampirised' by the end of the exercise.

At the end of the game think about how you felt about being 'vampirised'. Did you actually feel relief when you were 'bitten' and didn't have to avoid vampires anymore? Did you prefer being a vampire or a human? Write down your thoughts for homework.

## OR

Write a short story featuring the vampire as the hero or the villain.

# Characters

- The audience gets to know the **characters** in the play by listening to what they say, watching what they do and hearing what other characters say about them.

- An actor can change our view of a character by using an unexpected **tone** of voice. This is why it is important to see plays being performed as well as reading them.

- Sometimes what the character **says** and **does** may be contradictory – he or she might promise one thing to another character and then do the exact opposite!

- **Costumes**, **gestures**, and **expressions** also tell us about the character.

# P'tang Yang, Kipperbang

Jack Rosenthal

*Alan has fancied Ann for a long time. In a performance of their school play, he has failed to kiss her at an important moment. They are now walking home from school together.*

Ann: *Why*, though, Quack-Quack! Why didn't you do the kiss. You haven't said why. Did you just forget? *(Alan barely shrugs in reply. She tries again – hopefully.)* I mean there must be a reason. Everything has a reason … You can walk me home if you like.

Alan: *(Shrugs in reply to Ann's invitation.)* **Alright.** *(Alan and Ann walk on, as before.)*

Ann: What do you think was the reason?

Alan: I don't know.

Ann: *(Trying to jolly him out of his mood.)* You don't know much, then, do you!

Alan: *(Simply)* No. I don't. I know nothing. *(Pause)* I used to think I knew everything about everything. The world and that. But I don't. *(Pause)* Maybe I got it wrong.

Ann: Got *what* wrong?

Alan: Everything. Tommy. The world. Maybe it's all lies.

Ann: What is?

Alan: Everything I thought. About everything. *(She looks at him. He shivers, involuntarily.)*

Ann: You're shivering.

Alan: Yes.

Ann: Maybe you're sickening for something.

Alan: Maybe. *(They walk on in silence. After a moment or two …)* A few weeks ago I trod on a big, fat spider and hundreds of little ones came running out of it. I thought perhaps it was a miracle.

Ann:    *(Hotly)* I don't know about a miracle, it was sodding cruel!

Alan:   Accidental.

Ann:    *(Simmering down)* Oh. *(Pause)* It must just've been pregnant. You just gave it a sort of caesarean.

Alan:   Oh, I see.

Ann:    I don't think it'll have been a miracle. It's just Nature, really.

Alan:   Yes.

Ann:    Except Nature is a miracle, isn't it?

Alan:   *(Stopping, looks at her, smiles – albeit a little sadly.)* Yes, I forgot that. Yes it is. Supposedly. *(They're now at the gate of Ann's house. They stand for a moment in silence.)*

Ann:    Why didn't you want to kiss me? Am I that grotesque to the nth degree?

Alan:   *(Looking at her. He speaks quietly, solemnly, completely unselfconsciously, and very, very simply.)* You're beautiful, Ann. Sometimes I look at you and you're so beautiful I want to cry. And sometimes you look so beautiful I want to laugh and jump up and down, and run through the streets with no clothes on shouting 'P'tang, yang, kipperbang' in people's letterboxes. *(Pause)* But mostly you're so beautiful – even if it doesn't make *me* cry it makes my chest cry. Your lips are the most beautiful. Second is your nape.

Ann:    *(Slight pause)* My what?

Alan:   The back of your neck. It's termed the nape.

Ann:    Oh, my *nape*.

Alan:   And your skin. When I walk past your desk, I breathe in on purpose to smell your skin. It's the most beautiful smell there is.

Ann:    It's only Yardley's.

Alan:   It makes me feel dizzy. Giddy. You smell brand-new. You look brand-new. All of you. The little soft hairs on your arms.

Ann: That's *down*. It's not hairs. It's called down. Girls can have down.

Alan: But mostly it's your lips. I love your lips. That's why I've *always* wanted to kiss you. Ever since 3B. Just kiss. Not the other things. *(Pause)* Well, I *do. All* the other things. Sometimes I want to do them so much I feel I'm – do you have violin lessons?

Ann: *(Thrown)* What?

Alan: On the violin.

Ann: No. Just the recorder. Intermediate, Grade Two.

Alan: Well, on a violin there's the E string. That's the highest pitched and it's strung very tight and taut, and makes a kind of high, sweet scream. Well, sometimes I want you so much, that's what *I'm* like. *(A pause)*

Ann: *(Uncertainly)* Um … thank you.

Alan: I always wanted to tell you you were lovely. Personally, I always think it's dead weedy when Victor Mature – or whatsisname – Stewart Grainger – or someone says a girl's lovely. But you are. *(Pause)* And I know girls think it's weedy when boys call them sweet. But you are. *(Pause)* I don't expect I'll ever kiss you now in my whole life. Or take you to the pictures. Or marry you and do the *other* things to you. But I'll never forget you. And how you make me feel. Even when I'm 51 or something. *(A long pause. Whatever else is happening in the street – cars passing, people coming home from work, little kids playing – is unnoticed by them.)*

Ann: *(Quietly, gently)* Why didn't you kiss me then?

Alan: It's like cricketers. Well, I mean, it *isn't* like cricketers. Cyril Washbrook or Denis Compton or any of them … They face the bowler – and there are thousands of people watching … their families and friends and all the Australian fielders and the umpires and John Arlott and thousands of total strangers. And they don't care. Just keep their eye on the ball and lay their stroke. I don't know how they do it. I couldn't.

Ann: *(Pause)* Would you like to kiss me now? *(He shakes his head sadly.)* No one's watching. *(He shakes his head again.)* Why not? *(Her eyes looking into his, Ann starts drying her lips with the back of her hand. Gently, Alan takes her hand away from her lips and holds it by his side. He smiles tenderly at her. A long moment. Then sadly shakes his head.)*

Alan: I'm sorry, Ann. It's too late.

Ann: *(Tears starting into her eyes.)* It isn't even five o'clock!

Alan: I didn't mean that. Things are different now.

Ann: Why? What things?

Alan: You were right, you see, Ann. *Real* men *don't* mess about dreaming. I *could* kiss you … but it won't be like I dreamed it'd be. I know it won't. Nothing is. Kids kid themselves. *(A pause)*

Ann: *(Hotly)* I think you won't kiss me because I said you could!

Alan: What?

Ann: Because now I *want* you to.

Alan: *(Thrown; troubled)* Is that what happens?

Ann: I think you're just being sodding cruel again! Only this time on *purpose!*

Alan: Don't cry, Ann. *I* used to cry. Even in my sleep … dreaming. I won't any more, though. I've jacked in crying now. *(Ann looks into his eyes, bites back tears. Smiles sadly.)*

Ann: Would you like to say P'tang, yang, kipperbang? *(He smiles; shakes his head.)* My favourite words are yellow ochre, burnt sienna and crimson lake.

Alan: Very nice. *(Pause)* See you tomorrow. *(He turns to go.)*

Ann: Alan? *(He turns back. She kisses him, very briefly, on the cheek.)* For good luck, that's all. *(He smiles and starts back down the street. She watches him go for a moment, then turns and goes into her house.)*

1. At the beginning of the scene how can you tell that Alan is confused and upset?

2. Why is he bothered about the spider?

3. How does Alan really feel about Ann?

4. Why does he compare having to kiss Ann in the play to being a cricketer in a big match?

5. Why do you think Alan doesn't kiss Ann?

6. How can you tell that Alan thinks a lot? What kind of person is he? PQE

7. What impression do you get of Ann? PQE

8. Do you think Ann understands Alan? PQE

9. In your opinion, will their relationship change after this conversation?

10. Based on evidence from the text would you like either Alan or Ann as a boyfriend or girlfriend?

Imagine that you have been chosen to play the part of Alan or Ann for a classroom production of this scene. How would you play your part? You might refer to tone of voice, movement, costume, facial expression, etc.

**OR**

In pairs, prepare a short mime, which need not last longer than 30 seconds, in which one of you conveys to the audience that you *really* fancy or *really* hate the other person. How can you show us this, using only your facial expression and movement?

**OR**

Write Ann or Alan's diary entry on the evening after this conversation.

From a play you have studied choose **one** important relationship.

(i) Describe the main characteristics of this relationship throughout the play.

(ii) How does **either** the setting (time or place) **or** character have an influence on this relationship? Support your answer with reference to the text.

2009 H.L. Paper

# Casablanca

Julius J. Epstein, Philip G. Epstein, Howard Koch

*This is an extract from the screenplay of Casablanca. It is set during World War II when hundreds of people were trying to escape to America from Europe via Casablanca. Rick is a mysterious bar owner in the city. An old flame of his called Ilsa comes to him for help to get papers allowing her to leave Casablanca with her husband, Lazlo. Rick agrees to save her husband, but only if Ilsa stays behind with Rick in Casablanca. Rick gets papers from the corrupt chief of police Renault, and they reach the airport, but the German Major Strasser is not far behind …*

*A uniformed orderly uses a telephone near the hangar door.*
*On the airfield a transport plane is being readied.*

**Orderly:** Hello. Hello, radio tower? Lisbon plane taking off in ten minutes. East runway. Visibility: one and one half miles. Light ground fog. Depth of fog: approximately 500. Ceiling: unlimited. Thank you.

*He hangs up and moves to a car that has just pulled up outside the hangar.*
*Renault gets out while the orderly stands at attention.*
*He's closely followed by Rick, right hand in the pocket of his trench coat, covering Renault with a gun.*
*Laszlo and Ilsa emerge from the rear of the car.*

**Rick:** *(indicating the orderly)* Louis, have your man go with Mr Laszlo and take care of his luggage.

**Renault:** *(bowing ironically)* Certainly Rick, anything you say. *(to orderly)* Find Mr Laszlo's luggage and put it on the plane.

**Orderly:** Yes, sir. This way please.

*The orderly escorts Laszlo off in the direction of the plane.*
*Rick takes the letters of transit out of his pocket and hands them to Renault, who turns and walks toward the hangar.*

**Rick:** If you don't mind, you fill in the names. That will make it even more official.

**Renault:** You think of everything, don't you?

**Rick:** *(quietly)* And the names are Mr and Mrs Victor Laszlo.

*Renault stops dead in his tracks, and turns around.*
*Both Ilsa and Renault look at Rick with astonishment.*

**Ilsa:** But why my name, Richard?

**Rick:** Because you're getting on that plane.

**Ilsa:** *(confused)* I don't understand. What about you?

**Rick:** I'm staying here with him 'til the plane gets safely away.

*Rick's intention suddenly dawns on Ilsa.*

**Ilsa:** No, Richard, no. What has happened to you? Last night we said …

**Rick:** … Last night we said a great many things. You said I was to do the thinking for both of us. Well, I've done a lot of it since then and it all adds up to one thing. You're getting on that plane with Victor where you belong.

**Ilsa:** *(protesting)* But Richard, no, I, I …

Rick:   … You've got to listen to me. Do you have any idea what you'd have to look forward to if you stayed here? Nine chances out of ten we'd both wind up in a concentration camp. Isn't that true, Louis?

*Renault countersigns the papers.*

Renault:   I'm afraid Major Strasser would insist.

Ilsa:   You're saying this only to make me go.

Rick:   I'm saying it because it's true. Inside of us we both know you belong with Victor. You're part of his work, the thing that keeps him going. If that plane leaves the ground and you're not with him, you'll regret it.

Ilsa:   No.

Rick:   Maybe not today, maybe not tomorrow, but soon, and for the rest of your life.

Ilsa:   But what about us?

Rick:   We'll always have Paris. We didn't have, we'd lost it, until you came to Casablanca. We got it back last night.

Ilsa:   And I said I would never leave you.

Rick:   And you never will. But I've got a job to do, too. Where I'm going you can't follow. What I've got to do you can't be any part of. Ilsa, I'm no good at being noble, but it doesn't take much to see that the problems of three little people don't amount to a hill of beans in this crazy world. Someday you'll understand that. Now, now …

*Ilsa's eyes well up with tears.*
*Rick puts his hand to her chin and raises her face to meet his own.*

Rick:   Here's looking at you, kid.

*CUT TO*
*EXT. ROAD – NIGHT*

*Major Strasser drives at break-neck speed towards the airport.*
*He honks his horn furiously.*

*CUT TO*
*INT./EXT. AIRPORT HANGAR – NIGHT*

*Laszlo returns.*
*Rick walks into the hangar and Renault hands him the letters.*
*He walks back out to Laszlo.*

Laszlo:   Everything in order?

Rick:   All except one thing. There's something you should know before you leave.

Laszlo:   *(sensing what is coming)* Monsieur Blaine, I don't ask you to explain anything.

Rick:   I'm going to anyway, because it may make a difference to you later on. You said you knew about Ilsa and me.

Laszlo:   Yes.

Rick:   But you didn't know she was at my place last night when you were. She came there for the letters of transit. Isn't that true, Ilsa?

Ilsa:   *(facing Laszlo)* Yes.

| Rick: | *(forcefully)* She tried everything to get them, and nothing worked. She did her best to convince me that she was still in love with me, but that was all over long ago. For your sake, she pretended it wasn't, and I let her pretend. |
| Laszlo: | I understand. |
| Rick: | Here it is. |

*Rick hands the letters to Laszlo.*

| Laszlo: | Thanks. I appreciate it. |

*Laszlo extends his hand to Rick, who grasps it firmly.*

| Laszlo: | And welcome back to the fight. This time I know our side will win. |

*On the airfield the airplane engine turns over and the propellers start turning.*
*They all turn to see the plane readying for take-off.*
*Ilsa looks at Rick and he returns her stare with a blank expression.*
*He then glances at Laszlo, as does Ilsa.*
*Then Laszlo breaks the silence.*

| Laszlo: | Are you ready Ilsa? |
| Ilsa: | Yes, I'm ready. *(to Rick)* Goodbye, Rick. God bless you. |
| Rick: | You better hurry, or you'll miss that plane. |

*Rick watches as Ilsa and Laszlo walk very deliberately towards the plane.*

| Renault: | Well I was right. You are a sentimentalist. |
| Rick: | Stay where you are. I don't know what you're talking about. |

*Rick puts a cigarette in his mouth.*

| Renault: | What you just did for Laszlo, and that fairy tale that you invented to send Ilsa away with him. I know a little about women, my friend. She went, but she knew you were lying. |
| Rick: | Anyway, thanks for helping me out. |
| Renault: | I suppose you know this isn't going to be pleasant for either of us, especially for you. I'll have to arrest you of course. |
| Rick: | As soon as the plane goes, Louis. |

*The door to the plane is closed by an attendant and it slowly taxies down the field.*
*Suddenly a speeding car comes to a stop outside the hangar.*
*Strasser alights from the car and runs toward Renault.*

| Strasser: | What is the meaning of that phone call? |
| Renault: | Victor Laszlo is on that plane. |

*Renault nods toward the field.*
*Strasser turns to see the plane taxiing towards the runway.*

| Strasser: | Why do you stand here? Why don't you stop him? |
| Renault: | Ask Monsieur Rick. |

*Strasser looks briefly at Rick, then makes a step towards the telephone just inside the hangar door.*

| Rick: | Get away from that phone. |

*Strasser stops in his tracks, looks at Rick, and sees that he is armed.*

| Strasser: | *(steely)* I would advise you not to interfere. |
| Rick: | I was willing to shoot Captain Renault, and I'm willing to shoot you. |

*Strasser watches the plane in agony.*

*His eyes dart towards the telephone.*
*He runs toward it and desperately grabs the receiver.*

Strasser: Hello?

Rick: Put that phone down!

Strasser: Get me the Radio Tower!

Rick: Put it down!

*Strasser, one hand holding the receiver, pulls out a pistol with the other hand, and shoots quickly at Rick.*
*The bullet misses its mark.*
*Rick now shoots at Strasser, who crumples to the ground.*
*At the sound of an approaching car both men turn.*
*A police car speeds in and comes to a stop near Renault.*
*Four gendarmes hurriedly jump out.*
*In the distance the plane turns onto the runway.*
*The gendarmes run to Renault.*
*The first one hurriedly salutes him.*

Gendarme: Mon Capitaine!

Renault: Major Strasser's been shot.

*Renault pauses and looks at Rick.*
*Rick returns Renault's gaze with expressionless eyes.*

Renault: Round up the usual suspects.

Gendarme: Oui, mon Capitaine.

*The gendarmes take Strasser's body away and then drive off.*
*Renault walks inside the hangar, picks up a bottle of Vichy water and opens it.*

Renault: Well, Rick, you're not only a sentimentalist, but you've become a patriot.

Rick: Maybe, but it seemed like a good time to start.

Renault: I think perhaps you're right.

*As he pours the water into a glass, Renault sees the Vichy label and quickly drops the bottle into a trash basket which he then kicks over.*
*He walks over and stands beside Rick.*
*They both watch the plane take off, maintaining their gaze until it disappears into the clouds.*
*Rick and Louis slowly walk away from the hangar toward the runway.*

Renault: It might be a good idea for you to disappear from Casablanca for a while. There's a Free French garrison over at Brazzaville. I could be induced to arrange a passage.

Rick: My letter of transit? I could use a trip. But it doesn't make any difference about our bet. You still owe me ten thousand francs.

Renault: And that ten thousand francs should pay our expenses.

Rick: Our expenses?

Renault: Uh huh.

Rick: Louis, I think this is the beginning of a beautiful friendship.

*The two walk off together into the night.*

FADE OUT
**THE END**

1. Why does Rick want Renault to fill in the transit papers?

2. What does Rick think will happen to them if Ilsa stays in Casablanca?

3. What other arguments does Rick use to convince Ilsa to get on the plane?

4. Why does Rick shoot Strasser?

5. Do you think Rick loves Ilsa? Give reasons for your answer. PQE

6. Renault, the police chief, has a sense of humour. Can you find evidence of this? PQE

7. What is your impression of Rick? PQE

8. Would you like to watch this film? Give reasons for your answer. PQE

If you had to act in this scene, which character would you choose to be, and why?

*OR*

Imagine what would have happened if Strasser had managed to stop the plane from taking off. Write a scene describing the conversation that the characters would have in their jail cell.

*OR*

See if you can get a copy of the film Casablanca. Watch this scene in class. List five reasons why this scene is more interesting to watch than it is to read.

*OR*

Imagine you are directing this scene, and prepare a storyboard to help you. You need to decide which character is the most powerful/important. Think about the way you will give the audience this information through your use of the camera, and where you place the actors in each shot. Remember, you can use long shots, close-ups and editing to tell the story!

● Draw six to ten boxes in your copybook which you will use for the different shots in the scene.

● Use stick figures and labelling to indicate how you will direct the action.

*Remember, it's not important that you draw well for this exercise, as long as your instructions are clear!*

This scene includes some of the most famous quotes from movie history, including:

*'Here's looking at you kid.'*

and

*'I think this is the beginning of a beautiful friendship.'*

In groups of four make a list of every famous movie quote you can think of. Write out your quotes and pass them to the other groups. Have a competition to see which group can identify the origin of the most quotes.

Conflict occurs when people disagree with one another. It can also be caused by confusion within a person. When there is conflict on stage, the audience does not know what is going to happen next and this keeps their attention. This is called **tension** or **suspense**.

# The Prism

Dennis Sook

| | |
|---|---|
| Jane: | The doctor said we could stay here in the chapel and talk. |
| Roger: | Okay, sure. |
| Jane: | Oh, God. What are we going to do? |
| Roger: | I don't know. It's not fair. None of it. That poor little thing. It has a heart, and it is beating. How can that be? How can it have such a tiny, healthy heart and everything else be so … |
| Jane: | Maybe it's something we don't understand. |
| Roger: | We understand it well enough. It is what it is. It's got multiple birth defects. That's what the doctor said. |
| Jane: | Please don't call her 'it'. She has a name. Melanie. She is a human being. She's alive, and she belongs to you and me. |
| Roger: | That's not true. She doesn't belong to me. Nor to you either. She's no part of us. Just what do you suppose these doctors can do with surgery? Make her a whole person from assorted parts? You're mistaken if you think that. They can't do a damn thing. |
| Jane: | The doctor said the decision must be made now. Oh, God. |
| Roger: | 'Oh, God' is right. You're the one that believes that. Well, what does your God tell you to do? |
| Jane: | To keep her alive and to care for her forever. |
| Roger: | It's been seven days today. Seems appropriate to me that on the seventh day, your God rested. So, today he's resting. Resting where? Gone fishing? Out to lunch, back in an hour? Get Him here, because I want to talk to Him. Now. |
| Jane: | Don't. Don't talk like that. It's not God's fault. |
| Roger: | Then whose fault is it? |
| Jane: | We don't know why these things happen. |
| Roger: | Whose fault is it? Mine? Yours? |
| Jane: | It's not anybody's fault. |

Roger: I don't accept that.

Jane: Please.

Roger: Maybe we shouldn't have used birth control pills. Maybe you shouldn't have experimented with drugs back in your college days.

Jane: What?

Roger: You heard me.

Jane: Are you blaming me? Are you saying this is my fault? You took drugs, too, back then. Maybe it's your fault.

Roger: I need to know why our baby was born like this.

Jane: It's God's will. We must accept that. She is a special baby. There are special schools …

Roger: No, no, no, it's a mistake. Honest to Christ, they gave us the wrong one. I can't deal with this. I'm serious. I cannot handle this for the rest of my life. I refuse to be responsible for it, and nobody can make me.

Jane: But we are responsible for Melanie. We're all she has, and we are going to tell the doctor to do the operation. To do everything in his power to give her the best possible chance in the world.

Roger: Chance? What chance does it have? Chance for what? No, no, no, we are not going to.

Jane: We have to.

Roger: We don't have to. And we won't. It isn't fair to it … to her.

Jane: She didn't ask to be born; we wanted her. I love her. I don't care what you say, she has as much right to live as you do, and we'll tell the doctor to do whatever he can.

Roger: No we won't. If I have to, I'll … I will stop her living myself. And damn you.

Jane: No, you won't. You couldn't do that. God will give us the strength we need to …

Roger: I've heard all I want to hear about your absentee God. It doesn't exist.

Jane: Stop it. Stop it. God is that sweet little baby. God is you and me and our blessed little girl. Please, please, please. Let them help her.

Roger: It'll be alright. It'll be alright. I promise you. I promise. Alright. It will be alright. We'll talk to the doctor again. Just please, don't cry anymore.

1. Why do you think the doctor sent the parents to the chapel?

2. What is wrong with the baby?

3. How can you tell that Roger is angry?

4. What is the decision that they have to make?

5. What decision do they come to?

6. How does Jane feel about the baby? How does Roger feel? Why does this cause conflict?

7. Who do you feel most sympathy for in this scene?

8. How does the scene keep your interest?

9. What tone of voice do you think the actors should use for their last speeches?

Pretend that the baby has gone in for its operation.

- Place two chairs at the top of the class. This is now the waiting room.

- The teacher will pick two students to sit on the chairs. They are now the parents in the waiting room.

- In your copybook make two columns labelled 'Roger' and 'Jane'.

- Write the questions you would like to ask each character in the columns.

- The teacher will give you an opportunity to ask the parents in the waiting room your questions.

- They must answer honestly as the character.

- For homework, write a short description of one of the character's thoughts while waiting for their baby to come out of surgery.

***OR***

Write a letter to one of these characters offering them advice in this difficult situation.

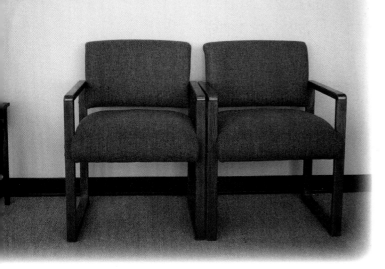

# Romeo and Juliet

William Shakespeare

*Juliet has secretly married Romeo without her parents' permission. Her mother has told her that it has been arranged for her to marry Paris. Then her father arrives …*

| | |
|---|---|
| Lady Capulet: | Here comes your father. Tell him so yourself, <br> And see how he will take it at your hands. <br> *(Enter Capulet and Nurse)* |
| Capulet: | … How now, wife <br> Have you delivered to her our decree? |
| Lady Capulet: | Ay, sir. But she will none, she gives you thanks. <br> I would the fool were married to her grave! |
| Capulet: | Soft! Take me with you, take me with you wife. <br> How? Will she none? Doth she not give us thanks? <br> Is she not proud? Doth she not count her blest, <br> Unworthy as she is, that we have wrought <br> So worthy a gentleman to be her brief? |
| Juliet: | Not proud you have, but thankful that you have. <br> Proud can I never be of what I hate, <br> But thankful even for hate that is meant love. |
| Capulet: | How, how, how, how, chopped logic? What is this? <br> 'Proud' – and 'I thank you' – and 'I thank you not' – <br> And yet 'not proud'? Mistress minion you, <br> Thank me no thankings, nor proud me no prouds, <br> But fettle your fine joints 'gainst Thursday next <br> To go with Paris to Saint Peter's Church, <br> Or I will drag thee on a hurdle thither. <br> Out, you green-sickness carrion! Out, you baggage! <br> You tallow-face! |
| Juliet: | Good father, I beseech you on my knees, <br> Hear me with patience but to speak a word. |
| Capulet: | Hang thee, young baggage! Disobedient wretch! <br> I tell thee what – get thee to church a'Thursday, <br> Or never after look me in the face. <br> Speak not, reply not, do not answer me! <br> My fingers itch. Wife, we scarce thought us blest <br> That God had lent us but this only child. <br> But now I see this one is one too much, <br> And that we have a curse in having her. <br> Out on her, hilding! |
| Nurse: | God in heaven bless her! <br> You are to blame, my lord, to rate her so. |
| Capulet: | And why, my Lady Wisdom? Hold your tongue, <br> Good Prudence. Smatter with your gossips, go! |

Nurse: I speak no treason.

Capulet: Oh, God-i-good-e'een!

Nurse: May one not speak?

Capulet: Peace, you mumbling fool!
Utter your gravity o'er a gossip's bowl,
For here we need it not.

Lady Capulet: You are too hot.

Capulet: God's bread! It makes me mad.
Day, night; hour, tide; work, play;
Alone, in company; still my care hath been
To have her matched. And now having provided
A gentleman of noble parentage,
Of fair demesnes, youthful, and nobly trained,
Stuffed, as they say, with honourable parts,
Proportioned as one's thought would wish a man –
And then to have a wretched puling fool
A whining mammet, in her fortune's tender,
To answer 'I'll not wed, I cannot love;
I am too young, I pray you pardon me'!
But, as you will not wed, I'll pardon you!
Graze where you will, you shall not house with me.
Look to't, think on't. I do not use to jest.
Thursday is near. Lay hand on heart. Advise.
An you be mine, I'll give you to my friend.
An you be not, hang, beg, starve, die in the streets,
For, by my soul, I'll ne'er acknowledge thee,
Nor what is mine shall never do thee good.
Trust to't. Bethink you. I'll not be foresworn. *(Exit Capulet)*

Juliet: Is there no pity sitting in the clouds
That sees into the bottom of my grief?
O sweet my mother, cast me not away!
Delay this marriage for a month, a week.
Or if you do not, make the bridal bed
In that dim monument where Tybalt lies.

Lady Capulet: Talk not to me, for I'll not speak a word.
Do as thou wilt, for I have done with thee.
*(Exit Lady Capulet)*

Juliet: O God! – O Nurse, how shall this be prevented?
My husband is on earth, my faith in heaven.
How shall that faith return again to earth
Unless that husband send it me from heaven
By leaving earth? Comfort me, counsel me.
Alack, alack, that heaven should practise stratagems
Upon so soft a subject as myself!

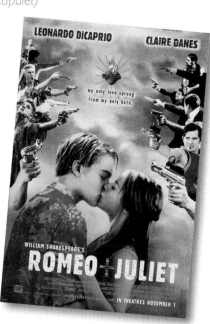

1. Why does Capulet feel that Juliet should give him thanks?

2. What words does Capulet use that indicate his anger towards Juliet?

3. How do the other characters' reactions tell you that Capulet is reacting very harshly?

4. What do Lord and Lady Capulet threaten to do if Juliet refuses to marry?

5. What is the source of conflict in this scene?

6. If you were directing this scene, what advice would you give to the actor playing the part of Capulet? Focus specifically on tone of voice, gesture, expression and movement.

7. What lighting and music would you choose to highlight the conflict between the characters in this scene?

Choose three words to describe the changing emotions that Juliet feels as this scene progresses.

- Now think of three freeze-frame positions that would show these emotions.

- Take a minute to practise your three positions, or describe them in your copybook.

- When the teacher calls on you, perform or describe your three positions for the class.

- Ask the class what words they would put with your positions.

For homework write an explanation of your choices using quotes and references from the scene.

**OR**

Move these characters to a different time and place. Re-write the scene as if they were in:

- *A trailer park in a very poor part of America*

- *A farm in rural Ireland*

- *An upper-class apartment in London*

- *An occupied country during World War II*

- *A spaceship circling Mars in the 25th century*

- *Anywhere else you can think of*

Try to recapture the essence of the conflict between a girl and her parents as she refuses the man they have chosen for her; but change the language.

**OR**

Re-read the scene. How would you make this scene dramatic on stage?

Name a play you have studied in which one character rebels against another. With which character did you have more sympathy? Give reasons for your answer.

2004 H.L. Paper

## Climax

A **climax** is the moment that all the tension has been building up to. It is an important, vital moment in the story.

# The Playboy of the Western World

J.M. Synge

*Christy Mahon, a young man from Kerry, has arrived in a remote part of Co. Mayo. It is the late 1800s. He is on the run because he believes that he has killed his father by hitting him over the head with a shovel. To his surprise the people admire him for doing such a terrible thing!*

*Before this scene, the audience has found out that Christy's father is still alive, and has come looking for him. Only Christy and a woman named the Widow Quin know the truth. Just at the moment when Christy is told he can marry the love of his life, Pegeen, the worst possible thing happens …*

| | |
|---|---|
| Michael: | *(… holding onto both of them)* … A daring fellow is the jewel of the world, and a man did split his father's middle with a single clout, should have the bravery of ten, so may God and Mary and St Patrick bless you, and increase you from this mortal day. |
| Christy and Pegeen: | Amen, O Lord! |
| | *(Hubbub outside.)* |
| | *(Old Mahon rushes in, followed by all the crowd, and Widow Quin. He makes a rush at Christy, knocks him down, and begins to beat him.)* |
| Pegeen: | *(Drags back his arm.)* Stop that, will you. Who are you at all? |
| Mahon: | His father, God forgive me! |
| Pegeen: | *(Drawing back)* Is it rose from the dead? |
| Mahon: | Do you think I look so easy quenched with the tap of a loy? *(Beats Christy again.)* |
| Pegeen: | *(Glaring at Christy)* And it's lies you told, letting on you had him slitted, and you nothing at all. |

| | |
|---|---|
| Christy: | *(Clutching Mahon's stick.)* He's not my father. He's a raving maniac would scare the world. *(Pointing to Widow Quin.)* Herself knows it is true. |
| Crowd: | You're fooling Pegeen! The Widow Quin seen him this day, and you likely knew! You're a liar! |
| Christy: | *(Dumbfounded)* It's himself was a liar, lying stretched out with an open head on him, letting on he was dead. |
| Mahon: | Weren't you off racing the hills before I got my breath with the start I had seeing you turn on me at all? |
| Pegeen: | And to think of the coaxing glory we had given him, and he after doing nothing but hitting a soft blow and chasing northward in a sweat of fear. Quit off from this. |
| Christy: | *(Piteously)* You've seen my doings this day, and let you save me from the old man; for why would you be in such a scorch of haste to spur me to destruction now? |
| Pegeen: | It's your treachery is spurring me, till I'm hard set to think you're the one I'm after lacing in my heart-strings a half-an-hour gone by. *(To Mahon.)* Take him on from this, for I think bad the world should see me raging for a Munster liar, and the fool of men. |
| Mahon: | Rise up now for retribution, and come on with me. |
| Crowd: | *(Jeeringly)* There's the playboy! There's the lad thought he'd rule the roost in Mayo. Slate him now, mister. |
| Christy: | *(Getting up in shy terror.)* What is it drives you to torment me here, when I'd asked the thunders of the might of God to blast me if I ever did hurt to any saving only the single blow. |
| Mahon: | *(Loudly)* If you didn't, you're a poor good-for-nothing, and isn't it by the like of you the sins of the whole world are committed? |
| Christy: | *(Raising his hands.)* In the name of the Almighty God … |
| Mahon: | Leave troubling the Lord God. Would you have him sending down droughts, and fevers, and the old hen and the cholera morbus? |
| Christy: | *(To Widow Quin.)* Will you come between us and protect me now? |
| Widow Quin: | I've tried a lot, God help me, and my share is done. |
| Christy: | *(Looking round in desperation.)* And I must go back into my torment is it, or run off like a vagabond straying through the Unions with the dusts of August making mudstains in the gullet of my throat, or the winds of March blowing on me till I'd take an oath I felt them making whistles of my ribs within? |
| Sara: | Ask Pegeen to aid you. Her like does often change. |
| Christy: | I will not then, for there's torment in the splendour of her like, and she a girl any moon of midnight would take pride to meet, facing southwards on the heaths of Keel. But what did I want crawling forward to scorch my understanding at her flaming brow? |
| Pegeen: | *(To Mahon, vehemently, fearing she will break into tears.)* Take on from this or I'll set the young lads to destroy him here. |

Mahon: *(Going to him, shaking his stick.)* Come on now if you wouldn't have the company to see you skelped.

Pegeen: *(Half laughing, through her tears.)* That's it, now the world will see him pandied, and he an ugly liar was playing odd the hero, and the fright of men.

Christy: *(To Mahon, very sharply.)* Leave me go!

Crowd: That's it. Now Christy. If them two set fighting, it will lick the world.

Mahon: *(Making a grab at Christy.)* Come here to me.

Christy: *(More threateningly.)* Leave me go, I'm saying.

Mahon: I will maybe, when your legs is limping, and your back is blue.

Crowd: Keep it up, the two of you. I'll back the old one. Now the playboy.

Christy: *(In a low, intense voice.)* Shut your yelling, for if you're after making a mighty man of me this day by the power of a lie, you're setting me on to think if it's a poor thing to be lonesome, it's worse to go mixing with the fools of the earth.

*(Mahon makes a move towards him.)*

*(Almost shouting)* Keep off … lest I do show a blow unto the lot of you would set the guardian angels winking in the clouds above. *(He swings round with a sudden rapid movement and picks up a loy.)*

Crowd: *(Half frightened, half amused.)* He's going mad! Mind yourselves! Run from the idiot!

Christy: If I'm such an idiot, I'm after hearing my own voice this day saying words would raise the topknot on a poet in a merchant's town. I've won your racing, and your lepping, and …

Mahon: Shut your gullet and come on with me.

Christy: I'm going, but I'll stretch you first. *(He runs at Old Mahon with the loy, chases him out of the door, followed by the crowd and the Widow Quin. There is a great noise outside, then a yell and then dead silence for a moment. Christy comes in, half dazed, and goes to the fire.)*

**DIVE IN!**

1. What is the first thing Christy's father (Old Mahon) does when he comes into the room?

2. How does Christy react when he sees his father?

3. What does Pegeen think of Christy when she finds out he hasn't killed his father?

4. How does Christy react when the crowd jeer him?

5. What do you think has happened by the end of this extract?

**TAKE THE PLUNGE!**

6. What is the mood when Michael is telling Christy and Pegeen they can get married?

7. How does the mood change?

8. The audience watching this play has been waiting for Old Mahon to reappear. Why do you think this might be the most important, vital moment in this story?

9. How do you think the crowd encourages the violence in this scene?

10. Would you like to find out how this story ends?

**WHY DON'T YOU...**

Pretend you are playing a part in this scene. Which character would you choose to play and why?

**OR**

What did you think of the language in this extract? Did you find it hard to understand? Was it realistic? Pick three examples of words that showed you the play was set long ago in Ireland.

**OR**

Imagine you are staging this scene. How would you use lighting, sound effects, music and movement to make it more dramatic?

# The Merchant of Venice

William Shakespeare

*Shylock is a Jewish moneylender in Venice. He has loaned Bassanio three thousand ducats. Antonio, Bassanio's friend, has promised that he will pay back 'a pound of his own flesh' if Bassanio does not return the money in time. Bassanio arrives too late, and Shylock refuses the money and goes to court to claim his fine, the pound of flesh, because he hates Antonio and wants him dead. Meanwhile, Portia, Bassanio's love, has disguised herself as a lawyer and has arrived to defend Antonio. The audience is waiting to find out if Shylock will get his way …*

| | |
|---|---|
| Shylock: | … We trifle time: I pray thee, pursue sentence. |
| Portia: | A pound of that same merchant's flesh is thine: |
| | The court awards it, and the law doth give it. |
| Shylock: | Most rightful judge! |
| Portia: | And you must cut this flesh from off his breast: |
| | The law allows it, and the court awards it. |
| Shylock: | Most learned judge! A sentence! Come, prepare! |
| Portia: | Tarry a little here; there is something else. |
| | This bond doth give here no jot of blood; |
| | The words expressly are 'a pound of flesh': |
| | Take then thy bond, take thou thy pound of flesh; |
| | But, in the cutting it, if thou dost shed |
| | One drop of Christian blood, thy lands and goods |
| | Are, by the laws of Venice, confiscate |
| | Unto the state of Venice. |
| Gratiano: | O upright judge! Mark, Jew: O learned judge! |
| Shylock: | Is that the law? |
| Portia: | Thyself shall see the act: |
| | For, as thou urgest justice, be assured |
| | Thou shalt have justice, more than thou desirest. |
| Gratiano: | O learned judge! Mark, Jew: a learned judge! |
| Shylock: | I take this offer, then; pay the bond thrice |
| | And let the Christian go. |
| Bassanio: | Here is the money. |
| Portia: | Soft! |
| | The Jew shall have all justice; soft! No haste: |
| | He shall have nothing but the penalty. |
| Gratiano: | O Jew! An upright judge, a learned judge! |

Portia:    Therefore prepare thee to cut off the flesh.
Shed thou no blood, nor cut thou less nor more
But just a pound of flesh: if thou takes more
Or less than a just pound, be it so much
As makes it light or heavy in the substance,
Or the division of the twentieth part
Of one poor scruple, nay, if the scale do turn
But in the estimation of a hair,
Thou diest and all thy goods are confiscate.

Gratiano:    A second Daniel, a Daniel, Jew!
Now, infidel, I have you on the hip.

Portia:    Why doth the Jew pause? Take thy forfeiture.

Shylock:    Give me my principal, and let me go.

| | |
|---|---|
| Bassanio: | I have it ready for thee; here it is. |
| Portia: | He hath refused it in the open court: |
| | He shall have merely justice and his bond. |
| Gratiano: | A Daniel, still say I, a second Daniel! |
| | I thank thee, Jew, for teaching me that word. |
| Shylock: | Shall I not have barely my principal? |
| Portia: | Thou shalt have nothing but the forfeiture, |
| | To be so taken at thy peril, Jew. |
| Shylock: | Why, then the devil give him good of it! |
| | I'll stay no longer question. |
| Portia: | Tarry, Jew: |
| | The law hath yet another hold on you. |
| | It is enacted in the laws of Venice, |
| | If it be proved against an alien |
| | That by direct or indirect attempts |
| | He seek the life of any citizen, |
| | The party 'gainst the which he doth contrive |
| | Shall seize one half his goods; the other half |
| | Comes to the privy coffer of the state; |
| | And the offender's life lies in the mercy |
| | Of the duke only, 'gainst all other voice. |
| | In which predicament, I say, thou stand'st; |
| | For it appears, by manifest proceeding, |
| | That indirectly and directly too |
| | Thou hast contrived against the very life |
| | Of the defendant; and thou hast incurred |
| | The danger formerly by me rehearsed. |
| | Down therefore and beg mercy of the duke. |
| Gratiano: | Beg thou mayst have leave to hang thyself: |
| | And yet, thy wealth being forfeit to the state, |
| | Thou hast not left the value of a cord; |
| | Therefore thou must be hanged at the state's charge. |
| Duke: | That thou shalt see the difference of our spirit |
| | I pardon thee thy life before thou ask it; |
| | For half thy wealth, it is Antonio's; |
| | The other half comes to the general state, |
| | Which humbleness may drive unto a fine. |
| Shylock: | I pray you, give me leave to go from hence; |
| | I am not well: send the deed after me, |
| | And I will sign it. |
| Duke: | Get thee gone, but do it. |

# Take the Plunge!

1. Why is Shylock pleased with the first two things that Portia says?

2. What unexpected point does Portia raise which changes everything?

3. Why does the court refuse to allow Shylock to take the money instead of the pound of flesh?

4. What other law does Portia prove Shylock has broken? What is the penalty?

5. Does the Duke show Shylock mercy?

6. The audience has been waiting throughout this play to see if Shylock will succeed in killing Antonio. Why is this scene an important, vital moment in the play?

7. Who do you feel sympathy for in this scene? Explain your answer.

8. This is a courtroom scene. How would you stage it to maximise dramatic tension?

Imagine that you are a journalist reporting on this court case. Write the article that you will submit to your editor. If you want to, you can pretend that you have interviewed some of the characters. You can write it in either broadsheet or tabloid style.

A freeze-frame is like a scene from a film that has been paused. You are going to pretend that you are frozen in a moment in the story. You decide what character each person in your group is playing. Remember to think about posture, gesture, expression and positions.

**OR**

Choose a moment from this scene and prepare a freeze-frame.

- Practise your moment.

- The teacher will call each group to the top of the classroom in turn.

- On the count of three you must freeze your moment and hold it still for 30 seconds.

- When the teacher points to you, you must explain who you are and what you are thinking at this moment in time.

For homework pretend you are the director of this scene. Write out how you would position the actors, what gestures and expressions they should use and what lighting, music or props they would need.

Select a play you have studied.

- Give an account of a dramatic scene or part of the play.

- How was the drama created?

Base your answer on the text studied. If you wish you may also make reference to a theatre performance or a film version you have seen of the play.

2002 H.L. Paper

# Humour

# Gregory's Girl

Bill Forsyth

*Gregory is a teenager in Scotland. His younger sister Madeline is nine years old, his father is a driving instructor. In this scene Gregory is getting ready to go to school. (Gregory is dressing in front of the mirror. Madeline is dressed for school and listens to his monologue.)*

Gregory: *(Just about to do up the buttons of his shirt)* Ooh dear me, almost forgot my twelve hour protector. That would never do. Just a little roll fights off the sweaty demon odours for a full twelve hours. Then, just a little dab to encourage the chesty follicles, and perhaps a quick whirl around the band of the Y-fronts and he's protected. One hundred per cent protection against all unsightly odours. Or is he? *(He attempts to smell his own breath. First by channelling it up his nostrils with his hands; then by exhaling loudly, then sniffing.)* Mm, can't smell a thing. Better give the shiny molars a polish, just to be on the safe side. *(He takes up an electric toothbrush. Elaborately selects the appropriate brush. Clicks it into place. Then switches on. He is in tune with this machine.)* Maximum revs. *(He changes gear.)* Massages the gums for the ultimate in oral gratification.

Madeline: You're not wearing that tie, are you?

Gregory: *(Surprised. Cannot find the switch.)* Please don't creep up on me like that. You could damage my delicate relationship with this finely tuned apparatus. What's wrong with the tie?

Madeline: It jars.

Gregory: So!

Madeline: It will set people's teeth on edge.

Gregory: It's a statement.

Madeline: Only to you. To everyone else it shows dreadful taste.

Gregory: Aren't you late for school or something?

Madeline: I'm waiting for somebody.

Gregory: Oh. Who?

Madeline: Richard. He walks me to school. *(The doorbell rings. The first few bars of 'Ode to Joy')* See you. *(She goes out.)*

Gregory: Bye … Walks her to school?

*(He ponders the purple tie. Abandons it. Undoes one shirt button. Then two. Then three. His vest shows. He adjusts it. Fails. Does up the third button, as his father comes in.)*

Father: Good God!

Gregory:  Hi, Mike!

Father:  Call me Dad, Gregory, or Pop or something … It makes me feel better when you call me Dad … or Father.

Gregory:  As you wish, Father. How are you anyway?

Father:  Fine. We're all well. Your mother was asking about you only the other day. I told her that we had met in the hallway, briefly, last Thursday and you looked fine … This is an added bonus. She'll be thrilled with the news of this unexpected sighting.

Gregory:  What keeps you hanging about the homestead?

Father:  'Returning to' not 'hanging about'. I have already taken Mr Clarke for his pre-test warm up, done an hour with Miss Bethnal and since my next client …

Gregory:  Client? Bit over the top, isn't it?

Father:  My next client happens to live nearby so I dropped in for a cup of coffee. Unfortunately the adaptor for the coffee machine seems to have walked, and, not unnaturally, I surmised that it might have walked here.

Gregory:  It doesn't need an adaptor.

Father:  It always did.

Gregory:  I have rewired the plug.

Father:  Ah!

Gregory:  It now works the coffee machine *and* the food processor.

Father:  Sounds dangerous.

Gregory:  It isn't.

Father:  While I'm here …

Gregory:  I haven't long.

Father:  No. I sense a powerful urgency. Since chance has thrown us together, why don't we *plan* to meet some time soon. Say breakfast later in the week. Eight o'clock in the kitchen, Friday? Your mother would like that.

Gregory:  Yes … that sounds fine.

Father:  It's a date then.

Gregory:  Yes. Look forward to it. I must be off. Remember to switch the filter valve to the left. Have a nice day you hear.

*(Gregory leaves. Father picks up the purple tie with disdain.)*

**DIVE IN!**

1. Who do you think Gregory is talking to at the beginning of the extract?

2. What advice does his sister give him?

3. Why is his father at home?

4. What do they agree to do next Friday?

**TAKE THE PLUNGE!**

5. Do you think Gregory is self-conscious? **P Q E**

6. Would you like Madeline for a younger sister? **P Q E**

7. What kind of person is Gregory's father? **P Q E**

8. In your opinion, do Gregory and his father get on well?

9. Do you think this is a 'happy family'?

10. Did you find this scene funny?

**WHY DON'T YOU...**

Write the conversation you might have with yourself in the mirror if you were getting ready for:

- *A big date*
- *A job interview*
- *A family wedding*
- *A court appearance*
- *A Cup Final*
- *A visit to the dentist*

**OR**

Prepare a mime of your morning routine. Try to show through movement and facial expression what you are feeling as you get ready for the day. Are you happy, excited, nervous, tired, grumpy, etc.?

# The Importance of Being Earnest

Oscar Wilde

*Mr Jack Worthing has just asked Lady Bracknell for permission to marry Gwendolen. This play is set in the late nineteenth century in England at a time when language and manners were extremely formal. Lady Bracknell's reaction to the proposal is to ask Jack a series of questions about his background. Don't be intimidated by the language or any parts you don't understand, just keep reading!*

| | |
|---|---|
| Lady Bracknell: | *(Sitting down)* You can take a seat, Mr Worthing. |
| | *(Looks in her pocket for note-book and pencil.)* |
| Jack: | Thank you, Lady Bracknell, I prefer standing. |
| Lady Bracknell: | *(Pencil and note-book in hand)* I feel bound to tell you that you are not down on my list of eligible young men, although I have the same list as the dear Duchess of Bolton has. We work together, in fact. However, I am quite ready to enter your name, should your answers be what a really affectionate mother requires. Do you smoke? |
| Jack: | Well, yes, I must admit I smoke. |
| Lady Bracknell: | I am glad to hear it. A man should always have an occupation of some kind. There are far too many idle men in London as it is. How old are you? |
| Jack: | Twenty-nine. |
| Lady Bracknell: | A very good age to be married at. I have always been of the opinion that a man who desires to get married should know either everything or nothing. Which do you know? |
| Jack: | *(After some hesitation)* I know nothing, Lady Bracknell. |
| Lady Bracknell: | I am pleased to hear it. I do not approve of anything that tampers with natural ignorance. Ignorance is like a delicate exotic fruit; touch it and the bloom is gone. The whole theory of modern education is radically unsound. Fortunately in England, at any rate, education produces no effect whatsoever. If it did, it would prove a serious danger to the upper classes, and probably lead to acts of violence in Grosvenor Square. What is your income? |
| Jack: | Between seven and eight thousand a year. |
| Lady Bracknell: | *(Makes a note in her book)* In land, or in investments? |

| | |
|---|---|
| Jack: | In investments, chiefly. |
| Lady Bracknell: | That is satisfactory. What between the duties expected of one during one's lifetime, and the duties exacted from one after one's death, land has ceased to be either a profit or a pleasure. It gives one position, and prevents one from keeping it up. That's all can be said about land. |
| Jack: | I have a country house with some land, of course, attached to it, about fifteen hundred acres, I believe; but I don't depend on that for my real income. In fact, as far as I can make out, the poachers are the only people who make anything out of it. |
| Lady Bracknell: | A country house! How many bedrooms? Well, that point can be cleared up afterwards. You have a town house, I hope? A girl with a simple, unspoiled nature, like Gwendolen, could hardly be expected to reside in the country. |
| Jack: | Well, I own a house in Belgrave Square, but it is let by the year to Lady Bloxham. Of course, I can get it back whenever I like, at six months' notice. |
| Lady Bracknell: | Lady Bloxham? I don't know her. |
| Jack: | Oh, she goes about very little. She is a lady considerably advanced in years. |
| Lady Bracknell: | Ah, nowadays that is no guarantee of respectability of character. What number in Belgrave Square? |
| Jack: | 149. |
| Lady Bracknell: | *(Shaking her head)* The unfashionable side. I thought there was something. However, that could be easily altered. |
| Jack: | Do you mean the fashion, or the side? |
| Lady Bracknell: | *(Sternly)* Both, if necessary, I presume. What are your politics? |
| Jack: | Well, I am afraid I really have none. I am a Liberal Unionist. |
| Lady Bracknell: | Oh, they count as Tories. They dine with us. Or come in the evening at any rate. You have of course no sympathy of any kind with the Radical Party? |
| Jack: | Oh! I don't want to put the asses against the classes, if that is what you mean, Lady Bracknell. |
| Lady Bracknell: | That is exactly what I do mean … ahem! … Are your parents living? |
| Jack: | I have lost both my parents. |
| Lady Bracknell: | Both? … To lose one parent may be regarded as misfortune … to lose both seems like carelessness. Who was your father? He was evidently a man of some wealth. Was he born in what the Radical papers call the purple of commerce, or did he rise from the ranks of the aristocracy? |
| Jack: | I am afraid that I really don't know. The fact is, Lady Bracknell, I said I had lost my parents. It would be nearer the truth to say that my parents seem to have lost me … I don't actually know who I am by birth. I was … well, I was found. |
| Lady Bracknell: | Found! |
| Jack: | The late Mr Thomas Cardew, an old gentleman of a very charitable and kindly disposition, found me, and gave me the name of Worthing, because he happened to have a first-class ticket for Worthing in his pocket at the time. Worthing is a place in Sussex. It is a seaside resort. |

| | |
|---|---|
| Lady Bracknell: | Where did this charitable gentleman who had a first-class ticket for this seaside resort find you? |
| Jack: | *(Gravely)* In a hand-bag. |
| Lady Bracknell: | A hand-bag? |
| Jack: | *(Very seriously)* Yes, Lady Bracknell. I was in a hand-bag – a somewhat large, black leather hand-bag, with handles to it – an ordinary hand-bag in fact. |
| Lady Bracknell: | In what locality did this Mr James, or Thomas, Cardew come across this ordinary hand-bag? |
| Jack: | In the cloak-room at Victoria Station. It was given to him in mistake for his own. |
| Lady Bracknell: | The cloak-room at Victoria Station? |
| Jack: | Yes. The Brighton line. |
| Lady Bracknell: | The line is immaterial. Mr Worthing, I confess that I feel somewhat bewildered by what you have just told me. To be born, or at any rate bred, in a hand-bag, whether it had handles or not, seems to me to display a contempt for the ordinary decencies of family life that reminds one of the worst excesses of the French Revolution. And I presume you know what that unfortunate movement led to? As for the particular locality in which the hand-bag was found, a cloak-room at a railway station might serve to conceal a social indiscretion – has probably, indeed, been used for that purpose before now – but it could hardly be regarded as an assured basis for a recognised position in good society. |
| Jack: | May I ask you then what you would advise me to do? I need hardly say I would do anything in the world to ensure Gwendolen's happiness. |
| Lady Bracknell: | I would strongly advise you, Mr Worthing, to try and acquire some relations as soon as possible, and to make a definite effort to produce at least one parent, of either sex, before the season is over. |
| Jack: | Well, I don't see how I could possibly manage to do that. I can produce the hand-bag at any moment. It is in my dressing-room at home. I really think that should satisfy you, Lady Bracknell. |
| Lady Bracknell: | Me, sir! What has it to do with me? YOU can hardly imagine that I and Lord Bracknell would dream of allowing our only daughter – a girl brought up with the utmost care – to marry into a cloak-room, and form an alliance with a parcel. *(Jack starts indignantly.)* Kindly open the door for me, sir. You will of course understand that for the future there is to be no communication between you and Miss Fairfax. |

1. How can you tell from the very beginning that Jack is getting off to a bad start with Lady Bracknell?

2. What is Lady Bracknell's attitude towards education?

3. Why does Lady Bracknell ask questions about Jack's income and land?

4. What is unusual about Jack's background?

5. What is Lady Bracknell's reaction to this information?

6. What kind of person is Lady Bracknell?
   PQE

7. How does Wilde exaggerate the snobbery of English society at this time?

8. You have been chosen to act the part of Jack. How will you play his character? Think about tone of voice, movement, costume, facial expression, etc.

9. How is the language of the extract different from the language that we use today? Select features of the language to illustrate the differences.

10. Did you find this extract funny? Explain your answer.

Think about the difficulties that you might have if producing this play. Focus on set and costumes.

**OR**

Write out the interview your mother or father might conduct the first time they meet your boyfriend or girlfriend.

**OR**

Imagine that a baby was found in a handbag in your town. Prepare the news report to be aired on the six o'clock news bulletin.

Name a play you have studied. Choose a scene from this play that you found either happy **or** sad. Describe how the playwright conveys this happiness **or** sadness.

# Closing Scene

The closing scene often contains an unexpected twist or a revelation. All the aspects of the story are concluded and the audience is expected to feel some emotion such as joy or sorrow. In the following scene there is an unexpected ending.

# The Plough and the Stars

## Act Four

Sean O'Casey

*In 1916 there was a rebellion against British rule in Ireland. There was very heavy fighting on the streets of Dublin. Over 200 ordinary people were killed by stray bullets. By the end of this play a character named Nora Clitheroe has lost her husband, her baby and her sanity. Her neighbour, Bessie Burgess, is trying to look after her. In this scene Nora is looking for her dead husband, but this is very dangerous because the British are trying to shoot an Irish sniper who they believe is in the building. They will shoot anyone they see.*

Nora: *(Staring in front of her and screaming)* Jack, Jack, Jack! My baby, my baby, my baby!

Bessie: *(Waking with a start)* You divil, are you afther gettin' out o' bed again!
*(She rises and runs towards Nora, who rushes to the window, which she frantically opens.)*

Nora: *(At window screaming)* Jack, Jack, for God's sake, come to me!

Soldiers: *(Outside, shouting)* Git away, git away from that window, there!

Bessie: *(Seizing hold of Nora)* Come away, come away, woman, from that window!

Nora: *(Struggling with Bessie)* Where is it; where have you hidden it? Oh Jack, Jack, where are you?

Bessie: *(Imploringly)* Mrs Clitheroe, for God's sake, come away!

Nora: *(Fiercely)* I won't; he's below. Let … me … go! You're thryin' to keep me from me husband. I'll follow him. Jack, Jack, come to your Nora!

Bessie: Hus-s-sh, Nora, Nora! He'll be here in a minute. I'll bring him to you, if only you'll be quiet – honest to God, I will.
*(With a great effort Bessie pushes Nora away from the window, the force used causing her to stagger against it herself. Two rifle shots ring out in quick succession. Bessie jerks*

*her body convulsively; stands stiffly for a moment, a look of agonised astonishment on her face, then she staggers forward, leaning heavily on the table with her hands.)*

Bessie: *(With an arrested scream of fear and pain)* Merciful God, I'm shot, I'm shot, I'm shot! … Th' life's pourin' out o' me! *(To Nora)* I've got this through … through you … through you, you bitch you! … O God, have mercy on me! … *(To Nora)* You wouldn't stop quiet, no, you wouldn't, you wouldn't, blast you! Look what I'm afther gettin', look at what I'm afther gettin' … I'm bleedin' to death, an' no one's here to stop th' flowin' blood! *(Calling)* Mrs Gogan, Mrs Gogan! Fluther, Fluther, for God's sake, somebody, a doctor, a doctor!

*(She staggers frightened towards the door, to seek for aid, but, weakening half-way across the room, she sinks to her knees, and bending forward, supports herself with her hands resting on the floor. Nora is standing rigidly with her back to the wall opposite, her trembling hands held out a little from the sides of her body, her lips quivering, her breast heaving, staring wildly at the figure of Bessie.)*

Nora: *(In a breathless whisper)* Jack, I'm frightened … I'm frightened, Jack … Oh, Jack, where are you?

Bessie: *(Moaningly)* This is what's afther comin' on me for nursin' you day an' night … I was a fool, a fool, a fool! Get me a dhrink o' wather, you jade, will you? There's a fire burnin' in me blood! *(Pleadingly)* Nora, Nora, dear, for God's sake, run out an' get Mrs Gogan, or Fluther, or somebody to bring a doctor, quick, quick, quick! *(Nora does not stir.)*

Bessie: Blast you, stir yourself, before I'm gone!

Nora: Oh, Jack, Jack, where are you?

Bessie: *(In a whispered moan)* Jesus Christ, me sight's goin'! It's all dark, dark! Nora, hold me hand! *(Bessie's body lists over and she sinks into a prostrate position onto the floor.)* I'm dyin', I'm dyin' … I feel it … Oh God, oh God! *(She feebly sings.)*
I do believe, I will believe
That Jesus died for me;
That on th' cross He shed His blood,
From sin to set me free …
I do believe … I will believe
… Jesus died … me;
… th' cross He shed … blood,
From sin … free.
*(She ceases singing, and lies stretched out, still and very rigid. A pause. Then Mrs Gogan runs in hastily.)*

Mrs Gogan: *(Quivering with fright)* Blessed be God, what's afther happenin'? *(To Nora)* What's wrong, child, what's wrong? *(She sees Bessie, runs to her and bends over the body.)* Bessie, Bessie! *(She shakes the body.)* Mrs Burgess, Mrs Burgess! *(She feels Bessie's forehead.)* My God, she's as cold as death. They're afther murdherin' th' poor inoffensive woman!

*(Sergeant Tinley and Corporal Stoddart enter agitatedly, their rifles at the ready.)*

Sergeant Tinley: *(Excitedly)* This is the 'ouse. That's the window!

Nora: *(Pressing back against the wall)* Hide it, hide it; cover it up, cover it up!

Corporal Stoddart: *(Going over to the body)* 'Ere. What's this? Who's this? *(Looking at Bessie)* Oh Gawd, we've plugged one of the women of the 'ouse.

Sergeant Tinley: Whoy the 'ell did she gow to the window? Is she dead?

Corporal Stoddart: Oh, dead as bedamned. Well, we couldn't afford to toike any chawnces.

Nora: *(Screaming)* Hide it, hide it; don't let me see it! Take me away, take me away, Mrs Gogan!

*(Mrs Gogan runs into the room, left, and runs out again with a sheet which she spreads over the body of Bessie.)*

Mrs Gogan: *(As she spreads the sheet)* Oh, God help her, th' poor woman, she's stiffenin' out as hard as she can! Her face has written on it th' shock o' sudden agony, an' her hands is whitenin' into th' smooth shininess of wax.

Nora: *(Whimperingly)* Take me away, take me away; don't leave me here to be lookin' and lookin' at it!

Mrs Gogan: *(Going over to Nora and putting her arm around her)* Come on with me, an' you can doss in poor Mollser's bed, till we gather some neighbours to come an' give the last friendly touches to Bessie in th' lonely layin' of her out.
*(Mrs Gogan and Nora go out slowly).*

Corporal Stoddart: *(Who has been looking around, to Sergeant Tinley)* Tea here, Sergeant. Wot abaht a cup of scald?

Sergeant Tinley: Pour it aht, Stoddart, pour it aht. I could scoff hanything just now.

*(Corporal Stoddart pours out two cups of tea, and the two soldiers begin to drink. In the distance is heard a bitter burst of rifle and machine-gun fire, interspersed with the boom, boom of artillery. The glare in the sky seen through the window flares into a fuller and a deeper red.)*

There gows the general attack on the Powst Office.

Voices: *(In a distant street)* Ambu … lance, Ambu … lance! Red Cro … ss, Red Cro … ss!

Voices of soldiers: *(At a barricade outside the house; singing)*

They were summoned from the 'illside,
They were called in from the glen,
And the country found 'em ready
At the stirring call for men.
Let not tears add to their 'ardship,
As the soldiers pass along,
And although our 'eart is breaking,
Make it sing this cheery song.

*(Joining in the chorus, as they sip the tea)*

Keep the 'owme fires burning, while your 'earts are yearning;
Though your lads are far away
They dream of 'owme;
There's a silver loining
Through the dark cloud shoining,
Turn the dark cloud inside out,
Till the boys come 'owme!

1. How does Bessie react when she sees Nora at the window?

2. How do you know that it is dangerous for Nora to be at the window?

3. What is Bessie's first reaction to being shot? Who does she blame?

4. How do you know that Bessie is religious?

5. Do you think the sergeant and corporal are worried that a woman has been shot? Explain your answer fully.

6. If you were a detective investigating Bessie's death what questions would you ask?

7. How do you think Nora would feel if she realised what she had caused? **PQE**

8. How do you think this ending would affect an audience?

9. The man who wrote this play, Sean O'Casey, believed that only ordinary people suffered in wars. How does this ending make this point? **PQE**

10. What did you notice about the way the characters spoke in this extract? **PQE**

Write a list of the sound effects you would have off-stage during this scene. How do you think these would add to the atmosphere?

**OR**

Improvise a death scene like Bessie's death in this extract. Imagine you have been murdered by poison, dagger or bullet and that you only have time to say one sentence before you die. What will you say? Act out your death scene for the class.

**OR**

Think about the ways a director might contrast the Dublin women with the English soldiers. You might want to think about language, costume, positions on stage, expressions and gestures.

In groups, make a list of the conflicts that are currently ongoing in the world. What do you know about them? Do people care about these conflicts? Tonight, find a newspaper and count how many articles there are about wars. Bring in one article if possible. If you can't find a newspaper you could use the Internet or watch the news.

257

> The main message of a play is called its **theme**. Read the next scene and think about what the writer is trying to say to us.

# The Freedom of the City

Brian Friel

*(The stage is in darkness except for the apron which is lit in cold blue.*

*Three bodies lie grotesquely across the front of the stage – Skinner on the left, Lily in the middle, Michael on the right. After a silence has been established we hear in the very far distance the wail of an ambulance siren.*

*A photographer, crouching for fear of being shot, runs on from the right and very hastily and nervously photographs the corpses, taking three or four pictures of each. His flash-bulb eerily lights up the stage each time.*

*When he gets the length of Skinner, a priest enters right, crouching like the photographer and holding a white handkerchief above his head. He gets down on his knees beside Michael, hastily blesses him and mumbles prayers into his ear. He then moves onto Lily and Skinner and goes through the same ritual with each.*

*While the priest crouches beside Michael, a spot picks out the judge high up in the battlements. And at the same moment a policeman in dark glasses enters from the left, removes his cap and faces the judge. The policeman reads from his notebook; the judge takes notes.*

*The judge is English, in his early sixties; a quick fussy man with a testy manner.)*

| | |
|---|---|
| Policeman: | Hegarty, my lord. |
| Judge: | Speak up, Constable, please. |
| Policeman: | Hegarty, my lord. |
| Judge: | Yes. |
| Policeman: | Michael Joseph. Unmarried. Unemployed. Lived with his parents. |
| Judge: | Age? |
| Policeman: | Twenty-two years, my lord. |
| Judge: | Was the deceased known to you personally, Constable B? |
| Policeman: | No, my lord. |
| Judge: | And when you arrived at the body, did you discover any firearms on his person or adjacent to his person? |
| Policeman: | I wasn't the first to get there, my lord. |
| Judge: | Would you answer my question? |
| Policeman: | I personally saw no arms, my lord. |

Judge: Thank you.

*(Three soldiers in full combat uniform run on from right. Two of them grab Michael by the feet and drag him off right, while a third, tense and scared, covers them with his rifle. The photographer runs off left. The priest moves to Lily.)*

Policeman: Doherty. Elizabeth. Married. Aged forty-three years.

Judge: Occupation?

Policeman: Housewife. Also a cleaning woman. Deceased lived with her family in a condemned property behind the old railway – a warehouse that was converted into eight flats and …

Judge: We are not conducting a social survey, Constable. Was the deceased known to you?

Policeman: No, my lord.

Judge: And did you discover any firearms on her person or adjacent to her person?

Policeman: I wasn't the first person on the scene, my lord.

Judge: I am aware of that, Constable.

Policeman: I saw no weapons, my lord.

*(The priest moves on to Skinner. The three soldiers return and drag Lily off.)*

Policeman: Fitzgerald. Adrian Casimir.

Judge: Pardon?

Policeman: Fitzgerald …

Judge: I've got that.

Policeman: Adrian Casimir.

Judge: Yes.

Policeman: Aged twenty-one. Single. No fixed address.

Judge: You mean he wasn't native to the city?

Policeman: He was, my lord. But he moved about a lot. And we haven't been able to trace any relatives.

Judge: Had the deceased a profession or a trade?

Policeman: No, my lord.

Judge: Was he bearing any firearms – when you got to him?

Policeman: Not when I got to him, my lord.

Judge: And was he known to you personally, Constable B?

Policeman: Yes, my lord.

Judge:    As a terrorist?

Policeman:    He had been in trouble many times, my lord. Petty larceny, disorderly behaviour – that sort of thing.

Judge:    I see. Thank you, Constable.

*(The priest goes off left. The policeman follows him. The three soldiers enter right and drag Skinner away as before. A ceremonial hat [the Mayor's] is lying beside Skinner's body. One of the soldiers takes it off with him.)*

Judge:    I should explain that I have permitted soldiers and policemen to give evidence under pseudonyms so that they may not expose themselves to the danger of reprisal. And before we adjourn for lunch, may I repeat once more and make it abundantly clear once more my words of the first day: that this tribunal of inquiry, appointed by her Majesty's Government, is in no sense a court of justice. Our only function is to form an objective view of the events which occurred in the City of Londonderry, Northern Ireland, on the tenth day of February 1970, when after a civil rights meeting British troops opened fire and three civilians lost their lives. It is essentially a fact-finding exercise; and our concern and our only concern is with that period of time when these three people came together, seized possession of a civic building, and openly defied the security forces. The facts we garner over the coming days may indicate that the deceased were callous terrorists who had planned to seize the Guildhall weeks before the events of February 10th; or the facts may indicate that the misguided scheme occurred to them on that very day while they listened to revolutionary speeches. But whatever conclusion may seem to emerge, it must be understood that it is none of our function to make moral judgements, and I would ask the media to bear this in mind. We will resume at 2.30.

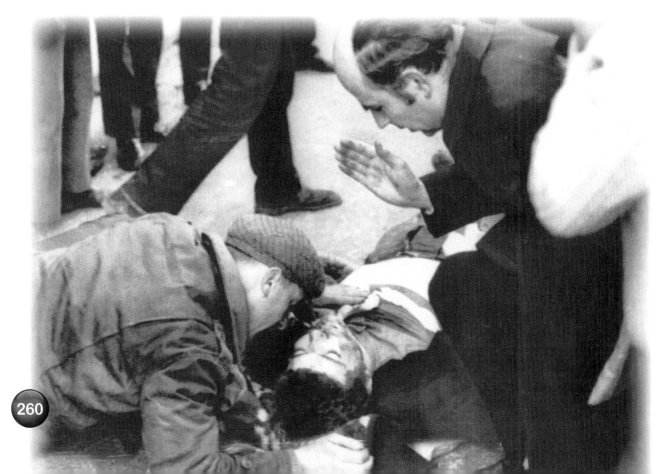

1. Re-read the opening line of the stage directions. How do you think an audience would feel when they see this opening scene?

2. How does the photographer's movement let you know that it is a dangerous place?

3. Why do you think the priest is holding a white handkerchief above his head?

4. How does the playwright let you know that the judge and policeman are not in the same place as the priest and photographer?

5. Who has been killed?

The photographer in this scene has taken photographs. Write the captions that you think would appear beneath three of them in tomorrow's paper.

**OR**

Write a letter of condolence to the family of one of the dead people expressing your sympathy and shock at their loss.

**OR**

In groups of four, think of other situations that you know of where injustice has occurred. Prepare a freeze-frame of the situation. Perform it for the class and then discuss the various situations that have arisen.

6. What did you notice about the type of language that the judge and policeman used when talking about the 'deceased'? **PQE**

7. Do you think this is a dramatic opening for a play? **PQE**

8. What does the judge tell us is happening in his final speech? Do you think the writer wants the audience to agree with him? **PQE**

9. Would you agree that the theme of this play appears to be 'justice and injustice'? Could you think of any other themes that are being explored? **PQE**

10. Would you like to see the rest of this play? Explain your answer.

Plays deal with interesting themes.

- Select a play you have studied.

- Outline a theme in it you found to be interesting.

- Would you consider the theme to be relevant to your own life and/or to the world around you?

Explain your answer with reference to the play.

# Unseen Drama

The questions on the unseen extract will focus on the following:

 The **opening** of a play has to catch our attention and help us form our first impressions. For example, in the extract from *Big Maggie* we meet the main character and we find out that the play is set in Ireland. The opening should also raise questions in the viewers' minds. In *Much Ado About Nothing* we are curious to find out what will happen when the soldiers arrive.

 How a play is **staged** and where it is **set** help the writer to tell the story and the audience to believe what they see on stage. The formal **set** and the **costumes** worn by Lady Bracknell and Jack in *The Importance of Being Earnest* will highlight the period and the society in which the play is set. **Lighting** could be used to create an eerie and a spooky **atmosphere** in *Vampire Dawn*.

 When we watch a play we are introduced to various **characters** and the **relationships** between them. We listen to what they say, watch what they do and hear what other people say about them. In *P'tang Yang, Kipperbang* Alan is a sensitive boy and this is obvious from what he says to Ann. The relationship between Rick and Ilsa is revealed in *Casablanca* as he persuades her to board the plane with her husband, Lazlo.

 Most plays contain **conflict.** When we watch people fight with each other or with themselves we don't know what will happen next and so we have to keep watching. This is called **tension** or **suspense.** For example, in *The Prism* there is conflict between a married couple about the future of their child. In *Romeo and Juliet* the conflict occurs between Juliet and her father about her arranged marriage.

 The **climax** of a play is the moment that all the tension and suspense has been leading up to. The reappearance of Christy's father in *The Playboy of the Western World* is the moment that the audience has been waiting for. In *The Merchant of Venice* all of the tension is resolved when Shylock is outwitted.

 The **language** used in a play tells us more about where it is set and the characters. In *The Plough and the Stars* the corporal and sergeant speak with Cockney accents, whereas in *The Importance of Being Earnest* the characters speak using very formal, 'posh' English.

 Sometimes the main **theme** or **message** in a play is very obvious. *Romeo and Juliet* is a famous play about love. The opening of *Freedom of the City* tells the audience that the play will be exploring violence and injustice.

# Studied Drama

Make sure that you prepare detailed notes on each of the following areas:

 The name of the **play** and the **playwright.**

 A short summary of the **plot-line.**

 Four or five **key scenes** which should deal with the following:

## The opening scene:

- Did it catch our attention?
- What questions does it raise?
- Where is it set?
- What characters are introduced?

## A scene suitable for staging:

- What era will you set it in?
- What type of set will you use?
- What costumes will the characters wear?
- How will you use lighting?
- Would music or sound effects be useful?

## A scene that tells us something important about an important character:

- What does the character say?
- What does the character do?
- How do other characters see him/her?
- What movements, gestures, tone of voice might an actor use when playing the character?

## A scene with conflict, tension or suspense:

- What is the source of the conflict?
- How is tension or suspense created?
- Describe the conflict.
- What is the outcome of the conflict?

## A climactic scene:

- What is the most exciting moment in the play?
- Why is it this scene, in your opinion?

## A scene that captures a major theme:

- Name a main theme in the play.
- Show how this scene explores that theme.

## The closing scene:

- Does this resolve the issues in the play?
- Are we left with questions?
- Is it the climactic scene?
- Were you satisfied with the ending?

*Remember a key scene can deal with more than one issue at a time! You should have at least two quotes for each key scene that you study.*

## The main characters:

- Describe your character at the **beginning** of the play.
- Outline how something **changes** or affects them during the play.
- Describe them at the **end** of the play.
- What was their **role** or dramatic purpose in the play (e.g. hero, villain)?

## Language:

- What does the language used tell us about **setting**?
- What does it say about the **characters** and the differences between them?
- Was it difficult or easy to understand? Did you like it?

# Poetry

In this chapter you will come across **poems**, on many topics including:

- Family and childhood
- Love
- War
- Death and grief
- Nature

You will learn how to identify **techniques** such as:

- Personification
- Assonance and alliteration
- Onomatopoeia

# Family and Childhood
## Poem from a Three Year Old
Brendan Kennelly

And will the flowers die?
And will the people die?

And every day do you grow old, do I
grow old, no I'm not old, do
flowers grow old?

Old things – do you throw them out?

Do you throw old people out?

And how you know a flower that's old?

The petals fall, the petals fall from flowers,
and do the petals fall from people too,
every day more petals fall until the
floor where I would like to play I
want to play is covered with old
flowers and people all the same
together lying there with petals fallen
on the dirty floor I want to play
the floor you come and sweep
with the huge broom.

The dirt you sweep, what happens that,
what happens all the dirt you sweep
from flowers and people, what
happens all the dirt? Is all the
dirt what's left of flowers and
people, all the dirt there in a
heap under the huge broom that
sweeps everything away?

Why you work so hard, why brush
and sweep to make a heap of dirt?
And who will bring new flowers?
And who will bring new people? Who will
bring new flowers to put in water
where no petals fall on to the
floor where I would like to
play? Who will bring new flowers
that will not hang their heads
like tired old people wanting sleep?
Who will bring new flowers that
do not split and shrivel every
day? And if we have new flowers,
will we have new people too to
keep the flowers alive and give
them water?

And will the new young flowers die?

And will the new young people die?

And why?

1. What is the child asking questions about?

2. Do you think the child understands what 'old' is?

3. Is there someone answering the child's questions? How do you know?

4. What does the child think dirt is?

5. Near the end of the poem, the child becomes worried about something. What is it?

6. How would you describe the tone of this poem? PQE

7. What connections does the child make between flowers and people? PQE

8. There is a simile in this poem, can you find and explain it? PQE

9. Even though this poem is written from the point of view of a three-year-old child, the reader can still see the attitude of the adult poet. How do you think the poet feels about the child he describes?

10. Does this poem remind you of any three year olds you know? Why?

When you talk to someone, you can change the meaning of what you say by changing your tone of voice. For example, you could say 'yes' in a happy tone, or 'yes' in a grumpy tone, letting your listener know how you are feeling. Poems also have a tone. This is the tone of voice of the poet or the speaker in the poem.

Try to remember things that really puzzled you when you were a small child. Write a paragraph describing these things.

**OR**

Imagine that you are babysitting the three-year-old child in the poem. Write out the conversation you have when you try to send him/her to bed.

**OR**

Write out the answers you would give to the questions in the poem.

# Truant

Phoebe Hesketh

*Sing a song of sunlight*
*My pocket's full of sky –*
*Starling's egg for April*
*Jay's feather for July.*
*And here's a thorn bush three bags full*
*Of drift-white wool.*

They call him dunce, and yet he can discern
Each mouse-brown bird,
And call its name and whistle back its call.
And spy among the fern
Delicate movement of a furred
Fugitive creature hiding from the day.
Discovered secrets magnify his play
Into a vocation.

Laughing at education
He knows where the redshank hides her nest, perceives
a red-patch tremble where a coot lays siege
To water territory.
Nothing escapes his eye:
A ladybird
Slides like a blood-drop down a spear of grass;
The sapphire sparkle of a dragon-fly
Redeems a waste of weeds.
Collecting acorns, telling the beads of the year
On yew tree berries, his mind's too full for
    speech.

Back in the classroom he can never find
Answers to dusty questions, yet he could
    teach,
Deeper than knowledge.
Geometry of twigs
Scratched on a sunlit wall;
History in stones,
Seasons told by the fields' calendar –
Living languages of Spring and Fall.

**DIVE IN!**

1. Do you know what a 'truant' is?

2. What is the song at the beginning of the poem about?

3. Who do you think calls the boy a dunce?

4. What special skills does the boy have?

5. Why do you think the boy laughs at education?

**TAKE THE PLUNGE!**

6. Re-read the opening song. It is a celebration of nature. What images can you find in the song to support this? **PQE**

7. There is an atmosphere of quiet and mystery created in the second verse. What words help to do this? **PQE**

8. What is the ladybird compared to in the third verse? Is this a good image? **PQE**

9. What are the 'beads of the year'? What comparison is being made here? **PQE**

10. How does the poet show that the world of nature is superior to the world of school in the final verse? Look closely at the language she uses. **PQE**

> When lots of words in a poem start with the same letter it is called alliteration. This gives a line a beat. In poetry this beat is called rhythm.

11. Can you find any examples of alliteration in this poem? What effect does it have? **PQE**

**WHY DON'T YOU...**

Write out the teacher's comments in a letter to this boy's parents, informing them that he has been skipping school.

**OR**

Pretend you are a cameraman filming the nature scenes described in this poem. Write the commentary which will be read out with your documentary.

**OR**

Read the following poem:

# Slow Reader

Allan Ahlberg

I – am – in – the – slow
read – ers – group – my – broth
er – is – in – the – foot
ball – team – my – sis – ter
is – a – ser – ver – my
lit – tle – broth – er – was
a – wise – man – in – the
in – fants – christ – mas – play
I – am – in – the – slow
read – ers – group – that – is
all – I – am – in – I
hate – it.

Do you remember learning to read? How does the rhythm of this poem help to make the memory more vivid? Can you see any connections between this poem and 'Truant'?

# Those Winter Sundays

Robert Hayden

Sundays too my father got up early
and put his clothes on in the blueblack cold,
then with cracked hands that ached
from labour in the weekday weather made
banked fires blaze. No one ever thanked him.

I'd wake and hear the cold splintering,
    breaking.
When the rooms were warm, he'd call,
and slowly I would rise and dress,
fearing the chronic angers of that house,

Speaking indifferently to him,
who had driven out the cold
and polished my good shoes as well.
What did I know, what did I know
of love's austere and lonely offices?

1. How does the poet show us that it is very cold?

2. Why does the father get up early?

3. When does the son get up?

4. Was the son grateful?

5. How does he feel *now* when he remembers this?

6. How do we know that the father has worked hard all week?

7. Do you think that he expected thanks?

8. Do you think this poem was written about recent times?

9. Why do you think the poem ends with a question?

10. Did this poem make you think about the things that your own parents do for you?

Write a letter from this boy, who is now grown up, to his father. What do you think he would say to him?

**OR**

Think about getting out of your bed on a cold winter's morning. Try to include sounds, smells, textures and tastes as well as what you see.

# Digging

Seamus Heaney

Between my finger and my thumb
The squat pen rests; snug as a gun.

Under my window, a clean rasping sound
When the spade sinks into gravelly
     ground:
My father, digging. I look down

Till his straining rump among the
     flowerbeds
Bends low, comes up twenty years away
Stooping in rhythm through potato drills
Where he was digging.

The coarse boot nestled on the lug, the shaft
Against the inside knee was levered firmly.
He rooted out the tall tops, buried the bright
edge deep
To scatter new potatoes that we picked
Loving their cool hardness in our hands.

The cold smell of potato mould, the squelch
and slap
Of soggy peat, the curt cuts of an edge
Through living roots awaken in my head.
But I've no spade to follow men like them.

By God, the old man could handle a spade.
Just like his old man.
My grandfather cut more turf in a day
Than any other man on Toner's bog.
Once I carried him milk in a bottle
Corked sloppily with paper. He straightened
up
To drink it, then fell to right away
Nicking and slicing neatly, heaving sods
Over his shoulder, going down and down
For the good turf. Digging.

Between my finger and thumb
The squat pen rests.
I'll dig with it.

**DIVE IN!**

1. What is in the poet's hand at the start of the poem?

2. Where is the poet and what is he looking at?

3. How do you know that he goes back in time in his memory?

4. What was the father digging 20 years ago?

5. How do you know that the poet is proud of his father?

6. What did the poet's grandfather dig?

7. Is the poet able to dig like his father and grandfather?

8. What decision does the poet reach at the very end of the poem?

A simile is a special kind of image. The poet creates a picture by comparing two things of different natures using the words 'like', 'as' or 'than'.

**TAKE THE PLUNGE!**

9. What comparison is made in the opening lines of the poem? **P Q E**

10. There are two types of 'digging' in this poem. Can you identify and explain them? **P Q E**

11. There are a number of sounds, smells and textures in this poem. Can you find them? How do they add to the descriptions? **P Q E**

12. Re-read the description of the grandfather digging turf. Make a note of the verbs used.

13. Do you think 'digging' is a good metaphor for writing poetry? Explain your answer.

**WHY DON'T YOU...**

Decide what you think is the main theme of the poem. It could be family, the craft of poetry writing, traditions or something else. Explain which theme you think is the strongest and say why.

**OR**

Try to remember a time when you were a child where you were given a job to do which you thought was very important, like Heaney bringing the milk to the men on the bog. Try to recapture your childish point of view and your fascination with the adults' work.

**TEST THE WATERS!**

From the poetry you have studied choose a poem which deals with either Youth or Old Age.

(a) What picture does this poem give of either youth or old age?

(b) What is your personal response to the picture of youth or old age given in this poem? Support your answer with reference to the poem.

2005 H.L. Paper

271

# Sport

# I'll stand the lot of you

Martin Hall

I'll stand the lot of you, I said
to the other kids. They said: Right!

I was Wolves 1957–58:
Finlayson; Stuart, Harris; Slater, Wright,
    Flowers;
Deeley, Broadbent, Murray, Mason, Mullen.
The other kids were Rest of the World:
Banks; Pele, Best; Best, Pele, Pele;
Best, Pele, Charlton, Pele, Best.
Jimmy Murray kicked off for Wolves.

Wolves were well on top in the opening
    minutes,
then Rest of the World broke away and
    scored
seven lucky goals. Wolves were in trouble!
But then tragedy struck Rest of the World:

Pele had to go and do their homework!
They were soon followed by Best and
    Charlton.
It was Wolves versus Banks!
Now Wolves were playing like a man
    possessed.
Soon they were all on level terms!
Seven-all, and only minutes to go,
when suddenly – sensation! Banks went off
to watch the Cup Final on television!
Seconds later, a pinpoint Mullen centre
found Peter Broadbent completely
    unmarked
in front of goal. What a chance!

He missed it,
And Wolves trooped sadly off
    toward their bike.

1. What challenge does the poet make at the start of the poem?

2. What team does the poet become?

3. Who are the other children's favourite players?

4. Why do you think 'Rest of the World' were able to score 'seven lucky goals'?

5. What happens to the 'Rest of the World' team?

6. Why is the end of the poem so funny?

7. How can you tell that the child is very familiar with football commentary? **PQE**

8. Do you think this child is very imaginative?

Pick your own ideal football team. Explain your choices. Make sure that you have suitably skilled players in each position.

**OR**

Remember back to when you were small. What were your favourite games? Try to write a description that captures the fun that you had.

**OR**

Imagine that a football commentator has come to comment on your class. Write the commentary that he/she would make on a typical day! Try to use the type of language and tone that a sports commentator would use.

In groups, prepare a freeze-frame from this poem.

A freeze-frame is like a scene from a film that has been paused. You are going to pretend that you are frozen in a moment in the poem. You decide which character each person in your group is playing. Remember to think about posture, gesture, expression and positions.

- Practise your moment.

- The teacher will call each group to the top of the classroom in turn.

- On the count of three you must freeze your moment and hold it still for 30 seconds.

- When the teacher points to you, you must explain who you are and what you are thinking at this moment in time.

For homework, pretend you are the director of this scene. Write out in full sentences how you would position the actors, what gestures and expressions they should use and what lighting, music or props they would need.

# New Season Ode

Thomas Keneally

We go to the cupboard,
   we take out club colours
and the air sings.

The season's close.
The pads are going on goalposts.
New lines are being marked,
Coaches hold heart-to-hearts
with old stars and new kids,
who might one day wear the best colours,
the green, the gold.
Our boys are running up sandhills.
Their legs pump,
'This season, this season, is our season'.
This year we all start equal.
Kids paint signs.
And I am seven again.
I know I will see heroes soon.
I feel the excitement.
I have hope in March,
and I might share the glory in September.

Blow that whistle ref!
Send that ball soaring!
Blow that whistle ref!

1. What preparations are being made for the new season?

2. What sport is the poet writing about?

3. The poet is Australian. Why does he call green and gold 'the best colours'?

4. How does the beginning of the season make the poet feel?

5. How does the poet make the ending exciting?

6. An **ode** is a poem of celebration. What is this poem celebrating?

7. How do you know that this season is being taken very seriously by everyone? **PQE**

8. Do you play sport? Did you like this poem?

Write your own 'New Season Ode' celebrating the beginning of one of your favourite pastimes. For example, debating, drama, athletics, GAA or anything else that gives you a sense of anticipation and excitement.

**OR**

Pretend that a new student has joined your class. Write out a clear set of instructions to help him/her learn a sport he/she is not familiar with. (See pages 160–161 in Chapter 2 for hints.)

**OR**

Pretend that you are the sports editor of the school magazine. Write an article about the school's victory or loss in an important sporting final.

Split into groups and read this poem out loud. Try to think of ways of capturing the mood of anticipation and excitement. You could:

- read a line each
- shout or whisper certain words or phrases
- read some words together and some words alone
- add sound effects.

*Try to capture the emotions in your voices.*

275

# Munster Final

Bernard O'Donoghue

*In memory of Tom Creedon, died 28 August 1983.*

The jarveys to the west side of the town
 Are robbers to a man, and if you tried
To drive through The Gap, they'd nearly strike you
With their whips. So we parked facing for home
And joined the long troop down the meadowsweet
And woodbine-scented road into the town.
By blue Killarney's lakes and glens to see
The white posts on the green! To be deafened
By the muzzy megaphone of Jimmy Shand
And the testy bray to keep the gangways clear.

As for Tom Creedon, I can see him still,
His back arching casually to field and clear.
'Glory Macroom! Good boy, Tom Creedon!'
We'd be back next year to try our luck in Cork.

We will be back next year, roaring ourselves
Hoarse, praying for better luck. After first Mass
We'll get there early; that's our only hope.
Keep clear of the carparks so we're not hemmed in,
And we'll be home, God willing, for the cows.

*Jarvey –*
someone who makes
a living by taking
tourists and visitors for
rides in a horse and
trap
*The Gap –*
The Gap of Dunloe

**DIVE IN!**

1. What might the jarveys do if you tried to drive through The Gap?

2. How do you know there is a large crowd going to the match?

3. Was Tom Creedon a good player?

4. Does the poet's team win the game?

5. What plans does the poet have for next year's match?

**TAKE THE PLUNGE!**

6. What do you think this poet does for a living? **PQE**

7. Look at the description of the setting in the first verse. What can you smell, see and hear that make this description more vivid?

8. Can you find any examples of alliteration?

9. The poet is obviously a religious person. How do you know this? **PQE**

**WHY DON'T YOU...**

Write a description of your experience of a GAA provincial final, if you have attended one. If not, write a description of some big event that you have attended. Try to capture the planning before the event, the feeling of the crowds and the emotions during and after the event.

**OR**

Think about the sports star, living or dead, that you admire most. Briefly outline his or her sporting achievements and why you find this person so inspirational.

**THRASH IT OUT!**

In groups, compose a chant for your school's sports teams, to be sung at matches. When you are ready perform it for the class.

**TEST THE WATERS!**

Choose any poem you have studied which you feel deserves a prize.

- Name the poem and poet.
- Describe what the poem is about.
- Say why you think it deserves a prize.

2004 O.L. Paper

# People
# Old Man

Jessica Siegal

Old man, once sturdy as a mountain
Now fragile as a twig.
It is many years and many storms till a mountain is worn
But a twig can suddenly go snap

Old man, whose white beard is tangled like a net
Meshed and tangled is he
Tangled like old yarn
But yarn can be snagged.

Old man, whose face is gnarled like an old tree
Gnarled and cracked his face is
Like a rotted tree stump
But a rotted tree stump can crumble to dust.

Old man, how many snaps can you withstand?
How much more snapping?
How long will this go on?
Before you too crumble into dust?

1. How has the old man changed since he was young?

2. What is the poet worried will happen to the old man?

3. Do you think the old man has had a hard life?

4. The old man is compared to a mountain and a twig in the first verse. What contrast is being created here? PQE

5. What imagery tells you that the old man is untidy? PQE

6. What do the adjectives in the third verse tell you about the old man? PQE

7. How is tension created in the final verse? PQE

8. How do you think the poet feels about the old man? PQE

Think of five questions you would like to ask the old man about his life. Write them out in the form of a poem.

**OR**

Interview an older person in your life. Maybe you could choose a grandparent, or a neighbour? Ask them about some of the following topics:

- School
- Pastimes
- Family
- Home
- Technology
- Work

Write a short essay on the differences between your life and the older person's life.

# The Slimming Poem

*Pam Ayres*

I'm a slimmer by trade, I'm frequently weighed,
I'm slim as a reed in the river.
I'm slender and lean, and hungry and mean.
Have some water, it's good for your liver.

Don't give me cheese rolls or profiteroles
Don't show me that jelly a shakin',
Don't give me cream crackers you picnic and snackers
Or great big ice-creams with a flake in.
Don't give me swiss roll or toad-in-the-hole
Don't show me that Black Forest gateau.

You sit and go mouldy you old garibaldi
You pastry all riddled with fat. Oh!
No, it's white fish for me, no milk in me tea
And if we don't like it we lump it.
No figs or sultanas, no mashed-up bananas
No pleasure and no buttered crumpet.

So don't get any bigger, me old pear-shaped figure
I can and I will become thinner.
So cheer up and take heart, pass the calorie chart,
Let's see what we're having for dinner!

1. Who is speaking in this poem?

2. Do you think he or she really hates food?

3. What does the speaker feel like when he/she thinks that he/she is fat?

4. Of all the foods mentioned in this poem, which would you find hardest to resist?

5. In this poem every second line rhymes. Give some examples. Do you think this makes the poem funnier?

6. Look at the simile in the second line. What quality of the reed does the slimmer compare herself to?

7. What words in the fourth verse might make a person feel either good or bad about themselves? **P Q E**

8. Do you think the person in this poem is happy and confident? **P Q E**

Pretend you live with this person. Write out the conversation you have after you've been served yet another tasteless dinner.

**OR**

Write a typical menu for one of your family's favourite meals.

# Phenomenal Woman

Maya Angelou

Pretty women wonder where my
secret lies.
I'm not cute or built to suit a
fashion model's size
But when I start to tell them,

They think I'm telling lies.
I say,
It's in the reach of my arms,
The span of my hips,
The stride of my step,
The curl of my lips.
I'm a woman
Phenomenally.
Phenomenal woman,
That's me.

I walk into a room
Just as cool as you please,
And to a man,
The fellows stand or
Fall down on their knees.
Then they swarm around me,
A hive of honey bees.
I say,
It's in the fire of my eyes,
And the flash of my teeth,
The swing in my waist,
And the joy in my feet.
I'm a woman
Phenomenally.
Phenomenal woman,
That's me.

Men themselves have
wondered
What they see in me.
They try so much
But they can't touch
My inner mystery.
When I try to show them
They say they still can't see.
I say,
It's in the arch of my back,
The sun of my smile,
The ride of my breasts,
The grace of my style.
I'm a woman
Phenomenally
Phenomenal woman,
That's me.

Now you understand
Just why my head's not bowed.
I don't shout or jump about
Or have to talk real loud.
When you see me passing
It ought to make you proud.
I say,
It's in the click of my heels,
The bend of my hair,
The palm of my hand,
The need of my care,
'Cause I'm a woman
Phenomenally.
Phenomenal woman,
That's me.

**DIVE IN!**

1. What do pretty women want to know about the phenomenal woman?

2. How do men react to her?

3. What do men wonder about her?

4. What has the poet tried to make 'you understand' in this poem?

**TAKE THE PLUNGE!**

5. What sort of woman is this? **PQE**

6. Do you think she is conventionally beautiful? **PQE**

7. Look at the way this poem is laid out on the page. Also notice the punctuation. How do these contribute to the rhythm? **PQE**

8. What do you think the woman's 'inner mystery' is? **PQE**

9. In what tone of voice should this poem be read?

> The theme of a poem is the main topic or issue of a poem. Just ask yourself, what is the poem really about? What message is the poem trying to give me?

10. What do you think Maya Angelou's message is in this poem?

**WHY DON'T YOU...**

Pretend that the 'Phenomenal Woman' is an agony aunt that the slimmer in 'The Slimming Poem' has written to. What reply will she send?

**OR**

Contrast the speaker in this poem to the speaker in 'The Slimming Poem'. Which person would you rather meet and why?

**THRASH IT OUT!**

In groups, prepare a rap and a walk to this poem. Think about beats that you could add to the poem – maybe by clicking your fingers or tapping the desk. Get one person to walk across the room while you are doing your rap – he or she must capture the confidence of the 'Phenomenal Woman'.

**TEST THE WATERS!**

Choose any poem you have studied which created vivid images of a person in your mind.

(a) Describe what images of the person come to mind from your chosen poem.

(b) Write about how two of these images contribute to your understanding of the person in the poem.

2008 H.L. Paper

**OR**

*'Poetry can tell us what human beings are.'* – Maya Angelou

(a) Select a poem you have studied which deals with a human being. Outline the picture you get of this person from the poem.

(b) How has the poet created this picture? Support your answer by reference to or quotation from the poem you have studied.

2003 H.L. Paper

283

# Bloody Men

Wendy Cope

Bloody men are like bloody buses –
You wait for about a year
And as soon as one approaches your stop
Two or three others appear.

You look at them flashing their indicators,
Offering you a ride.
You're trying to read the destinations,
You haven't much time to decide.
If you make a mistake, there is no turning
  back.
Jump off, and you'll stand there and gaze
While the cars and the taxis and lorries go by
And the minutes, the hours, the days.

1. What are men compared to in this poem?

2. In the first verse how are men like buses?

3. Why don't you have 'much time to decide'?

4. Do you really wait for 'about a year' for buses? Or could the poet be talking about something else?

5. Draw two columns and list the ways in which men and buses are the same.

6. It is scary getting off a bus when you don't know where you are. Why is it scary leaving a relationship? **P Q E**

7. Is Wendy Cope being funny all the time in this poem or is there a slightly serious message? **P Q E**

Write a poem with the title *'Bloody … are like bloody …'* using two of the following ideas, or any other ideas you have:

- *Children*  · *Animals*  · *Exams*
- *Storms*  · *Discos*  · *Parents*
- *Girlfriends*  · *Porches*  · *Swimming pools*

**OR**

Describe a typical bus journey that you make.

**OR**

Write a letter of complaint to a bus company about its poor service, lack of timekeeping and generally low standards.

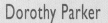

# Symptom Recital

Dorothy Parker

I do not like my state of mind;
I'm bitter, querulous, unkind.
I hate my legs, I hate my hands,
I do not yearn for lovelier lands.
I dread the dawn's recurrent light;
I hate to go to bed at night.
I snoot at simple, earnest folk.
I cannot take the simplest joke.
I find no peace in paint or type.
My world is but a lot of tripe.
I'm disillusioned, empty-breasted.
For what I think, I'd be arrested.
I am not sick, I am not well.
My quondam dreams are shot to hell.
My soul is crushed, my spirit sore;
I do not like me any more.
I cavil, quarrel, grumble, grouse.
I ponder on the narrow house.
I shudder at the thought of men.
I'm due to fall in love again.

*quondam —*
former

1. How can you tell that this person is not very happy?

2. Which line did you think was the most negative?

3. Were you surprised at the ending?

4. This poem is called 'Symptom Recital'. What is the poet showing symptoms of? **P Q E**

5. How does the rhyme add to the humour? Use examples to back up your answer.

6. Do you think the poet wants to fall in love again?

Imagine that the poet has now fallen in love. Write her new 'Symptom Recital'.

**OR**

Pretend that you have just spent 30 minutes on the phone with this poet. Write out some of the conversation that you imagine you have had. You don't have to be sympathetic!

# Calypso

W.H. Auden

Dríver drive faster and make a good rún
Down the Springfield Line under the shíning sún.

Fly like an aéroplane, dón't pull up short
Till you brake for Grand Céntral Státion, New Yórk.

For thére in the míddle of that waiting-háll
Should be stánding the óne that Í love best of áll.

If he's nót there to méet me when Í get to town,
I'll stánd on the síde-walk with téars rolling dówn.

For hé is the óne that I love to look ón,
The ácme of kindness and pérfectión.

He présses my hánd and he sáys he loves mé,
Which I fínd an admiráble pecúliarity.

The wóods are bright gréen on both sídes of the líne;
The trées have their lóves though they're dífferent from míne.

But the póor fat old bánker in the sún-parlour cár
Has nó one to lóve him excépt his cigár.

If Í were the Héad of the Chúrch or the Státe,
I'd pówder my nóse and just téll them to wáit.

For lóve's more impórtant and pówerful thán
Even a príest or a póliticián.

1.  Split into groups and read 'Calypso' out loud. Try to think of ways of emphasising the beat. Watch the words with the accents over them. These must be stressed.
    You could:

    - Read a line each.
    - Shout certain words or phrases.
    - Read some words together and some words alone.
    - Add sound effects.

2.  Why is the poet in a hurry.

3.  How will the speaker react if the loved one is not there?

4.  Who does the poet feel sorry for?

Think about how the poet is filled with a sense of anticipation as he/she waits for his/her train to get to Grand Central Station. Can you describe a time when you were waiting for something important to happen in your life?

**OR**

Write a short story entitled 'Waiting at the Station'.

**OR**

Bring a song into class that you think has a really good rhythm or beat to it. Lots of rap and R&B music is good for this.

The beat of a poem is called the rhythm.

5.  A 'Calypso' is a type of Caribbean song with a strong rhythm. How does this match the mood of the poem?

6.  The poet is travelling on a train. Why do you think it is useful to know this?

7.  How can you tell that the poet is very much in love?

8.  What does this poem claim about love?

# He wishes for the cloths of heaven

W.B. Yeats

Had I the heavens' embroidered cloths.
Enwrought with golden and silver light,
The blue and the dim and the dark cloths
Of night and light and the half-light,
I would spread the cloths under your feet:
But I, being poor, have only my dreams;
I have spread my dreams under your feet;
Tread softly because you tread on my dreams.

**DIVE IN!**

1. What is the most precious item that you own?

2. Valentine's Day is when people in love exchange gifts. What are the most traditional gifts?

3. What gift would the poet offer his loved one if he had it?

**TAKE THE PLUNGE!**

4. What do you think the 'heavens' embroidered cloths' might be?

5. When is the sky golden? When is it silver?

6. There are three different 'cloths' mentioned in the third and fourth lines. List them and their colours or shades.

7. Up to this point in the poem the poet has been comparing different types of sky to different types of cloth. This is a metaphor. In the last three lines of the poem he compares the cloths to something else. What does he compare them to?

8. What is he really offering this lady?

9. How do you think the poet is feeling in the last line of the poem? Is he confident? **P Q E**

10. Do you think she will accept his offer?

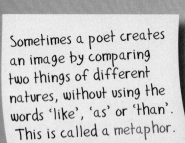

Sometimes a poet creates an image by comparing two things of different natures, without using the words 'like', 'as' or 'than'. This is called a metaphor.

Look out the window at the sky today. If you can't see out of a window imagine a sky. What kind of cloth is the sky today? If the sky could be any type of cloth, what type would you choose?

**OR**

Dreams are often seen as being fragile and delicate. Yeats compares them to cloths as cloths are easily damaged or torn and so are dreams. Can you think of other things that you could compare dreams to? Explain briefly why you chose each object.

**OR**

Imagine that you are the person who has received the poem. Write the letter you are sending in reply. Will you accept or reject the offer?

W.B. Yeats fell madly in love with a woman named Maud Gonne. The only problem was that she didn't love him back. This is called unrequited love. In 'He wishes for the cloths of heaven', Yeats offered Maud Gonne his love. In 'When you are old', we find out what happened.

# When you are old

W.B. Yeats

When you are old and grey and full of sleep,
And nodding by the fire, take down this book,
And slowly read, and dream of the soft look
Your eyes had once, and of their shadows deep;

How many loved your moments of glad grace,
And loved your beauty with love false or true,
But one man loved the pilgrim soul in you,
And loved the sorrows of your changing face;

And bending down beside the glowing bars,
Murmur, a little sadly, how Love fled
And paced upon the mountains overhead
And hid his face among a crowd of stars.

1. Have you ever thought about what it will be like to be old? Do you like the thought of being old?

2. Think of five advantages of being old. Now think of five disadvantages.

3. The poet is imagining what will happen in the future. How do we know this?

4. What words in the first verse tell you that Yeats is describing an older Maud Gonne?

5. What will she be thinking and dreaming about according to Yeats? **P Q E**

6. In the second verse, what does Yeats say other people love about Maud Gonne? **P Q E**

7. What does he love about her? How is his love better than the love of others?

8. How do we know that Yeats is telling Maud Gonne that she will regret rejecting him? **P Q E**

9. How do you know that Yeats is hurt? **P Q E**

10. Who do you feel sorry for?

Pick a song about unrequited love. Bring in the song and explain the singer's or the writer's attitude based on the lyrics. Make sure you write this out as a proper paragraph with points, quotes and explanations.

**OR**

Re-write this poem as though it were a celebration of her acceptance of his love. Begin *When we are old and grey and full of sleep …*

# Poem

Ted Kooser

Get your tongue
out
of my mouth;
I'm kissing you
goodbye.

# Shall I Compare Thee

### William Shakespeare

Shall I compare thee to a summer's day?

Thou art more lovely and more temperate:

Rough winds do shake the darling buds of May,

And summer's lease hath all too short a date:

Sometime too hot the eye of heaven shines,

And often is his gold complexion dimmed;

And every fair from fair sometime declines,

By chance, or nature's changing course untrimmed.

But thy eternal summer shall not fade,

Nor lose possession of that fair thou ow'st,

Nor shall death brag thou wander'st in his shade,

When in eternal lines to time thou grow'st;

    So long as men can breathe, or eyes can see,

    So long lives this, and this gives life to thee.

# Take the Plunge!

1. In the first two lines the poet asks a question and then answers it. Explain this question and answer in your own words.

2. Why is May not perfect?

3. How does Shakespeare personify the sun?

4. Read the line 'And every fair from fair sometime declines'. Fair is another word for beauty. What do you think the poet is saying here?

5. Shakespeare boasts that his love's beauty 'shall not fade'. How can he make such a boast?

Imagine you have received this poem from an admirer. How does it make you feel?

**OR**

Write your own poem entitled 'Shall I compare thee …' using any comparison you like. Here are some suggestions!

- A Meath jersey
- A 99 cone
- A jaguar
- A red hot volcano
- A winter's morning
- A work of art
- A cuddly teddy bear
- A meteor
- A crashing wave
- A flying kite

**OR**

Write an introduction for this poem that you would use if you were editing an anthology of poetry for young people.

A sonnet is a poem of fourteen lines which is supposed to obey certain rules. A Shakespearean sonnet is divided into three quatrains (four lines of verse) and a rhyming couplet (two lines). Each quatrain develops an idea and the rhyming couplet sums up the poem.

6. What two imperfections of summer are mentioned in the first quatrain?

7. A lease is a legal agreement to use something for a specific amount of time. How can 'summer' have a 'lease'?

8. What is the sun compared to in the second quatrain? Why is this an appropriate image when dealing with beauty?

9. The third quatrain begins with 'But'. How does this indicate a change in Shakespeare's argument?

10. What do you think of the claim made in the rhyming couplet? What tone of voice do you think these lines should be read in?

11. Look at the words at the end of each line. Can you find any words that rhyme? Is there a pattern?

Shakespearean sonnets have a set rhyming scheme. It is generally abab cdcd efef gg. Look again at 'Shall I Compare Thee'. Can you see this rhyming scheme in the poem?

12. This poem is not just about admiration of a loved one. There are other messages. Could you suggest any of them?

# The Thickness of Ice

Liz Loxley

At first we'll meet as friends
(Though secretly I'll be hoping
We'll become much more
And hoping that you're hoping that too).

At first we'll be like skaters
Testing the thickness of ice
(With each meeting
We'll skate nearer the centre of the lake).

Later we will become less anxious to
   impress,
Less eager than the skater going for gold,
(The triple jumps and spins
Will become an old routine:
We will be content with simple
   movements).

Later we will notice the steady thaw,
The creeping cracks will be ignored,
(And one day when the ice gives way
We will scramble to save ourselves
And not each other).

Last of all we'll meet as acquaintances
(Though secretly we will be enemies,
Hurt by missing out on a medal,
Jealous of new partners).

Last of all we'll be like children
Having learnt the thinness of ice,
(Though secretly, perhaps, we may be
   hoping
To break the ice between us
And maybe meet again as friends).

1. What is the poet hoping in the first verse?

2. How do you know that they are both a little bit scared in the second verse?

3. What tells you that the couple are becoming more comfortable with each other?

4. Which lines prove that they don't love each other anymore?

5. What does the word 'acquaintances' suggest in the second last verse? How are they feeling secretly?

6. What has to happen if they can meet again as friends?

7. The poet compares the couple to a pair of figure skaters. What is the first stage in their relationship?

8. Why do they need 'thick ice' at this stage?

9. What do they do at first to impress each other and how does this change?

10. What do the 'creeping cracks' in the ice represent in the fourth verse?

11. How is the image of competitive skaters used to show their pain at the end of the poem?

12. At the beginning of this poem, the thickness of ice supported the relationship. By the end of the poem, the ice is doing something completely different. What is this?

Say whether you think this poem accurately reflects the stages of a relationship. What do you think is the best stage of a relationship?

**OR**

Write a short story about the relationship described in the poem.

**OR**

Look at the lines

*Last of all we'll meet as acquaintances,*
*(Though secretly we will be enemies,*

Write out the extremely polite dialogue that might take place during a chance meeting between two enemies who have to pretend to be friendly. How will you convey the hatred between them if they can't be openly hostile? Your dialogue could be acted out for the class.

Poets often use symbols to represent an idea or a concept, for example, a dove represents peace. In the beginning of this poem, ice symbolises the strength of the love between the two people. However, by the end of the poem it has come to represent a barrier between them. The poet has cleverly changed the meaning of the symbol during the poem.

From the poetry you have studied, choose a poem which made you feel either happy or sad. Explain how the poem had this effect on you.

1995 O.L. Paper

*OR*

Being in love has always inspired men and women to express their feelings in verse.

Select a love poem you have studied.

(a) Describe what happens in this poem.

(b) How does the lover express her/his feelings?

(c) Would you like to have this poem written for you for St Valentine's Day? Give reasons for your answer.

2004 H.L. Paper

*OR*

Take any poem you have studied which deals with wishes *or* thoughts.

(a) What are the poet's main wishes OR thoughts in the poem?

(b) Describe how *either* the imagery *or* the language of the poem contributes to the poet's expression of his/her thoughts or wishes. Explain your answer with reference to the poem.

2006 H.L. Paper

# Late Fragment

Raymond Carver

And did you get what
you wanted from this life, even so?
I did.
And what did you want?
To call myself beloved, to feel myself
beloved on the earth.

# War and Violence

*The first three poems in this section are all set during World War I and capture the attitudes of soldiers who fought in that conflict.*

**WHY DON'T YOU...** Try reading this poem out loud in the 'poshest' accent you can do.

## Base Details*

Siegfried Sassoon

If I were fierce, and bald, and short of breath,
   I'd live with scarlet Majors at the Base,
And speed glum heroes up the line to death.
   You'd see me with my puffy petulant face,
Guzzling and gulping in the best hotel,
   Reading the Roll of Honour. 'Poor young chap,'
I'd say – 'I used to know his father well;
   Yes, we've lost heavily in this last scrap.'
And when the war is done and youth stone dead,
I'd toddle safely home and die – in bed.

\* During World War I the standard military tactic was for the senior officers to remain back at base while the ordinary soldiers were sent to do the actual fighting in the trenches. It was thought that the officers were too valuable to risk.

1. What sort of person do you picture as a Major after reading this poem? Draw a little caricature of the character.

A caricature is an exaggerated, cartoonish portrait of a person, usually emphasising their worst points.

Write the letter that you think the Major might have sent to the young chap's father reporting his death.

**OR**

Does anything really get on your nerves? Why not write a paragraph or two giving the 'base details' of this annoyance?

**OR**

Write a poem about a political leader whose actions you disagree with. Try to caricature the leader, imitating Siegfried Sassoon.

2. Is the speaker in the poem actually a Major?

3. What do you think the speaker's attitude is towards the officers? PQE

4. How does the poet describe the ordinary soldiers being sent to the front line? PQE

5. Find an example of alliteration in the poem. What effect does this have?

6. What do you think of the Major's reaction to the death of the soldier? PQE

7. What tone of voice is the poet using in the last two lines of the poem? PQE

A pun is a play on words with the same sounds but different meanings.

8. Can you suggest how the title 'Base Details' might be a pun? Does the word 'base' have more than one meaning?

*Brian Cowen*

*Barack Obama*

# Dulce et Decorum Est

Wilfred Owen

ent double, like old beggars under sacks,
Knock-kneed, coughing like hags, we cursed through sludge,
Till on the haunting flares we turned our backs,
And towards our distant rest began to trudge.
Men marched asleep. Many had lost their boots
But limped on, blood-shod. All went lame; all blind;
Drunk with fatigue; deaf even to the hoots
Of tired, outstripped Five-Nines* that dropped behind.

Gas! Gas! Quick, boys! – An ecstasy of fumbling,
Fitting the clumsy helmets just in time;
But someone still was yelling out and stumbling,
And flound'ring like a man in fire or lime …
Dim, through the misty panes and thick green light,
As under a green sea, I saw him drowning.
In all my dreams, before my helpless sight,
He plunges at me, guttering, choking, drowning.

If in some smothering dreams, you too could pace
Behind the wagon that we flung him in,
And watch the white eyes writhing in his face,
His hanging head, like a devil's sick of sin;
If you could hear, at every jolt, the blood
Come gargling from the froth-corrupted lungs,
Obscene as cancer, bitter as the cud
Of vile, incurable sores on innocent tongues, –
My friend, you would not tell with such high zest
To children ardent for some desperate glory,
The old Lie: *Dulce et decorum est*
*Pro patria mori.**

*Five-Nines –*
the calibre of shell used by the enemy which made a distinctive whistling noise as it fell through the air.

* *Dulce et decorum est pro patria mori –* it is sweet and proper to die for the fatherland. (From 'Odes' III (ii), by Horace)

1. In groups of five or more, prepare a freeze-frame of the first verse of this poem.

2. Take notes on the other groups as they perform their freeze-frames. What do you notice?

3. Pick out individual soldiers in the different freeze-frames that can be described with some of the adjectives in the first verse, for example, 'bent double', 'knock-kneed'.

During World War I it was considered deeply unpatriotic to criticise the war effort. However, more and more of the men at the front were beginning to question what was happening as millions of men were slaughtered. Wilfred Owen's poem was extremely shocking and revolutionary when it was first printed. Do you think it is an effective protest against the war? How does he try to convince his readers that war is wrong and futile?

**OR**

How would you protest against a war if all criticisms were censored by the media? Are there any conflicts today which you feel are unjustified? Write a brief paragraph about this topic.

**OR**

Look again at the second verse. See if you can find a piece of music that matches the atmosphere of that moment. Bring it in and play it for the class, explaining your choice.

4. The soldiers in the first verse are returning from front-line action in World War I. How do you know they are exhausted? **P** **Q** **E**

5. In the first two lines the soldiers are compared to two different kinds of people. Who are they and why are the comparisons effective?

6. Why are the men marching 'blood-shod'?

7. Using your own words, describe the state the men are in at the end of this verse.

8. What is the effect of the exclamation marks at the start of the second verse?

9. What do you think happens in the second verse?

10. List all the verbs in this verse. What do you notice about them?

11. Who is the poet talking to in the third verse? What is his attitude towards the listener? **P** **Q** **E**

12. In your opinion, what was the most visceral part of the description of the man's death?

13. Why is *'Dulce et decorum est pro patria mori'* an old lie?

*This poem is about Robert Gregory, the son of one of W.B. Yeats's great friends, Lady Gregory. Robert Gregory died while flying a plane in World War I.*

# An Irish Airman Foresees His Death

W.B. Yeats

I know that I shall meet my fate
Somewhere among the clouds above;
Those that I fight I do not hate,
Those that I guard I do not love;
My country is Kiltartan Cross,
My countrymen Kiltartan's poor,
No likely end could bring them loss
Or leave them happier than before.
Nor law, nor duty bade me fight,
Nor public men, nor cheering crowds,
A lonely impulse of delight
Drove to this tumult in the clouds;
I balanced all, brought all to mind,
The years to come seemed waste of breath,
A waste of breath the years behind
In balance with this life, this death.

**DIVE IN!**

1. Have you ever flown in a plane? If you have, can you remember how you felt the first time? If you haven't, would you like to? Give reasons for your answer.

2. Do you think the pilot in the poem is a typical soldier? Why or why not?

**TAKE THE PLUNGE!**

3. What do you think the pilot expects to happen to him? Look closely at the first two lines.

4. How does the pilot feel about the people in the war? PQE

5. The Gregory family were from Kiltartan in Co. Sligo. How do you know this place was important to them?

6. Since he was an Irishman, Robert Gregory would not have been conscripted to fight in World War I. What line tells us this?

7. Why does he suggest that he joined the air force? PQE

8. How does the pilot feel about flying? PQE

9. What does the pilot feel about his future and growing old? PQE

10. Choose some examples of rhyme and describe how they add to the poem. PQE

**WHY DON'T YOU...**

Have you ever stood at the edge of a cliff and wondered what it would be like to jump off? Why are we sometimes tempted to do very dangerous or reckless things? Make a list of extreme sports. Are there any you would like to do? Why?

**OR**

Imagine that you own an extreme sports tour company. Prepare the insurance form that you will ask your clients to sign before they take part in the activities you have organised. This must protect you from being sued if anyone is seriously injured or killed, as well as inform your clients of the risks involved.

**OR**

Think of an activity that makes you feel as if you were flying. Write a brief four-line poem describing the sensation.

**TEST THE WATERS!**

Choose a poem which describes:
- An event **OR**
- A place **OR**
- A person

How does the poet describe the event, or the place, or the person.

Did you like the poem? Give a reason for your answer.        2001 O.L. Paper

**OR**

Poems deal with many interesting themes.

- Select a poem you have studied.
- Outline a theme you found interesting.
- Would you consider the theme to be relevant to your own life and/or to the world around you? Explain your answer with reference to the poem.

*The following two poems recreate moments of horrendous violence from opposing viewpoints.*

# The Black and Tans* Deliver her Cousin's Son

Catherine Byron

*Galway 1921*

'Didn't she step out into the yard
      God love her
and see her own son's brains
scattered like mash about the flags?
And didn't she then kneel down
and gather the soggy shards
of her womb's child into her apron
carefully, as a girl gathers
mushrooms in the September fields?
And didn't she then stifle
the outbreath of her grieving
till only a whistle
or whimper of her lamentation
was heard in that place lest
the soldiers note her the more?'

\* In the 1920s, Ireland fought a war of Independence against England. In an attempt to control the country the English government created a new armed police force. They were nicknamed the 'Black and Tans' after the colour of their uniform. They were renowned for their vicious and brutal methods.

1. What struck you first about this poem?

2. What words or images shocked you?

3. Have you ever read another poem about violence in Ireland?

Write the report that the leader of the Black and Tan division would send to his superiors describing this event.

**OR**

Re-write this event as a short scene from a play or a short story.

4. Who is speaking in the poem? How do you know someone is speaking?

5. How do you think the speaker feels about the events he/she is describing? **PQE**

6. The language used in this poem lets you know that the speaker is Irish. Can you find any examples of this?

7. The poet uses very visceral imagery. What image do you find most violent? **PQE**

8. The poet conveys the tenderness the woman feels for her son by comparing her actions to what?

9. How do you know the woman is afraid? **PQE**

10. How did this poem make you feel?

# The One Twenty Pub

Wislawa Szymborska

The bomb is primed to go off at one twenty.
A time-check: one sixteen.
There's still a chance for some to join
the pub's ranks, for others to drop out.

The terrorist watches from across the street.
Distance will shield him
from the impact of what he sees:

A woman, turquoise jacket on her shoulder
enters; a man with sunglasses departs.
Youths in tee-shirts loiter without intent.

One seventeen and four seconds.
The scrawny motorcyclist, revving up
to leave, won't believe his luck;
but the tall man steps straight in.

One seventeen and forty seconds.
That girl, over there with the walkman
 – now the bus has cut her off.
One eighteen exactly.
Was she stupid enough to head inside?
Or wasn't she? We'll know before long,
when the dead are carried out.

It's one nineteen.
Nothing much to report
until a muddled barfly* hesitates,
fumbles with pockets, and, like
a blasted fool, stumbles back
at one nineteen and fifty seconds
to retrieve his goddamn cap.
One twenty
How time drags when …
Any moment now.
Not yet.
Yes.
        Yes,
                there
                        it
                                goes.

* *barfly* –
slang for an alcoholic

*(version from the Polish
by Dennis O'Driscoll)*

**DIVE IN!**

1. Can you name any terrorist atrocities that have happened during your lifetime?

2. How did you react when you heard about them?

**TAKE THE PLUNGE!**

3. In the first verse we find out the meaning of the poem's title. What is it?

4. What do you think of the lines:

   *There's still a chance for some to join*

   *the pub's ranks, for others to drop out.*

5. Who is watching the pub, and why?

6. How does he feel about what he is seeing?

7. In the third verse, why does the poet describe all the people to us?

8. In the fifth verse, what is the terrorist's attitude to the girl with the walkman? **P Q E**

9. What is ironic about the barfly's actions?

10. How does the shape of the last verse contribute to the sense of anticipation? **P Q E**

11. Were you surprised that this poem was written by someone from Poland? Where do you think of when you hear the word 'terrorism'?

12. Who do you have sympathy for in the poem, and why?

**WHY DON'T YOU...**

Imagine that it is the day after the bomb exploded in the pub.

● Put an empty chair at the top of the class. This is now the hot seat.

● When a person sits in the hot seat he or she becomes a character from the poem.

● The teacher will select people to sit in the hot seat.

● Write the questions you would like to put to the following people:

   (a) The terrorist

   (b) The woman with the turquoise jacket

   (c) The man with the sunglasses

   (d) One of the youths

   (e) The scrawny motorcyclist

   (f) The girl with the walkman

   (g) The barfly

Take it in turns to ask the person in the hot seat your questions.

Afterwards, write a brief description of one character based on his/her answers.

305

*Soldiers react in different ways to the choices that they face during war. In the next two poems we see two very different reactions to a similar situation.*

# Happy Days with the Sendero Luminoso

Gerry Murphy

Not wanting to alienate the villagers
    we approached the village elder
and asked, *very* politely
if we could spend a few days
recuperating in his village
after our latest battle
with the fascist government thugs.
He answered, that however much
he supported our heroic struggle, and there was
    nobody
who supported it more than he, nevertheless
he had to consider the welfare of the villagers
and could not be seen to take sides,
since the army would inevitably learn of our stay,
come and shoot him and destroy his village.
We could only interpret this as a lack of
    revolutionary
fervour amongst the peasantry and further evidence
of a growing apathy towards the struggle.

So we shot him and destroyed his village.

1. When you read the title of this poem what did you expect it to be about?

2. How did the last line of this poem make you feel?

3. Where do you think this poem is set?

Irony occurs when people say things that can be taken at face value, but may also have a second and contradictory level of meaning.

The atmosphere of a poem is linked to the setting of the poem. Where the poem is taking place can influence our feelings.

Imagine you are a foreign journalist who is in the area when this village is destroyed. Write the newspaper article that you will send to your editor outlining the facts and details of this atrocity.

**OR**

Think about the saying: 'When elephants fight, it's the grass that gets trampled.' Is this an accurate description of what happens to the people of this village? Can you think of any other place in the world today where this might also apply? Write out your thoughts.

4. What is the attitude of the speaker to the villagers in the first few lines? **PQE**

5. Why does this group of soldiers need to rest?

6. How does the village elder respond to the soldiers' request? **PQE**

7. What is the village elder afraid of?

8. Why do the soldiers kill him and the villagers?

9. Where does the attitude of the speaker towards the villagers change? **PQE**

10. What is the tone of this poem at the beginning and at the end?

# Conquerors

Henry Treece

By sundown we came to a hidden village
Where all the air was still
And no sound met our tired ears, save
For the sorry drip of rain from blackened trees
And the melancholy song of swinging gates.
Then through a broken pane some of us saw
A dead bird in a rusting cage, still
Pressing his thin tattered breast against the bars,
His beak wide open. And
As we hurried through the weed-grown street,
A gaunt dog started up from some dark place
And shambled off on legs as thin as sticks
Into the wood, to die at least in peace.
No one had told us victory was like this;
Not one amongst us would have eaten bread
Before he'd filled the mouth of the grey child
That sprawled, stiff as stone, before the shattered door.
There was not one who did not think of home.

1. When you read the title of this poem what did you expect it to be about?

2. How did the last line of this poem make you feel?

3. Where do you think this poem is set?

4. There is a very distinct atmosphere at the beginning of this poem. How would you describe it?

5. What are the only sounds that are mentioned as the soldiers enter the village? What sounds do you think are missing?

6. What do you think the bird in the cage symbolises?

7. In your opinion, why are the men hurrying?

8. Look carefully at the description of the dog. What words catch your attention?

9. How do the 'conquerors' feel about their victory? PQE

10. Why do they 'think of home'?

11. Look at the poet's use of alliteration in his description of the deserted village. Pick two examples of alliteration and explain how they add to the atmosphere of the poem. PQE

Think about the soldiers in 'Happy Days with the Sendero Luminoso' and compare their attitude to the attitude of those in 'Conquerors'. What are the differences between the two groups of soldiers?

**OR**

In groups, discuss the irony present in both of these poems. Draw up a number of points to illustrate how the irony works. Present your findings to the class and write a paragraph on irony in both poems for homework.

**OR**

Write the diary entry of one of the soldiers from 'Conquerors' as he recorded it in his journal the night after visiting the village.

*The next three poems deal with the aftermath of war. Read the poem below in silence.*

# Pigtail

Tadeusz Rózewicz (translated by Adam Czerniawski)

When all the women in the transport
had their heads shaved
four workmen with brooms made of birch twigs
swept up
and gathered up the hair

Behind clean glass
the stiff hair lies
of those suffocated in gas chambers
there are pins and side combs
in this hair.

The hair is not shot through with light
is not parted by the breeze
is not touched by any hand
or rain or lips
In huge chests
clouds of dry hair
of those suffocated
and a faded plait
a pigtail with a ribbon
pulled at school
by naughty boys.

*The Museum, Auschwitz, 1948*

1. Draw a sketch of an image that you saw in this poem.

2. Have you heard of Auschwitz? If you haven't, ask your teacher to explain it or look it up in your history book.

3. What do the first lines of the poem tell us happened to women upon their arrival at Auschwitz?

4. In the second verse what has happened to the hair?

5. How does the poet emphasise the lack of life in this hair? PQE

6. What piece of hair stands out and why? PQE

7. How did this poem make you feel?

Write the caption that you would put underneath this display in the Auschwitz museum.

**OR**

The pigtail in this poem represents the loss of innocence and freedom of the children killed in Auschwitz. What object would you choose to represent your life and why would you choose it?

Select a poem you have studied which deals with either war OR peace.

(i) What does the poet say about either war or peace in the poem?

Support your answer by reference to the poem.

(ii) What effect did this poem have on you?

Explain your answer by reference to the poem.

2009 H.L. Paper

**OR**

Choose a poem that you think has an interesting title.

(i) Considering the poem as a whole, explain how the title is interesting.

(ii) Name two other features of your chosen poem which appeal to you and explain why they appeal to you.

2007 H.L. Paper

*Sign at the entrance to Auschwitz. It translates as Work Brings Freedom.*

# The End and the Beginning

Wislawa Szymborska

(translated from the Polish by Stanislaw Baravczak
and Clare Cavanagh)

After every war
someone's got to tidy up.
Things won't pick
themselves up, after all.

Someone's got to shove
the rubble to the roadsides
so that the carts loaded with corpses
can get by.

Someone's got to trudge
through the sludge and ashes,
through the sofa springs,
the shards of glass,
the bloody rags.

Someone's got to lug the post
to prop the wall,
someone's got to glaze the window,
set the door in its frame.

No sound bites, no photo opportunities
and it takes years.
All the cameras have gone
to other wars.

The bridges need to be rebuilt,
the railroad stations, too.
Shirt sleeves will be rolled
to shreds.

Someone, broom in hand,
still remembers how it was.
Someone else listens, nodding
his unshattered head.
But others are bound to be bustling nearby
who'll find all that
a little boring.

From time to time someone still must
dig up a rusted argument
from underneath a bush
and haul it off to the dump.

Those who knew
what this was all about
must make way for those
who know little.
And less than that.
And at last nothing less
than nothing.

Someone's got to lie there
in the grass that covers up
the causes and effects
with a cornstalk in his teeth,
gawking at the clouds.

1. Do you like tidying your bedroom? Who does most of the housework in your home? In general, do people like tidying up?

2. Make a list of the jobs that would have to be done to tidy up your school hall after a disco.

3. Now imagine that you have to 'tidy up' a city after a riot. Make out that list.

Imagine that you live in the world of the black and white photograph below. Describe a day in your life.

**OR**

Pretend that you are the leader of a country which has just signed a peace treaty after a long and destructive conflict. Write the radio speech that you will deliver to your people to inspire them to begin the process of rebuilding their country.

**OR**

Write an informative report for the UN looking for funds to help reconstruct your damaged country. You must outline the problems you face and what you would do with any money received.

4. Is the speaker's tone in the first verse full of self-pity? How would you describe the tone?

5. What is the first job that needs to be done and why is this important?

6. In the third and fourth verse there is a mixture of ordinary, everyday things and the remains of war. What are these things?

7. Who was there during the war but has now gone? Why is their disappearance important?

8. There is evidence in the poem that some people need to remember the war and that others need to forget. Where is this evidence? **PQE**

9. What do you think the poet means in the verse when he says 'someone still must dig up a rusted argument …'? **PQE**

10. What eventually happens to the knowledge about the war?

11. Who do you think the poet might be talking about in the last verse? There can be more than one answer to this!

*Many of the poems in this section are very bleak. This next poem reminds us that no matter how bad things get there is always hope.*

# Though there are torturers

Michael Coady

Though there are torturers in the
world
There are also musicians.

Though, at this moment, men
Are screaming in prisons
There are jazzmen raising storms
Of sensuous celebration
And orchestras releasing
Glories of the spirit.

Though the image of God
Is everywhere defiled
A man in West Clare
Is playing the concertina,
The Sistine Choir is levitating
Under the dome of St Peter's
And a drunk man on the road
Is singing for no reason.

1. This poem is full of opposites. Which one was your favourite?

2. Re-write this poem with the title 'Though there is the Junior Cert …

314

# Death and Grief

# The Identification

Roger McGough

So you think it's Stephen?
Then I'd best make sure
Be on the safe side as it were.
Ah, there's been a mistake. The hair
you see, it's black, now Stephen's fair …
What's that? The explosion?
Of course, burnt black. Silly of me.
I should have known. Then let's get on.

The face, is that a face I ask?
that mask of charred wood
blistered, scarred could
that have been a child's face?
The sweater, where intact, looks
in fact all too familiar.
But one must be sure.

The scoutbelt. Yes that's his.
I recognise the studs he hammered in
not a week ago. At the age
when boys get clothes-conscious
now you know. It's almost
certainly Stephen. But one must
be sure. Remove all trace of doubt.
Pull out every splinter of hope.

Pockets. Empty the pockets.
Handkerchief? Could be any schoolboy's.
Dirty enough. Cigarettes?
Oh this can't be Stephen.
I don't allow him to smoke you see.
He wouldn't disobey me. Not his father.
But that's his penknife. That's his alright.
And that's his key on the keyring
Gran gave him just the other night.
Then this must be him.

I think I know what happened
… … about the cigarettes
No doubt he was minding them
for one of the older boys.
Yes that's it.
That's him.
That's our Stephen.

# Take the Plunge!

1. Who do you think is speaking in this poem?

2. How do you know that you are hearing only one side of a conversation?

3. Why does the speaker think that it is not Stephen at first?

4. Is the face of the body recognisable?

5. What age do you think Stephen is?

6. What things in Stephen's pockets suggest that it is not him and what things suggest that it is him?

7. Why do you think the speaker makes an excuse for Stephen having cigarettes in his pocket? Does it really make any difference?

8. Do you think that 'The Identification' is a good title for the poem? **P Q E**

9. There is a line repeated which shows us that the person keeps trying to convince himself that this is not Stephen. Can you find it?

10. What do you think the person means when he says, 'Remove all trace of doubt. Pull out every splinter of hope'? What do you think of when you think of a splinter?

11. How did this poem make you feel?

Write a newspaper report about the accident that killed Stephen.

**OR**

Remember that there was someone with the father as he identified his son's body. Write that person's diary entry on the evening of the identification.

# Mid-Term Break

Seamus Heaney

I sat all morning in the college sick bay
Counting bells knelling classes to a close.
At two o'clock our neighbours drove me
   home.

In the porch I met my father crying –
He had always taken funerals in his stride –
And Big Jim Evans saying it was a hard
   blow.

The baby cooed and laughed and rocked the
   pram
When I came in, and I was embarrassed
By old men standing up to shake my hand

And tell me they were 'sorry for my trouble'.
Whispers informed strangers I was the
   eldest,
Away at school, as my mother held my hand

In hers and coughed out angry tearless
   sighs.
At ten o'clock the ambulance arrived
With the corpse, stanched and bandaged by
   the nurses.

Next morning I went up into the room.
   Snowdrops
And candles soothed the bedside; I saw him
For the first time in six weeks. Paler now,

Wearing a poppy bruise on his left temple,
He lay in the four foot box as in his cot.
No gaudy scars, the bumper knocked him
   clear.
A four foot box, a foot for every year.

# Take the Plunge!

**DIVE IN!**

1. Where is the poet at the start of the poem and how do you think he is feeling?

2. What tells you that something is terribly wrong in the second paragraph?

3. What makes the poet feel very awkward?

4. How is his mother reacting to the tragedy?

5. How long had it been since he had seen his brother?

6. How did his brother die?

7. What age was the poet's brother?

The main emotion in a poem is called the mood.

**TAKE THE PLUNGE!**

8. There is an ominous mood in the first verse. Can you pick any words or phrases that help to create this? **P Q E**

9. There is a contrast in the third verse. What is it and how is it created? **P Q E**

10. When he visits his brother's room there is a very distinct atmosphere. Could you describe it in your own words?

11. What do you associate the words 'Mid-Term Break' with? Do you think this is an appropriate title for this poem?

12. The final line of this poem is not easy to forget. Why do you think this is?

**WHY DON'T YOU…**

Imagine that you were at school with the young Seamus Heaney. Write the letter of condolence that you would send to him.

***OR***

Describe your plans for your next mid-term break.

# Funeral Blues

W.H. Auden

Stop all the clocks, cut off the telephone,
Prevent the dog from barking with a juicy bone,
Silence the pianos and with muffled drum
Bring out the coffin, let the mourners come.

Let aeroplanes circle moaning overhead
Scribbling on the sky the message He Is Dead,
Put crêpe bows round the white necks of public doves,
Let the traffic policemen wear black cotton gloves.

He was my North, my South, my East and West,
My working week and my Sunday rest,
My noon, my midnight, my talk, my song;
I thought that love would last forever: I was wrong.

The stars are not wanted now: put out every one;
Pack up the moon and dismantle the sun;
Pour away the ocean and sweep up any wood.
For nothing now can come to any good.

**DIVE IN!**

1. Why does the poet want everything to stop in the first verse?

2. How would he like to let everybody know that 'He Is Dead'?

3. The person who died was very important to the poet. How does the poet show us this?

4. What are the good things that the poet can no longer appreciate in the final verse?

**TAKE THE PLUNGE!**

5. In the first two verses the poet gives a series of orders. What tone of voice do you think he is using? What does this tell us about how he is feeling?

6. Pick the most striking command and explain why it got your attention. **P Q E**

7. Are the poet's orders going to be obeyed? Why not?

8. The poet uses metaphors to explain the depth of his love in the third verse. Which of the comparisons is your favourite, and why? **PQE**

9. Why has he been proven wrong in thinking that 'love would last forever'? **PQE**

10. Imagine the world without stars, moon or sun, sea or land. What kind of place would it be? Would it even be a place? What word would you choose to describe the poet's view of the world in the last verse?

Imagine somebody you love has died. What would your orders to the rest of the world be? How would you let the world know your loved one was gone? Make a list.

***OR***

Write a radio announcement informing listeners that the world is going to end tomorrow. What advice will you give people?

***OR***

This poem is extremely popular and famous. Can you suggest any reasons for this?

*Read this poem quietly to yourself.*

# The Bustle in a House

Emily Dickinson

The Bustle in a House
The Morning after Death
Is solemnest of industries
Enacted upon Earth –

The Sweeping up the Heart
And putting Love away
We shall not want to use again
Until Eternity.

Write down what this poem made you think and feel.

# 'Do not stand at my grave and weep'

Anon

Do not stand at my grave and weep;
I am not there. I do not sleep.
I am a thousand winds that blow.
I am diamond glints on snow.
I am sunlight on ripened grain.
I am the gentle autumn rain.
When you awaken in the morning's hush
I am the swift uplifting rush
Of quiet birds in circled flight.
I am the soft stars that shine at night.
Do not stand at my grave and cry;
I am not there. I did not die.

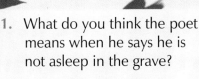

1. What do you think the poet means when he says he is not asleep in the grave?

2. The metaphors in this poem explain the parts of the person's spirit that live on. *'I am a thousand winds that blow'*, tells us that the poet's spirit is now free like the wind. Take each of the other metaphors and say what *quality* of his spirit the poet says is still alive.

3. Why do you think the poet wrote this poem?

Think about your best qualities.

- Write down any words that come into your head, for example, 'strong'.

- Now look at your words and jot down any things that you associate with those words, for example, when I look at the word 'strong' I think of 'rocks' and 'oak trees'.

- Try to link the two concepts into an image, like the poet has done above. For example, 'I am the oak that stands tall and proud', or 'I am the rock that the sea can't break.'

- Write a poem like the one above.

**OR**

Imagine that you are writing your will. What are your most precious possessions and who are you going to leave them to?

321

## Citizen of the World

Dave Calder

when you are very small
maybe not quite born
your parents move
for some reason you never understand they move
from their own town
from their own land
and you grow up in a place
that is never quite your home

and all your childhood people
with a smile or a fist say
you're not from here are you
and part of you says fiercely yes I am
and part of you feels no I'm not
I belong where my parents belonged

but when you go to their town, their country
people there also say
you're not from here are you
and part of you says no I'm not
and part of you feels fiercely yes I am

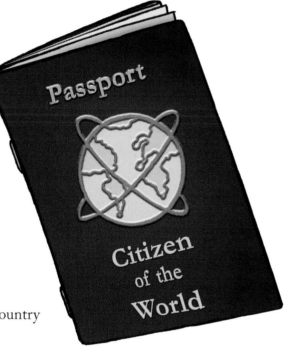

and so you grow up both and neither
and belong everywhere and nowhere much the same
both stronger and weaker for the lack of ground
able to fly but not to rest
and all over the world, though you feel alone
are millions like you, like a great flock of swallows
soaring or falling exhausted, wings beating the rhythm
of the wind that laughs at fences or frontiers,
whose home is itself, and the whole world it moves over.

1. Why do you think this child's parents moved?

2. What does the poet mean when he says people speak 'with a smile or a fist'?

3. Does the poet feel like he belongs to the country his parents brought him to or the country they left?

Pretend you are the person in this poem. Write the story of your first visit to the country your parents came from.

**OR**

Are you a citizen of Ireland? What does it mean to you to be Irish or not Irish? Is there another country you would like to be a citizen of? Why?

4. Why do you think this poem is called 'Citizen of the World'?

5. Do children have any choice about where they are born or where they are brought up?

6. Why is the poet 'able to fly but not to rest'?

7. What does the poet compare the millions like him to? Is it a good image for people like him? Why? **PQE**

8. Why does the wind laugh at fences or frontiers? **PQE**

9. Does this poem end on a positive or negative note? **PQE**

10. Has this poem made you think? What about?

*Get into groups and take it in turns to read this next poem out loud. Don't try to figure out what the words mean, just read them the way they are spelt.*

# The Wild Trabler

Nan Joyce

The wild trabler the wild
trabler is a man dat fit when he is drunk
and ol ws shoten dat pepel tinkes he is ful of heat
But no gust a man dat life left be hind
a man hum never had a chanc in life since he wos born
on wonte out cast in hes on cuntrey senc he was a child
he was regetd leven wild lick the birds
ben hunted lick a wild anamel Pepel snar at hem
and a fard of hem Lif never brot hem aney hapnes
he corses the day he wos boorn He som times ask God
why he was put on ert he is on happy man hum never had
a tru frend den he turns to the onley frend
he has, the frend dat makes hem laf and cry and happy
for whil. A frend dat wil bring hem tloser to det.
Dis is a wild man.

DIVE IN!

1. The words in this poem are spelt differently. Why did the poet do this?

2. Was it easier to understand this poem when you were reading it yourself or when someone else read it to you?

*Now read the second version of this poem!*

The Wild Traveller. The wild traveller
is a man that fights when he is drunk
and always shouting, that people think
he is full of hate. But no,
Just a man that life left behind
A man who never had a chance in life
Since he was born. Unwanted, outcast
In his own country since he was a child
He was rejected, living wild like the birds
Being hunted like a wild animal.
People snarl at him and are afraid of him.
Life never brought him any happiness.
He curses the day he was born.
He sometimes asks God why he was put on earth.
He is an unhappy man who never had a true friend
Then he turns to the only friend he has. The friend
That makes him laugh and cry and happy for a while
A friend that will bring him closer to death.
This is a wild man.

3. Why do people think the Wild Traveller is full of hate? P Q E

4. Is he full of hate? P Q E

5. What has made him 'wild'? P Q E

6. Who or what do you think is his 'only friend'?

7. Does the poet capture the loneliness of the life of a Traveller? P Q E

8. Which version of this poem do you prefer? Why?

Have a class discussion on the topic, 'The treatment of Travellers in Ireland is racist'. You could divide into teams, research the topic and hold a debate. Remember that there are two sides to every argument.

Write to Nan Joyce telling her how the poem made you feel.

**OR**

Imagine that the Traveller man in this poem has come to visit your class.

- Put an empty chair at the top of the class. This is now the hot seat.

- The teacher will select people to sit in the hot seat. When a person sits in the hot seat he or she is the Traveller man.

- Write the questions you would like to put to him about his life and his experiences.

Take it in turns to ask the person in the hot seat your questions.

Afterwards, write an account of the interview with the Traveller for your school magazine, explaining what you have learnt.

# A Letter To My Mother

Eva Johnson

*Up until the 1970s the Australian Government had a policy of removing Aboriginal children from their parents to be brought up by white people. They believed this would help Aboriginal people to integrate into 'normal' society. This poem tells the story of one such child.*

I not see you long time now, I not see you long time now
White fulla bin take me from you, I don't know why
Give me to the Missionary to be God's child.
Give me new language, give me new name
All time I cry, they say – 'that shame'
I go to city down south, real cold
I forget all them stories, my Mother you told
Gone is my spirit, my dreaming, my name
Gone to these people, our country to claim
They gave me white mother, she give me new name
All time I cry, she say – 'that shame'
I not see you long time now, I not see you long time now.


I grow as a Woman now, not Piccaninny no more
I need you to teach me your wisdom, your lore
I am your Spirit, I'll stay alive
But in white fulla way, you won't survive
I'll fight for Your land, for your Sacred sites
To sing and to dance with the Brolga in flight
To continue to live in your own tradition
A culture for me was replaced by a mission
I not see you long time now, I not see you long time now.
One day your dancing, your dreaming, your song
Will take me your Spirit back where I belong

*Native children of Hermannsburg/ Newlands, John, Sir/1920 PICPIC/64581 169 LOC Album 282/ National Library of Australia*

My Mother, the earth, the land – I demand

Protection from aliens who rule, who command

For they do not know where our dreaming began

Our destiny lies in the laws of White Man

Two Women we stand, our story untold

But now as our spiritual bondage unfold

We will silence this Burden, this longing, this pain

When I hear you my Mother give me my Name

I not see you long time now, I not see you long time now.

1. Where does the white fellow take the child?

2. What is the white people's reaction to the child's tears?

3. As a grown woman, why does she now need her mother?

4. Do the white people succeed in making the child forget her origins? **P Q E**

> The words people use, the way they pronounce them, and even their grammar, can vary. These variations are called dialects.

5. How does this poet use dialect effectively? Why does she use it?

6. One line is repeated several times in the poem. What is the effect of this?

7. In the last verse the poet's mother is her link to the land. Where is this evident? **P Q E**

8. *There is a contrast between the vulnerability of the child in the first verse and the defiance of the grown woman in the other verses. Discuss this statement.* **P Q E**

9. What words or phrases in the poem show us that the poet comes from a completely different culture to ours? **P Q E**

10. What did you think of this poem?

Write the mother's poem to her daughter.

**OR**

Imagine you are an Australian Government official. Write your report on how you think the child, Eva Johnson, is settling into her new home.

**OR**

Watch the film *Rabbit-Proof Fence* and write a review of it.

# Nature

## December

R. Southey

A wrinkled crabbed man they picture thee,
Old Winter, with a rugged beard as grey
As the long moss upon the apple-tree;
Blue-lipt, an ice drop at thy sharp blue nose,
Close muffled up, and on thy dreary way
Plodding along through sleet and drifting snows.
They should have drawn thee by thy high-heap't hearth
Old Winter! seated in thy great armed chair;
Watching the children at their Christmas mirth; -
Or circled by them as thy lips declare
Some merry jest, or tale of murder dire,
Or troubled spirit that disturbs the night;
Pausing at times to rouse the smouldering fire,
Or taste the old October brown and bright.

**DIVE IN!**

1. What does the poet say people compare Winter to?

2. How does the poet say Winter should be pictured?

3. Does the poet have sympathy for Winter?

**TAKE THE PLUNGE!**

> When something that isn't human is given human characteristics it is called personification.

4. In the first six lines, what sort of old man does the poet personify Winter as? **PQE**

5. How does his personification of Winter change in the rest of the poem? **PQE**

6. In the second personification of Winter, what type of character does the poet describe?

7. When do you think this poem was written? Choose examples from the language of the poem to back up your answer. **PQE**

8. Do you like this poem? Why or why not?

**WHY DON'T YOU...**

Try to personify one of the following:

- The Sun
- Summer
- The Junior Certificate
- Sunset
- Death
- The Ocean

***OR***

Write a short description of an old person that you know.

***OR***

Write a brief newspaper article about the dangers of cold weather for old people.

*Before reading this next poem:*

Write down as many words as you can think of to describe snow. Try to think about texture, taste, and smell, as well as sight.

# Snow

Walter de la Mare

No breath of wind,
No gleam of sun –
Still the white snow
Whirls softly down –
Twig and bough
And blade and thorn
All in an icy
Quiet, forlorn,
Whispering, rustling,
Through the air,
On sill and stone,
Roof – everywhere,
It heaps its powdery
Crystal flakes
Of every tree
A mountain makes;
Till pale and faint
At shut of day,
Stoops from the West
One wintry ray,
And, feathered in fire,
Where ghosts the moon,
A robin shrills
His lonely tune.

# Take the Plunge!

1. How many of your 'snow words' appeared in this poem?

2. Were there any words in this poem that you thought were unusual?

3. How do you know that it is very quiet and silent at the start of this poem? **PQE**

4. Pick out two words that make gentle sounds.

5. What happens to the trees when the snow falls on them?

6. Can you find the only clear sound in the poem? **PQE**

7. How many colours do you think are in this poem? **PQE**

- Find two examples of rhyme in this poem.

- Look for the major contrast between the images at the beginning and end of this poem. What creates this contrast?
(Hint: think about colour and sound.)

When a word imitates the sound it is describing it is called onomatopoeia. For example, the tick-tock of the clock, the buzzing of the bee.

- Pick out as many examples of onomatopoeia as you can find in this poem.

# The Snow

Emily Dickinson

It sifts from Leaden Sieves –
It powders all the Wood.
It fills with Alabaster Wool
The wrinkles of the road –

It makes an Even Face
Of Mountain, and of Plain –
Unbroken Forehead from the East
Unto the East again –

It reaches to the Fence –
It wraps it Rail by Rail,
Till it is lost in Fleeces –
It deals Celestial Vail

To Stump and Stack – and Stem –
A Summer's empty Room –
Acres of Joints, where Harvests were,
Recordless, but for them.

It Ruffles Wrists of Posts
As Ankles of a Queen –
Then stills its Artisans – like Ghosts –
Denying they have been –

*Alabaster is cold, hard, white stone*
*An artisan is a very skilled craftsman*

**DIVE IN!**

1. Emily Dickinson didn't give her poems titles. Someone else called this poem 'The Snow'. What title would you give it?

2. Pick out any line or word from this poem that catches your attention.

3. Do you like it when it snows? Why or why not?

**TAKE THE PLUNGE!**

4. (a) In the first line of the poem what is the snow compared to?

   (b) What is the sky compared to?

   (c) Do you think this is a good metaphor for describing snow falling?

5. Why is the phrase 'alabaster wool' unusual?

6. In the second verse what is the landscape compared to? What does the snow do to the landscape? **P Q E**

7. If you face 'east' and turn in a full circle you will come 'Unto the East again'. What is the poet trying to emphasise with this phrase in verse two?

8. (a) What texture of snow does the word 'fleeces' suggest?

   (b) What quality of snow does the word 'ruffles' capture?

   (c) What image does the word 'vail' create?

9. Why does the line 'To Stump and Stack – and Stem' stand out?

10. What do you think 'A Summer's empty Room' might be? Remember there were harvests in it!

11. How are the posts personified? What kind of material is normally ruffled?

12. What do you think happens at the end of this poem? What word makes it sound mysterious?

13. There is an elusive feminine presence in this poem. Can you find any traces of her?

When a vowel sound (a, e, i, o, u), is repeated in a line it is called assonance. For example, lone-show, brave-vain. Notice it is the vowel sound and not just the vowel letter that creates assonance. Words that rhyme often have assonance; this makes them sound the same. For example, 'The cat sat on the mat.'

● Make a list of all the verbs in this poem. In what way is the verb 'stills' different from all the others?

● Find three examples of alliteration (p. 268). Do they add rhythm to the poem?

● Find three examples of assonance. Do they add rhyme to the poem?

● Pick your favourite metaphor from this poem and explain why you chose it.

Name a poem you have studied where the poet was inspired by any ONE of the following:

● Something the poet saw
● Something the poet felt
● Something the poet heard
● Something the poet remembered

Refer to the poem you have chosen, and say clearly:

– What the poem was about
– How the poet described things
– Why you *liked* or *disliked* the poem             2000 O.L. Paper

**OR**

Choose any poem you have studied which has interesting sound effects or musical qualities. Describe these sound effects or musical qualities and explain how they enrich the poem.

2008 H.L. Paper

**OR**

Choose any poem you have studied which is 'wonder-filled' or captures the 'whoosh of the imagination'.

(i) Describe what happens in this poem.

(ii) How does the poet fill the poem with wonder or show the imagination at work?

# Valley of Oranges

Kathleen Keyes

I picked the orange that
Hung loosely from its bough
Through an open window
As we travelled, slowly, by train
In warm sunshine.
It felt rounded and firm to the touch of
    my cheek
Skin on skin
Intoxicating with the
    penetrating scent of
Orange zest
It splashed to the lap of my dress
Rolling about in a sea of blue silk.

In the shade of a tree
The peel came away, softly,
As a shearer takes wool from a sheep.
Our train had stopped in a place, where
    trees,
Bent from the weight of hanging fruit
Huddle together sharing their secrets.
Mine was a velvet segment
Heavy, bulging with juice and the
Pulp of sweet citrus orange.
A cold half-moon on my tongue
Releasing its tangy goodness
Streaming on taste buds
The flickering stars
Busily soaking it up
While my train had
    slipped away.

335

1. Suggest a country where this poem could have taken place.

2. Would you like to visit the country that you have named? Why or why not?

3. Which of your senses is appealed to first in the poem?

4. Why do you think the person in the poem puts the orange next to her cheek?

5. What other words used to describe the orange catch your attention and why? **PQE**

6. What does the poet compare her dress to? Why do you think this comparison came into her mind?

7. The poet compares the peeling away of the orange skin to a completely different activity. What is it?

8. How does the poet personify the trees in the place where they stop?

9. Pick out words describing the orange that make your mouth water. **PQE**

10. Even though the poem is set in the day time, the poet uses imagery from the night to describe the sensation of eating the orange. Identify this imagery and explain the comparisons. **PQE**

11. Why is it important that this journey happens on a train rather than in a car?

12. What do you think is the significance of the train slipping away at the end of the poem?

Write a menu of your favourite meal with descriptions of each course. You are trying to sell the food so make it sound as appealing as possible.

**OR**

Write a short story about someone's journey on a train or a bus.

**OR**

Why not try reading this poem in groups and then preparing a freeze-frame of any part of it?

- Practise your moment.
- The teacher will call each group to the top of the classroom in turn.
- On the count of three you must freeze your moment and hold it still for 30 seconds.
- When the teacher points to you, you must explain who you are and what you are thinking at this moment in time.

A freeze-frame is like a scene from a film that has been paused. You are going to pretend that you are frozen in a moment in the poem. You decide what character each person in your group is playing. Remember to think about posture, gesture, expression and positions.

# Blackberry-Picking

Seamus Heaney

Late August, given heavy rain and sun
For a full week, the blackberries would ripen.
At first, just one, a glossy purple clot
Among others, red, green, hard as a knot.
You ate that first one and its flesh was sweet
Like thickened wine: summer's blood was in it
Leaving stains upon the tongue and lust for
Picking. Then red ones inked up and that hunger
Sent us out with milk-cans, pea-tins, jam-pots
Where briars scratched and wet grass bleached our boots.
Round hayfields, cornfields and potato-drills
We trekked and picked until the cans were full,
Until the tinkling bottom had been covered
With green ones, and on top big dark blobs burned
Like a plate of eyes. Our hands were peppered
With thorn pricks, our palms sticky as Bluebeard's.

We hoarded the fresh berries in the byre,
And when the bath was filled we found a fur,
A rat-grey fungus, glutting in our cache.
The juice was stinking too. Once off the bush
The fruit fermented, the sweet flesh would turn
    sour.
I always felt like crying. It wasn't fair
That all the lovely canfuls smelt of rot.
Each year I hoped they'd keep, knew they
    would not.

**DIVE IN!**

1. What sort of weather was needed for the blackberries to ripen?

2. What did the poet do with the first blackberry?

3. List the containers the children used to collect the blackberries.

4. Where did they go to find the blackberries?

5. Where did they keep the blackberries when they were picked?

6. What happens at the end of the poem?

**TAKE THE PLUNGE!**

7. In the first six lines the poet uses words associated with blood. Can you find any examples of these?

8. Look at the poet's use of colour. List all the colours you can find in the poem.

9. How does the poet convey the children's eagerness to pick the blackberries? **PQE**

10. Do you like the description of the containers filling up with blackberries? Give reasons for your answer. **PQE**

11. The tone of the poem changes in the second verse. Can you find where this happens? **PQE**

12. The poet doesn't just use his sense of sight when describing the blackberry picking. Re-read the poem and note when he uses his sense of:

    (a) Touch

    (b) Hearing

    (c) Smell

    (d) Taste

**WHY DON'T YOU...**

Seamus Heaney says that the children ended up with 'palms sticky as Bluebeard's'. Bluebeard was an infamous pirate who killed hundreds of victims. Write an entry in Bluebeard's ship's log describing a successful attack on a rich sailing ship. If you're stuck for ideas think of the film *Pirates of the Caribbean*.

*OR*

Think of an activity that you used to do every summer holidays when you were small. Try to re-create the atmosphere and your feelings about that activity.

# The Early Purges

Seamus Heaney

I was six when I first saw kittens drown.
Dan Taggart pitched them, 'the scraggy wee shits',
Into a bucket; a frail metal sound,

Soft paws scraping like mad. But their tiny din
Was soon soused. They were slung on the snout
Of the pump and the water pumped in.

'Sure, isn't it better for them now?' Dan said.
Like wet gloves they bobbed and shone till he sluiced
Them out on the dunghill, glossy and dead.

Suddenly frightened, for days I sadly hung
Round the yard, watching the three sogged remains
Turn mealy and crisp as old summer dung

Until I forgot them. But the fear came back
When Dan trapped big rats, snared rabbits, shot crows
Or, with a sickening tug, pulled old hens' necks.

Still, living displaces false sentiments
And now, when shrill pups are prodded to drown
I just shrug, 'Bloody pups'. It makes sense:

'Prevention of cruelty' talk cuts ice in town
Where they consider death unnatural
But on well-run farms pests have to be kept down.

339

# Take the Plunge!

1. What did the young boy see when he was six?

2. How does it make him feel?

3. What else makes him feel that way?

4. How does his attitude change?

5. In the first two verses what details make the killing of the kittens more shocking? **PQE**

6. What are the dead kittens compared to in the third and fourth verses? What is the effect of these comparisons? **PQE**

7. In your opinion what kind of person is Dan? **PQE**

8. How does the poet use sound to convey the death of the animals? Remember to think about:

   ● Onomatopoeia (p. 332)

   ● Assonance (p. 334)

   ● Alliteration (p. 268)

9. The adult writer says, '… on well-run farms pests have to be kept down.' Do you think he really believes this?

10. Why do you think the poem is called 'The Early Purges'.

Think about a pet or an animal that you have encountered in your life. You may have loved or hated the animal. Describe the encounter, trying to recapture your feelings.

### OR

Write the script for a radio campaign by the Irish Society for the Prevention of Cruelty to Animals. You want to raise awareness of the fact that a pet given for Christmas is f or life.

Split the class in half. One half must imagine that they come from the country and live on farms, the other half must imagine they live in town. Have a debate on the topic:

*The prevention of cruelty to animals is essential.*

# Revelation

Liz Lochhead

I remember once being shown the black bull
when a child at the farm for eggs and milk.
They called him Bob – as though perhaps
you could reduce a monster
with the charm of a friendly name.
At the threshold of his outhouse, someone
held my hand and let me peer inside.
At first, only black
and the hot reek of him. Then he was immense,
his edges merging with the darkness, just
a big bulk and a roar to be really scared of,
a trampling, and a clanking tense with the chain's jerk.
His eyes swivelled in the great wedge of his tossed head.
He roared with rage. His nostrils gaped like wounds.

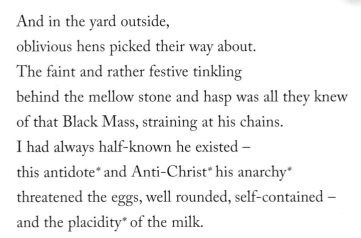

And in the yard outside,
oblivious hens picked their way about.
The faint and rather festive tinkling
behind the mellow stone and hasp was all they knew
of that Black Mass, straining at his chains.
I had always half-known he existed –
this antidote* and Anti-Christ* his anarchy*
threatened the eggs, well rounded, self-contained –
and the placidity* of the milk.

I ran, my pigtails thumping on my back in fear,
past the big boys in the farm land
who pulled the wings from butterflies and
blew up frogs with straws.
Past thorned hedge and harried nest,
scared of the eggs shattering –
only my small and shaking hand on the jug's rim
in case the milk should spill.

*antidote* –
something that cancels
everything out

*Anti-Christ* –
the devil

*anarchy* –
a state of total and
utter chaos, lack of
control

*placidity* –
peace

1. Is there any animal that you are scared of?

2. Do you think the description of the bull in the first verse is frightening?

3. How old do you think the girl is?

4. Why is the girl at the farm?

5. What does she think of the name they have given the bull?

6. What is the first thing she notices about the bull?

7. What sounds can she hear? **PQE**

8. What words capture the anger and violence of the bull? **PQE**

9. The poet uses religious imagery to describe the bull in the second verse. Why do you think she calls him an Anti-Christ?

10. There are two different worlds in this farmyard. Explain how the poet creates this contrast in the second verse. Look closely at the language used. **PQE**

11. In the final verse the girl is not just afraid of the bull. What else is she scared of?

12. Can you find three examples of alliteration in this poem? Do these add to the rhythm?

13. What did you think of this poem?

Write the dialogue between the girl and her mother when she returns home from the farm.

**OR**

Write a description of an imaginary encounter with a dangerous animal.

**OR**

Your family has bought an unusual pet which you can no longer keep. Write the advertisement that you would place in the classified section of a newspaper to try to sell it.

# Life Paths

# The Road Not Taken

Robert Frost

Two roads diverged in a yellow wood,
And sorry I could not travel both
And be one traveller, long I stood
And looked down one as far as I could
To where it bent in the undergrowth;

Then took the other, as just as fair,
And having perhaps the better claim,
Because it was grassy and wanted wear;
Though as for that, the passing there
Had worn them really about the same,

And both that morning equally lay
In leaves no step had trodden black.
Oh, I kept the first for another day!
Yet knowing how way leads on to way,
I doubted if I should ever come back.

I shall be telling this with a sigh
Somewhere ages and ages hence:
Two roads diverged in a wood, and I –
I took the one less travelled by,
And that has made all the difference.

1. Why does the traveller pause at the fork in the road?

2. How does he decide which road to take?

3. Does he think he will get to travel the other path in the future?

4. At one level this poem is about going for a walk in a wood and choosing a path. What other meaning do you think it has?

5. The poet chooses the harder road. Why do you think he does this?

6. Look carefully at the last two lines. What do you think they mean?

An allegory is a story that has two levels of meaning.

Write a story about a choice that you made which you now regret.

**OR**

Look at the map on the right. Write a clear set of directions that will get somebody from A to B.

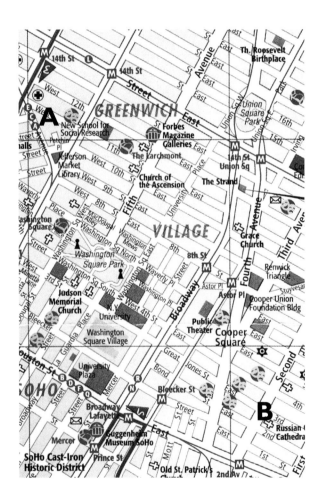

# The door

Miroslav Holub
(translated from the Czech by Ian Milner)

Go and open the door.
   Maybe outside there's
   a tree, or a wood,
   a garden,
   or a magic city.

Go and open the door.
   Maybe a dog's rummaging.
   Maybe you'll see a face,
or an eye,
or the picture
   of a picture.

Go and open the door.
   If there's a fog
   it will clear.

Go and open the door.
   Even if there's only
   the darkness ticking,
   even if there's only
   the hollow wind,
even if
   nothing
      is there,
go and open the door.

At least
there'll be
a draught.

# Take the Plunge!

**DIVE IN!**

1. Who is the poet speaking to?

2. What might you see if you open the door?

3. What is the worst thing that could happen?

**TAKE THE PLUNGE!**

4. Like 'The Road Not Taken' this poem has a deeper message. What do you think it is?

5. There is a moment of humour in the poem. Where is it?

6. Which of the images struck you most and why?

**WHY DON'T YOU...**

Explain what you would like to find on the other side of your 'door'.

**OR**

Write a story where the opening of a door is important. This can be an actual or symbolic opening.

# Overheard in County Sligo

Gillian Clarke

*I married a man from County Roscommon
and I live at the back of beyond*
with a field of cows and a yard of hens
and six white geese on the pond.

At my door's a square of yellow corn
caught up by its corners and shaken,
and the road runs down through the open gate
and freedom's there for the taking.

I had thought to work on the Abbey stage
or have my name in a book,
to see my thought on the printed page,
or still the crowd with a look.

But I turn to fold the breakfast cloth
and to polish the luster and brass,
to order and dust the tumbled rooms
and find my face in the glass.

I ought to feel I'm a happy woman
for I lie in the lap of the land,
and I married a man from County Roscommon
and I live in the back of beyond.

**DIVE IN!**

1. Irish people use the phrase 'the back of beyond'. What do they mean?

2. Does the setting sound pretty?

3. What had been the woman's ambitions?

4. What does she do now?

5. Is she happy? **P Q E**

**TAKE THE PLUNGE!**

6. Why do you think the poet called this poem 'Overheard in County Sligo'?

7. Is there a hint in this poem that the woman might leave? **P Q E**

8. Look carefully at the description of the door. What is it compared to? **P Q E**

9. This poem has a good rhythm and rhyme. How is this achieved? (Remember the importance of assonance and alliteration!) **P Q E**

**WHY DON'T YOU...**

Think about the choice this woman made. Imagine you are back at the point in time when she makes this choice. Write the story of her decision. *You might like to read the story 'The Gift of the Magi' in Chapter 6 for inspiration.*

**OR**

Write a poem entitled 'Overheard Backstage in the Abbey'.

**OR**

Write an entry in a tourist brochure promoting the attractions of rural Ireland.

# Painting

*Look carefully at the painting below. Then answer the questions that follow.*

1. When do you think this painting is set?

2. What is the man in the foreground doing?

3. What do you see in the bay?

4. Look very carefully in the bottom right-hand corner underneath the ship. What can you see in the water?

5. This painting is called *The Fall of Icarus*. Is this the title you would expect?

6. Why do you think Brueghel, the painter, made Icarus such an insignificant part of the painting?

*Icarus was the son of an Ancient Greek called Dedalus. The two men were captured by enemies and, in order to escape their prison, Dedalus made two sets of wings. Unfortunately, Icarus flew too close to the sun and the wax on his wings melted, so he fell into the sea and drowned. This was seen as a punishment from the gods because Icarus had become too proud.*

*This poem was written by W.H. Auden after seeing the painting* The Fall of Icarus.

# Musée des Beaux Arts

W.H.Auden

About suffering they were never wrong,
The old Masters: how well they understood
Its human position: how it takes place
While someone else is eating or opening a window or just walking dully along;
How, when the aged are reverently, passionately waiting
For the miraculous birth, there always must be
Children who did not specially want it to happen, skating
On a pond at the edge of the wood:
They never forgot
That even the dreadful martyrdom must run its course
Anyhow. In a corner, some untidy spot
Where the dogs go on with their doggy life and the torturer's horse
Scratches its innocent behind on a tree.
In Breughel's Icarus, for instance: how everything turns away
Quite leisurely from the disaster; the ploughman may
Have heard the splash, the forsaken cry,
But for him it was not an important failure; the sun shone
As it had to on the white legs disappearing into the green
Water, and the expensive delicate ship that must have seen
Something amazing, a boy falling out of the sky,
Had somewhere to get to and sailed calmly on.

**TAKE THE PLUNGE!**

1. Auden says that the 'old Masters' understood that human suffering *'takes place While someone else is eating … or just walking dully along'*. How is the same point made in Brueghel's painting? **PQE**

2. Many paintings focus on religious themes. In light of this, what might the *'miraculous birth'* and *'the dreadful martyrdom'* be referring to?

3. What was happening while the *'miraculous birth'* and *'dreadful martyrdom'* were taking place? Was everyone taking notice of these special events? **PQE**

4. Look at Auden's description of the painting in the last eight lines.

   (a) What does he imagine the ploughman's attitude was?

   (b) What effect does his description of Icarus have?

   (c) Why does the ship sail *'calmly on'*?

5. What do both Brueghel's painting and Auden's poem say about life and suffering?

**WHY DON'T YOU …**

Write a story entitled 'Life goes on …'

*OR*

Pretend you're a sailor on the ship in the painting. Try to tell the captain of the ship that you saw a boy with wings fall out of the sky. Write out the conversation that you have.

*OR*

Write a poem inspired by one of the paintings below.

**TEST THE WATERS!**

From the poetry you have studied choose a poem which is set in an interesting time or place.

(a) Describe this setting.

(b) What does this setting contribute to the effectiveness of the poem? Give reasons for your answer based on the evidence from the poem. 2005 H.L. Paper

*OR*

If you could invite a poet of your choice to your school, who would you choose?

(a) Explain your choice of poet with reference to the poet's work.

(b) Choose your favourite poem by this poet and explain why you like it so much. Support your answer by reference to the poem. 2006 H.L. Paper

# Unseen Poetry

When answering the question on Unseen Poetry in the exam look out for the following:

 The **theme** of the poem is the main topic or issue in the poem. Just ask yourself what is the poem really about? For example, in 'Phenomenal Woman', Maya Angelou is saying that true beauty comes from within.

 A poem is a series of word pictures. We see them with our imagination instead of with our eyes. We call these pictures **images**.

 A **simile** is a special kind of image. The poet creates a picture by comparing two things of different natures using the words 'like', 'as' or 'than'. In the poem 'Digging', Seamus Heaney says that the pen rests in his hand 'snug as a gun'.

 Sometimes a poet creates an image by comparing two things of different natures, *without* using the words 'like', 'as' or 'than'. This is called a **metaphor**. In 'He wishes for the cloths of heaven', W.B. Yeats says 'Tread softly because you tread on my dreams'. He is comparing the delicacy of his dreams to fragile cloths.

 When an inanimate object is given human characteristics it is called **personification**. In 'December', the month is described as a crabby old man.

 When lots of words in a poem start with the same letter it is called **alliteration**. This gives the line a beat. In poetry this is called **rhythm**. For example, the poem 'Truant' opens with the line 'Sing a song of sunlight'.

 When a vowel sound (a, e, i, o, u) is repeated in a line it is called **assonance**. Notice it is the vowel sound and not just the vowel letter that creates assonance. Words that **rhyme** often have assonance; this makes them sound the same. For example, Emily Dickinson says that snow 'sifts from Leaden Sieves'.

When a word imitates the sound it is describing it is called **onomatopoeia**. Walter de la Mare describes how the snow was 'whispering' and 'rustling' as it fell. These verbs recreate the sound of snow falling softly.

 When you talk to someone you can change the meaning of what you say by changing your tone of voice. Poems also have a **tone**. This is the tone of voice of the poet, or the speaker in the poem. In Brendan Kennelly's 'Poem From a Three Year Old', he captures the persistent, questioning **tone** of a small child.

 The main emotion in the poem is called the **mood**. In 'Mid-Term Break', there is a **mood** of sorrow.

 The **atmosphere** of the poem is linked to the setting of the poem. The soldiers' discovery of a massacred village in 'Conquerors' creates an **atmosphere** of horror and regret.

# Studied Poetry

For the question on studied poetry make sure you have covered the following:

 A range of themes, for example, love, war, death, childhood.

 More than one poem by one poet, for example, W.B. Yeats, W.H. Auden, Seamus Heaney.

 The themes, tones and techniques used by poets.

 Quotations from each poem.

# Fiction

In this chapter you will study the **importance** of:

- Good openings
- Character creation
- Atmospheric settings

You will **learn** how to identify moments of:

- Tension
- Climax
- Conflict

# Opening

# Lemonade

Raymond Carver

When he came to my house months ago to measure my walls for bookcases, Jim Sears didn't look like a man who'd lose his only child to the high waters of the Elwha river. He was bushy-haired, confident, cracking his knuckles, alive with energy, as we discussed tiers, and brackets, this oak stain compared to that. But it's a small town, this town, a small world here. Six months later, after the bookcases have been built, delivered and installed, Jim's father, a Mr Howard Sears, who is 'covering for his son' comes to paint our house. He tells me – when I ask, more out of small-town courtesy than anything, 'How's Jim?' – that his son lost Jim Jr in the river last spring. Jim blames himself. 'He can't get over it, neither,' Mr Sears adds. 'Maybe he's gone on to lose his a little too,' he adds, pulling on the bill of his Sherwin-Williams cap.

Jim had to stand and watch as the helicopter grappled with, then lifted, his son's body from the river with tongs. 'They used like a big pair of kitchen tongs for it, if you can imagine. Attached to a cable. But God always takes the sweetest ones, don't He?' Mr Sears says. 'He has his own mysterious purposes.' 'What do you think about it?' I want to know. 'I don't want to think,' he says. 'We can't ask or question His ways. It's not for us to know. I just know he has taken him home now, the little one.'

He goes on to tell me that Jim Sr's wife took him to thirteen foreign countries in Europe in the hopes it'd help him get over it. But it didn't. He couldn't. 'Mission unaccomplished,' Howard says. Jim's come down with Parkinson's disease. What next? He's home from Europe now, but still blames himself for sending Jim Jr back to the car that morning to look for that thermos of lemonade. They didn't need any lemonade that day! Lord, lord, what was he thinking of, Jim Sr has said a hundred – no, a thousand – times now, and to anyone who will still listen. If only he hadn't made lemonade in the first place that morning! What could he have been thinking about? Further, if they hadn't stopped the night before at the Safeway store, and if that bin of yellowy lemons hadn't stood next to where they kept the oranges, apples, grapefruit and bananas.

That's what Jim Sr had really wanted to buy, some oranges and apples, not lemons for lemonade, forget lemons, he hated lemons – at least now he did – but Jim Jr he liked lemonade, always had. He wanted lemonade.

'Let's look at it this way,' Jim Sr would say, 'those lemons had to come from someplace, didn't they? The Imperial Valley probably, or else over near Sacramento; they raise lemons there, right?' They had to be planted and irrigated and watched over and then pitched into sacks by field workers and weighed then dumped into boxes and shipped by rail or truck to this godforsaken place where a man can't do anything but lose his children! Those boxes would've been off-loaded from the truck by boys not much older than Jim Jr himself. They had to be uncrated and poured all yellow and lemony-smelling out of their crates by those boys, and washed and sprayed by some kid who was still living, walking around town, living and breathing, big as you please. Then they were carried into the store and placed in that bin under that eye-catching sign that said Have You Had Fresh Lemonade Lately? As Jim Sr's reckoning went, it harks all the way back to first causes, back to the first lemon cultivated on earth. If there hadn't been any lemons on earth, and there hadn't been any Safeway store, well, Jim would still have his son, right? And Howard Sears would still have his grandson, sure. You see, there were a lot of people involved in this tragedy. There were the farmers and the pickers of lemons, the truck drivers, the big Safeway store … Jim Sr, too, he was ready to assume his share of responsibility, of course. He was the most guilty of all. But he was still in his nosedive, Howard Sears told me. Still, he had to pull out of this somehow and go on. Everybody's heart was broken, right. Even so.

Not long ago Jim Sr's wife got him started in a little wood-carving class here in town. Now he's trying to whittle bears and seals, owls, eagles, seagulls, anything, but he can't stick to any one creature long enough to finish the job, is Mr Sear's assessment. The trouble is, Howard Sears goes on, every time Jim Sr looks up from his lathe, or his carving knife, he sees his son breaking out of the water downriver, and rising up – being reeled in, so to speak – beginning to turn and turn in circles until he was up, way up above the fir trees, tongs sticking out of his back, and then the copter turning and swinging upriver, accompanied by the roar and whap-whap of the chopper blades. Jim Jr passing now over the searchers who line the bank of the river. His arms are stretched out from his sides, and drops of water fly out from him. He passes overhead once more, closer now, and then returns a minute later to be deposited, ever so gently laid down, directly at the feet of his father. A man who, having seen everything now – his dead son rise from the river in the grip of metal pitchers and turn and turn in circles flying above the tree line – would like nothing more now than to just die. But dying is for the sweetest ones. And he remembers sweetness, when life was sweet, and sweetly he was given that other lifetime.

1. What kind of man was Jim Sears?

2. Why is Jim Sr's father 'covering for his son'?

3. How did Jim Sr's wife try to help him cope with the tragedy?

4. Why did Jim Sr decide to make lemonade?

5. What hobby had Jim Sr tried to take up?

6. Re-read the opening sentence. Did you think this was a good opening for a short story? Why or why not? **P Q E**

7. How do the first two paragraphs make the reader want to find out more about Jim Sr and the tragic accident? **P Q E**

8. Why does Jim Sr blame himself for his son's death? **P Q E**

9. What series of events does Howard blame for Jim Jr's death? **P Q E**

10. Do you think 'Lemonade' is a good title for this story? Why or why not?

Write the newspaper article that might have appeared describing the events in this short story. (Use the information on the Inverted Pyramid, page 181, to help you write the article.)

***OR***

Design a poster aimed at raising awareness of water safety on Irish beaches, rivers and lakes.

***OR***

Read this description of a famous idea known as *The Butterfly Effect*.

*If a butterfly flutters its wings in the Amazonian rainforest it may change the course of a tornado in Texas. Tiny events can have huge consequences.*

Try to write a short story showing how a tiny event results in massive changes in a character's life.

In pairs:

- Read the opening lines of the seven examples of fiction in this section.

- Write each line in your copybook.

- Rank them in order of preference.

- Write down the reasons for your choice.

- Report back to the class.

Write about the best opening you have come across in a book or short story, explaining why it encouraged you to keep reading.

## Setting

# The Lumber-Room

Saki

The children were to be driven, as a special treat, to the sands at Jagborough. Only Nicholas was not to be of the party; he was in disgrace. Only that morning he had refused to eat his wholesome bread-and-milk on the seemingly frivolous ground that there was a frog in it. Older and wiser and better people had told him that there could not possibly be a frog in his bread-and-milk and that he was not to talk nonsense; he continued, nevertheless, to talk what seemed the veriest nonsense, and described with much detail the colouration and markings of the alleged frog. The dramatic part of the incident was that there really was a frog in Nicholas's basin of bread-and-milk; he had put it there himself, so he felt entitled to know something about it. The sin of taking a frog from the garden and putting it into a bowl of wholesome bread-and-milk was enlarged on at great length, but the fact that stood out clearest in the whole affair, as it presented itself to the mind of Nicholas, was that the older, wiser, and better people had been proved to be profoundly in error in matters about which they had expressed the utmost assurance.

'You said there couldn't possibly be a frog in my bread-and-milk; there was a frog in my bread-and-milk,' he repeated, with the insistence of a skilled tactician who does not intend to shift from favourable ground.

So his boy-cousin and girl-cousin and his quite uninteresting younger brother were to be taken to Jagborough sands that afternoon and he was to stay at home. His cousins' aunt, who insisted, by an unwarranted stretch of the imagination, in styling herself his aunt also, had hastily invented the Jagborough expedition in order to impress on Nicholas the delights that he had justly forfeited by his disgraceful conduct at the breakfast-table. It was her habit, when one of the children fell from grace, to improvise something of a festival nature from which the offender would be rigorously debarred; if all the children sinned collectively they were informed of a circus in a neighbouring town, a circus of unrivalled merit and uncounted elephants, to which, but for their depravity, they would have been taken that very day.

A few decent tears were looked for on the part of Nicholas when the moment for the departure of the expedition arrived. As a matter of fact, however, all the crying was done by his girl-cousin who scraped her knee rather painfully against the step of the carriage as she was scrambling in.

'How she did howl!' said Nicholas cheerfully, as the party drove off without any of the elation of high spirits that should have characterised it.

'She'll soon get over that,' said the soi-disant aunt. 'It will be a glorious afternoon for racing about over those beautiful sands. How they will enjoy themselves!'

'Bobby won't enjoy himself much, and he won't race much either,' said Nicholas with a grim chuckle. 'His boots are hurting him. They're too tight.'

'Why didn't he tell me they were hurting?' asked the aunt with some asperity.

'He told you twice, but you weren't listening. You often don't listen when we tell you important things.'

'You are not to go into the gooseberry garden,' said the aunt, changing the subject.

'Why not?' demanded Nicholas.

'Because you are in disgrace,' said the aunt loftily.

Nicholas did not admit the flawlessness of the reasoning; he felt perfectly capable of being in disgrace and in a gooseberry garden at the same moment. His face took on an expression of considerable obstinacy. It was clear to his aunt that he was determined to go into the gooseberry garden, 'Only,' as she remarked to herself, 'because I have told him he is not to.'

Now the gooseberry garden had two doors by which it might be entered, and once a small person like Nicholas could slip in there he could effectually disappear from view amid the masking growth of artichokes, raspberry canes, and fruit bushes. The aunt had many other things to do that afternoon, but she spent an hour or two in trivial gardening operations among flower beds and shrubberies, whence she could keep a watchful eye on the two doors that led to the forbidden paradise. She was a woman of few ideas, with immense powers of concentration.

Nicholas made one or two sorties into the front garden wriggling his way with obvious stealth of purpose towards one or other of the doors, but never able for a moment to evade the aunt's watchful eye. As a matter of fact, he had no intention of trying to get into the gooseberry garden, but it was extremely convenient for him that his aunt should believe that he had; it was a belief that would keep her in self-imposed sentry-duty for the greater part of the afternoon. Having thoroughly confirmed and fortified her suspicions, Nicholas slipped back into the house and rapidly put into execution a plan of action that had long germinated in his brain. By standing on a chair in the library, one could reach a shelf on which reposed a fat, important-looking key. The key was as important as it looked; it was the instrument

which kept the mysteries of the lumber-room secure from unauthorised intrusion, which opened a way for only aunts and suchlike privileged persons. Nicholas had not had much experience of the art of fitting keys into keyholes and turning locks, but for some days past he had practised with the key of the schoolroom door; he did not believe in trusting too much to luck and incident. The key turned stiffly in the lock, but it turned. The door opened, and Nicholas was in an unknown land, compared with which the gooseberry garden was a stale delight, a mere material pleasure.

Often and often Nicholas had pictured to himself what the lumber-room might be like, that region that was so carefully sealed from youthful eyes and concerning

which no questions were ever answered. It came up to his expectations. In the first place it was large and dimly lit, one high window opening on to the forbidden garden being its only source of illumination. In the second place it was a storehouse of unimagined treasures. The aunt-by-assertion was one of those people who think that things spoil by use and consign them to dust and damp by way of preserving them. Such parts of the house as Nicholas knew best were rather bare and cheerless, but here were wonderful things for the eye to feast on. First and foremost there was a piece of framed tapestry that was evidently meant to be a firescreen. To Nicholas it was a living, breathing story; he sat down on a roll of Indian hangings, glowing in wonderful colours beneath a layer of dust, and took in all the details of the tapestry picture. A man, dressed in the hunting costume of some remote period, had just transfixed a stag with an arrow; it could not have been a difficult shot because the stag was only one or two paces away from him; in the thickly growing vegetation that the picture suggested, it would not have been difficult to creep up to a feeding stag, and the spotted dogs that were springing forward to join in the chase had evidently been trained to keep to heel till the arrow discharged. That part of the picture was simple, if interesting, but did the huntsman see, what Nicholas saw, that four galloping wolves were coming in his direction through the wood? There might be more than four of them hidden behind the trees, and in any case would the man and his dogs be able to cope with the four wolves if they made an attack? The man had only two arrows left in his quiver, and he might miss with one or both of them; all one knew about his skill in shooting was that he could hit a large stag at a ridiculously short range.

Nicholas sat for many golden minutes revolving the possibilities of the scene; he was inclined to think that there were more than four wolves and that the man and his dogs were in a tight corner.

But there were other objects of delight and interest claiming his instant attention: there were quaint twisted candlesticks in the shape of snakes, and a teapot fashioned like a china duck, out of whose open beak the tea was supposed to come. How dull and shapeless the nursery teapot seemed in comparison! And there was a carved sandal-wood box packed tight with aromatic cotton-wool, and between the layers of cotton-wool were little brass figures, hump-necked bulls and peacocks and goblins delightful to see and to handle. Less promising in appearance was a large square book with plain black covers; Nicholas peeped into it, and behold it was full of coloured pictures of birds. And such birds! In the garden, and in the lanes where he went for a walk, Nicholas came across a few birds, of which the largest were an occasional magpie or wood-pigeon; here were herons and bustards, kites, toucans, tiger-bitterns, brush turkeys, ibises, golden pheasants, a whole portrait gallery of undreamed-of creatures. And as he was admiring the colouring of the mandarin duck and assigning a life-history to it, the voice of his aunt in shrill vociferation of his name came from the gooseberry garden without. She had grown suspicious at his long disappearance and had leapt to the conclusion that he had climbed over the wall behind the sheltering screen of the lilac bushes; she was now engaged in an energetic and rather hopeless search for him among the artichokes and raspberry canes.

'Nicholas, Nicholas!' she screamed, 'you are to come out of this at once. It's no use trying to hide there; I can see you all the time.'

It was probably the first time for twenty years that any one had smiled in the lumber-room.

Presently the angry repetitions of Nicholas's name gave way to a shriek, a cry for somebody to come quickly. Nicholas shut the book, restored it carefully to its place in a corner, and shook some dust from a neighbouring pile of newspaper over it. Then he crept from the room, locked the door and replaced the key exactly where he had found it. His aunt was still calling his name when he sauntered into the front garden.

'Who's calling?' he asked.

'Me,' came the answer from the other side of the wall, 'Didn't you hear me? I've been looking for you in the gooseberry garden, and I've slipped into the rain-water tank. Luckily there's no water in it, but the sides are slippery and I can't get out. Fetch the little ladder from under the cherry tree –'

'I was told I wasn't to go into the gooseberry garden,' said Nicholas promptly.

'I told you not to, and now I tell you that you may,' came the voice from the rain-water tank, rather impatiently.

'Your voice doesn't sound like aunt's,' objected Nicholas. 'You may be the Evil One tempting me to be disobedient. Aunt often tells me that the Evil One tempts me and that I always yield. This time I'm not going to yield.'

'Don't talk nonsense,' said the prisoner in the tank. 'Go and fetch the ladder.'

'Will there be strawberry jam for tea?' asked Nicholas innocently.

'Certainly there will be,' said the aunt, privately resolving that Nicholas should have none of it.

'Now I know that you are the Evil One and not aunt,' shouted Nicholas gleefully. 'When we asked aunt for strawberry jam yesterday she said there wasn't any. I know there are four jars of it in the store cupboard, because I looked, and of course you know it's there, but she doesn't because she said there wasn't any. Oh, Devil, you have sold yourself!'

There was an unusual sense of luxury in being able to talk to an aunt as though one was talking to the Evil One, but Nicholas knew, with childish discernment, that such luxuries were not to be over-indulged in. He walked noisily away, and it was a kitchenmaid, in search of parsley, who eventually rescued the aunt from the rain-water tank.

Tea that evening was partaken of in a fearsome silence. The tide had been at its highest when the children had arrived at Jagborough Cove, so there had been

no sands to play on – a circumstance that the aunt had overlooked in the haste of organising her punitive expedition. The tightness of Bobby's boots had had a disastrous effect on his temper the whole of the afternoon, and altogether the children could not have been said to have enjoyed themselves. The aunt maintained the frozen muteness of one who has suffered undignified and unmerited detention in a rain-water tank for thirty-five minutes. As for Nicholas, he, too, was silent in the absorption of one who has much to think about; it was just possible, he considered, that the huntsman would escape with his hounds, while the wolves feasted on the stricken stag.

1. What had Nicholas done at breakfast time that got him into trouble?

2. Is Nicholas upset when the others leave for the beach?

3. How does Nicholas distract his Aunt from the lumber-room?

4. What evidence is there that Nicholas has planned his trip to the lumber-room for a long time?

5. Why doesn't Nicholas rescue his Aunt?

6. How would you describe the Aunt in this story? 🅟🅠🅔

7. What details in this story indicate that Nicholas is an intelligent, imaginative boy? 🅟🅠🅔

8. How do you know that this story is set in the past? 🅟🅠🅔

9. Re-read the description of the lumber-room. What details bring the setting to life for the reader? 🅟🅠🅔

10. Did you think this story was funny? Why or why not?

Write a story based around any object or objects from the lumber-room.

*OR*

Write the script for a radio advertisement inviting people to a car boot sale in your area.

*OR*

Notice that Saki manages to capture the point of view of a child in this story. A junk room becomes a treasure because of the power of the imagination. Try writing a description of one of the following places from the point of view of a young child, perhaps attempting to re-capture something you were fascinated by as a child.

- The beach
- The garden shed
- A classroom
- The wardrobe
- The park
- The amusement arcade
- The circus
- A building site
- The shopping centre

# Conflict

# New Boy

Roddy Doyle

## 1   He is very late

He sits.

He sits in the classroom. It is his first day.

He is late.

He is five years late.

And that is very late, he thinks.

He is nine. The other boys and girls have been like this, together, since they were four. But he is new.

—We have a new boy with us today, says the teacher-lady.

—So what? says a boy who is behind him.

Other boys and some girls laugh. He does not know exactly why. He does not like this.

—Now now, says the teacher-lady.

She told him her name when he was brought here by the man but he does not now remember it. He did not hear it properly.

—Hands in the air, she says.

All around him, children lift their hands. He does this too. There is then, quite quickly, silence.

—Good, says the teacher-lady. —Now.

She smiles at him. He does not smile. Boys and girls will laugh. He thinks that this will happen if he smiles.

The teacher-lady says his name.

—Stand up, she says.

Again, she says his name. Again, she smiles. He stands.

He looks only at the teacher-lady.

—Everybody, this is Joseph. Say Hello.

—Hello!

—HELLO!

—**HELL-OHH!**

— Hands in the air!

The children lift their hands. He also lifts his hands. There is silence. It is a clever trick, he thinks.

—Sit down, Joseph.

He sits down. His hands are still in the air.

—Now. Hands down.

Right behind him, dropped hands smack the desk. It is the so-what boy.

—Now, says the teacher-lady.

She says this word many times. It is certainly her favourite word.

—Now, I'm sure you'll all make Joseph very welcome. Take out your *Maths Matters*.

—Where's he from, Miss?

It is a girl who speaks. She sits in front of Joseph, two desks far.

—We'll talk about that later, says the teacher-lady.

—But maths first.

This is the first part of her name. Miss.

—Miss, Seth Quinn threw me book out the window.

—Didn't!

—Yeh did.

—Now!

Joseph holds his new book very tightly. It is not a custom he had expected, throwing books out the windows. Are people walking past outside warned that this is about to happen? He does not know. He has much to learn.

—Seth Quinn, go down and get that book.

—I didn't throw it.

—Go on.

—It's not fair.

—Now.

Joseph looks at Seth Quinn. He is not the so-what boy. He is a different boy.

—Now. Page 37.

No one tries to take Joseph's book. No more books go out the window.

He opens his book at page 37.

The teacher-lady talks at great speed. He understands the numbers she writes on the blackboard. He understands the words she writes. LONG DIVISION. But he does not understand what she says, especially when she faces the blackboard. He does not put his hand up. He watches the numbers on the blackboard. It is not so very difficult.

A finger pushes into his back. The so-what boy. Joseph does not turn.

—Hey. Live-Aid.

Joseph does not turn.

The so-what boy whispers.

—Live-Aid. Hey, Live-Aid. Do they know it's Christmas?

It is Monday, the 10th day of January. It is sixteen days after Christmas. This is a very stupid boy.

But Joseph knows that this is not to do with Christmas or the correct date. He knows he must be careful.

The finger prods his back again, harder, very hard.

—Christian Kelly!

—What?

It is the so-what boy. His name is Christian Kelly.

—Are you annoying Joseph there?

—No.

—Is he, Joseph?

Joseph shakes his head. He must speak. He knows this.

—No.

—I'm sure he's not, she says.

This is strange, he thinks. Her response. Is it another trick?

—Sit up straight so I can see you, Christian Kelly.

—He was poking Joseph's back, Miss.

—Shut up.

…

—Now!

Miss the teacher-lady stares at a place above Joseph's Head. There is silence in the classroom. The hands in the air trick is certainly not necessary.

—God give me strength, she says.

But why? Joseph wonders. What is she about to do? There is nothing very heavy in the classroom.

She stares again. For six seconds, exactly. Then she taps the blackboard with a piece of chalk.

—Take it down.

He waits. He watches the other children. They take copybooks from their schoolbags. They open the copybooks. They draw the margin. They stare at the blackboard. They write. They stare again. They write again. They write. A girl in the desk beside him takes a pair of glasses from a small black box that clicks loudly when she opens it. She puts the glasses onto her face. She looks at him. Her eyes are big. She smiles.

—Specky fancies yeh.

It is Christian Kelly.

—You're dead.

## 2 The Finger

This is the dangerous boy who sits behind Joseph. This boy has just told Joseph that he is dead. Joseph must understand this statement, very quickly.

He does not turn to look at Christian Kelly.

Miss, the teacher-lady, has wiped the figures from the blackboard. She writes new figures. Joseph sees: these are problems to be solved. There are ten problems. They are not difficult.

What did Christian Kelly mean? *You are dead.* Joseph thinks about these words and this too is not difficult. It is very clear that Joseph is not dead. So, Christian Kelly's words must refer to the future. *You will be dead.* All boys must grow and eventually die – Joseph knows this; he has seen dead men and boys. Christian Kelly's words are clearly intended as a threat, or promise. I will kill you. But Christian Kelly will not murder Joseph just because the girl with magnified eyes smiled at him. I will hurt you. This is what Christian Kelly means.

Joseph has not yet seen this Christian Kelly.

It is very strange. Joseph must protect himself from a boy he has not seen. Perhaps not so very strange. He did not see the men who killed his father.

The girl with the magnified eyes smiles again at Joseph. This time Christian Kelly does not speak. Joseph looks again at his copybook.

He completes the seventh problem. 751 divided by 15. He knows the answer many seconds before he writes it down. He already knows the answer to the ninth problem – 761 divided by 15 – but he starts to solve the eighth one first. He is quite satisfied with the progress. It is many months since Joseph sat in the classroom. It is warm here. January is certainly a cold month in this country.

Christian Kelly is going to hurt him. He has promised this. Joseph must be prepared.

—Finished?

It is the teacher-lady. The question is for everybody.

Joseph looks. Many of the boys and girls still lean over their copybooks. Their faces almost touch the paper.

—Hurry up now. We haven't all day.

—Hey.

The voice comes from behind Joseph. It is not loud.

Joseph turns. He does this quickly. He sees this Christian Kelly.

—What's number four?

Quickly Joseph decides.

—Seventeen, he whispers.

He turns back, to face the blackboard and the teacher-lady.

—You're still dead. What's number five?

—Seventeen.

—How can—

—Also seventeen.

—No talk.

Joseph looks at the blackboard.

—It better be.

—Christian Kelly.

It is the teacher-lady.

—What did I say? she asks.

—Don't know, says Christian Kelly.

—No talk.

—I wasn't—

—Just finish your sums. Finished, Joseph?

Josephs nods.

—Good lad. Now. One more minute.

Joseph counts the boys and girls. There are twenty-three children in the room. This sum includes Joseph. There are five desks without occupants.

—That's plenty of time. Now. Pencils down. Down.

One boy sits very near the door. Unlike Joseph, he wears the school sweater. Like Joseph, he is black. A girl sits behind Joseph, beside a big map of this country. She, also, is black. She sits beside the map. And is she Irish?

—Now. Who's first?

Miss, the teacher-lady, smiles.

Children lift their hands.

—Miss, Miss. Miss, Miss.

Joseph does not lift his hand.

—We'll get to the shy ones later, says the teacher-lady.

—Hazel O'Hara.

Hands go down. Some children groan.

The girl with the magnified eyes removes her glasses. She puts them into the box. It clicks. She stands up.

—Good girl.

She walks to the front of the room.

What do Irish children look like? Like this Hazel O'Hara? Joseph is not sure. Hazel's hair is almost white. Her skin is very pink right now; she is very satisfied. She is standing beside the teacher-lady and she is holding a piece of white chalk.

—Now, Hazel. Are you going to show us all how to do number one?

Hazel O'Hara nods.

—Off you go.

Christian Kelly does not resemble Hazel O'Hara.

—Hey.

Joseph watches Hazel O'Hara progress.

—Hey.

Hazel O'Hara's demonstration is both swift and accurate.

Joseph turns to look at Christian Kelly.

—Yes, he whispers.

—D'you want that?

Christian Kelly is holding up a finger, very close to Joseph's face. There's something on the finger's tip. Joseph hears another voice.

—Kelly's got snot on his finger.

Joseph turns, to face the blackboard. He feels the finger on his shoulder. He hears laughter – he feels the finger press his shoulder.

He grabs.

He pulls.

—What's going on there?

Christian Kelly is on the floor, beside Joseph. Joseph holds the finger. Christian Kelly makes much noise.

The teacher-lady now holds Joseph's wrist.

—Let's go. Now. Hand in the air! Everybody!

Joseph releases Christian Kelly's finger. He looks at Hazel O'Hara's answer on the blackboard. It is correct.

## 3  You're Definitely Dead

Joseph looks at the blackboard. Miss still holds his wrist. There is much noise in the room.

He sees boys and girls stand out of their seats. Other children lean across their neighbours' desks. They all want to see Christian Kelly.

Christian Kelly remains on the floor. He also makes much noise.

—Me finger! He broke me finger!

—Sit down!

It is Miss.

—Hands in the air!

She no longer holds Joseph's wrist. Joseph watches children sit down. He sees hands in the air. He looks at his hands. He raises them.

—Joseph?

He looks at Miss. She kneels beside Christian Kelly. She holds the finger. She presses the knuckle. Christian Kelly screams.

—There's nothing broken, Christian, she says. —You'll be grand.

—It's sore!

—I'm sure it is, she says.

She stands. She almost falls back as she does this. She puts one hand behind her. She holds her skirt with the other hand.

Joseph hears a voice behind him. It is a whisper. Perhaps it is Seth Quinn.

—I seen her knickers.

She is now standing. So is Christian Kelly.

—What colour?

Miss shouts.

—Now!

Christian Kelly rubs his nose with his sleeve. He looks at Joseph. Joseph looks at him. There is silence in the classroom.

—That's better, says Miss. —Now. Hands down. Good. Joseph.

Joseph hears the whisper-voice.

—Yellow.

Joseph looks up at Miss. She is looking at someone behind him. She says those words again.

—God give me strength.

She speaks very quietly. She turns to Christian Kelly. She puts her hand on his shoulder.

—Sit down, Christian.

Christian Kelly goes to his desk, behind Joseph. Joseph does not look at him.

—Now, Joseph. Stand up.

Joseph does this. He stands up.

—First. Christian is no angel. Are you, Christian?

—I didn't do anything.

She smiles at Christian. She looks at Joseph.

—You have to apologise to Christian, she says.

Joseph speaks.

—Why?

She looks surprised. She inhales, slowly.

—Because you hurt him.

This is fair, Joseph thinks.

—I apologise, he says.

A boy speaks.

—He's supposed to look at him when he's saying it.

Miss, the teacher-lady, laughs. This surprises Joseph.

—He's right, she says.

Joseph turns. He looks at Christian Kelly. Christian Kelly glances at Joseph. He then looks at his desk.

—I apologise, says Joseph

—He didn't mean to hurt you, says Miss.

Joseph speaks.

—That is not correct, he says.

—Oh now, says Miss.

Many voices whisper.

—What did he say?

—He's in for it now.

—Look at her face.

—Now!

Joseph looks at Miss's face. It is extremely red. She speaks.

—We'll have to see about this.

Her meaning is not clear.

—Get your bag.

Joseph picks up his school-bag. Into this bag he puts his new *Maths Matters* book and copybook and pencil.

—Come on now.

Is he being expelled from this room? He does not know.

He hears excited voices.

—She's throwing him out.

—Is she throwing him out?

He follows Miss to the front of the room.

—Now, she says. —We'd better put some space between you and Christian.

Joseph is very happy. He is to stay. And Christian Kelly will no longer sit behind him.

But then there is Seth Quinn.

A girl speaks. She is a very big girl.

—He should sit beside Pamela.

Many girls laugh.

—No, says the black girl who sits beside the map.

Joseph understands. This is Pamela.

—Leave poor Pamela alone, says Miss. —There.

Miss points.

—Beside Hazel.

Joseph watches the girl called Hazel O'Hara. She moves her chair. She makes room for Joseph. She wears her glasses. Her eyes are very big. Her hair is very white. Her skin is very pink indeed.

—Look at Hazel, says the big girl. —She's blushing.

…

Joseph sits beside Hazel O'Hara.

—Hands in the air!

Joseph raises his hand. He hears a voice he knows.

—You're definitely dead.

Joseph looks at the clock. It is round and it is placed on the wall, over the door.

—Don't listen to that dirt-bag, says Hazel O'Hara.

It is five minutes after ten o'clock. It is an hour since Joseph was brought to this room by the man. It certainly has been very eventful.

—Joseph?

It is Miss.

—Yes? says Joseph.

—I'm not finished with you yet, says Miss. —Stay here at little break.

What is this little break? Joseph does not know. The other boys in the hostel did not tell him about a little break.

—Now, says Miss. —At last. The sums on the board. Who did the last one?

—Hazel.

—That's right. Who's next?

Hands are raised. Some of the children lift themselves off their seats.

—Miss!

—Miss!

—Seth Quinn, says Miss.

—Didn't have my hand up.

—Come on, Seth.

Joseph hears a chair being pushed. He does not turn.

## 4 Milk

The boy called Seth Quinn walks to the front of the room. He is a small, angry boy. His head is shaved. His nose is red. He stands at the blackboard but he does not stand still.

—So, Seth, says Miss, the teacher-lady.

—What?

—Do number three for us.

She holds out a piece of chalk. Seth Quinn takes it but he does not move closer to the blackboard.

Beside Joseph, Hazel O'Hara whispers.

—Bet he gets it wrong.

Joseph does not respond. He looks at Seth Quinn.

—Well, Seth? says Miss.

Joseph knows the answer. He would very much like to whisper it to Seth Quinn.

Miss holds out her hand. She takes back the chalk.

—Sit down now, Seth, she says.

—Told you, says Hazel O'Hara.

Joseph watches Seth Quinn. He walks past Joseph. He looks at the floor. He does not look at Joseph.

Maybe we'll have less guff out of Seth for a while, says Miss.

Joseph decides to whisper.

—What is guff?

—It's a culchie word, Hazel O'Hara whispers back.

—It means talking, if you don't like talking. She says it all the time.

—Thank you, says Joseph, very quietly.

—Jaysis, says Hazel O'Hara. —You're welcome.

—Now, says Miss. —Little break.

Some of the children stand up.

—Sit down, says Miss.

This, Joseph thinks, is very predictable.

Miss waits until all the children sit again.

—Now, she says. —We didn't get much work done yet today. So you'll want to pull up your socks when we get back. Now, stand.

*Pull up your socks*. This must mean work harder. Again, Joseph feels that he is learning. He does not stand up.

—Dead.

It is Christian Kelly, as he passes Joseph.

The room is soon empty. Joseph and Miss are alone.

It is very quiet.

—Well, Joseph, she says. —What have you to say for yourself?

Joseph does not speak. She smiles.

—God, she says. —I wish they were all as quiet as you. How are you finding it?

Joseph thinks he knows what this means.

—I like school very much, he answers.

—Good, she says. —You'll get used to the accents.

—Please, says Joseph. —There is no difficulty.

—Good, she says. — Now.

She steps back from Joseph's desk. Does this mean that he is permitted to go? He does not stand.

She speaks.

—Look, Joseph. I know a little bit about why you're here. Why you left your country.

She looks at Joseph.

—And if you don't want to talk about it, that's grand.

Joseph nods.

—I hope you have a great time here. I do.

She is, Joseph thinks, quite a nice lady. But why did she embarrass Seth Quinn?

—But, she says.

Still, she smiles.

—I can't have that behaviour, with Christian, in the classroom. Or anywhere else.

—I apologise.

She laughs.

—I'm not laughing at you, she says. —It's lovely. You're so polite, Joseph.

She says nothing for some seconds. Joseph does not look at her.

—But no more fighting, she says. —Or pulling fingers, or whatever it was you did to Christian.

Joseph does not answer.

—You've a few minutes left, says Miss. —Off you go.

—Thank you, says Joseph.

He stands, although he would prefer to stay in the classroom.

He walks out, to the corridor.

He remembers the way to the schoolyard. It is not complicated. He goes down a very bright staircase. He passes a man. The man smiles at Joseph. Joseph reaches the bottom step. The door is in front of him. He sees children outside, through the window. The schoolyard is very crowded.

He is not afraid of Christian Kelly.

He reaches the door.

But he does not wish to be the centre of attention.

He cannot see Christian in the schoolyard. He pushes the door. He is outside. It is quite cold.

Something bright flies past him. He feels it scrape his face as it passes. He hears a smack behind him, close to his ear. And his neck is suddenly wet, and his hair. And his sleeve.

He looks.

It is milk, a carton. There is milk on the glass and on the ground but there is also milk on Joseph. He is quite wet, and he is also the centre of attention. He is surrounded.

—Kellier did it.

—Christian Kelly.

Even in the space between Joseph and the door, there are children. Joseph does not see Christian Kelly. He removes his sweatshirt, over his head, and feels the milk on his face. He must wash the sweatshirt before the milk starts to smell. He touches his shoulder. His shirt is also very wet. It too must be washed.

He is very cold.

There is movement, pushing. Children move aside. Christian Kelly stands in front of Joseph. And behind Christian Kelly, Joseph sees Seth Quinn.

## 5   The Bell

Christian Kelly stands in front of Joseph. Seth Quinn stands behind Christian Kelly.

All the children in the school, it seems, are watching. They stand behind Joseph, pressing. They are also beside him, left and right, and in front, behind Christian Kelly. Joseph knows: something must happen, even if the bell rings and announces the conclusion of this thing called little break. The bell will not bring rescue.

Joseph remembers another bell.

For one second there is silence.

Then Joseph hears a voice.

—Do him.

Joseph does not see who has spoken. It was not Christian Kelly and it was not Seth Quinn.

He hears other voices.

—Go on, Kellier.

—Go on.

—Chicken.

Then Joseph hears Christian Kelly. He sees his lips.

—I told you.

Joseph remembers the soldier.

The soldier walked out of the schoolhouse. He held the bell up high in the air. It was the bell that called them all to school, every morning. It was louder than any other sound in Joseph's village, louder than engines and cattle. Joseph loved its peal, its beautiful ding. He never had to be called to school. He was there every morning, there to watch the bell lifted and dropped. Joseph's father was the teacher.

—I told you, says Christian Kelly.

Joseph does not respond. He knows: anything he says will be a provocation. He will not do this.

There is a surge of children, behind Christian Kelly. He is being pushed. Christian Kelly must do something. He must hit Joseph. Joseph understands this. Someone pulls at Joseph's sweatshirt. He has been holding the sweatshirt at his side. He does not look; he does not take his eyes off Christian Kelly, or Seth Quinn. Someone pulls again, but not too hard. He or she is offering to hold it. Joseph lets go of the sweatshirt. His hands are free. He is very cold. He looks at Christian Kelly. He knows. This is not what Christian Kelly wants. Christian Kelly is frightened.

The soldier held the bell up high. He let it drop; he lifted it. The bell rang out clearly. There were no car or truck engines in the air that morning. Just gunfire and, sometimes, the far sound of someone screaming or crying. The bell rang out but no children came running. Joseph hid behind the school wall. The soldier was grinning. More soldiers came out of the schoolhouse. They fired their guns into the air. The soldier dropped the bell. Another soldier aimed at it and fired.

Christian Kelly takes the step and pushes Joseph. Joseph feels the hand on his chest. He steps back. He stands on a foot, behind him. Christian Kelly's hand follows Joseph. Joseph grabs the hand, and one of the fingers.

This is a very stupid boy indeed.

Joseph watches Christian Kelly. He sees the sudden terror.

Christian Kelly realises that he has made an important mistake. Once again, he has delivered his finger to Joseph.

It is now Joseph's turn. He must do something.

The soldiers had gone. Joseph waited. He wanted to enter the schoolhouse; he wanted to find his father. But he was frightened. The bullet noise was still alive in his ears, and the laughing soldiers, his father's bell – Joseph was too frightened. He was ashamed, but he could not move. He wanted to call out to his father but his throat was blocked and too dry. He had dirtied himself, but he could not move.

Children shout but Joseph does not look or listen. He looks straight at Christian Kelly. He knows: he cannot release the finger. It will be weakness. Seth Quinn stands behind Christian Kelly. He stares at Joseph.

The school bell rings. It is a harsh electric bell.

No one moves.

The bell continues to ring. Joseph continues to look at Christian Kelly.

The bell stops.

He found his father behind the schoolhouse. He knew it was his father, although he did not see the face. He did not go closer. He recognised his father's trousers. He recognised his father's shirt and shoes. He ran.

Christian Kelly tries to pull back his finger. Joseph tightens his hold. He hears children.

—This is stupid.

—Are yis going to fight, or what?

There are fewer children surrounding them. The children stand in lines in the schoolyard. They wait for the teachers to bring them back into the school. Joseph and Christian Kelly are alone now, with Seth Quinn.

—Let him go.

It is Seth Quinn. He has spoken to Joseph.

—Seth Quinn!

It is Miss, the teacher-lady. She is behind Joseph. Christian Kelly tries to rescue his finger.

—And Christian Kelly.

Miss sees Christian Kelly's finger in Joseph's fist.

—Again?

Joseph knows what she will say.

—God give me strength.

He is learning very quickly.

## 6  Robbing a Bank

Miss, the teacher-lady, follows the other boys and girls into the classroom. She stops at the door and turns to Joseph, Christian Kelly and Seth Quinn.

—Not a squeak out of you, she says. —Just stand there.

She is looking at Joseph. Does she think that he will run away?

She walks into the room. Joseph remains in the corridor.

—Now!

Joseph hears the noise of the children sitting down, retrieving books from schoolbags. He hears Miss.

—Open up page 47 of *Totally Gaeilge.* Questions one to seven. I'll be right outside and listening out for any messing.

Joseph does not look at Christian Kelly or Seth Quinn. They do not speak. They face the classroom door but cannot see inside.

Miss has returned.

—Now, she says.

She stands in front of them.

—I didn't do anything, says Christian Kelly.

—Shut up, Christian, for God's sake.

Joseph looks at Miss. She does not look very angry.

—We have to sort this out, boys, she says.

—I didn't—

—Christian!

It is, perhaps, a time when she will say *God give me strength.*

But she doesn't. She looks at Seth Quinn.

—Seth, she says. —What happened?

—Nothing.

Christian Kelly is looking at the floor. Seth Quinn is looking at Miss.

—It was a funny sort of nothing I saw, says Miss.

—Well, Joseph. Your turn. What happened?

—Nothing happened, says Joseph.

Miss says nothing, for three seconds. These seconds, Joseph thinks, are important. Because, in that time, the three boys become united. This is what Joseph thinks. They are united in their silence. They do not like one another but this does not matter. They stand there together, against Miss.

She looks at the three boys.

—You're great lads, she says.

Joseph does not think that she is sincere.

—What'll I do with you? she says.

Again, the boys say nothing.

—Seth?

Seth Quinn shrugs.

—Joseph?

Joseph looks at her. He does not speak. He will not speak. He will be punished but he is not frightened or very concerned. He is, at this moment, quite happy.

—Nothing to say for yourself? says Miss.

Joseph shakes his head. He looks at the floor. There are many loud noises coming from the classroom. Joseph hopes that these will distract Miss. She does not speak. He hears her breathe. He looks at her feet. They do not move.

She speaks.

—Right, so. If that's the way you want it—

—Miss?

Joseph looks. It is Hazel O'Hara, the girl with the magnified eyes. She is at the door.

—Yes, Hazel? says Miss

—I seen it.

—Now, Hazel—

—But I seen it. Christian Kelly pushed—

—Back inside, Hazel.

—But he—

—Hazel!

Hazel lifts her very big eyes and makes a clicking sound with her mouth. She turns and walks back into the classroom. They hear her.

—She's a b****, that one. I was only telling her.

Miss follows Hazel. She rushes into the classroom.

—Hands in the air!

Seth Quinn speaks.

—She thinks she's robbing a … bank.

Christian Kelly laughs quietly. Seth Quinn laughs quietly. Joseph smiles.

They listen to Miss. They cannot see.

—Hazel O'Hara!

—What?

Joseph laughs. It is like listening to a radio programme.

—I heard what you said, Hazel O'Hara!

—It was a private conversation.

He laughs because other boys are also laughing. He hears the snort. He also snorts.

—Don't you dare talk to me like that!

—Like what?

Joseph looks at Christian Kelly. He looks at Seth Quinn. They laugh, with him. Their shoulders shake.

—Stand up! says Miss.

—I *am* standing.

—Hands in the air!

—She's an eejit, whispers Christian Kelly.

The three boys laugh together.

It is quiet in the classroom.

Seth Quinn whispers, —Now.

And—

—Now, says Miss, inside the room.

This is, perhaps, the funniest thing Joseph has ever heard. He laughs so much, he cannot see. He wipes his eyes. The other boys also wipe their eyes. He tries to stop. He knows that Miss will soon reappear.

He stops.

Then he says it.

—Now.

He thinks suddenly of his father; a great weight drops through his chest. He cries now as he laughs. He feels the weight, the sadness, fall right through him. He wipes his eyes. He continues to laugh. Many times, Joseph made his father laugh. He remembers the sound of his father's laughter; he sees his father's face.

He laughs. He wipes his eyes. He looks at the other boys. They are looking at the classroom door.

Miss stands in front of Joseph.

He stops laughing. He waits.

He is surprised. She does not seem angry. She looks at Joseph for some long time.

—The three musketeers, she says. —In you go.

She stands aside.

Christian Kelly enters the room. Joseph follows Christian Kelly. Seth Quinn follows Joseph.

1. How do you know that it is Joseph's first day in a new school?

2. Are the class well behaved?

3. How does the reader know that Joseph may not understand everything that is going on?

4. Why does Christian Kelly tell Joseph he's 'dead'?

5. What first gets Joseph into trouble with the teacher?

6. How does the teacher try to help Joseph?

7. Why does Joseph refuse to fight Christian?

8. Why does Hazel get into trouble?

9. What unites Joseph, Christian and Seth in front of the teacher?

10. Why do they start to laugh?

11. There is tension between Joseph and the class from very early in the story. Can you find the moment when the conflict begins?

12. Why does Joseph take the threat 'you're dead' so seriously? **PQE**

13. How do you know that Joseph has hidden strength? **PQE**

14. Does the teacher help to resolve the conflict? **PQE**

15. Did you think this was a realistic depiction of a classroom conflict? Why or why not?

Re-write a shortened version of this story from Christian's point of view.

**OR**

Write an account of the funniest moment you've ever experienced.

**OR**

Imagine that you have to flee your home and your country. You can only bring five items with you. They must be things you can carry. What would you bring and why?

The main **conflict** which appears in this story is between Joseph and the other boys. Very often it is the conflict in a tale which makes it interesting. The opposing sides create tension.

Notice that this story relies heavily on dialogue, even though it is punctuated in an unconventional manner. Examine:

- the conversations between the teacher and the students

- the conversations between the students themselves

- the conversations between Joseph and the other characters

In groups, re-write a piece of the dialogue as a play script and then act it out for the class.

# Suspense and Tension

# The Sniper

Liam O'Flaherty

*This story is set during the Irish Civil War, when the Irish army split in two. Men who had only months previously fought together against the British now fought against each other.*

The long June twilight faded into night. Dublin lay enveloped in darkness, but for the dim light of the moon that shone through the fleecy clouds, casting a pale light as of approaching dawn over the streets and the dark waters of the Liffey. Around the beleaguered Four Courts the heavy guns roared. Here and there through the city machine-guns and rifles broke the silence of the night, spasmodically, like dogs barking on lone farms. Republicans and Free Staters were waging civil war.

On a roof-top near O'Connell Bridge a Republican sniper lay watching. Beside him lay his rifle and over his shoulder were slung a pair of field-glasses. His face was the face of a student – thin and ascetic, but his eyes had the cold gleam of a fanatic. They were deep and thoughtful, eyes of a man who is used to looking at death.

He was eating a sandwich hungrily. He had eaten nothing since morning. He had been too excited to eat. He finished the sandwich, and taking a flask of whiskey from his pocket, he took a short draught. Then he returned the flask to his pocket. He paused for a moment considering whether he should risk a smoke. It was dangerous. The flash might be seen in the darkness and there were enemies watching.

He decided to take the risk. Placing a cigarette between his lips, he struck a match, inhaled the smoke hurriedly and put out the light. Almost immediately a bullet flattened itself against the parapet of the roof. The sniper took another whiff and put out the cigarette. Then he swore softly and crawled away to the left.

Cautiously he raised himself and peered over the parapet. There was a flash and a bullet whizzed over his head. He dropped immediately. He had seen the flash. It came from the opposite side of the street. He rolled over the roof to a chimney stack in the rear, and slowly drew himself up behind it, until his eyes were level with the top of the parapet. There was nothing to be seen – just the dim outline of the opposite house-top against the blue sky. His enemy was under cover.

Just then an armoured car came across the bridge and advanced slowly up the street. It stopped on the opposite side of the street fifty yards ahead. The sniper could hear the dull panting of the motor. His heart beat faster. It was an enemy car. He wanted to fire, but he knew it was useless. His bullets would never pierce the steel that covered the grey monster.

Then around the corner of a side street came an old woman, her head covered by a tattered shawl. She began to talk to the man in the turret of the car. She was pointing to the roof where the sniper lay. An informer. The turret opened. A man's head and shoulders appeared, looking towards the sniper. The sniper raised his rifle and fired. The head fell heavily on the turret wall. The woman darted towards the side street. The sniper fired again. The woman whirled round and fell with a shriek in the gutter. Suddenly from the opposite roof a shot rang out and the sniper dropped his rifle with a curse. The rifle clattered to the roof. The sniper thought the noise would wake the dead. He stooped to pick the rifle up. He couldn't lift it. His forearm was dead. 'Christ,' he muttered, 'I'm hit.'

Dropping flat on to the roof, he crawled back to the parapet. With his left hand he felt the injured forearm. The blood was oozing through the sleeve of his coat. There was no pain – just a deadened sensation, as if the arm had been cut off.

Quickly, he drew his knife from his pocket, opened it on the breastwork of the parapet and ripped open the sleeve. There was a small hole where the bullet had entered. On the other side there was no hole. The bullet had lodged in the bone. It must have fractured it. He bent the arm below the wound. The arm bent back easily. He ground his teeth to overcome the pain.

Then, taking out his field dressing, he ripped open the packet with his knife. He broke the neck of the iodine bottle and let the bitter fluid drip into the wound. A paroxysm of pain swept through him. He placed the cotton wadding over the wound and wrapped the dressing over it. He tied the end with his teeth.

Then he lay still against the parapet, and closing his eyes he made an effort of will to overcome the pain.

In the street beneath, all was still. The armoured car had retired speedily over the bridge, with the machine-gunner's head hanging lifeless over the turret. The woman's corpse lay still in the gutter.

The sniper lay for a long time nursing his wounded arm and planning escape. Morning must not find him wounded on the roof. The enemy on the opposite roof covered his escape. He must kill that enemy and he could not use his rifle. He had only a revolver to do it. Then he thought of a plan.

Taking off his cap, he placed it over the muzzle of his rifle. Then he pushed the rifle slowly upwards over the parapet, until the cap was visible from the opposite side of the street. Almost immediately there was a report, and a bullet pierced the centre of the cap. The sniper slanted the rifle forward. The cap slipped down into the street. Then catching the rifle in the middle, the sniper dropped his left hand over the roof and let his hand hang lifelessly. After a few moments he let the rifle drop into the street. Then he sank to the roof, dragging his hand with him.

Crawling quickly to the left, he peered up at the corner of the roof. His ruse had succeeded. The other sniper, seeing the cap and rifle, thought that he had killed his man. He was now standing before a row of chimney pots, looking across with his head clearly silhouetted against the western sky.

The Republican sniper smiled and lifted his revolver above the edge of the parapet. The distance was about fifty yards – a hard shot in the dim light, and his right arm was paining him like a thousand devils. He took steady aim. His hand trembled with eagerness. Pressing his lips together, he took a deep breath through his nostrils and fired.

He was almost deafened with the report and his arm shook with the recoil.

When the smoke cleared, he peered across and uttered a cry of joy. His enemy had been hit. He was reeling over the parapet in his death agony. He struggled to keep his feet, but he was slowly falling forward, as if in a dream. The rifle fell from his grasp, hit the parapet, fell over, bounded off the pole of a barber's shop beneath and then clattered on to the pavement.

Then the dying man on the roof crumbled up and fell forward. The body turned over in space and hit the ground with a dull thud. He lay still.

The sniper looked at his enemy falling and he shuddered. The lust of battle died in him. He became bitten by remorse. The sweat stood out in beads on his forehead. Weakened by his wound and by the long summer day of fasting and watching on the roof, he revolted from the sight of the shattered mass of his dead enemy. His teeth chattered. He began to gibber himself, cursing the war, cursing himself, cursing everybody.

He looked at the smoking revolver in his hand and with an oath he hurled it to the roof at his feet. The revolver went off with the concussion, and the bullet whizzed past the sniper's head. He was frightened back to his senses by the shock. His nerves steadied. The cloud of fear scattered from his mind and he laughed.

Taking the whiskey flask from his pocket, he emptied it at a draught. He felt reckless under the influence of the spirits. He decided to leave the roof and look for his company commander to report. Everywhere around was quiet. There was not much danger in going through the streets. He picked up his revolver and put it in his pocket. Then he crawled down through the sky-light to the house beneath.

When the sniper reached the laneway on the street level, he felt a sudden curiosity as to the identity of the enemy sniper whom he had killed. He decided that he was a good shot whoever he was. He wondered if he knew him. Perhaps he had been in his own company before the split in the army. He decided to go over to have a look at him. He peered around the corner into O'Connell Street. In the upper part of the street there was heavy firing, but around here all was quiet.

The sniper darted across the street. A machine-gun tore up the ground around him with a hail of bullets, but he escaped. He threw himself downwards beside the corpse. The machine-gun stopped.

Then the sniper turned over the dead body and looked into his brother's face.

1. What time of day is it at the start of the story?

2. How do we know the sniper has been on the roof for a long time?

3. Why is he worried about smoking a cigarette?

4. Who dies first? Why?

5. Why does the sniper need to escape from the roof?

6. In your own words, explain how he tricks the other sniper.

7. How does he feel after he kills his opponent?

8. What makes him check the identity of the other sniper?

9. Were you surprised by the ending?

10. How did the story make you feel?

11. Re-read the description of the sniper. What details does the writer include to make him more realistic? 🅟🅠🅔

12. How does the writer build up the tension in the third paragraph? 🅟🅠🅔

13. Look again at the description of the armoured car. Several images are used to convey a sense of menace. Identify these and explain them.

14. Examine the verbs and adverbs used to describe the sniper's actions when he is injured. Pick three words that you think are effective.

> A **denouement** is the final moment in a story when a complicated plot is finally resolved.

15. Why do you think this story is remembered for its denouement?

Identify four key moments where you feel the suspense and tension increase in this story. Explain your choices.

*OR*

Imagine that the sniper is captured. He is condemned to death by firing squad. Write the speech he will make before his execution.

*OR*

Picture the sniper as an old man. He has had to live with his actions for many years. You are a researcher for a history documentary and you are interviewing him about his role in the Civil War. This is the first time he has spoken publicly. Write out the interview.

Re-read the part where the sniper shoots his enemy. In pairs, prepare a freeze-frame of one of the moments from this passage. Note that the entire paragraph is like a slow-motion clip from a film.

A **freeze-frame** is like a scene from a film that has been paused. You are going to pretend that you are frozen in a moment in the story. You decide what character each person in your group is playing. Remember to think about posture, gesture, expression and positions.

● Practise your moment.

● The teacher will call each group to the top of the classroom in turn.

● On the count of three you must freeze your moment and hold it still for 30 seconds.

● When the teacher points to you, you must explain who you are and what you are thinking at this moment in time.

For homework, pretend you are the director of this scene. Write out in full sentences how you would position the actors, what gestures and expressions they should use and what lighting, music or props they would need.

Describe briefly your favourite moment in a short story and explain why it is your favourite.

2004 O.L. Paper

*OR*

Choose a short story you have studied which contains a strong element of surprise.

(a) Describe the setting of the short story.

(b) Describe the events leading up to the surprise in the short story.

(c) How did the surprise in the short story affect one or more of the characters?

2004 H.L. Paper

This is a famous Irish short story. It describes complicated **relationships** between a number of characters. All the main characters are introduced in the first paragraph of this story. Write their names at the top of five columns. (The narrator's name is Bonaparte.) Jot down words that come into your head to describe these people as you read through the rest of the story.

# Guests of the Nation

Frank O'Connor

## I

At dusk the big Englishman, Belcher, would shift his long legs out of the ashes and say 'Well, chums, what about it?' and Noble and myself would say 'All right, chum' (for we had picked up some of their curious expressions), and the little Englishman, Hawkins, would light the lamp and bring out the cards. Sometimes Jeremiah Donovan would come and supervise the game, and get excited over Hawkins' cards, which he always played badly, and shout at him as if he was one of our own, 'Ah, you divil, why didn't you play the tray?'

But ordinarily Jeremiah was a sober and contented poor devil like the big Englishman, Belcher, and was looked up to only because he was a fair hand at documents, though he was slow even with them. He wore a small cloth hat and big gaiters over his long pants, and you seldom saw him with his hands out of his pockets. He reddened when you talked to him, tilting from toe to heel and back, and looking down all the time at his big farmer's feet. Noble and myself used make fun of his broad accent, because we were both from the town.

I could not at the time see the point of myself and Noble guarding Belcher and Hawkins at all, for it was my belief that you could have planted that pair down anywhere from this to Claregalway and they'd have taken root there like a native weed. I never in my short experience saw two men take to the country as they did.

They were passed onto us by the Second Battalion when the search for them became too hot, and Noble and myself, being young, took them over with a natural feeling of responsibility, but Hawkins made us look like fools when he showed us that he knew the country better then we did.

'You're the bloke they call Bonaparte,' he says to me. 'Mary Brigid O'Connell told me to ask you what you'd done to the pair of her brother's socks you borrowed.'

For it seemed, as they explained it, that the Second had little evenings, and some of the girls of the neighbourhood turned up, and, seeing they were such decent chaps, our fellows could not leave the two Englishmen out. Hawkins learned to dance 'The Walls of Limerick', 'The Siege of Ennis' and 'The Waves of Tory' as well as any of them, though he could not return the compliment, because our lads at that time did not dance foreign dances on principle.

So whatever privileges Belcher and Hawkins had with the Second they just took naturally with us, and after the first couple of days we gave up all pretence of keeping an eye on them. Not that they could have got far, because they had accents you could have cut with a knife, and wore khaki tunics and overcoats with civilian pants and boots, but I believe myself they never had any idea of escaping and were quite content to be where they were.

It was a treat to see how Belcher got off with the old woman in the house where we were staying. She was a great warrant to scold, and cranky even with us, but before she ever had a chance of giving our guests, as I may call them, a lick of her tongue, Belcher had made her his friend for life. She was breaking sticks, and Belcher, who had not been more than ten minutes in the house, jumped up and went over to her.

'Allow me, madam,' he said, smiling his queer little smile. 'Please allow me,' and he took the hatchet from her. She was too surprised to speak, and after that, Belcher would be at her heels, carrying a bucket, a basket or a load of turf. As Noble said, he got into looking before she leapt, and hot water, or any little thing she wanted, Belcher would have ready for her. For such a huge man (and though I am five foot ten myself I had to look up at him) he had an uncommon lack of speech. It took us a while to get used to him, walking in and out like a ghost, without speaking. Especially because Hawkins talked enough for a whole platoon, it was strange to hear Belcher with his toes in the ashes come out with a solitary 'Excuse me, chum,' or 'That's right, chum.' His one and only passion was cards, and he was a remarkably good card player. He could have skinned myself and Noble, but whatever we lost to him, Hawkins lost to us, and Hawkins only played with the money that Belcher gave him.

Hawkins lost to us because he had too much old gab, and we probably lost to Belcher for the same reason. Hawkins and Noble argued about religion into the early hours of the morning, and Hawkins worried the life out of Noble, who had a brother a priest, with a string of questions that would puzzle a cardinal. Even in treating of holy subjects, Hawkins had a deplorable tongue. I never met a man who could mix such a variety of cursing and bad language into any argument. He was a terrible man, and a fright to argue. He never did a stroke of work, and when he had no one else to argue with, he got stuck into the old woman.

He met his match in her, for when he tried to get her to complain profanely of the drought she gave him a great comedown for blaming it entirely on Jupiter Pluvius (a deity neither Hawkins nor I had ever heard of, though Noble said that among the pagans, it was believed that he had something to do with the rain). Another day he was swearing at the capitalists for starting the German war when the old lady laid down her iron, puckered up her little crab's mouth and said: 'Mr Hawkins, you can say what you like about the war, and think you'll deceive me because I am only a simple poor countrywoman, but I know what started the war. It was the Italian Count that stole the heathen divinity out of the temple of Japan. Believe me, Mr Hawkins, nothing but sorrow and want can follow people who disturb the hidden powers.'

A queer old girl all right.

## II

One evening we had our tea and Hawkins lit the lamp and we all sat into cards. Jeremiah Donovan came in too, and sat and watched us for a while, and it suddenly struck me that he had no great love for the two Englishmen. It came as a surprise to me because I had really noticed nothing of it before.

Late in the evening a really terrible argument blew up between Hawkins and Noble about capitalists and priests and love of country.

'The capitalists pay the priests to tell you about the next world so that you won't notice what the b******s are up to in this,' said Hawkins.

'Nonsense, man!' said Noble, losing his temper. 'Before ever a capitalist was thought of people believed in the next world.'

Hawkins stood up as though he were preaching.

'Oh, they did, did they?' he said with a sneer. 'They believed all the things you believe – isn't that what you mean? And you believe that God created Adam, and Adam created Shem and Shem created Jehoshophat. You believe all that silly old fairytale about Eve and Eden and the apple. Well listen to me, chum! If you're entitled to a silly belief like that I'm entitled to my own silly belief – which is that the first thing your God created was a bleeding capitalist, with morality and Rolls Royce complete. Am I right, chum?' he says to Belcher.

'You're right, chum,' says Belcher with a smile, and he got up from the table to stretch his legs into the fire and stroke his moustache. So, seeing that Jeremiah Donovan was going, and that there was no knowing when the argument about religion would be over, I went out with him. We strolled down to the village together, and then he stopped, blushing and mumbling, and said I should be behind, keeping guard. I didn't like the tone he took with me, and anyway I was bored with life in the cottage, so I replied by asking what the hell we wanted to guard them for at all.

He looked at me in surprise and said: 'I thought you knew we were keeping them as hostages.'

'Hostages?' I said.

'The enemy have prisoners belonging to us, and now they're talking of shooting them,' he said. 'If they shoot our prisoners, we'll shoot theirs.'

'Shoot Belcher and Hawkins?' I said.

'What else did you think we were keeping them for?' he said.

'Wasn't it very unforeseen of you not to warn Noble and myself of that in the beginning?' I said.

'How was it?' he said. 'You might have known that much.'

'We could not know it, Jeremiah Donovan,' I said. 'How could we when they were on our hands so long?'

'The enemy have our prisoners as long and longer,' he said.

'That's not the same thing at all,' I said.

'What difference is there?' said he.

I couldn't tell him, because I knew he wouldn't understand. If it was only an old dog you had to take to the vet's, you'd try and not get too fond of him, but Jeremiah Donovan was not a man who would ever be in danger of that.

'And when is this to be decided?' I said.

'We might hear tonight,' he said. 'Or tomorrow or the next day at latest. So if it's only hanging round that's a trouble to you, you'll be free soon enough.'

It was not the hanging round that was a trouble to me at all by this time. I had worse things to worry about. When I got back to the cottage the argument was still on. Hawkins was holding forth in his best style, maintaining that there was no next world, and Noble was saying that there was; but I could see that Hawkins had had the best of it.

'Do you know what, chum?' he was saying with a saucy smile. 'I think you're just as big a bleeding unbeliever as I am. You say you believe in the next world, and you know just as much about the next world as I do, which is sweet damn-all. What's heaven? You don't know. Where's heaven? You don't know. You know sweet damn-all! I ask you again, do they wear wings?'

'Very well, then,' said Noble. 'They do. Is that enough for you? They do wear wings.'

'Where do they get them then? Who makes them? Have they a factory for wings? Have they a sort of store where you hand in your chit and take your bleeding wings?'

'You're an impossible man to argue with,' said Noble. 'Now, listen to me –' And they were off again.

It was long after midnight when we locked up and went to bed. As I blew out the candle I told Noble. He took it very quietly. When we'd been in bed about an hour he asked if I thought we should tell the Englishmen. I didn't, because I doubted if the English would shoot our men. Even if they did, the Brigade officers, who were always up and down to the Second Battalion and knew the Englishmen well, would hardly want to see them plugged. 'I think so too,' said Noble. 'It would be great cruelty to put the wind up them now.'

'It was very unforeseen of Jeremiah Donovan, anyhow,' said I.

It was next morning that we found it so hard to face Belcher and Hawkins. We went about the house all day, scarcely saying a word. Belcher didn't seem to notice; he was stretched into the ashes as usual, with his usual look of waiting in quietness for something unforeseen to happen, but Hawkins noticed and put it down to Noble's being beaten in the argument the night before.

'Why can't you take the discussion in the proper spirit?' he said severely. 'You and your Adam and Eve! I'm a Communist, that's what I am. Communist or Anarchist, it all comes to much the same thing.' And he went around the house, muttering when the fit took him: 'Adam and Eve! Adam and Eve! Nothing better to do with their time than pick bleeding apples!'

## III

I don't know how we got through that day, but I was very glad when it was over, the tea things were cleared away, and Belcher said in his peaceable way: 'Well, chums, what about it?' We sat around the table and Hawkins took out the cards, and just then I heard Jeremiah Donovan's footsteps on the path and a dark presentiment crossed my mind. I rose from the table and caught him before he reached the door.

'What do you want?' I asked.

'I want those two soldier friends of yours,' he said, getting red.

'Is that the way, Jeremiah Donovan?' I asked.

'That's the way. There were four of our lads shot this morning, one of them a boy of sixteen.'

'That's bad,' I said.

At that moment Noble followed me out, and the three of us walked down the path together, talking in whispers. Feeney, the local intelligence officer, was standing by the gate.

'What are you going to do about it?' I asked Jeremiah Donovan.

'I want you and Noble to get them out; tell them they're being shifted again; that'll be the quietest way.'

'Leave me out of that,' said Noble, under his breath. Jeremiah Donovan looked at him hard.

'All right,' he says. 'You and Feeney get a few tools from the shed and dig a hole by the far end of the bog. Bonaparte and myself will be after you. Don't let anyone see you with the tools. Wouldn't like it to go beyond ourselves.'

We saw Feeney and Noble go round to the shed and went in ourselves. I left Jeremiah Donovan to do the explanations. He told them that he had orders to send them back to the Second Battalion. Hawkins let out a mouthful of curses, and you could see that though Belcher didn't say anything, he was a bit upset too. The old woman was for having them stay in spite of us and she didn't stop advising them until Jeremiah Donovan lost his temper and turned on her. He had a nasty temper, I noticed. It was pitch-dark in the cottage by this time, but no one thought of lighting the lamp, and in the darkness the two Englishmen fetched their topcoats and said goodbye to the old woman.

'Just as a man makes a home of a bleeding place, some b****** at headquarters thinks you're too cushy and shunts you off,' said Hawkins, shaking her hand.

'A thousand thanks, madam,' said Belcher. 'A thousand thanks for everything' – as though he'd made it up.

We went round to the back of the house and down towards the bog. It was only then that Jeremiah Donovan told them. He was shaking with excitement.

'There were four of our fellows shot in Cork this morning and now you're to be shot as a reprisal.'

'What are you talking about?' snaps Hawkins. 'It's bad enough being mucked about as we are without having to put up with your funny jokes.'

'It isn't a joke,' says Donovan. 'I'm sorry, Hawkins, but it's true,' and begins on the usual rigmarole about duty and how unpleasant it is. I never noticed that people who talk a lot about duty find it much of a trouble to them.

'Oh, cut it out!' said Hawkins.

'Ask Bonaparte,' said Donovan, seeing that Hawkins wasn't taking him seriously. 'Isn't it true Bonaparte?'

'It is,' I said, and Hawkins stopped.

'Ah, for Christ's sake, chum!'

'I mean it, chum,' I said.

'You don't sound as if you meant it.'

'If he doesn't mean it, I do,' said Donovan, working himself up.

'What have you against me, Jeremiah Donovan?'

'I never said I had anything against you. But why did your people take out four of your prisoners and shoot them in cold blood?'

He took Hawkins by the arm and dragged him on, but it was impossible to make him understand that we were in earnest. I had the Smith and Wesson in my pocket and I kept fingering it and wondering what I'd do if they put up a fight for it and ran, or wishing to God they'd do one or the other. I knew if they did run for it, that I'd never fire on them. Hawkins wanted to know was Noble in it, and when we said yes, he asked us why Noble wanted to plug him. Why did any of us want to plug him? What had he done to us? Weren't we all chums? Didn't we understand him and didn't he understand us? Did we imagine for one instant that he'd shoot us for all the so-and-so officers in the so-and-so British army?

By this time we'd reached the bog, and I was so sick I couldn't even answer him. We walked along the edge of it in the darkness, and every now and then Hawkins would call a halt and begin all over again, as if he was wound up, about our being chums, and I knew that nothing but the sight of the grave would convince him that we had to do it. And all that time I was hoping that something would happen; that they'd run for it or that Noble would take over the responsibility from me. I had the feeling that it was worse on Noble than on me.

## IV

At last we saw the lantern in the distance and made towards it. Noble was carrying it, and Feeney was standing somewhere in the darkness behind him, and the picture of them so still and silent in the bogland brought it home to me that we were in earnest, and banished the last bit of hope I had.

Belcher, on recognising Noble, said 'Hallo, chum,' in his quiet way, but Hawkins flew at him at once, and the argument began all over again, only this time Noble had nothing to say for himself and stood with his head down, holding the lantern between his legs.

It was Jeremiah Donovan who did the answering. For the twentieth time, as though it was haunting his mind, Hawkins asked if anybody thought he'd shoot Noble.

'Yes, you would,' said Jeremiah Donovan.

'No, I wouldn't, damn you!'

'You would, because you'd know you'd be shot for not doing it.'

'I wouldn't, not if I was to be shot twenty times over. I wouldn't shoot a pal. And Belcher wouldn't – isn't that right Belcher?'

'That's right, chum,' Belcher said, but more by way of answering the question than of joining in the argument. Belcher sounded as though whatever unforeseen thing he'd always been waiting for had come at last.

'Anyway, who says Noble would be shot if I wasn't? What do you think I'd do if I was in his place, out in the middle of a blasted bog?'

'What would you do?' asked Donovan.

'I'd go with him wherever he was going, of course. Share my last bob with him and stick by him through thick and thin. No one can ever say of me that I let down a pal.'

'We've had enough of this,' said Jeremiah Donovan, cocking his revolver. 'Is there any message you want to send?'

'No, there isn't.'

'Do you want to say your prayers?'

Hawkins came out with a cold-blooded remark that even shocked me and turned on Noble again.

'Listen to me, Noble,' he said. 'You and me are chums. You can't come over to my side, so I'll come over to your side. That shows you I mean what I say? Give me a rifle and I'll go along with you and the other lads.'

Nobody answered him. We knew there was no way out.

'Hear what I'm saying?' he said. 'I'm through with it. I'm a deserter or anything else you like. I don't believe in your stuff, but it's no worse than mine. That satisfy you?'

Noble raised his head, but Donovan began to speak and he lowered it again without replying.

'For the last time, have you any messages to send?' said Donovan in a cold, excited sort of voice.

'Shut up, Donovan! You don't understand me, but these lads do. They're not the sort to make a pal and kill a pal. They're not the tools of any capitalist.'

I alone of the crowd saw Donovan raise his Webley to the back of Hawkins' neck, and as he did so I shut my eyes and tried to pray. Hawkins had begun to say something else when Donovan fired, and as I opened my eyes at the bang, I saw Hawkins stagger at the knees and lie out flat at Noble's feet, slowly and as quiet as a kid falling asleep, with the lantern light on his lean legs and bright farmer's boots. We all stood very still, watching him settle out in the last agony.

Then Belcher took out a handkerchief and began to tie it about his own eyes (in our excitement we'd forgotten to do the same for Hawkins), and, seeing it wasn't big enough, turned and asked for the loan of mine. I gave it to him and he knotted the two together and pointed his foot at Hawkins.

'He's not quite dead,' he said. 'Better give him another.'

Sure enough, Hawkins's left knee was beginning to rise. I bent down and put my gun to his head; then, recollecting myself, I got up again. Belcher understood what was in my mind.

'Give him his first,' he said. 'I don't mind. Poor b******, we don't know what's happening to him now.'

I knelt and fired. By this time I didn't seem to know what I was doing. Belcher, who was fumbling a bit awkwardly with the handkerchief, came out with a laugh as he heard the shot. It was the first time I had heard him laugh and it sent a shudder down my back; it sounded so unnatural.

'Poor bugger!' he said quietly. 'And last night he was so curious about it all. It's very queer, chums, I always think. Now he knows as much about it as they'll ever let him know, and last night he was all in the dark.'

Donovan helped him to tie the handkerchiefs about his eyes. 'Thanks chum,' he said. Donovan asked if there were any messages he wanted sent.

'No, chum,' he said. 'Not for me. If any of you would like to write to Hawkins's mother, you'll find a letter from her in his pocket. He and his mother were great chums. But my missus left me eight years ago. Went away with another fellow and took the kid with her. I like the feeling of a home, as you may have noticed, but I couldn't start another again after that.'

It was an extraordinary thing, but in those few minutes Belcher said more than in all the weeks before. It was just as if the sound of the shot had started a flood of talk in him and he could go on the whole night like that, quite happily, talking about himself. We stood around like fools now that he couldn't see us any longer. Donovan looked at Noble, and Noble shook his head. Then Donovan raised his Webley, and at that moment Belcher gave his queer laugh again. He may have thought we were talking about him, or perhaps he noticed the same thing I'd noticed and couldn't understand it.

'Excuse me, chums,' he said. 'I feel I'm talking a hell of a lot, and so silly, about my being so handy about the house and things like that. But this thing came on me suddenly. You'll forgive me, I'm sure.'

'You don't want to say a prayer?' asked Donovan.

'No, chum,' he said. 'I don't think it would help. I'm ready, and you boys want to get it over.'

'You understand that we're only doing our duty?' said Donovan.

Belcher's head was raised like a blind man's, so that you could only see his chin and the top of his nose in the lantern light.

'I never could make out what duty was myself,' he said. 'I think you're all good lads, if that's what you mean. I'm not complaining.'

Noble, just as if he couldn't bear any more of it, raised his fist at Donovan, and in a flash Donovan raised his gun and fired. The big man went over like a sack of meal, and this time there was no need of a second shot.

I don't remember much about the burying, but that it was worse than all the rest because we had to carry them to the grave. It was mad lonely with nothing but a patch of lantern light between ourselves and the dark, and birds hooting and screeching all round, disturbed by the guns. Noble went through Hawkins's belongings to find the letter from his mother, and then joined his hands together. He did the same with Belcher. Then, when we'd filled in the grave, we separated from Jeremiah Donovan and Feeney and took our tools back to the shed. All the way we didn't speak a word. The kitchen was dark and cold as we'd left it, and the old woman was sitting over the hearth, saying her beads. We walked past her into the room, and Noble struck a match to light the lamp. She rose quietly and came to the doorway with all her cantankerousness gone.

'What did ye do with them?' she asked in a whisper, and Noble started so much that the match went out in his hand.

'What's that?' he asked without turning round.

'I heard ye,' she said.

'What did you hear?' asked Noble.

'I heard ye. Do ye think I didn't hear ye, putting the spade back in the houseen?'

Noble struck another match and this time the lamp lit for him.

'Was that what ye did to them?' she asked.

Then, by God, in the very doorway, she fell on her knees and began praying, and after looking at her for a minute or two Noble did the same by the fireplace. I pushed my way out past her and left them at it. I stood at the door, watching the stars and listening to the shrieking of the birds dying out over the bogs. It is so strange what you feel at times like that that you can't describe it. Noble says he saw everything ten times the size, as though there were nothing in the whole world but that little patch of bog with the two Englishmen stiffening into it, but with me it was as if the patch of bog where the Englishmen were was a million miles away, and even Noble and the old woman, mumbling behind me, and the birds and the bloody stars were all far away, and I was somehow very small and very lost and lonely like a child astray in the snow. And anything that happened to me afterwards, I never felt the same about again.

1. When does the reader realise that Belcher and Hawkins are prisoners?

2. How do we know that Belcher and Hawkins have been in Ireland for a good while?

3. Why does Bonaparte believe that they will not try to escape?

4. Why does Hawkins always lose at cards?

5. What do Hawkins and Noble always argue about?

6. In Part II what does Jeremiah Donovan tell Bonaparte that shocks him?

7. How does Hawkins react when he realises what is going to happen?

8. Belcher's reaction is different; in what way?

9. Why do you think Belcher suddenly starts talking?

10. How did the ending make you feel?

11. Re-read the first description of Jeremiah Donovan. As the story progresses and we learn more about him how does our view of him change? ⓟⓠⓔ

12. What do you think of the character of Hawkins? Were you sorry to see him die? ⓟⓠⓔ

13. We only really get to know Belcher at the end of the story. What were our first impressions of him and how were they changed? ⓟⓠⓔ

14. The story is told from Bonaparte's point of view. What effect does this have of your view of him as a character? ⓟⓠⓔ

15. How have Bonaparte and Noble changed by the end of this story? ⓟⓠⓔ

16. Pick the moment that you would consider to be the climax of this story, and explain why you chose this moment. ⓟⓠⓔ

17. The description of the shooting of Hawkins is very graphic. Re-read that passage and pick out the details that you think make it shocking.

18. What do you believe Frank O'Connor wanted you to think about after you had read this story? ⓟⓠⓔ

19. Why do you think he called this story 'Guests of the Nation'? ⓟⓠⓔ

20. Did you find any aspects of this story difficult? Explain why.

The climax is the moment that all the tension has been building up to. It is an important, vital moment in the story.

# Take the Plunge!

This story won international awards when it was published. Why do you think that was?

**OR**

Write a shortened version of this story from Jeremiah or Belcher's point of view.

**OR**

Write the IRA's press release announcing the 'executions' of the two English hostages and the corresponding British Army Statement condemning the 'murders'.

In pairs, prepare the conversation that you think might have taken place between Bonaparte and Noble if they met for the next time twenty years after the events in this story.

Think about a short story you have studied in which a friendship develops or fails between two people.

Say who the people are and why, in your opinion, the friendship developed or failed.

2003 O.L. Paper

**OR**

Select from your course a short story which you found to be very sad, very funny or both and explain, with supporting reference, the skill of the writer in bringing about the particular effect.

1999 H.L. Paper

# Resolution

# The Mile

George Layton

What a rotten report. It was the worst report I'd ever had. I'd dreaded bringing it home to my mum to read. We were sitting at the kitchen table having our tea, but neither of us touched anything. It was gammon and chips as well, with a pineapple ring. My favourite. We have gammon every Friday, because my Auntie Doreen works on the bacon counter at the Co-op, and she drops it in on her way home. I don't think she pays for it.

My mum was reading the report for the third time. She put it down on the table and stared at me. I didn't say anything. I just started at my gammon and chips and pineapple ring. What could I say? My mum looked so disappointed. I really felt sorry for her. She was determined for me to do well at school, and get my 'O' Levels, then get my 'A' Levels, then go to university, then get my degree, and then get a good job with good prospects …

'I'm sorry, Mum …'

She picked up the report again, and started reading it for the fourth time.

'It's no good reading it again, Mum. It's not going to get any better.'

She slammed the report back on the table.

'Don't you make cheeky remarks to me. I'm not in the mood for it!'

I hadn't meant it to be cheeky, but I suppose it came out like that.

'I wouldn't say anything if I was you, after reading this report!'

I shrugged my shoulders.

'There is nothing much I can say, is there?'

'You can tell me what went wrong. You told me you worked hard this term!'

I had told her I'd worked hard, but I hadn't.

'I did work hard, Mum.'

'Not according to this.'

She waved the report under my nose.

'You're supposed to be taking your 'O' Levels next year. What do you think is going to happen then?'

I shrugged my shoulders again, and stared at my gammon and chips.

'I don't know.'

She put the report back on the table. I knew I hadn't done well in my exams because of everything that had happened this term, but I didn't think for one moment I'd come bottom in nearly everything. Even Norbert Lightowler had done better that me.

'You've come bottom in nearly everything. Listen to this.'

She picked up the report again.

'Maths – Inattentive and lazy.'

I knew what it said.

'I know what it says, Mum.'

She leaned across the table, and put her face close to mine.

'I know what it says too, and I don't like it.'

She didn't have to keep reading it.

'Well, stop reading it then.'

My mum just gave me a look.

'English Language – He is capricious and dilettante. What does that mean?'

I turned my pineapple ring over with my fork. Oh heck, was she going to through every rotten subject?

'Come on – English Language – Mr Melrose says you're "capricious and dilettante". What does he mean?'

'I don't know!"

I hate Melrose. He's really sarcastic. He loves making a fool of you in front of other people. Well, he could stick his 'capricious and dilettante', and his rotten English Language, and his set books, and his horrible breath that nearly knocks you out when he stands over you.

'I don't know what he means.'

'Well, you should know. That's why you study English Language, to understand words like that. It means you mess about, and don't frame yourself.'

My mum kept reading every part of the report over and over again. It was all so pointless. It wasn't as if reading it over and over again was going to change anything. Mind you, I kept my mouth shut. I just sat there at my tea. I knew her when she was in this mood.

'What I can't understand is how come you did so well at Religious Instruction? You got seventy-five percent.'

I couldn't understand that either.

'I like Bible stories, Mum.' She wasn't sure if I was cheeking her or not. I wasn't.

'Bible stories? It's all I can do to get you to come to St Cuthbert's one Sunday a month with me and Auntie Doreen.'

That was true, but what my mum didn't know was that the only reason I went was because my Auntie Doreen slips me a few bob!

'And the only reason you go then is because your Auntie Doreen gives you pocket money.'

'Aw, that's not true, Mum.'

Blimey! My mum's got eyes everywhere.

She put the report back into the envelope. Hurray! The Spanish Inquisition was over. She took it out again. Trust me to speak too soon.

'I mean, you didn't even do well at sport, did you? "Sport – He is not a natural athlete." Didn't you do anything right this term?'

I couldn't help smiling to myself. No, I'm not a natural athlete, but I'd done one thing right this term. I'd shown Arthur Boocock that he couldn't push me around any more. That's why everything else had gone wrong. That's why I was 'lazy and inattentive' at Maths, and 'capricious and dilettante' at English Language. That's why this last term had been so miserable, because of Arthur blooming Boocock.

He'd only come into our class this year because he'd been kept down. I didn't like him. He's a right bully, but because he's a bit older and is good at sport and running and things, everybody does what he says.

That's how Smokers' Corner started.

Arthur used to pinch his dad's cigarettes and bring them to school, and we'd smoke them at playtime in the shelter under the woodwork classroom. We called it Smokers' Corner.

It was daft really. I didn't even like smoking; it gives me headaches. But I joined in because all the others did. Well, I didn't want Arthur Boocock picking on me.

We took it in turns to stand guard. I liked it when it was my turn; it meant I didn't have to join in the smoking.

Smokers' Corner was at the top end of the playground, opposite the girls' school. That's how I first saw Janis. It was one playtime. I was on guard, when I saw these three girls staring at me from an upstairs window. They kept laughing and giggling. I didn't take much notice, which was a good job because I saw Melrose coming across the playground with Mr Rushton, the deputy head. I ran into the shelter and warned the lads.

'Arthur, Tony – Melrose and Rushton are coming!'

There was no way we could've been caught. We knew we could get everything away before Melrose or Rushton or anybody could reach us, even if they ran across the playground as fast as they could. We had a plan, you see.

First, everybody put their cigarettes out, but not on the ground; with your fingers. It didn't half hurt if you didn't wet them enough. Then Arthur would open a little iron door that was in the wall next to the boiler house. Norbert had found it ages ago. It must've been there for years. Tony reckoned it was some sort of oven. Anyway, we'd empty our pockets and put all the cigarettes inside. All the time we'd be waving our hands about to get rid of the smoke, and Arthur would squirt the fresh-air spray he'd nicked from home. Then we'd shut the iron door and start playing football or tig.

Melrose never let on why he used to come storming across the playground. He never said anything, but we knew he was trying to catch the Smokers, and he knew we knew. All he'd do was give us all the look in turn, and march off. But on that day, the day those girls had been staring and giggling at me, he did say something.

'Watch it! All of you. I know what you're up to. Just watch it. Specially you, Boocock.'

We knew why Melrose picked on Arthur Boocock.

'You're running for the school on Saturday, Boocock. You'd better win or I'll want to know the reason why.'

Mr Melrose is in charge of athletics, and Arthur holds the school record for the mile. Melrose reckons he could run for Yorkshire one day if he trains hard enough.

I didn't like this smoking lark, it made me cough, gave me a headache, and I was sure we'd get caught one day.

'Hey, Arthur, we'd better pack it in. Melrose is going to catch us one of these days.'

Arthur wasn't bothered.

'Ah you! You're just scared, you're yeller!'

Yeah, I was blooming scared.

'I'm not. I just think he's going to catch us.'

Then Arthur did something that really shook me. He took his right hand out of his blazer pocket. For a minute I thought he was going to hit me, but he didn't. He put it to his mouth instead, and blew out some smoke. He's mad. He'd kept his cigarette in his hand in his pocket all the time. He's mad. I didn't say anything though. I was scared he'd thump me.

On my way home after school that day, I saw those girls. They were standing outside Wilkinson's sweetshop, and when they saw me they started giggling again. They're daft, girls. They're always giggling. One of them, the tallest, was ever so pretty though. The other two were all right, but not as pretty as the tall girl.

It was the other two that were doing most of the giggling.

'Go on, Glenda, ask him.'

'No, you ask him.'

'No, you're the one who wants to know. You ask him.'

'Shurrup!'

The tall one looked as embarrassed as I felt. I could see her name written on the school bag: Janis Webster.

The other two were still laughing, and telling each other to ask me something. I could feel myself going red. I didn't like being stared at.

'Do you two want to photograph me or summat?'

They giggled even more.

'No, thank you, we don't collect photos of monkeys, do we, Glenda?'

The one called Glenda stopped laughing and gave the other one a real dirty look.

'Don't be so rude, Christine.'

Then this Christine started teasing her friend Glenda.

'Ooh, just because you like him, Glenda Bradshaw, just because you fancy him.'

I started walking away. Blimey! If any of the lads came by and heard this going on, I'd never hear the end of it. The one called Christine started shouting after me.

'Hey, my friend Glenda thinks you're ever so nice. She wants to know if you want to go out with her.'

Blimey! Why did she have to shout so the whole street could hear? I looked round to make sure nobody like Arthur Boocock or Norbert or Tony were about. I didn't want them to hear these stupid lasses saying things like that. I mean, we didn't go out with girls, because … well … we just didn't.

I saw the pretty one, Janis, pulling Christine's arm. She was telling her to stop embarrassing me. She was nice that Janis, much nicer than the other two. I mean, if I was forced to go out with a girl, you know if somebody said, 'You will die tomorrow if you don't go out with a girl', then I wouldn't have minded going out with Janis Webster. She was really nice.

I often looked out for her after that, but when I saw her, she was always with the other two. The one time I did see her on her own, I was walking home with Tony and Norbert and I pretended I didn't know her, even though she smiled and said hello. Of course, I sometimes used to see her at playtime, when it was my turn to stand guard at Smokers' Corner. I liked being on guard twice as much now. As well as not having to smoke, it gave me a chance to see Janis. She was smashing. I couldn't get her out of my mind. I was always thinking about her, you know, having daydreams. I was forever 'rescuing' her.

One of my favourite rescues was where she was being bullied by about half-a-dozen lads, not hitting her or anything, just mucking about. And one of them was always Arthur Boocock. And I'd go up very quietly and say, 'Are these lads bothering you?' And before she had time to answer, a fight would start, and I'd take them all on. All six at once, and it would end up with them pleading for mercy. And then Janis would put her hand on my arm and ask me to let them off … and I would. That was my favourite rescue.

That's how the trouble with Arthur Boocock started.

I'd been on guard one playtime, and had gone into one of my 'rescues'. It was the swimming-bath rescue. Janis would be swimming in the deep end, and she'd get into trouble, and I'd dive in and rescue her. I'd bring her to the side, put a towel around her, and walk off without saying a word. Bit daft really, because I can't swim. Not a stroke. Mind you, I don't suppose I could beat up six lads on my own either, especially if one of them was Arthur Boocock. Anyway, I was just pulling Janis out of the deep end when I heard Melrose shouting his head off.

'Straight to the Headmaster's study. Go on, all three of you.'

I looked round, and I couldn't believe it. Melrose was inside Smokers' Corner. He'd caught Arthur, Tony and Norbert. He was giving Arthur a right crack over the head. How had he caught them? I'd been there all the time … standing guard … thinking about Janis … I just hadn't seen him coming … oh heck …

'I warned you, Boocock, all of you. Go and report to the Headmaster!'

As he was going past me, Arthur showed me his fist. I knew what that meant.

They all got the cane for smoking, and Melrose had it in for Arthur even though he was still doing well at his running. The more Melrose picked on Arthur, the worse it was for me, because Arthur kept beating me up.

That was the first thing he'd done after he'd got the cane – beaten me up. He reckoned I'd not warned them about Melrose on purpose.

'How come you didn't see him? He's blooming big enough.'

'I just didn't.'

I couldn't tell him that I'd been daydreaming about Janis Webster.

'He must've crept up behind me.'

Arthur hit me, right on my ear.

'How could he go behind you? You had your back to the wall. You did it on purpose, you yeller-belly!'

And he hit me again, on the same ear.

After that, Arthur hit me every time he saw me. Sometimes, he'd hit me in the stomach, sometimes on the back of my neck. Sometimes, he'd raise his fist and I'd think he was going to hit me, and he'd just walk away, laughing. Then he started taking my spending money. He'd say, 'Oh, you don't want that, do you?' and I'd say, 'No, you have it, Arthur.'

I was really scared of him. He made my life a misery. I dreaded going to school, and when I could, I'd stay at home by pretending to be poorly. I used to stick my fingers down my throat and make myself sick.

I suppose that's when I started to get behind with my school work, but anything was better that being bullied by that rotten Arthur Boocock. And when I did go to school, I'd try to stay in the classroom at playtime, or I'd make sure I was near the teacher who was on playground duty. Of course, Arthur thought it was all very funny, and he'd see if he could hit me without the teacher seeing, which he could.

Dinner time was the worst because we had an hour free before the bell went for school dinners, and no one was allowed to stay inside. It was a school rule. That was an hour for Arthur to bully me. I used to try and hide but he'd always find me.

By now it didn't seem to have anything to do with him being caught smoking and getting the cane. He just seemed to enjoy hitting me and tormenting me. So I stopped going to school dinners. I used to get some chips, or a Cornish pasty, and wander around. Sometimes I'd go into town and look at the shops, or else I'd go in the park and muck about. Anything to get away from school and Arthur Boocock.

That's how I met Archie.

There's a running track in the park, a proper one with white lines and everything, and one day I spent all dinner time watching this old bloke running round. That was Archie. I went back the next day and he was there again, running round and round, and I got talking to him.

'Hey, mister, how fast can you run a mile?'

I was holding a bag of crisps, and he came over and took one. He grinned at me.

'How fast can *you* run a mile?'

I'd never tried running a mile.

'I don't know, I've never tried.'

He grinned again.

'Well, now's your chance. Come on, get your jacket off.'

He was ever so fast and I found it hard to keep up with him, but he told me I'd done well. I used to run with Archie every day after that. He gave me an old track-suit top, and I'd change into my shorts and trainers and chase round the track after him. Archie said I was getting better and better.

'You'll be running for Yorkshire one of these days.'

I laughed and told him to stop teasing me. He gave me half an orange. He always did after running.

'Listen, lad, I'm serious. It's all a matter of training. Anybody can be good if they train hard enough. See you tomorrow.'

That's when I got the idea.

I decided to go in for the mile in the school sports at the end of term. You had to be picked for everything else, but anybody could enter the mile.

There were three weeks to the end of term and in that three weeks I ran everywhere. I ran to school. I ran with Archie every dinner time. I went back and ran on the track after school. Then I'd run home. If my mum wanted anything from the shops, I'd run there. I'd get up really early in the mornings and run before breakfast. It was always running. I got into tons of trouble at school for not doing my homework properly, but I didn't care. All I thought about was the mile.

I had daydreams about it. Always me and Arthur, neck and neck, and Janis would be cheering me on. Then I dropped Janis from my daydreams. She wasn't important any more. It was just me and Arthur against each other. I was sick of him and his bullying.

Arthur did well at sports day. He won the high jump and the long jump. He was picked for the half mile and the four-forty, and won them both. Then there was the announcement for the mile.

'Will all those competitors who wish to enter the open mile please report to Mr Melrose at the start.'

I hadn't let on to anybody that I was going to enter, so everybody was very surprised to see me when I went over in my shorts and trainers – especially Melrose. Arthur thought it was hilarious.

'Well, look who it is. Do you want me to give you half a mile start?'

I ignored him, and waited for Melrose to start the race. I surprised a lot of people that day, but nobody more than Arthur. I stuck to him like a shadow. When he went forward, I went forward. If he dropped back, I dropped back. This went on for about half the race. He kept giving me funny looks. He couldn't understand what was happening.

'You won't keep this up. Just watch.'

And he suddenly spurted forward. I followed him, and when he looked round to see how far ahead he was, he got a shock when he saw he wasn't.

It was just like my daydreams. Arthur and me, neck and neck, the whole school cheering us on, both of us heading for the last bend. I looked at Arthur and saw the tears rolling down his cheeks. He was crying his eyes out. I knew at that moment I'd beaten him. I don't mean I knew I'd won the race. I wasn't bothered about that. I knew I'd beaten him, Arthur. I knew he'd never hit me again.

That's when I walked off the track. I didn't see any point in running the last two hundred yards. I suppose that's because I'm not a natural athlete …

'"Sport – He is not a natural athlete." Didn't you do anything right this term?'

Blimey! My mum was still reading my report. I started to eat my gammon and chips. They'd gone cold.

**DIVE IN!**

1. Why is the narrator's mother annoyed with him?

2. Why does the narrator start smoking?

3. What are the names of the three girls the narrator keeps meeting, and which one does he like?

4. How do the teachers catch the boys smoking?

5. Why do things get worse for the narrator after this?

**WHY DON'T YOU …**

Write your own story beginning with the words, 'What a rotten report …'

*OR*

Write the conversation that you imagine the narrator and Janis Webster might have had immediately after the race.

*OR*

Write an article for a school magazine reporting on the race in this story, or on a sporting event that your school has been involved in.

**TAKE THE PLUNGE!**

6. Why is the narrator's report so bad? **P Q E**

7. How does the narrator decide to get his own back on Arthur?

> The **resolution** in a story is the part where the conflict and questions are resolved. If these are successfully dealt with the story can come to a satisfactory conclusion.

8. This story is resolved in an unexpected way. Did you think this was a satisfactory conclusion? Why or why not? **P Q E**

## Theme

# The Gift of the Magi

O. Henry

*This story is set in New York in the early 1900s.*

One dollar and eighty-seven cents. That was all. And sixty cents of it was in pennies. Pennies saved one and two at a time by bulldozing the grocer and the vegetable man and the butcher until one's cheek burned with the silent imputation of parsimony that such close dealing implied. Three times Della counted it. One dollar and eighty-seven cents. And the next day would be Christmas.

There was clearly nothing left to do but flop down on the shabby little couch and howl. So Della did it. Which instigates the moral reflection that life is made up of sobs, sniffles, and smiles, with sniffles predominating.

While the mistress of the home is gradually subsiding from the first stage to the second, take a look at the home. A furnished flat at $8 per week. It did not exactly beggar description, but it certainly had that word on the look out for the mendicancy squad.

In the vestibule below was a letter-box into which no letter would go, and an electric button from which no mortal finger could coax a ring. Also appertaining thereunto was a card bearing the name 'Mr James Dillingham Young'.

The 'Dillingham' had been flung to the breeze during a former period of prosperity when its possessor was being paid $30 per week. Now, when the income was shrunk to $20, the letters of 'Dillingham' looked blurred, as though they were thinking seriously of contracting to a modest and unassuming D. But whenever Mr James Dillingham Young came home and reached his flat above he was called 'Jim' and greatly hugged by Mrs James Dillingham Young, already introduced to you as Della. Which is all very good.

Della finished her cry and attended to her cheeks with the powder rag. She stood by the window and looked out dully at a grey cat walking a grey fence in a grey backyard. Tomorrow would be Christmas day, and she had only $1.87 with which to buy Jim a present. She had been saving every penny she could for months, with this result. Twenty dollars a week doesn't go far. Expenses had been greater than she had calculated. They always are. Only $1.87 to buy a present for Jim. Her Jim. Many a happy hour she had spent planning for something nice for him. Something fine and rare and sterling – something just a little bit near to being worthy of the honour of being owned by Jim.

There was a pier-glass between the windows of the room. Perhaps you have seen a pier-glass in an $8 dollar flat. A very thin and very agile person may, by observing his reflection in a rapid sequence of longitudinal strips, obtain a fairly accurate conception of his looks. Della, being slender, had mastered the art.

Suddenly she whirled from the window and stood before the glass. Her eyes were shining brilliantly, but her face had lost its colour within twenty seconds. Rapidly she pulled down her hair and let it fall to its full length.

Now, there were two possessions of the James Dillingham Youngs in which they both took a mighty pride. One was Jim's gold watch that had been his father's and his grandfather's. The other was Della's hair. Had the Queen of Sheba lived in the flat across the airshaft, Della would have left her hair hang out the window some day to dry just to depreciate Her Majesty's jewels and gifts. Had King Solomon been the janitor, with all his treasures piled up in the basement, Jim would have pulled out his watch every time he passed, just to see him pluck his beard from envy.

So now Della's beautiful hair fell about her, rippling and shining like a cascade of brown waters. It reached below her knee and made itself almost a garment for her. And then she did it up again nervously and quickly. Once she faltered for a minute and stood while a tear or two splashed on the worn red carpet.

On went her old brown jacket; on went her old brown hat. With a whirl of skirts and with the brilliant sparkle still in her eyes, she fluttered out of the door and down the stairs to the street.

Where she stopped the sign read: 'Mme. Sofronie. Hair Goods of All Kinds.' One flight up Della ran, and collected herself, panting. Madame, large, too white, chilly, hardly looked the 'Sofronie'.

'Will you buy my hair?' asked Della.

'I buy hair,' said Madame. 'Take yer hat off and let's have a sight at the looks of it.'

Down rippled the brown cascade.

'Twenty dollars,' said Madame, lifting the mass with a practised hand.

'Give it to me quick,' said Della.

Oh, and the next two hours tripped by on rosy wings. Forget the hashed metaphor. She was ransacking the stores for Jim's present.

She found it at last. It surely had been made for Jim and no one else. There was none like it in any of the stores, and she had turned all of them inside out. It was a platinum fob chain simple and chaste in design, properly proclaiming its value by substance alone and not by meretricious ornamentation – as all good things should do. It was even worthy of The Watch. As soon as she saw it she knew that it must be Jim's. It was like him. Quietness and value – the description applied to both. Twenty-one dollars they took from her for it, and she hurried home with the 87 cents. With that chain on his watch Jim might be properly anxious about the time in any company. Grand as the watch was, he sometimes looked at it on the sly on account of the old leather strap that he used in place of a chain.

When Della reached home her intoxication gave way a little to prudence and reason. She got out her curling irons and lighted the gas and went to work repairing the ravages made by generosity added to love. Which is always a tremendous task, dear friends – a mammoth task.

Within forty minutes her head was covered with tiny, close-lying curls that made her look wonderfully like a truant schoolboy. She looked at her reflection in the mirror long, carefully, and critically.

'If Jim doesn't kill me,' she said to herself, 'before he takes a second look at me, he'll say I look like a Coney Island chorus girl. But what could I do – oh! what could I do with a dollar and eighty seven cents?'

At seven o'clock the coffee was made and the frying pan was on the back of the stove, hot and ready to cook the chops.

Jim was never late. Della doubled the fob chain in her hand and sat on the corner of the table near the door that he always entered. Then she heard his step on the stair away down on the first flight, and she turned white for just a moment. She had a habit of saying little silent prayers about the simplest everyday things, and now she whispered: 'Please God, make him think I am still pretty.'

The door opened and Jim stepped in and closed it. He looked thin and very serious. Poor fellow, he was only twenty-two – and to be burdened with a family! He needed a new overcoat and he was without gloves.

Jim stepped inside the door, as immovable as a setter at the scent of a quail. His eyes were fixed upon Della, and there was an expression in them that she could not read, and it terrified her. It was not anger, nor surprise, nor disapproval, nor horror, nor any of the sentiments that she had been prepared for. He simply stared at her fixedly with that peculiar expression on his face.

Della wriggled off the table and went for him.

'Jim, darling,' she cried, ' don't look at me that way. I had my hair cut off and sold it because I couldn't have lived through Christmas without giving you a present. It'll grow out again – you won't mind, will you? I just had to do it. My hair grows awfully fast. Say "Merry Christmas!" Jim, and let's be happy. You don't know what a nice – what a beautiful, nice gift I've got for you.'

'You've cut off your hair?' asked Jim laboriously, as if he had not arrived at that patent fact yet even after the hardest mental labour.

'Cut it off and sold it,' said Della. 'Don't you like me just as well anyhow? I'm me without my hair, ain't I?'

Jim looked about the room curiously.

'You say your hair is gone?' he said with an air almost of idiocy.

'You needn't look for it,' said Della. 'It's sold, I tell you – sold and gone, too. It's Christmas Eve, boy. Be good to me, for it went for you. Maybe the hairs of my head were numbered,' she went on with a sudden serious sweetness, 'but nobody could ever count my love for you. Shall I put the chops on, Jim?'

Out of his trance Jim seemed quickly to wake. He enfolded his Della. For ten seconds let us regard with discreet scrutiny some inconsequential object in the other direction. Eight dollars a week or a million a year – what is the difference? A mathematician or a wit would give you the wrong answer. The magi bought valuable gifts, but that was not among them. This dark assertion will be illuminated later on.

Jim drew a package from his overcoat pocket and threw it upon the table.

'Don't make any mistake, Dell,' he said, 'about me. I don't think there's anything in the way of a haircut or a shave or a shampoo that could make me like my girl any less. But if you'll unwrap that package you may see why you had me going awhile at first.'

White fingers and nimble tore at the string and paper. And then an ecstatic scream of joy; and then, alas! a quick feminine change to hysterical tears and wails necessitating the immediate employment of all the comforting powers of the lord of the flat.

For there lay The Combs – the set of combs, side and back, that Della had worshipped for long in a Broadway window. Beautiful combs, pure tortoiseshell, with jewelled rims – just the shade to wear in the beautiful vanished hair. They were expensive combs, she knew, and her heart had simply craved and yearned over them without the least hope of possession. And now they were hers, but the tresses that should have adorned the coveted ornaments were gone.

But she hugged them to her bosom, and at length she was able to look up with dim eyes and a smile and say: 'My hair grows so fast, Jim!'

And then Della leaped up like a little singed cat and cried, 'Oh, oh!'

Jim had not yet seen his beautiful present. She held it out eagerly to him upon her open palm. The dull precious metal seemed to flash with a reflection of her bright and ardent spirit.

'Isn't it a dandy, Jim? I hunted all over town to find it. You'll have to look at the time a hundred times a day now. Give me your watch. I want to see how it looks on it.'

Instead of obeying, Jim tumbled down in the couch and put his hands under the back of his head and smiled.

'Dell,' said he, 'let's put our presents away and keep 'em awhile. They're too nice to use at present. I sold the watch to get the money to buy your combs. And now suppose you put the chops on.'

The magi, as you know, were wise men – wonderfully wise men – who brought the gifts to the Babe in the manger. They invented the art of giving Christmas presents. Being wise, their gifts were no doubt wise ones, possibly bearing the privilege of exchange in case of duplication. And here I have lamely related to you the uneventful chronicle of two foolish children in a flat who most unwisely sacrificed for each other the greatest treasures of their house. But in a last word to the wise of these days, let it be said that of all who give gifts these two were the wisest. Of all who give and receive gifts, such as they are wisest. Everywhere they are wisest. They are the magi.

1. Why does Della need the money?

2. What are the couple's two most precious possessions?

3. Why does she compare Jim to the watch chain? **PQE**

4. Why is she nervous about Jim's return?

5. How does Jim react when he sees Della?

6. Did you think there was a sad or happy ending to this story?

7. There is a very distinctive narrator in this story. He speaks directly to the reader. Pick out an example of this and say what you think it tells us about the narrator.

8. Based on the story, what type of person is Della? **PQE**

9. Do you think Della and Jim have a good relationship? **PQE**

10. Were you able to predict the ending of this story? Did you enjoy the twist?

> The main message of a story is called its theme. You have to ask yourself, what issue does the writer want me to think about?

11. The theme of this story is made very clear in the last paragraph. Can you identify it and explain it in your own words?

Write a modern version of this story set in Ireland. See if you can imitate the conversational style of the author. You don't have to use words as big as O. Henry's!

### OR

Think about the best gift anyone ever gave you. Was it monetary value which made it precious or was it the thought that went into it? Write a thank you letter to the person explaining why the gift meant so much to you.

# Unseen Fiction

*When answering this question look for the following aspects of the extract:*

 The **opening** of a novel or short story introduces us to characters and immediately shows us their situation. It also makes us ask questions so that we will read further to find the answers. For example, the beginning of 'Lemonade' makes us curious to find out more about the accident.

 Where the story takes place is called a **setting**. An unusual setting makes the reader curious. We are as interested in the mysteries of 'The Lumber-Room' as Nicholas.

 We find out about the **characters** in a story through what they say, do and what others say about them. Often characters play a specific **role**, for example, hero, heroine or villain. In 'New Boy', Joseph is the hero of the novel.

 Certain stories create a distinct **atmosphere** which is often linked to the setting. In 'The Sniper', the pale moonlit streets create an atmosphere of menace.

 **Tension** occurs when the excitement in a story builds up and we know that something is going to happen. In 'Guests of the Nation', we, like Becher, are waiting 'for something unforeseen to happen'.

 A **climax** is a moment that tension builds up to. It is an important, vital moment in the story. For example, in 'Guests of the Nation', the **climax** is the moment when Donovan raises 'his Webley to the back of Hawkin's neck'.

 **Conflict** can occur between characters or within a character. This also creates tension and makes characters more real. In 'New Boy', Joseph has to resolve the **conflict** between himself and Christian, but in a way that does not make him appear weak.

 The **denouement** or **resolution** is the way in which the story is wrapped up. For example, in 'The Sniper', the reader is surprised when they discover the identity of the dead man. Sometimes the resolution will try to teach us a **moral**. In 'Gift of the Magi', Della and Jim 'are the magi', because they give away their most precious possession to show their love for one another.

 The main message of a story is called its **theme**.

# Studied Fiction

*In preparing for this question it is best if you make out your own notes using the following headings as guidelines:*

# Plot

State the basic details of the story in one paragraph.

 **Opening**

- State what questions are raised.
- Show how the setting is introduced and give specific examples.
- Show how the characters are introduced, state your first impressions and use quotes.
- State whether or not you think it is an effective opening.

 **Closing**

- State whether or not there was tension and excitement.
- Were all the questions raised in the novel/short story answered?
- How had the main characters changed? Had lessons been learnt?
- Decide if there was a moral to the story.
- State if you were satisfied with the ending, and why.

# Setting

 **Social Setting**

- State where and when the novel/short story was set and give examples.
- What were the attitudes of the society being described?
- How is the world in this novel/short story different from your world?

 **Important Places**

- Describe in detail the most important places in the novel/short story. Pick two or three examples.
- Was vivid imagery or descriptive language used?

*You must re-read the descriptions of these places, keeping an eye out for things you can see, hear, smell, taste and touch. Sometimes imagery is used. Try to pick out a good quote for each setting.*

# Characters

 **Narrator** – establish who the narrator is or from whose point of view the story is told.

 **Main Characters** – pick three main characters:
- Describe your first impression of this character.
- Pick out critical moments which change them or affect them.
- Describe them at the end of the novel/short story.
- What did the type of language they used tell us about them?
- Decide if they had a particular role in the novel/short story and, if so, explain it.
- State how they related to the other characters and how they influenced each other.

**Make sure that you have quotes or specific examples for each point.**

# Relationships

 List the most important relationships in the novel/short story:
- Describe the relationship at the beginning of the novel/short story.
- Pick out critical moments that change the relationship.
- Describe the relationship at the end of the novel/short story.
- Describe how the characters influenced each other.

**Make sure that you have quotes or specific examples for each point.**

# Atmosphere

 Pick out key moments of **suspense** or **tension**:
- Establish the source of the tension.
- How does the setting contribute to the atmosphere?
- Describe the climax.

**Make sure that you have quotes or specific examples for each point.**

# Conflict

 Pick out examples of conflict:

- Is the conflict between certain characters?
- Is there conflict between a certain character and society?
- Is a character experiencing inner conflict?
- Is the conflict resolved satisfactorily or not?
- How did it add to your enjoyment of the book?

**Make sure that you have quotes or specific examples for each point.**

# Theme

 Decide what is the main message of the novel/short story:

- How did the setting contribute to this theme?
- How did the writer use the characters to explore the theme?
- What had we learned by the end of the novel/short story?

**Make sure that you have quotes or specific examples for each point.**

# 7 Grammar

In this chapter you will come across ways to improve your **punctuation** and **grammar**, including exercises on:

- Capital letters, full stops and commas
- Nouns and pronouns
- Verbs, adverbs and adjectives

You will **learn** how to:

- Use prepositions, conjunctions and apostrophes
- Recognise different forms of the past tense
- Punctuate dialogue correctly

although
whereve
whereas
until

# Capital Letters

**Capital letters** are used:

- At the beginning of a sentence.
- For names of:
  - people and places (Martin, Ann, New York, Sligo)
  - book and film titles (The Merchant of Venice, Shrek)
  - days and months (Thursday, July)
  - brand names (Adidas, Coca-Cola).

Re-write the following sentences, putting in or removing **capital letters** where necessary:

1. LAURA AND ANN VISITED KERRY, CORK AND GALWAY WHEN THEY TOURED AROUND IRELAND.

2. niamh and liam went to see catwoman in the cinema and bought pizzas in domino's afterwards.

3. I HAVE TO VISIT DOCTOR SMITH ON MONDAY THE SEVENTEENTH OF OCTOBER.

4. i can't wait for the coca-cola cup final between manchester united and arsenal.

5. ELVIS PRESLEY LOVED MCDONALD'S BURGERS; HE WOULDN'T EAT ANY OTHER TYPE.

6. i can't find my ralph lauren top or my wrangler jeans; i'll have to wear my diesel shorts instead.

7. IN THE ANDES MOUNTAINS OF PERU THE SNOW STAYS ON THE PEAKS FROM MAY TO OCTOBER.

8. i love walking around supermarkets and looking at the food. my favourites are dunnes, roches, superquinn, tesco and super valu.

9. I HAVE TO REVIEW A BOOK BY THE END OF MAY. I DON'T KNOW WHETHER TO DO *HARRY POTTER AND THE PRISONER OF AZKABAN* OR *TO KILL A MOCKINGBIRD*.

10. my favourite adverts are the ones for ballygowan water and volkswagen cars.

®

Correct the following passage, putting in **capital letters** wherever they are missing:

*the windows of my cortina didn't wind down. the doors rattled. the exhaust pipe had holes in it that made the machine sound like a kalashnikov AK 47, and caused british soldiers at the checkpoints near swanlibar no end of anxiety. but if you put four girls in the back seat, and three more in the front passenger seat, and put the philomena begley tape up to maximum volume, then the cortina became a dream machine. heavier on the road, it glided along, freewheeled down the hills silently. not a rattle could be heard above the steel guitar of daniel o'hara. glangevlin at the time was like an extended family. people belonged to each other. the girls took a lift from me on weekend nights to the mayflower ballroom in drumshanbo, or the ballroom of romance in glenfarne. at the end of the night they all gathered with their men along the long bench by the wall of the tearoom, drinking mugs of tea.* ®

# Full Stops

**Full stops** are used:

- To mark the end of a sentence, e.g. 'The demonstration is now over.'

- After initials, e.g. T. Bear, G. Byrne, T. Cruise.

- For abbreviations, e.g. Thurs. (Thursday), U.C.C. (University College Cork), Prof. (Professor).

- To let the reader know that you should take a long breath, and to help make sense of the sentence.

Re-write the following sentences using the necessary **full stops** and **capital letters**:

1. sinéad came all the way from the island of jersey to visit the new campus at dcu

2. molly and daragh travelled the whole way to cairns in australia just to scuba dive on the great barrier reef

3. i know why saint patrick is the patron saint of ireland, but why is saint george the patron saint of england?

4. mr moran lives on the ennis road but doctor moran has her surgery on oak avenue in co limerick

5. the fbi were called in to investigate financial irregularities in the vgi banking group ®

Re-write the following passage, writing out all the abbreviations fully and putting in the necessary **capital letters**. Remember the rules of punctuation!

the g.a.a. pres. mr s. kennedy has asked the taoiseach ms f. carey to travel with other ministers from the u.s.a. and the e.u. to a meeting on the development of internet sporting organisations. the meeting is due to take place on fri. the seventeenth of july in new york in the park heights hotel on park avenue. ®

# Commas

**Commas** are used:

- To mark a short pause in a sentence, e.g. 'The delays in our justice system are not just dangerous, they are criminal.'

- Between words in a list replacing 'and', e.g. instead of saying, 'Apples and oranges and pears and plums are all delicious fruits' you can say, 'Apples, oranges, pears and plums are all delicious fruits'. *Notice there is no comma in front of the LAST 'and'.*

- To indicate when someone has finished speaking when writing dialogue, e.g. 'The Olympics have been ruined by the drug-taking scandals,' complained the sports commentator.

Re-write these sentences, putting **commas** in the correct places:

1. The skills of a good gymnast include flexibility suppleness strength stamina and artistic flair.

2. Whether the footballer committed the foul or not is irrelevant what matters is that his team lost.

3. 'Pass the salt please' said Sarah.

4. I didn't leave my book upstairs I left it in school.

5. The special offers in-store today are six-packs of crisps at twenty per cent off apples at a discount rate and legs of lamb at half price.

Re-write the following passage, putting **commas** in where you think they are needed:

The dirty grey skies showed no sign of clearing. Moving along inch by inch the cars slowly reached the roundabout. The windscreen wipers went to and fro to and fro squeaking annoyingly as they did so. Glancing to the right I noticed the woman next to me was busy applying her make-up. 'That's not very safe' I said to my companion. In the space of five minutes she used moisturiser foundation eye-shadow mascara and lipstick. I still couldn't believe it we hadn't reached the roundabout by the time she was finished.

# Nouns

A **noun** is the name of a person, place or thing.

There are four types of nouns.

A **common noun** is any ordinary object (chair, egg, tree).

A **proper noun** is a specifically named object like a person (**S**tephen), a place (**A**merica), a day (**S**t **P**atrick's **D**ay) or a month (**O**ctober). All proper nouns have capital letters.

An **abstract noun** is the name of a quality or emotion (intelligence, strength, kindness).

A **collective noun** is a name for a group of similar objects that form a whole (a *flock* of sheep, a *gang* of thieves, a *pride* of lions, a *murder* of crows).

Draw four columns in your copybook with the headings 'Common', 'Proper', 'Abstract' and 'Collective'. Put the following **nouns** into the correct columns:

| | | | | | |
|---|---|---|---|---|---|
| deck-chair | nurse | steward | Thursday | shoal | hatred |
| bench | mercy | ruby | jar | Donegal | child |
| empathy | box | laboratory | steel | John | pencil |
| team | ice | horde | bicycle | Nike | pack |
| Hallowe'en | New Orleans | rubbish | group | sadness | pony |
| bunch | cat | knowledge | rug | lunacy | chicken |
| tea | day | Sally | | | ® |

**1.** Complete the following word puzzle using **common nouns**. Choose the words that fit in the empty spaces and re-write the passage in your copybook.

*cashier, queue, menu, sandwiches, cup, bill*

*When the man walked into the café he looked carefully at the _____ on the wall. There were lots of different types of _____. He ordered a roll and a _____ of coffee and joined the _____ where he waited to pay the _____. The _____ came to nearly five euro.*

**2.** From this passage pick out the **proper nouns** and list them in your copybook.

*Martin, Ann and Colm couldn't wait for Christmas. They had already written their letters to Santa Claus in Lapland. Those letters had been posted way back in October. They were also going to do special Christmas shopping with their Aunt Betty in Cork.*

**3.** Read the following passage and list any **abstract nouns** you find in your copybook:

*The eyes of the young child revealed her innocence and naivety. But these would not protect or shield her from the brutality and harshness of the real world. Her sweet love and kindness would, over time, be engulfed by a tide of bitterness and cynicism.*

**4.** In your copybook fill in the **collective nouns** that go with the groups of objects below.

- An _____ of soldiers
- A _____ of fish
- A _____ of people
- A _____ of locusts
- An _____ of spectators
- A _____ of cattle
- A _____ of cardinals
- A _____ of kittens
- A _____ of dolphins
- A _____ of grapes

Ⓡ

# Pronouns

A **pronoun** is used instead of a noun in a sentence.

There are three types of pronouns: personal, possessive and relative.

**1. Personal pronouns** are used when you speak about yourself or another person, e.g. *I, you, they, me, us, them, myself, herself, yourselves.*

Write a list of the **personal pronouns** that you can find in these sentences.

1. I can't believe that you went to all this trouble.

2. When they walked in the door we were absolutely shocked.

3. Emily and myself went over to Rachel's house where she cooked a great meal just for us.

4. Between ourselves, I think that the way they behaved was disgraceful, but I can't say that to them.

5. 'You asked me too late, so now I have made other arrangements,' she said.

---

2. **Possessive pronouns** indicate the owner of something, e.g. 'They are my shoes' could be replaced by 'They are *mine*.' 'That's Kevin's new car' could be replaced by 'That's *his* car.'

Re-write the following passage into your copybook, filling in the missing **possessive pronouns**:

theirs, ours, yours, mine, hers, yours

*At four o'clock I went looking for my school-bag and I couldn't see it. Then John walked by the window with it. 'Hey, that bag's _____', I shouted at him. 'How can it be _____, my name is on it', he replied. 'Emer's is the same too.' But when I checked with Emer she was sure that the bag she had was _____. She asked the twins about _____ but they said, 'We have _____'. Just when I was about to give up, the P.E. teacher walked in from the gym, held out my bag, and asked me, 'Is this _____?'*

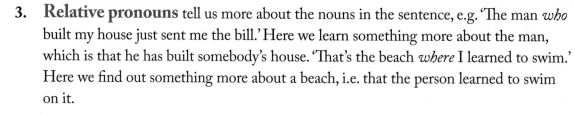

---

3. **Relative pronouns** tell us more about the nouns in the sentence, e.g. 'The man *who* built my house just sent me the bill.' Here we learn something more about the man, which is that he has built somebody's house. 'That's the beach *where* I learned to swim.' Here we find out something more about a beach, i.e. that the person learned to swim on it.

The five most important relative pronouns are **who, which, where, whose** and **that.**

Pick out the **relative pronouns** in the following passage:

*The chef who won that famous cookery award works in the restaurant where they serve very unusual salads. When we went there we ate a meal which was very nice. However, it has to be said, it was a treat that cost a fortune. The guy whose restaurant it is must be loaded!* ®

# Verbs

A **verb** is an action word. Every sentence must contain a verb. Verbs change depending on whether we are speaking about the past, present or future.

The athlete **ran** a record-breaking race. *(past)*

I **go** to the cinema whenever there is a horror film on. *(present)*

I **will visit** my granny during the summer holidays. *(future)*

1. Put the following **verbs** into a sentence about the past.
   - study
   - wash
   - eat
   - jump
   - go
2. Put the following verbs into a sentence about the present.
   - listen
   - speak
   - watch
   - cough
   - swim
3. Put these verbs into a sentence about the future.
   - paint
   - surf
   - play
   - dodge
   - write

Pick out the **verbs** from the following passage and list them in order in your copybook.

*The knife was in my sack. It took an age to let go a hand and slip the strap off my shoulder, and then repeat it with the other hand. I braced the rope across my thigh and held on to the plate with my right hand as hard as I could. Fumbling at the catches on the rucksack, I could feel the snow slowly giving way beneath me. Panic threatened to swamp me. I felt in the sack, searching desperately for the knife. My hand closed round something smooth and pulled it out. The red plastic handle slipped in my mitt and I nearly dropped it. I put it in my lap before tugging my mitt off with my teeth. I had already made the decision. There was no other option left to me. The metal blade stuck to my lips when I opened it with my teeth.* ®

# Adverbs

An **adverb** tells you more about the action.

The little boy played **happily** on the swings.

The mother **gently** rocked the baby to sleep.

The choir sang the Christmas carols **sweetly**.

Think of **adverbs** to describe these verbs, and put them into sentences.

- burn
- snow
- score
- kick
- scream
- cook
- fall
- hit
- rain
- crash
- laugh
- whisper

Write out the sentences below in your copybook, using the following **adverbs**:

ravenously, nervously, reluctantly, fussily, painfully

1. Michael _____ headed off to school on Monday morning.
2. Amy ate her dinner _____ as she hadn't had food since breakfast.
3. Fiona made her way home _____ after spraining her ankle.
4. When people have an interview they sit _____ in the waiting room.
5. The bride re-adjusted her veil _____ so that she would look perfect for her big day. ®

# Adjectives

An **adjective** is a word that describes a noun.

Read this sentence:

The girl ate the toffee.

Now read this sentence with adjectives:

The greedy, hungry girl ate the sticky, luscious toffee.

Make the sentences below more descriptive by adding some **adjectives**. Remember to put a **comma** between two adjectives, but not between the last adjective and the noun.

1. The girl skipped down the street.

2. Claire spent the night in hospital.

3. The ship sailed over the ocean.

4. The apple bounced off the table and onto the floor.

5. The music could be heard across the road.

Put ten of these **adjectives** into sentences.

*impatient, fizzy, fat, friendly, optimistic, bitter, strong, disgusting, depressed, dangerous, deadly, difficult, calm, serene, upset, soft, uncomfortable, tight, safe, cosy, sensitive, salty, frustrated, spicy, awful, bouncy, bright, jealous*

# Tenses

When we want to write about things that have already happened we use the **past tense**.

Look at this sentence from a story:

She jumped over the wall.

If this story had been written in the **present tense** the sentence would read:

She jumps over the wall.

Put the sentences below into the **past tense**.

1. Conor loves going to Donegal to see his granny.

2. Chloe reads books at bedtime.

3. Rosalie studies archaeology in college.

4. Daire runs round the garden in circles after the dog.

5. It rains in Kerry during the summer.

6. The sun shines and we laugh and play.

7. At the disco everyone dances and has a good time.

8. The dentist says that sugar is bad for my teeth.

9. Nine out of ten cats prefer our product.

10. The programme that is on the TV is very interesting.

Ⓡ

You have just been using what is called the **past simple tense**. This means that you are describing something that happened in the past, but there is no indication that it will happen again in the future.

Sometimes we want to write in the past tense while also letting the reader know that what happened might happen again in the future.

Look at this sentence again:

She jumped over the wall.

This is the **past simple tense** because she jumped over the wall once, but there is no indication that she will jump over it again.

Now, if that sentence was written like this …

She has jumped over the wall.

… it suggests that she may jump over the wall again at some point in the future even though she is not jumping over it right now.

This tense is called the present perfect simple tense! Don't worry about the name but try to remember what it does.

Draw three columns in your copybook and try changing the list of verbs below from the **present tense** into the **past simple** and then the **present perfect simple**. Look back at the examples if you get confused. Watch out for verbs that change a lot in the different tenses, like 'I see'. These are called **irregular verbs**.

| Present | Past Simple | Present Perfect Simple | Present | Past Simple | Present Perfect Simple |
|---------|-------------|------------------------|---------|-------------|------------------------|
| I paint | I painted | I have painted | I listen | | |
| I knit | I knitted | I have knitted | I fight | | |
| I see | I saw | I have seen | I am | | |
| I smile | | | I want | | |
| I go | | | I attack | | |
| I take | | | I grow | | |
| I cry | | | I admire | | |
| I whisper | | | I write | | |
| I tear | | | | | |

Ⓡ

Correct the following passage. Re-write it in your copybook using the **past simple** and the **present perfect simple**.

I been going to drama classes since I was four and I done all sorts of things. I seen lots of plays with my drama group. I sleeped in lots of different hotels when I travelled around and I winned lots of awards and competitions. My teacher says that I been the best student she ever teached. ®

# Question Marks and Exclamation Marks

**Question marks** and **exclamation marks** are sometimes used instead of full stops.

We use **question marks** to show that we have asked a question.

What age are you?

We use **exclamation marks**:

● to emphasise a point, e.g. Ireland won the World Cup!

● or to give a command, e.g. Mind the gap!

● or to express surprise or humour, e.g. You must be joking!

Re-write the following sentences, using either a **question mark** or an **exclamation mark**, depending on whether you think the sentence is a question or a statement:

1. Do you know at what time the next bus departs

2. Is that all the money you have

3. That was definitely a foul, referee

4. There is no way I'm going to bed this early

5. She is a lovely girl

6. Why did the chicken cross the road

7. To get to the other side

8. Stop talking this instant

9. Get in line

10. What page are we on ®

# Prepositions

Have you ever noticed all the really small words that there are in the English language? Some of these are **prepositions**. A **preposition** joins a noun or a pronoun to the rest of a sentence.

Some important prepositions are: **on, at, up, over, into, through, by.**

Look at the way this sentence changes if you change the preposition:

The cow jumped **over** the moon.

The cow jumped **under** the moon.

The cow jumped **on** the moon.

The cow jumped **by** the moon.

The cow jumped **into** the moon.

1. In your copybook list the main **prepositions** that you can find in this passage.

   *My father has just finished cutting the grass. I hear the crunch of gravel and the rattly echo of the mower's hard wheels as he pushes them over the driveway and into the grey cinder-block garage. He is wearing what he always wears in my childhood memories of him in the summer: a white V-neck T-shirt and baggy grey work pants. His hair is black and cut flat on top. He is a lean six-footer with neck and arms browned and freckled by the sun, his left arm more so because of the way he angles it out of the window of the car whenever he is driving. Parking the mower marks the end of his labour for the week. In my memory he is smiling that jaunty off-to-the-side smile, one I could never confuse with anyone else's.*

2. Put some of the following **prepositions** into a short paragraph beginning with this sentence:

   When I go shopping I look out for …

   - by
   - on
   - into
   - with
   - under
   - up
   - of

   - in
   - from
   - onto
   - before
   - above
   - down
   - at

Ⓡ

# Conjunctions

**Conjunctions** are words or phrases that join together two parts of a sentence.

The most common ones are: **and, but, because**.

Look at these sentences.

I study English **and** French.

I speak English **but** not French.

I speak English **because** I was born here and not in France.

*There are **many** conjunctions in the English language.*

Try to put these ten **conjunctions** into the sentences below.

as long as, therefore, whereas, unless, during, although, albeit, wherever, as far as, until

1. You will find flies _____ there is rubbish.

2. One of the twins loves broccoli _____ the other eats no vegetables.

3. I kept running for _____ I could.

4. She is going to the cinema tonight _____ I know.

5. Hitler wanted to rule the world _____ World War Two started.

6. There is still poverty in the Developing World _____ many have made contributions to help it.

7. He finally apologised for his rudeness _____ two weeks too late.

8. He sneezed constantly _____ the concert.

9. _____ she went to the Gaeltacht, she hated Irish.

10. You won't be going to the party _____ you finish your homework.

®

Therefore

as far as

although

whereas     until     wherever

albeit

# Apostrophes

An **apostrophe** is used for two things:

1. To show that something or someone **owns** another thing:

    *Joseph's book* (The book belonging to Joseph)

    *The car's speed* (The speed belonging to the car)

    So if you are ever stuck, ask yourself if you can rephrase it 'the x belonging to y' or 'the x of y'.

    If more than one person or thing owns another thing then the **apostrophe** comes **after** the 's'. Look at the example:

    *Katie and Amy, two sisters, share a toy. It is the **girls' toy**.*

    Whereas:
    *Jack has his own toy. It is the **boy's toy**.*

2. When a word or two words are shortened, an **apostrophe** is put in instead of the missing letters:

    I do not $\longrightarrow$ I don't

    He is $\longrightarrow$ He's

    She would $\longrightarrow$ She'd

    They are $\longrightarrow$ They're

    There is one infamous exception!

The two words 'it' and 'is'.

'It is a nice day' becomes '**It's** a nice day' when shortened.

# BUT

… in the sentence 'the dog ate its dinner' you **do not use an apostrophe** as that would be wrong. The dog did not eat it is dinner, it ate its dinner. So even though the dinner belonged to the dog it still does not get an apostrophe. Confused? Don't be, <u>it's</u> the only exception!

The **apostrophes** in these signs have been used incorrectly or left out altogether. Correct the signs, inserting apostrophes in the right place or removing them if necessary.

- TURNIP'S REDUCED
- GROCERS ASSOCIATION
- TROUSERS' FOR SALE
- PUPIL'S ENTRANCE
- MEMBER'S BAR
- TODAYS BREAD TODAY
- LADIES LOO
- TOMS' GARAGE
- IRELANDS BEST ICE-CREAM
- CITIZENS ADVICE BUREAU

The **apostrophes** in this passage have also been used incorrectly. Re-write the following passage, inserting apostrophes where necessary and removing any unnecessary ones:

*Monday mornings' in my house are my least favourite time of the week. Its always mayhem. My three sister's insist on hogging the bathroom and my brothers' voice can be heard shouting at them all over the house. My mother says that its too much for her, shes' going to go insane and itll be all our fault. Dads already gone by the time I get up. Hes working funny hours at the moment and its strange not to say goodbye to him in the morning. Mind you, he got a nice new car; I love its fancy interior. I also love it's chrome wheels. My brother thinks hes going to get to drive it but he does'nt have a hope! Im going to do my driving test next week, and theyre all convinced I'm going to fail.*

BATHROOM

# Writing Dialogue

We use **inverted commas**, or **quotation marks**, ' ', for two reasons:

● When we want to write down directly what someone said, e.g. *'Help,' said Louise, 'I've fallen off the ship!'*

What the person actually said goes inside the inverted commas. Notice that the comma and exclamation mark also go inside the inverted commas.

● When we are using *quotations*, e.g. *'Romeo, Romeo, wherefore art thou Romeo?'* This is something Juliet says in Shakespeare's famous play.

The other important thing to remember is that when a new person speaks you *must* begin a **new line**.

Re-write the following dialogue, inserting **inverted commas** where necessary:

*Everything is normal, the doctor was saying. Just lie back and relax. His voice was miles away in the distance and he seemed to be shouting at her. You have a son.*

*What?*

*You have a fine son. You understand that, don't you? A fine son. Did you hear him crying?*

*Is he all right, Doctor?*

*Of course he is all right.*

*You are certain he is all right?*

*I am quite certain.*

*Is he still crying?*

*Try to rest. There is nothing to worry about.*

*Why has he stopped crying, Doctor? What happened?*

*Don't excite yourself, please. Everything is normal.*

*I want to see him. Please let me see him.*

*Dear lady, the doctor said, patting her hand. You have a fine strong healthy child. Don't you believe me when I tell you that?*

*What is the woman over there doing to him?*

*Your baby is being made to look pretty for you, the doctor said. We are giving him a little wash, that is all. You must spare us a moment or two for that.*

*You swear he is all right?*

*I swear it. Now lie back and relax. Close your eyes. Go on, close your eyes. That's right. That's better. Good girl …*

*I have prayed and prayed that he will live, Doctor.*

*Of course he will live. What are you talking about?*

*The others didn't.*

*What?*

Ⓡ